Teaching Peace

Nonviolence and the Liberal Arts

Edited by J. Denny Weaver
and Gerald Biesecker-Mast

ROWMAN & LITTLEFIELD PUBLISHERS, INC.
Lanham • Boulder • New York • Oxford

ROWMAN & LITTLEFIELD PUBLISHERS, INC.

Published in the United States of America
by Rowman & Littlefield Publishers, Inc.
A wholly owned subsidiary of The Rowman & Littlefield Publishing Group, Inc.
4501 Forbes Boulevard, Suite 200, Lanham, Maryland 20706
www.rowmanlittlefield.com

PO Box 317
Oxford
OX2 9RU, UK

British Library Cataloguing in Publication Information Available

Library of Congress Cataloging-in-Publication Data

Teaching peace : nonviolence and the liberal arts / edited by J. Denny Weaver and Gerald
  Biesecker-Mast.
    p. cm.
  Includes bibliographical references and index.
  ISBN 0-7425-1456-0 (hardcover : alk. paper) — ISBN 0-7425-1457-9 (pbk. : alk. paper)
  1. Nonviolence. 2. Nonviolence—Study and teaching. 3. Nonviolence—Religious
aspects—Christianity. I. Weaver, J. Denny, 1941– II. Biesecker-Mast, Gerald, 1965–

HM1281.T4 2003
303.6'1—dc21   2003004922

Printed in the United States of America

∞™ The paper used in this publication meets the minimum requirements of American
National Standard for Information Sciences—Permanence of Paper for Printed Library
Materials, ANSI/NISO Z39.48-1992

In memory of
John Howard Yoder,
Who taught us that when living in the "politics of Jesus"
We can see the whole world

Contents

Preface

The roots of this book go back many years. Both editors grew up in conservative Mennonite congregations whose separatist traditions they have sought to transcend, but which nonetheless implanted in them a commitment to the nonviolence of Jesus. Each editor can point to additional life experiences that stimulated the growth of a nonviolent worldview. Weaver notes three: (1) Hearing veterans of the civil rights movement speak of nonviolent resistance and realizing that the traditional Mennonite idea of nonresistance has often allowed violence, including the systemic violence of racism, to continue unchallenged; (2) being in Algeria as a conscientious objector with the Mennonite Central Committee during the Vietnam War in the mid-1960s but not having an answer to the Algerians' pride in their revolutionary war that they perceived had achieved independence from France; (3) having to teach theology as a newly minted Ph.D. and wondering whether or how nonviolence might shape the theological enterprise. Biesecker-Mast was studying American political communication with a view toward a career either in journalism or in public policy development when he encountered the voices of social activists like Ron Sider and John Perkins who critiqued American foreign and domestic policies for their violence against the poor and disenfranchised. As a college student, Biesecker-Mast became involved in numerous public protests against the Reagan administration's support for the counterrevolutionary contras in Nicaragua. Then while studying public policy in a Washington-based semester program, he encountered John Howard Yoder's *Politics of Jesus* which convinced him that the form of Christian political involvement is as important as the goal of that involvement, that form for Christians being the pattern of Jesus who witnessed against the evil and injustice of his society but when given the opportunity to bring about the reign of God by force, rejected that violent option and instead went to the cross loving his political and social enemies.

The paths of Weaver and Biesecker-Mast first crossed at academic conferences, pursuing questions of the meaning of Anabaptist history and the meaning
and practice of nonviolence. These conversations intensified when Biesecker-
Mast joined Bluffton College faculty in 1995.

Founded in 1899, Bluffton College is a church-related college belonging to
Mennonite Church USA. *Dancing with the Kobzar,*[1] written by the author of one
of the chapters to follow, describes how the college has always maintained a commitment to nonviolence in the midst of the vicissitudes of economic depression,
world wars, and fluctuating enrollment. Thus the commitment to nonviolence reflected in this book speaks for the long tradition of the college. However, taking
that insight into the many disciplines of the liberal arts curriculum introduces a
new level of understanding of the meaning and significance of nonviolence. This
specific discussion began to take shape with a curriculum revision a few years
ago that sought to make the college's mission an integral, visible element of the
General Education curriculum.

A brief paper that Weaver presented at a conference for new faculty at Mennonite colleges precipitated the development of the book project. The paper became the stimulus for an all-day workshop in October 2000 in Bluffton, during
which Bluffton faculty engaged in focused discussion about how explicit they
could be in making nonviolence a beginning perspective from which to understand their disciplines. Out of that day-long event came the decision to develop
the chapters for this book.

Learning from the project has occurred at several levels. Even though faculty
were long committed to nonviolence, articulating the specific impact of nonviolence on their disciplines compelled them to achieve new levels of insight and
to push into areas heretofore not thought pertinent to the discussion of nonviolence. Developing the project has also produced a great deal of cross-disciplinary
interaction, as faculty discussed the chapters with each other and developed
deeper understanding of nonviolence on a wide scale. Such learning would no
doubt take place with other faculties who sought to apply nonviolence to the curriculum of their institutions, we believe. Since the chapters of this book are conversation starters that can only begin to explore the many possibilities in any discipline, we do hope that faculty at other institutions extend and revise these
ideas. Interest and imagination can and will multiply the findings of the chapters
of this book many times across the curriculum. Of most significance for this
learning are the students who will leave college with significantly heightened
awareness both of nonviolence as a worldview and of the extent to which prevailing assumptions in most disciplines accommodate violence. And the learning from such discussions demonstrates something else for faculty and students
alike—one does not need to be a trained theologian or ethicist to begin a meaningful and fruitful discussion about the impact of nonviolence across the academic curriculum, even though the involvement of ethicists and theologians is
ultimately desirable. In addition to rudimentary knowledge of a discipline, one

needs primarily a willingness to think about nonviolence and the imagination to look for ways to apply it and make it real.

This book is truly a collective effort, which would not exist without the work and support of many people. We are grateful to Bluffton President Lee Snyder, who gave her warm support to this project from the beginning, and to Academic Dean John Kampen, whose sage counsel was to "do it right," and who also authorized us to serve as editors. Associate Dean Robert Peiffer procured the foundation money that underwrote the expenses for the all-day workshop in October 2000. The book would obviously not exist without our faculty colleagues, whose insight and commitment made it possible and who added the writing of these chapters to already busy schedules, then accepted our editorial oversight as we shaped the chapters into an integrated manuscript. We thank student assistants Cynthia Wiltheiss and Jennifer Gingerich, who assisted with editorial tasks, and Karen Bontrager, who contributed her time to work on the index. Sally Weaver Sommer provided valuable input at several points in the production of this volume. Thanks to Jon Stealey for his professional production of photographs. In addition to coauthoring the essay on nonviolence, Glen Stassen contributed additional assistance and support for the project.

This book reflects our lifelong belief that nonviolence is true because it is integral to the story of Jesus Christ, who makes God's reign present in the world. It expresses the Christian profession that in Christ "all things are become new" since "God was in Christ, reconciling the world to himself" (2 Corinthians 5: 17–19). At this point we are grateful to John Howard Yoder who, more than any other individual, has contributed to our understanding that the rejection of violence belongs integrally to the story of Jesus Christ. For that reason we dedicate this book to the memory of John Howard Yoder. John Howard Yoder also had an ecumenical vision that posed the "politics of Jesus" as a challenge to all Christians. Inspired by that vision of Yoder, it is our prayer that this book serve our colleagues everywhere and do for those who read it what the preparation has done for us, namely to deepen our understanding that nonviolence truly has the potential to touch most disciplines of the academic curriculum and thus to touch most dimensions of our lives as Christians. May that learning inspire and multiply Christians committed to nonviolence and peace as a way of knowing.

> J. Denny Weaver and Gerald Biesecker-Mast
> Bluffton College
> January 2003

NOTES

1. Perry Bush, *Dancing with the Kobzar: Bluffton College and Mennonite Higher Education, 1899–1999,* Studies in Anabaptist and Mennonite History, no. 38 (Telford, Pa.: Pandora Press U.S.; copublished with Herald Press and Faith & Life Press, 2000).

INTRODUCTION

1

Christian Nonviolence and the Enlightenment Crisis

Gerald Biesecker-Mast

ENLIGHTENMENT VIOLENCE
AND THE CRITIQUE OF MODERNITY

"The Enlightenment has always aimed at liberating men from fear and establishing their sovereignty. Yet the fully enlightened earth radiates disaster triumphant."[1] Thus wrote Max Horkheimer and Theodor Adorno in 1945, following the unprecedented violence of World War II, with its breathtaking application of modern technologies to the task of efficient killing in the death camps of the Holocaust and in the nuclear incineration of Hiroshima and Nagasaki. This pronouncement of Horkheimer and Adorno was prophetic, for the decades to follow would witness an increasingly broad and decisive loss of confidence in the methodologies and techniques associated with modern science, at least as privileged instruments for access to Truth.

Whatever else can be said about postmodernity, either as theory or as condition, no characterization is perhaps more widely accepted than that the postmodern world has relativized and particularized the previously assumed universality of the truths associated with the practice of reason in general and of the scientific method in particular.[2] There is no privileged access to the reality or the truth of the cosmos, no absolute point of reference, no final court of appeal, postmoderns have learned. All truths are perspectival, based in the commitments and priorities and orientations of the researcher or seeker, and thereby open to challenge or subversion by alternative perspectives. From such assumptions competing and even mutually exclusive conclusions have multiplied across the landscape of academia. Postmodernism can be argued to promote either nihilism or a recovery of religious faith.[3] To postmodernism is attributed both consumer culture and various countercultures.[4] Postmodernism has been heralded as both the harbinger of interdisciplinarity and the end of collegiality.[5]

Yet few analyses of the postmodern condition, especially regarding the academy, have taken up in detail the explicit link between the Enlightenment and violence articulated by Horkheimer and Adorno already in 1945. Certainly, the host of postcolonial studies has called attention to the relationship between techniques of reason and imperial politics, between research about subjects and the domination of subjects.[6] And while such analyses of domination imply a critique of Enlightenment violence, they are often less explicit about the exact relationship between a logic of mastery and the existence of violence. More often the question is focused on who or what is excluded by a particular research project or, conversely, who or what is privileged. Surely the presence of exclusion and domination is crucial data to notice and document. Yet the project proposed by this book seeks to extend such observations that document the violence of present techniques of knowledge toward the reconstruction of alternative nonviolent methods of learning and teaching.

CHRISTIAN NONVIOLENCE
AND HIGHER EDUCATION

The specific orientation for knowledge offered in this book as an alternative to violence-accommodating methodologies and pedagogies has its roots in a particular tradition of Christian theology and hermeneutics whose contemporary form derives from the Anabaptist movements of the sixteenth century and is expressed more broadly in that loose coalition of contemporary communities of interpretation known as the Historic Peace Churches—Brethren, Mennonites, and Quakers who have made conscientious objection to war a central feature of their Christian faith—as well as in such groups as the Fellowship of Reconciliation that bring together pacifist people of faith from numerous denominational backgrounds.[7] That tradition is perhaps most distinguished by its repeated refusal to permit political relationships among allied or warring nations to justify acceptance of warfare as a valid expression of national policy or personal relationship to others who may be classified as "enemies." In other words, within this tradition commitment to peace is based less on an optimistic view of human nature than it is on the "nonconformity" of Christian churches to the warring ways of the broader society and recognition of God's peaceable reign where it becomes visible in the world. [8]

Early Anabaptist writers like Menno Simons state such nonconformist premises with language contrasting "two opposing princes and two opposing kingdoms: the one is the Prince of Peace; the other the prince of strife."[9] Another Anabaptist text depicts "two assemblies, or classes of people": those who were "born by nature to seize and destroy" and those with "no desire for revenge."[10]

Such texts, which constitute nonviolence as the central feature that distinguishes the people of God from the violence-promoting assumptions of the present social order, clearly assume that the follower of Jesus who seeks the way of peace does so in contrast to popular opinion, conventional wisdom, and all of the social and political practices associated with the "prince of strife." They also make statements about what is "natural" for children of God and what is "natural" for those who rebel against God's rule.

For some peace church Christians this nonconformist orientation has meant clinging to rural and agricultural lifestyles and avoiding many of the troubling features of modernity. Guy Hershberger offered an exemplary statement of this attitude of particular rather than broad cultural engagement in his classic work *War, Peace, and Nonresistance*:

> Therefore, the Christian youth of today who would make a permanent contribution to American life is wise if he understands that the most constructive work which can be done is not to be found in those glamorous and spectacular enterprises associated with urban industry, military service, and the affairs of state, but rather in the quiet and more fundamental task of building the small Christian community.[11]

Such a claim is consistent with the ideals that have constituted the more conservative or old-order members of the historic peace churches.

By way of contrast progressives within the historic peace churches have tended to emphasize that peace commitments should be brought aggressively into a relationship of engagement with the problems and possibilities of modern and postmodern cultures, a posture that is consistent with movement toward greater activism and involvement among peace churches and groups committed to nonviolence described in chapter 2. An example of a peace church theologian who advocates such involvement is Gordon Kaufman, who has argued vigorously that pacifist Christians must avoid the temptation to withdraw from society, except as a short-term strategy, and instead "be the very instrument through which nonresistant love actually enters into the power struggles and clashes in this world to redeem them."[12] For Kaufman, as for many members of the peace churches today, bringing nonviolence to bear on the complex problems of the contemporary world involves risking loss of purity in order to "remain a significant and effective agent" of God's redemption.[13] While Hershberger's views assume the primacy of the church as a believer's reference point, Kaufman expects that the rules and expectations of modern professional or political organizations may relativize the church's authority, including even its pacifist commitments. Kaufman goes so far as to suggest that a pacifist Christian secretary of state might take leadership in making war, since he would be acting on behalf of a nonpacifist nation.[14]

An alternative to both Hershberger and Kaufman is offered by J. Denny Weaver who argues that Christian pacifism ought to be grounded in a church that is both an alternative to the violence of the surrounding society and an activist challenge to those violent dimensions of the social order—a church he describes as a socially active alternative community by way of contrast to a withdrawn alternative community or a church identified with the institutions of society. As Weaver puts it, "The activist alternative community proclaims the gospel both to call people into the church (in agreement with the withdrawn alternative community) but also to transform the society, with the socially active alternative community functioning as the agent of change."[15]

This socially active alternative community is an essential resource for peace witness in higher education. We know that being for peace is meaningless unless that peace commitment is made in the context of struggle against the sins of society and of humankind, including the overreaching of political and economic powers and the exploitation of the poor and the voiceless. Furthermore, we know that for Christians this struggle for peace must be rooted in communities of faith because such a difficult struggle cannot be sustained by individuals acting alone. And finally, as John Kampen argues in chapter 4 of this book, that truth is not to be found floating high above the hope and terror of human struggle but rather in the midst of it. And so we should not expect the project of peaceable education to be free of controversy or immune to the problems of the communities from which its students and faculty are drawn. Peaceable education is about a collective yet vulnerable engagement with the surrounding world, not protectionist withdrawal from it. Yet such an education should not permit the institutions and practices of the secular order to have the final word in determining the convictions and values according to which students will recognize truth and make professional decisions.

CHRISTIAN WORLDVIEWS
AND CULTURAL ENGAGEMENT

Christian nonviolence rooted in biblical nonconformity and practiced in the context of a socially active alternative community is a commitment that is made against the common sense and mainstream wisdom of the social order—that is, the given "natural" order. This is a crucial observation for it distinguishes Christian nonviolence from a problematic, although understandable, tendency that has prevailed throughout much of the Christian tradition: to integrate or assimilate such distinctive Christian commitments as nonviolence with structures of knowledge and power considered to be broader, wider, and more universal than the world over which Jesus is Lord, which is the world described in the Bible and the church.

In Christian higher education, especially among evangelical colleges associated with the Council of Christian Colleges and Universities, much emphasis is placed on the "integration of faith and learning," which means that faculty and students are encouraged to think creatively and critically in their scholarship about the ways in which faith shapes their learning and understanding.[16] On the one hand, this emphasis has enabled many colleges and universities to be explicit about their religious commitments and to avoid the tendency toward secularization that George Marsden has noted among so many educational institutions originally founded by churches. On the other hand, because this logic of integration has been typically articulated by scholars shaped by Calvinism and Reformed theology, it is usually mobilized on behalf of conservative rather than liberationist social agendas, sometimes explicitly rejecting the more radical Anabaptist critiques of social and political systems—for example, the institutions and commercial enterprises associated with the military.[17]

Such accounts of "integrated" Christian faithfulness typically begin with the creation, rather than with the birth, life, death, and resurrection of Jesus.[18] God created the world as good, according to such accounts, but after the fall human sin distorted the institutions and cultures that ordered the created world. In such accounts, the redemption provided by Jesus' death and resurrection is narrated as substitutionary atonement, with little attention if any given to the actual teachings and practices of Jesus as recorded in the Synoptic Gospels.[19] Instead of attending to Jesus' teachings, the Reformed perspective on the creation emphasizes that God's plan of redemption made it possible for Christians to see within the corrupted creation the original intention of the creator. Thus, according to this view, Christians must now work at restoring all of life to God's good original intention. While all Christians agree that the salvation accomplished by Jesus includes a dimension of restoration, the Reformed emphasis on the original creation more than Jesus' incarnation dismisses the actual ways in which God's will for humankind was made manifest in Jesus' earthly life and teachings. Making the restored creation the initial point of departure tends also to reduce the significance of Jesus' body—the church—as the primary agent of God's transformation. As this "all of life redeemed" perspective is usually interpreted, the church is just one of many human institutions that God seeks to redeem rather than the front edge of God's reign in the world. And so it is viewed as wrong, according to this perspective, to say that certain institutions—the military, for example, or police forces that rely on deadly force—should be rejected in principle as legitimate vocations for Christians. Such a radical view is not seen to acknowledge properly the goodness of all God's creation and is accused of focusing too narrowly on the church as God's primary agent of mission and transformation.

While the advantage of the Reformed perspective is that it provides an obvious motivation for the integration of Christian faith across all of the disciplines associated with the cultivation of creation, it can be interpreted as too eager to accept the broad outlines of the status quo as basic reflections of God's original intention, even if corrupted in the specific details. Perhaps this tradition of thought also too easily dismisses Anabaptist arguments for nonviolent and nonconformist discipleship as sectarian avoidance of social responsibility and engagement. The Dutch Reformed theologian Abraham Kuyper, for example, in an article on common grace rightly insisted that it was wrong to limit the practice of Christian faith only to the spheres of responsibility associated with the church, thereby assuming that in the "secular" spheres a Christian would simply conduct himself or herself as anyone else would.[20] But Kuyper unfairly associates this church–world dualism with Anabaptism:

> You only have to take a small step more before landing in the Anabaptist position which concentrated all sanctity in the human soul and dug a deep chasm between this inward-looking spirituality and life all around. Then scholarship becomes unholy; the development of art, trade, and business becomes unholy; unholy also the functions of government; in short, all that is not directly spiritual and aimed at the soul.[21]

This sort of misreading of Anabaptism has become so widespread that many who claim an Anabaptist faith heritage have come to accept this critique as common sense. Yet, when one examines early Anabaptist statements about the relationship between church and world, one is impressed more by the spirit of antagonism to specific practices deemed unholy, rather than an unqualified rejection of all that is outside the "spiritual" realm of piety and the church per se.[22]

The sword, for example, is said in article seven of the definitive Schleitheim *Articles* to be ordered by God and potentially used for the good; however, the Christian disciple rejects the sword as outside of Christ's higher law of love.[23] In other words, Anabaptism recognizes God's creative work throughout the whole world but is nevertheless selective about the particular means by which Christians seek to advance that work, a selectiveness established by the practices and commitments identified with the story of Jesus.[24] A contemporary Mennonite theologian, Duane Friesen, has shown recently that an Anabaptist theology of culture can be fully engaged with the philosophical, political, and aesthetic practices of the social order while at the same time refusing thoroughgoing assimilation to the status quo.[25] He calls on contemporary Anabaptists to be discriminating in their involvement with the broader culture, recognizing the exilic status of the church on the one hand, while seeking the peace of the city on the other.

Not surprisingly, a recent commentary by a Reformed philosopher on a collection of personal statements by Anabaptist scholars about the relationship between their academic disciplines and Christian faith reflects doubt about whether scholarship rooted in Anabaptism really has anything substantively distinctive to offer to the world of scholarship. Although the writer enthusiastically affirms the commitments of the Anabaptist tradition, he notes that while "the particular social and theological teachings of the radical Reformation have exercised a profound effect on the formation and work of the contributors whose essays are collected here . . . yet, the results of their scholarship seldom bear clear identifying marks of these influences."[26] The writer concludes that "perhaps the Anabaptist character that can be found in the work of these scholars, and of others whom they cite, is to be found less in any specific content than in the spirit in which they undertake their intellectual work."[27] A close rereading of the essays in question and certainly the appearance of the book in hand demonstrates that an Anabaptist worldview, especially its prioritization of nonviolence, does indeed offer not only a different spirit but a different content.

THE WORLD AS IT "IS"
AND THE EYES OF PEACE

Peace church colleges and Christian colleges who wish to teach nonviolence need to engage the world with the rigor and risk encouraged by Kaufman, yet with the qualifying force of the dual citizenship called for by Friesen and Weaver. In such a context students would come to understand the good creation of God in all of its glory and fallenness; at the same time they would be urged to consider the higher way of Christ as embodied by the church. More than seeking in the creation a dim reflection of God's original intention, such students would be urged to identify with the new creation that is to come and that is already recognizable in the work of the church.

At Bluffton College, for example, undergraduates can obtain a criminal justice major in which they study the realities, both good and evil, of the American criminal justice system. Along the way they are also introduced to alternative models of justice, models that grow out of the higher way of Christian forgiveness and restitution found in the life of the church and given expression by such church outreaches as the Victim Offender Reconciliation Program. This approach mirrors the kind of learning that can happen in academic departments that seek to encourage nonconformity to worldly violence in their curricula. Whether students are studying human communication, physics, history, music, or educational theory, they are also provided with resources for understanding and cultivating the material and social landscape of God's good-but-fallen creation at the same time that they are urged toward a life of faith that strives for Christ's perfect peace.

Such an approach to education and scholarship begins with the assumption that "people who bear crosses are working with the grain of the universe," as stated eloquently by John Howard Yoder, and elaborated in Stanley Hauerwas's recent Gifford Lectures, entitled *With the Grain of the Universe*.[28] The "grain of the universe" can be understood as an eschatological characterization of the direction in which history is ultimately headed or it can be interpreted as an ontological claim about the "natural" order of the universe and the ground of existence or being. Whether the grain of the universe is considered along eschatological or teleological lines, which was clearly Yoder's orientation, or whether that "grain" is described in ontological terms, as Hauerwas—following John Milbank—seems to favor, there is clearly now a precedent for asserting a comprehensive view of reality that assumes the ultimate futility of violence as a method of solving human problems or constructing human projects.[29] The chapters in this volume assume that futility and vary in their orientation toward ontological nonviolence or eschatological nonviolence.

The book begins with a chapter by social ethicists Glen Stassen and Michael Westmoreland-White that describes the complex and emerging meanings of violence and nonviolence as they have been used in the context of historical struggles for justice and peace. According to Stassen and Westmoreland-White, violence is best defined according to two criteria—the presence of overpowering force and the consequent harm or destruction to humans. Nonviolence by contrast seeks not only to avoid the use of destructive overpowering force but also to actively challenge the use of such force everywhere. Put differently nonviolence has been both a strategy and a goal for an increasing number of historical movements for peace and democracy, including Gandhi's struggle against British imperialism in India, King's civil rights movement in the United States, and the antiapartheid movement in South Africa. For Stassen and Westmoreland-White, the practices of nonviolence, or what they call just peacemaking, are not simply "ideals" but are social and political paradigms that are increasingly being used to challenge authoritarian regimes and build just and peaceful democratic societies throughout the world.[30]

Part II of this book, on nonviolence in the Bible and theology, continues this discussion of foundational understandings of violence and nonviolence with three chapters that describe the biblical and theological premises for nonviolence as a worldview. These three chapters, authored by theologian J. Denny Weaver and biblical scholars David Janzen and John Kampen, make the case for two critical and distinctive propositions about Christian nonviolence that, if taken seriously, can shape the whole curriculum of an educational institution. These two propositions are: (1) Christian nonviolence is based in the specific centrality of nonviolence to the life and teachings of Jesus and, as such, to the salvation of humankind accomplished on the cross (Weaver and Janzen); and (2) Christian nonviolence addresses the violence of the world from within the controversial context of struggle against the sins of society and of humankind, including the overreaching of political and economic powers and the exploitation of the poor and the voiceless (Kampen).

These two propositions—that nonviolence is central to the story of Jesus and that nonviolence is a feature of the struggle for justice and liberation—are crucial qualifiers of the peace this book promotes. These two qualifiers insist that Christian peacemaking and peace teaching must transcend the temptation to reduce peace to the secular art of diplomacy or to the humanistic practice of liberal tolerance, even though such skills are valuable crafts necessary for the survival of democratic and multicultural societies, as Stassen and Westmoreland-White have demonstrated.

Part III of the book addresses the presence or absence of nonviolence in particular historical and political contexts, from the American Civil War to the war in Kosovo to the Bush administration's war on terrorism. Historian Perry Bush demonstrates how a commitment to nonviolence leads to a more negative evaluation of modern warfare than is usually proposed by contemporary history textbooks. Political historian James Satterwhite explains how American and United Nations policies toward Serbia and Kosovo prior to the outbreak of violent conflict neglected the nonviolent liberationist movements in Kosovo as valid partners for restoring peace and justice. Political and social theorist Daniel Wessner critiques the Bush doctrine of preemptive strike from a methodological and pedagogical stance he calls "critically embodied studies." These chapters demonstrate the obvious relevance of a nonviolent worldview to understanding the apparently violence-filled world of politics and international relations as well as to analyzing and narrating the past, especially military history.

In part IV, an approach to the humanities is sketched with particular examples drawn from theoretical and methodological issues within the academic disciplines of Communication and English. Susan Biesecker-Mast's chapter compares the standard Greco-Roman philosophical assumptions of the Western rhetorical tradition with the nonviolent rhetoric of Jesus and the argument for the impossible that appears in the biblical tradition. Jeff Gundy articulates an approach both to reading and to teaching literature that on the one hand highlights the critique of violence and possibilities for nonviolence that appear in the plots and characters of novels and stories and on the other hand offers to students a vulnerable exploration of such texts in the classroom, an exploration that is open to the challenge of contrasting experiences, identities, and opinions. Cynthia Bandish focuses on the theological assumptions behind the plots of Gothic novels, assumptions which both affirm and subvert a just-war ethic.

Part V is concerned especially with how the creation of art and the teaching of the arts promotes or undermines peaceful imaginations and perspectives on the world and the self. Gregg Luginbuhl describes the aesthetics of both violence and peace in his interpretation of numerous paintings and sculptures. Melissa Friesen advocates an alternative to a popular theory of actor training—The Method—that she argues tends toward psychological violence by encouraging actor roles to overcome personal identities through the purposeful violation of social boundaries. Mark Suderman explains how violence and peace are represented in choral music—both in terms of lyrical content and musical form—and takes up numerous practical pedagogical issues faced by choir directors in music selection, ensemble development, and choir relationships.

With part VI, the book turns to the social sciences and their efforts to describe patterns and habits of human relationships. James Harder's chapter demonstrates how the economic paradigms associated with global marketization neglect to account for the social and economic violence that accompanies the privileging of "flexible" and "free flowing" global capital over local and democratic decision making. Jeff Gingerich argues for the replacement of a retributive justice paradigm in criminal justice studies and practice with a restorative justice model that focuses on restoration and healing between victims and offenders. Pamela Nath notices the absence of attention in standard psychology textbooks to the psychology of violence and war and suggests beginning strategies for turning the discipline and its classrooms toward a better understanding of the psychology of violence and of peace. Ronald Friesen examines the reluctance of mainstream economics texts to address the economics of war and peace and suggests how economic analysis of the cost of war can strengthen antiwar arguments.

Part VII addresses the hard sciences with particular attention to biology and mathematics. Angela Montel's chapter highlights the use of violent metaphors in the field of cell biology, suggesting that such metaphors contribute to and are also a reflection of a broader political atmosphere in which violence is seen as "natural"; she offers alternative "nonviolent" images and metaphors of cell behavior. Todd Rainey explains how the "conflict resolution" behavior of certain primates contests the dominant assumption that human "animality" is a root of human violence. Two chapters by mathematicians—Stephen Harnish and Darryl Nester—demonstrate opportunities for such an apparently "objective" discipline as mathematics to promote peace: explaining how mathematical theory resolves tensions between mutually exclusive domains, which suggests that it is both logical and realistic to search for "third" option solutions to seemingly intractable conflicts, and showing how the selection and application of examples both challenges conventional assumptions about the success of violence and promotes nonviolence as a norm.

Finally, the book concludes with two chapters that deal with the teaching and promotion of nonviolence in professional programs. In part VIII the first chapter, by Gayle Trollinger, describes how a college education department uses the rigorous expectations of a state licensing program as an occasion to integrate the teaching of conflict resolution skills across a curriculum that prepares students for teaching careers in increasingly violent school systems. The final chapter, by George Lehman, envisions an alternative management model that emphasizes human dignity and well-being as organizational goals that would trump profit and growth as the primary criteria for decision making. Considered together these chapters suggest one way to address the destruction and violence associated with the Enlightenment project. While not denying the fruitful contributions to human well-being associated with the Enlightenment, the chapters assume that "pure reason" is not a sufficient ground for peaceful and ethical engagement with the world—either as scholars or as professionals. Looking at the world "with the eyes of peace," as these writers do, qualifies that Enlightenment project by putting reason in the service of peace and ultimately under the Lordship of the Prince of Peace. We invite others who share such a peaceable vision to join us in this project.

NOTES

1. Max Horkheimer and Theodor Adorno, *Dialectic of Enlightenment* (New York: Continuum, 1991; original German edition, 1944), 3.

2. For a particularly readable and insightful analysis of the development of Enlightenment reason as well as a nuanced critique of its overextended claims, see Stephen Toulmin, *Cosmopolis: The Hidden Agenda of Modernity* (Chicago: University of Chicago Press, 1992).

3. See Mark Taylor, *Erring: A Postmodern A/theology* (Chicago: University of Chicago Press, 1984); and John Caputo, *On Religion* (London: Routledge, 2001).

4. See Ernesto Laclau and Chantal Mouffe, *Hegemony and Socialist Strategy: Toward a Radical Democratic Politics* (London: Verso, 1985); and Jean Baudrillard, *The Consumer Society* (London: Sage Publications, 1998).

5. See Sande Cohen, *Academia and the Luster of Capital* (Minneapolis: University of Minneapolis Press, 1993); and Noam Chomsky and Donald Macedo (editor), *Chomsky on MisEducation* (Lanham, Md.: Rowman& Littlefield, 2000).

6. See Edward Said, *Orientalism* (New York: Vintage Books, 1978); and Gayatri Chakravorty Spivak, *A Critique of Postcolonial Reason* (Cambridge: Harvard University Press, 1999).

7. For a succinct statement drafted by representatives from all of these groups, see Douglas Gwyn, George Hunsinger, Eugene F. Roop, and John Howard Yoder, *A Declaration on Peace: In God's People the World's Renewal Has Begun* (Scottdale, Pa.: Herald Press, 1991).

8. That is the central argument of Gwyn, et al., *A Declaration on Peace*. Demonstrating the possibility of a Christian worldview shaped by nonviolence involves two distinct but related tasks. One is to show that in spite of the many claims to the contrary, Christian nonviolence is intrinsic to the story of Jesus and locates its foundation in that story more than in a particular historical tradition such as the peace churches. At the same time, it is also important to show that Christian nonviolence has been enfleshed by historic movements such as Anabaptism. Both these tasks appear in this introduction.

9. Leonard Verduin, trans., and J. C. Wenger, ed., *The Complete Writings of Menno Simons* (Scottdale, Pa.: Herald Press, 1956), 554.

10. Thieleman J. van Braght, *The Bloody Theater or Martyrs Mirror* (Scottdale, Pa.: Herald Press, 1985), 472.

11. Guy F. Hershberger, *War, Peace, and Nonresistance* (Scottdale, Pa.: Herald Press, 1946), 309–310.

12. Gordon Kaufman, *Nonresistance and Responsibility and Other Mennonite Essays* (Newton, Mass.: Faith and Life Press, 1979), 115.

13. Kaufman, *Nonresistance*, 115.

14. Kaufman, *Nonresistance*, 93.

15. J. Denny Weaver, "The Socially Active Community: An Alternative Ecclesiology," in *The Limits of Perfection,* ed. Rodney J. Sawatsky and Scott Holland (Waterloo, Ont.: Institute of Anabaptist-Mennonite Studies, 1993), 91.

16. The discussion in the remainder of this section draws on and extends material I first published in an article entitled "The Radical Mission of Teaching and Thinking: The Anabaptist Difference in Mennonite Higher Education," *The Mennonite* (February 2, 1999), 4–6.

17. My examples here are focused on the context of Protestant institutions associated with the Council of Christian Colleges and Universities. I have not addressed other traditions of integrating faith and learning such as the venerable Catholic natural law tradition.

18. See for example the study guides published by members of the Coalition for Christian Outreach in the early 1980s and promoted at Christian College Coalition (now the Council of Christian Colleges and Universities) member institutions, especially in the Midwest: Bradshaw Frey, William Ingram, Thomas E. McWhertor, and William David Romanowski, *All of Life Redeemed* (Jordan Station, Ont.: Paideia Press, 1983); and Bradshaw Frey, William Ingram, Thomas McWhertor, and William David Romanowski, *At Work and at Play* (Jordan Station, Ont.: Paideia Press, 1986). *All of Life Redeemed* notably focuses on the fall and restoration of creation through the substitutionary atonement of Jesus and only mentions obedience to the teachings of Jesus in passing at the very conclusion of the book. Neither book gives any explicit attention to the teachings and ministry of Jesus as found for example in the Sermon on the Mount. Nevertheless, both books made a considerable contribution to the struggle of Christian college students and intellectuals to consider seriously the relationship of faith to learning.

19. Frey et al., *All of Life Redeemed*, 18–20.

20. I draw from this nineteenth-century Dutch Reformed theologian partly because he represents the emphatic Reformed rejection of Anabaptist theology and partly because he has become an influential source among intellectuals associated with the Council of Christian Colleges and Universities.

21. James D. Bratt, ed., *Abraham Kuyper: A Centennial Reader* (Grand Rapids, Mich.: Eerdmans, 1998), 172.

22. For a sustained analysis of early Anabaptist texts regarding the relationship between the nonviolence of the church on the one hand and the sword of governance on the other, see my "Anabaptist Separation and Arguments Against the Sword in the Schleitheim *Brotherly Union*," *Mennonite Quarterly Review* 64.3 (July 2000), 381–402.

23. John Howard Yoder, ed. and trans., *The Legacy of Michael Sattler* (Scottdale, Pa.: Herald Press, 1973), 39.

24. Notably, a prominent Reformed theologian has recently acknowledged the misreading of Anabaptism promulgated by the Reformed tradition and has specifically cited the Schleitheim *Brotherly Union* as an example of Anabaptist acknowledgement of God's work in the world "outside of the perfection of Christ." See Richard Mouw, *He Shines in All That's Fair* (Grand Rapids, Mich.: Eerdmans, 2002), 21.

25. Duane Friesen, *Artists, Citizens, Philosophers* (Scottdale, Pa.: Herald Press, 2000), 23–42.

26. David A. Hoekema, "Contours of the Christian Mind, Anabaptist and Reformed," in *Minding the Church: Scholarship in the Anabaptist Tradition,* ed. David Weaver Zercher (Telford, Pa.: Pandora Press U.S., 2002), 248.

27. Hoekema, "Contours," 248–249.

28. John Howard Yoder, "Armaments and Eschatology," *Studies in Christian Ethics* 1 (1988), 58; Stanley Hauerwas, *With the Grain of the Universe* (Grand Rapids, Mich.: Brazos Press, 2001).

29. For the ontological approach to proclaiming nonviolence, see John Milbank's magisterial work *Theology and Social Theory* (Oxford: Blackwell, 1993). For an alternative, eschatological approach, see David Toole, *Waiting for Godot in Sarajevo* (Boulder, Colo.: Westview, 1998).

30. The chapter by Stassen and Westmoreland-White is an excellent example of what John Howard Yoder has called for elsewhere: to recognize how the biblical paradigm for reconciliation can be recognized as a model "for the life of the larger society" in concrete material practices that are recognizable in the world around us. See John Howard Yoder, *Body Politics* (Scottdale, Pa.: Herald Press, 2001), x–13.

I

WHAT IS NONVIOLENCE?

2

Defining Violence and Nonviolence

Glen H. Stassen and
Michael L. Westmoreland-White

Defining violence is not as easy as one might think. Like most everything else truly important, violence gets defined differently according to the loyalties, interests, and basic convictions of those who do the defining.

A commitment to continuing the status quo influences some to define violence as whatever violates the usual order of things. A generation ago, persons with such a commitment to the status quo often saw the speech and marching of committed nonviolent protestors against segregation as violent. By contrast, a commitment to justice that criticizes the status quo influences others of us to emphasize structural violence—the violence that the forces of domination in the status quo do anonymously to their victims. Valuing human life leads to a definition of violence that emphasizes violation of persons, valuing property focuses on destruction of material assets, and valuing the created order includes violence to nature in the definition. However, we do not want to deconstruct the meaning so far that "violence is merely in the eye of the beholder," and "one person's violence is another's liberation." We need a clear definition of violence so we can diagnose and understand our times and our cultures.

One subconscious influence that sometimes skews definitions of violence is the desire to defend past actions or present policies as moral. In order to reduce that defensive distortion, we need to separate definition from denunciation. We need to be clear that defining an act as violent is not enough to establish that it is wrong. Many people justify killing in a just war. They agree that war is violent— it involves bombing, shooting, destroying—but they argue that this violence is justified to prevent a greater violence. This claim actually involves two separate arguments: a definition of violence and a contention that some violence, unfortunately, is needed for the greater good. However, claiming that all violence is wrong also requires two separate arguments: one to define what is violent and another to explain why all violence is wrong. If we confuse these two arguments and assume from the start that all violence is wrong, then people who defend certain kinds of violence will want to skew the definition defensively so that their preferred kind of violence is hidden from view by the definition. If these arguments are blurred, for example, then killing two persons during a robbery is violence, but killing a million persons in the Vietnam War is not violence. Or shouting loud epithets during a protest demonstration is violence, but the racial and class injustice that causes a million infants to die without proper health care is not violence. Or death caused by gross structural injustice is violence, but guerrilla warfare by "freedom fighters" is not violence. These examples show that a definition of violence can blind us to the very ethical arguments we need to carry out. In order to get a clear definition, as helpful as possible for ethical clarification, we need to separate the question of definition from the argument about what kind of violence may or may not be justified.

DESTRUCTION OR DEATH BY
MEANS THAT OVERPOWER CONSENT

We contend that an adequate definition of violence has two dimensions: (1) destruction to a victim and (2) by overpowering means. *Violence is destruction to a victim by means that overpower the victim's consent.* Several conversations contribute to that definition.

Some argue that to kill someone by bludgeoning is violent but to kill by quietly slipping poison in a drink is not violent—it is quiet and peaceful. Because we have a strong loyalty to human dignity and life, because we see violence as abuse or violation primarily of human persons, we think it odd to say poisoning is not violent. Accordingly, "quiet and peaceful" is not the opposite of violence. The key is whether killing is involved, not whether killing occurs loudly or quietly. The idea of violating a victim appears in psychiatrist James Gilligan's comment that a violent death involves any of many "nonnatural forms of death."[1] To the idea of violating a victim, David Stassen adds the concept of potential harm when he defines violence as "any aggressive, potentially harmful or fatal act committed either directly or indirectly against a person or group of people."[2] Thus shooting at someone and missing, which makes the act potentially but not actually fatal, is still an act of violence.

In an award-winning essay in the Council for Philosophical Studies Competition a generation ago, Ronald Miller defined violence as any act that is capable of injuring, damaging, or destroying and is done with that intent.[3] This is the "destruction to a victim" part of the definition that we suggested above.

Then Miller adds what we have called the overpowering means: "an act of violence must involve great force." However, we believe that stressing "great force" causes Miller problems. It causes him to suggest that purposely neglecting persons in need of care—children, sick, aged—is "action with intent to injure them" (abuse of persons) but not an act of violence, because it lacks force (the means). He admits his definition leads him into a difficulty: pulling a trigger (in shooting), flipping a switch (to an ICBM), or dropping a cyanide pill in water (in poisoning) "are not in themselves acts of force," but they "all are acts that under the proper circumstances we do call acts of violence." He resolves the problem by saying that since such acts physically overpower persons, they can be described as forceful. And they result "in injury, damage, and destruction," and so are violent.[4]

Miller does nicely in distinguishing violence from force and coercion. *Force*, he argues, is any act in which a person intends to overpower a person or inanimate object physically. *Coercion* is any act in which a person intends to cause another person, by threat, injury, or force, to do something different from what he or she was doing. If five men prevent a person from jumping off a bridge by picking him up and carrying him away from the ledge, this is force and coercion, but it is not violence.[5]

Failing to distinguish between force, coercion, and violence leads some to argue that violence is justified because of the need to use force and coercion against criminals. Some argue that because a nonviolent boycott or demonstration coerces people, it is violent. But force and coercion do not necessarily involve violence, in the sense of injury to a person. It is not violent when a parent coerces a child into doing her or his homework or prevents the child from running into oncoming traffic.

Robert Audi corrects Miller's argument in two ways.[6] First, Audi lists a number of cases, nearly all of which would "under any conditions whatsoever, be clear cases of violence." These include psychological violence: "'tearing someone apart' psychologically. . . . Suppose a man screams abusive epithets at his wife, humiliates her, and provokes her to a psychological breakdown, which he exacerbates by continuing his vilification. Surely he would be doing her violence, though he might leave her physically untouched."[7] So violence need not involve physical force.

Second, Audi says that violence need not be intentional. "If in a rage one inadvertently and unintentionally tramples three children and knocks over two old ladies, one would still be guilty of violence; and if a pilot unintentionally released his bombs over a crowded city, he would surely be responsible for doing violence to the people below." Thus "Violence is the physical attack upon, or the vigorous physical abuse of, or the sharp, caustic, psychological attack upon a person or animal, or the highly vigorous, or incendiary, or malicious and vigorous, destruction or damaging of property or potential property. In addition, . . . violence to animate beings tends to involve or cause their suffering or injury or both."[8] It strikes us, however, that psychological violence of the sort that Audi described to one's wife (or children) need not be sharp and caustic, if it is systematic and manipulative enough to destroy their personhood.

Audi concludes: "The notion of vigorous abuse comes very close to forming a kind of core" or unity of the definition. This names our two qualities: destruction to a victim, by means that are "vigorous." Except *vigor* is not exactly the point. According to Audi, quietly and secretly poisoning and thus killing one's wife, if the poison is not forced physically down her throat, is at best a borderline case of violence.[9] But from our perspective, this is not a fully satisfactory definition. It seems clear that to poison one's wife quietly is still to do her unambiguous violence. In spite of himself, Audi is still thinking in the shadow of the assumption that violence requires physical force, even though he has argued clearly that some violence is psychological and not physical. This assumption leads to his odd hesitation about naming killing by poison as violence and thus also his rejection of the concept of structural violence.[10]

We propose to clear up these internal confusions by returning to Miller's way out of the difficulty and developing it further: the key is not whether the means employed include physical force, but whether they violate (overpower) the victim's ability to consent or the victim's human dignity and human rights.

Consider assisted suicide. Suppose a person whose body is deteriorating from an incurable disease clearly tells several witnesses in a thoughtful and cogent way, persistently over an extended period of time, that she wants to die. Suppose she enters into a pact with a medically knowledgeable person to provide some poison, and there are several witnesses. In this case, consent is clear. If that medically knowledgeable person assists the sick person to take the poison and the person dies, we may believe that assistance was wrong, but the label we would apply to the act would probably not be "violence." What is missing is not simply physical force; poisoning someone without knowledge or consent, even without use of physical force, would be violence against that person. But in the case of assisted suicide, knowledge and consent are present. It is the knowledge and consent that cause us not to call this violence. There is no act of overpowering that person's consent.

Perhaps more importantly, with the idea in mind that violence need not employ physical means to overpower the victim's ability to consent or to violate his or her human dignity and rights, we can clearly include such structural or systemic practices as poverty, racism, and sexism in the category of violence. A number of the chapters in this book deal with responses to such violence.

SOCIAL FUNCTION

Thus far we have been discussing in a philosophical and somewhat hypothetical fashion how the concept of violence functions in ordinary language and widely shared moral understanding. The two philosophical essays by Miller and Audi come from a previous generation, before our increased awareness of the violence in our society and culture. The following now focuses on how the term functions socially. We may find a confirmation of the idea that violence is an "act of overpowering the victim's consent."

Violence functions in an authoritarian way—it is a means of domination. By whatever means, it overpowers the consent or the considered judgment or the human rights of its victims. Violence does not require presence of sudden force. Quiet poison is violent. A wrecking ball and bulldozer against my home is surely force, but not necessarily violent, if I want it razed in order to construct a much nicer dwelling in its place. The key is the authoritarian function—if it is done against my considered judgment, my human rights, then it is violent. The point is: violence is damage, destruction, or death by means that are authoritarian in the sense of overpowering consent and human dignity.

The definitions of Miller and Audi a generation ago, defining violence as individual intentional acts using physical force (especially Miller), caused them to stumble over their own awareness of psychological violence and acts of violence that did not use force. It also caused them to shy away from discussing structural violence. We have seen that their own evidence contradicted the requirement of intentionality and of physical force. Hence we can see that authoritarian structures that cause destruction, damage, and death to persons are clearly violence.

James Juhnke and Carol Hunter's description of the violent dimensions of United States culture covers well the physical and systemic or structural dimensions of violence:

> Every day, on average, more than 6,000 Americans suffer physical injury from violent assault. . . . At its peak in the 1980s, our homicide rate was about fifteen times that of industrial nations such as France, Japan, Germany, and the United Kingdom. American citizens own more than two hundred million guns. More than a decade after the end of the Cold War, the United States has 7,200 nuclear warheads deployed, sufficient to destroy all civilization on planet earth. . . . For many, the only way we can conceive of fighting violence is with more violence. The result, not surprisingly, is more violence.
> We have . . . created a culture that supports an incredible amount of violence: the systemic violence of poverty, hunger, unemployment, homelessness and racism and the individual violence of guns, drugs, homicide, rape and domestic abuse.[11]

For these reasons, we define "violence," whether systemic and structural or individual, direct or indirect, as "*destruction to a victim or victims by means that overpoer the victim's consent.*"

DEFINING NONVIOLENCE AS "PEACEMAKING INITIATIVES"

Nonviolence is not well defined simply as the absence of violence just as *shalom* is not adequately defined as the absence of war. In biblical literature, and especially in the prophets, *shalom* requires the presence of justice, of peaceful and perhaps covenantal community relationships, and well-being.[12] We use nonviolence to refer to initiatives and practices of peacemaking. These peacemaking initiatives actively transform violent conflicts or those that could become violent into relationships of relative justice and relative community well-being.

Terminology changes over time as concepts develop and are clarified through both dialogue and disagreement. Nineteenth-century abolitionists, feminists, and pacifists like Adin Ballou and William Lloyd Garrison spoke of "nonresistance," a term derived from traditional translations of Matthew 5:39 as "Do not resist evil."[13] In this terminology, they were following the understanding of traditionally Christian pacifist groups such as Mennonites, Hutterites, Amish, Church of the

Brethren, and Friends/Quakers, all of whom tended to see Jesus as teaching "nonresistance," whether or not they were active in work for peace and justice. Even though individuals and groups in these traditions sometimes engaged in actions that today would be labeled "active nonviolent direct action," they still spoke in terms of "nonresistance." To others, however, nonresistance sounded like cooperating with sin or aiding oppressors. When Protestant theologian Reinhold Niebuhr broke with his earlier pacifism and left the Fellowship of Reconciliation (an interfaith pacifist group), he insisted that strict adherence to Jesus' teaching of nonresistance both rendered one irrelevant to the world of power politics (except as a critique) and neglected the biblical mandate to seek justice in the world. Niebuhr also contended that those who engaged in active forms of nonviolence failed to see that what Jesus condemned was coercion and that violent coercion and nonviolent coercion differed only in scale but not in kind.[14] Although Niebuhr's position was ably answered both by G. H. C. MacGregor[15] and by John Howard Yoder,[16] Guy Hershberger, a Mennonite theologian who disagreed with Yoder, basically agreed with Niebuhr that the true Christian position was apolitical nonresistance rather than politically engaged pacifism or nonviolent resistance.[17]

Recently, Walter Wink has challenged the traditional translation of *antistenai* in Matthew 5:39. Rather than the reading "do not resist," Wink claims that *antistenai* means "*violent* resistance," "rebellion," and "uprising," which results in Matthew 5:39 reading, "Do not *violently* resist evil." Thus, the claim that Jesus taught nonresistance rather than nonviolent resistance is mistaken, whether argued in *defense* (Hershberger) or *criticism* of apolitical nonresistance.[18]

Practitioners and theorists alike have sought terminology more adequate than "nonresistance." Early in his South African campaigns, Mohandas K. Gandhi called his approach "passive resistance," but became dissatisfied with that term almost immediately. Before long, he coined the term *satyagraha* from two Sanskrit words meaning "truth," and "force" or "aggression." Thus *satyagraha* means "truth-force" and is intimately intertwined with the Hindu and Jain concept of *ahimsa* or "not harming." All contemporary advocates of nonviolence emphasize that it is an active process, not to be confused with passivity, that it requires courage and does not work with cowardice, that it requires discipline and strength of will, and that, just as with war or violent conflict, it entails risks of injury or death to its practitioners. In their important book, *On the Moral Nature of the Universe*, Nancey Murphy and George F. R. Ellis distinguish between refraining from violent retaliation when attacked, which they call "nonviolent resistance," and planned campaigns to right wrongs, protect the innocent, or to interfere with objectionable processes using a variety of nonviolent methods, which they call "nonviolent direct action." The distinction is useful, but since many advocates of such campaigns call their work "nonviolent resistance," one must not expect terminological purity in the literature.[19] Others distinguish between nonviolence as a "way of life," and as a tactic or strategy in defense of political communities or in movements for social change, or both.[20] Obviously, one can be committed to nonviolence both as a way of life and as a political strategy, but some are committed only to one or the other. Some who join in movements for nonviolent social change for pragmatic reasons later become committed to nonviolence in other areas of life.

CONTEMPORARY APPROACHES TO NONVIOLENCE

Throughout human history, individuals and groups have handled conflict in multitudinous ways: evasion or flight, submission or voluntary subordination of goals and interests to the stronger party, mediation and conflict resolution, and direct engagement in struggle, whether violent or nonviolent. Violent struggles—wars, riots, violent revolutions, terror tactics—dominate the history books,[21] but the use of nonviolent direct action in struggle is at least as old as the Hebrew midwives, Shiphrah and Puah, who defied Pharaoh's order to kill all the newborn male Hebrew babies (Ex. 1:15–22), and includes the civil disobedience of Shadrach, Meshach, and Abednego (Daniel 3) and Daniel himself (Daniel 6). Building on work by André Trocmé and the Jewish scholar Milton Konvitz, John Howard Yoder pointed to two examples of nonviolent civil disobedience by Jews against Roman rule that would have been known to the original readers of the Gospels. Both events, the first a spontaneous mass action in which unarmed Jews bared their necks to Pilate's troops rather than have Caesar's image placed in the Temple and the second a planned, prolonged general strike by the Jews rather than obey the Emperor Caligula's demand that he be worshipped by his subjects, are detailed by Josephus.[22] Ched Myers interprets several sections of Mark's Gospel in terms of nonviolent direct action campaigns by Jesus and the disciples (e.g., Mark 1:21–3:35; Mk. 11:1–13:3; Mk. 14:1–16:8).[23] In various cultures and contexts throughout history, sporadic uses of nonviolent direct action have occurred. Nevertheless, as a *systematic theory of struggle*, nonviolent direct action is a modern phenomenon. It has roots in the nineteenth-century abolitionist movement, especially in the thought and action of such key figures as Adin Ballou, William Lloyd Garrison, Sarah and Angelina Grimké, Sojourner Truth, and (until he abandoned nonviolence to support John Brown's raid on Harper's Ferry and then the Civil War) Frederick Douglass.[24] The nineteenth-century feminist and women's suffrage movement also contributed to the rise of nonviolence theory, as did some of the writings of Count Leo Tolstoy and the essay "On Civil Disobedience" by Henry David Thoreau, who penned it as an explanation for his war tax resistance during the Mexican-American War.[25]

Nonviolent direct action on a mass scale has experienced its greatest growth in both practice and theory in the twentieth century, partly as a transformative response to the experience of that century as the most violent century in human history. In a book and a PBS miniseries, Peter Ackerman and Jack Duvall examine numerous campaigns of nonviolent direct action, from the democratic revolution against Czarist rule in Russia in 1905 (before the later Communist takeover), to the German *Ruhrkampf* in 1923, which nonviolently resisted French invasion for war reparations at the cost of German starvation, to the

Gandhi-led movement for self-rule in India, to three nonviolent campaigns of resistance to the Nazis,[26] to El Salvador's nonviolent removal of military dictatorship in 1944, to the Civil Rights movement in the U.S. South, to the nonviolent strands of the campaign against apartheid in South Africa, to the nonviolent revolution in the Philippines in 1986, and more. Ackerman and Duvall document successful nonviolent direct action campaigns in every decade of the bloody twentieth century, on every continent, and in many different contexts. They also show how these campaigns influenced each other as the century progressed.[27]

The labor movement clearly added both tactics and energy to nonviolent direct action. Early in its history, the more authoritarian labor advocates did not trust democratic processes to bring justice to labor strife and argued that only violence could achieve justice. Striking workers responded with retaliatory violence to the violence of strikebreakers and police. But labor violence only gave justification to bringing in the National Guard with bayonets to drive away the strikers. Learning from the failure of this authoritarian function of violence, labor adopted nonviolent strategies—strikes, work slowdowns, boycotts, picketing, democratic appeals to the public, organized collective bargaining, and labor law reform—all tactics that would become classic components of nonviolent campaigns for social justice. In 1923, Clarence Marsh Case (1874–1946), Quaker minister, sociologist, and professor, published the first systematic analysis of the various methods and dynamic mechanisms in mass nonviolent direct action.[28] Arguing that past studies of conflict had overlooked the importance of "antagonistic cooperation," Case placed methods of social change on a scale from persuasion to violent coercion.

PERSUASION

1. By argument

2. By suffering

   a) Nonresistant suffering or martyrdom when injury inflicted by opponent

   b) Self-inflicted, for example, a hunger strike

NONVIOLENT COERCION

1. Indirect action: strike, boycott, noncooperation

2. Political action through institutions and culture—combines partisan persuasion and impersonal coercion of law and established traditions, involving the threat or use of force or "legitimate violence" by police, courts, and prisons

3. Social coercion:

   a) Ostracism

   b) Collective pressure through "passive resistance"

VIOLENT COERCION

1. Threat of violence or force
2. Use of violence of force

Case was the first to classify coercive tactics like strikes and boycotts as examples of nonviolent action. His work had an enormous impact on pacifists who sympathized with the labor movement and paved the way for greater development of nonviolence theory in future movements. Case also discussed the efficacy of nonviolent action and dispelled the myth that its practitioners were cowards.

More influential was Mohandas K. Gandhi (1869–1948) and the movements he led in South Africa and India. In his youth and during his stay in Britain, Gandhi struggled to find his spiritual bearings, exploring not only his own Hindu *Upanishads* and the *Bhagavad-Gita* but also the story of the Buddha, the life and message of Jesus of Nazareth as he found it in the Gospels, and the writings of Tolstoy.[29] Gandhi was also a keen observer and analyst of historical events and studied the largely nonviolent tactics of the first Russian revolution in 1905.[30]

From 1893 to 1914, Gandhi worked to help Indians resist increasing discrimination by white South Africans. During this time, he was clarifying his spiritual and moral vision, gradually simplifying his needs and possessions, and founding two ashrams (religious communities), Phoenix near Durban (1904) and Tolstoy Farm (1910) near Johannesburg. These experiments in communal living clarified his spiritual vision, gave experiences to people in cooperation as equals across lines of race, class, and caste, and provided an alternative economy to the system of oppression. The creation of alternative institutions even while seeking wider reform has become a vital component of most successful nonviolent movements. In 1907–1908, Gandhi led his first campaign of nonviolent direct action, persuading Indians in South Africa to resist the injustice of the Transvaal "Black Act" by refusing to register as the act demanded and by dramatically burning certificates of registration. This led to a series of actions of civil disobedience with resultant jailings. As others would do in later movements, Gandhi transformed a punishment that had been a mark of deep shame into a badge of honor in the fight against injustice.

For Gandhi, ultimate Truth (God) could not be fully apprehended by any mortal. Even one's opponents had portions of Truth and could be one's teachers. Therefore, truthseeking must be nonviolent, because violence would prevent one from seeking the truth of the adversary and from being able to communicate with the adversary the truth one had found, including the truth that the adversary is treating one unjustly. The satyagrahi or "truth warrior" nonviolently confronts the oppressor with the reality of the humanity of the victims and invites the oppressor to recover from oppression's distorting effect on his own humanity by correcting the oppressive conditions. By 1914 Gandhi's experiments (watched with fascination all over the world) had convinced him of both the morally transforming effect of satyagraha on all parties and its political efficacy. He had created a new sense of Indian unity in South Africa, though rifts remained between "African born" and newer arrivals. He had further managed to effect some changes in laws which discriminated against Indians in South Africa, though not on as wide a scale as he wanted and without changing the attitudes of most whites or creating a successful coalition between Indians and other nonwhite racial groups in South Africa.[31]

Returning to India in 1915 and spending the next five years in relative obscurity, Gandhi founded an ashram and a journal. In 1920, he assumed an unexpected dominance in the Indian National Congress, which was the main organ of Indian nationalist hopes for independence from Great Britain. He advised those who attended to take up a campaign of noncooperation with the British Raj. In 1917, 1918, and 1928, he led several completely nonviolent and highly successful local campaigns on single issues. In 1920–1922, 1930–1934, and 1940–1942, he led three major all-India campaigns of nonviolent resistance to the British, but none succeeded in staying disciplined to nonviolence. This failure distressed Gandhi greatly, and he often responded to riots by his followers with fasts and hunger strikes until peaceful means were again adopted. Other times, he called off campaigns rather than let them degenerate into violent rioting. He experimented with a wide range of symbolic and small-scale modes of satyagraha, such as refusing to wear foreign cloth, selling banned books, making salt illegally, or observing _hartal_, a cessation of public business as a sign of grief. Only rarely did he sanction the nonpayment of taxes or similar forms of outright civil disobedience because he knew that most of the masses did not have the inner discipline for such nonviolence. He would sometimes limit the numbers and types of people permitted to become satyagrahis, as in his 1930 march to the sea to make salt (in defiance of a British salt monopoly). When he did sanction mass nonviolent action, he made great efforts to educate the participating public in nonviolence, both in relation to the British and to the many Indian divisions of caste and religion, always sharpest between Hindus and Muslims. Along with these direct action campaigns, Gandhi also advocated an alternative economics (the "positive program") of simple living that would be sustainable for all India and break down the vast disparities of wealth and starvation. Gandhi believed the economics of the industrial West, in either capitalist or socialist form, was unsustainable and inherently violent.[32]

By themselves, Gandhi's satyagraha campaigns did not free India from the British, and the independence that came in 1947 was not the _swaraj_ (freedom) that Gandhi envisioned but the "brown Raj" of domination that he feared as early as 1909. Further, continuing religious intolerance and the effects of caste traditions grieved him, as did India's adoption of Western-style industrial economics, whether leaning to the democratic socialist or to the capitalist side. The division of India in 1947–1948 into Muslim East and West Pakistan and Hindu India, in a violent disruption that would today be called "ethnic cleansing," caused Gandhi great distress. His continual espousal of religious freedom and mutual respect earned him an assassin's bullet by an authoritarian Hindu nationalist in 1948. But Gandhi's legacy cannot be overestimated. His nonviolent campaigns and writings have been studied repeatedly by widely disparate groups involved in various forms of nonviolent struggle all over the world.[33]

The movement which became the next most famous and dramatic nonviolent struggle for human rights was the Civil Rights movement in the U.S., more often called by its participants "the Freedom Movement," since they were struggling not only for legal recognition of civil rights and liberties of African Americans, but for equality and a nonracist society. Historians usually date this struggle as 1954 to 1968, but the movement's beginnings can be traced to the 1940s. It is often believed that Gandhian methods were introduced either by Martin Luther King Jr. or by white Northern advisers, but this is also a distortion. Sudarshan Kapur has shown that African Americans were keenly interested observers of Gandhi's campaigns at least as early as his return to India. Numerous African American newspapers and journals covered Gandhi sympathetically from 1919 forward, and editors often advocated Gandhian strategies in the U.S. for African American emancipation. Further, a number of African American leaders visited Gandhi or his followers prior to World War II and probed his ideas on nonviolence and the meaning of direct action, discussed the problems of training individuals and communities to carry out a nonviolent desegregationist struggle, and reflected with Gandhi on the applicability of nonviolent direct action to injustice on a mass scale in the United States.[34] A number of Gandhians from India also came to the United States prior to 1955 and brought the message of the Mahatma and his nonviolent campaign to African Americans. Madeleine Slade (1892–1982), a British disciple and coworker with Gandhi, communicated the meaning and relevance of his work to African American students and faculty at Howard University and spoke in several churches and African American social clubs on the same topic in 1934. In the early 1940s, Krishnalal Shridharani (1911–1960), a veteran satyagrahi of the 1930 salt march campaign, established close ties between the two movements by coming to the U.S. and participating in several desegregation campaigns led by the Congress of Racial Equality (CORE). Founded in 1942 by James Farmer, Bayard Rustin, and George Houser, who were staff members of the Fellowship of Reconciliation (FOR)—the well-known religious pacifist organization—CORE based its campaigns on the systematic study of Gandhian nonviolence strategy as outlined by Shridharani in his 1939 work, *War Without Violence*, the first systematic analysis of Gandhi's methods in English.[35]

James Farmer founded CORE because, at that time, most white pacifists, although in favor of Gandhian nonviolence *theoretically*, still found demonstrations and confrontational techniques too much like violence. (Earlier, veteran pacifist and radical labor activist A. J. Musté had found pacifist commitment to labor to be similarly lukewarm.[36]) CORE was meant to organize a mass nonviolent movement for racial equality, and Farmer was not too worried that most of the rank and file were not complete pacifists. In 1947, CORE organized a "Journey of Reconciliation" from Washington, D.C., to Louisville, Kentucky, and back with both African American and white passengers. The journey was to test the 1946 U.S.

Supreme Court decision banning segregated seating on interstate buses. With few arrests and relatively little violence by local whites, the journey did not get the national attention that CORE hoped, but it did provide a model for the later Freedom Rides of the 1960s, in which CORE played a vital part.

The Freedom Movement sprang forth in earnest, however, with the 1955–1956 boycott of city buses in Montgomery, Alabama, sparked by the arrest of seamstress Rosa Parks (1913–), secretary of the Montgomery chapter of the NAACP, who had training in nonviolence at the Highlander Folk School in Monteagle, Tennessee, a Christian-based school for radical social change. Parks's arrest for refusing to move from the "white" to the "Negro" section of the segregated city bus outraged the Montgomery African American community. Along with NAACP leader E. D. Nixon (1899–1987), Jo Ann Robinson (now Jo Ann Robinson Gibson) of the Women's Political Caucus organized the bus boycott in protest.[37] The movement soon brought the leadership of the young Rev. Dr. Martin Luther King Jr. to the fore.

King had been introduced to Gandhi's ideas during his college days at Morehouse and had read his writings as well as secondary works on Gandhi after hearing a lecture on Gandhi at Howard University by its president Mordecai Johnson. King was not a complete disciple of nonviolence until after assuming leadership of the Montgomery Bus Boycott. Later, after several conversations with Bayard Rustin of the War Resisters League and Glenn Smylie of FOR, and more reading and contemplation on the subject, King adopted nonviolence as a lifestyle as well as a strategy for social change. He joined FOR and not only led the freedom struggle through many nonviolent campaigns but also spoke out against the War in Vietnam and the nuclear arms race and, at the time of his assassination in 1968, was trying to form a mass movement for economic justice for poor people of all races and ethnic groups.[38]

Many millions of persons, white as well as black, were directly involved in the movement, marching, picketing, boycotting, sitting in, submitting to jail. These were deeply formative experiences. The rest of the nation experienced it through the media or direct observation. As a result, "nonviolence" no longer means merely "not doing violence," but actively engaging in peacemaking initiatives.

But there is much more to the story. Nonviolent direct action has spread globally and has been dramatically effective in toppling dictatorships and moving nations toward peace and justice.[39] Movements in which nonviolence had a key impact include the overthrow of dictators Ferdinand Marcos in the Philippines in 1986, and Pinochet in Chile in 1988; the aborted nonviolent movement in China in 1989 and the continuing nonviolent struggle in Tibet, symbolized by the exiled spiritual leader, the fourteenth Dalai Lama (winner of the 1989 Nobel Peace Prize); the continuing nonviolent movement for democracy in Burma led by Aung San Suu Kyi (winner of the 1991 Nobel Peace Prize); the nonviolent revolution in Indonesia in 1998; the nonviolent movement for the independence of East Timor (finally realized in 2000 with aid from the conflict resolution team sent by the Carter Center and from humanitarian intervention led by Australia under the auspices of the United Nations) which led to a joint 1996 Nobel Peace Prize to Roman Catholic Bishop Carlos Belo and the journalist José Ramos-Horta for nonviolent leadership.

The first (1990–1991) Palestinian Intifada was largely nonviolent with no terrorist attacks or suicide bombings (although the media focused on rock-throwing children and youths) and led to the Oslo process—unlike the current violent Intifada, which has led to ever worse conditions for Palestinians as well as Israelis.

In South Africa, the early movement of the African National Congress (ANC) was based on Gandhian nonviolence. After the Sharpeville massacre of 1968, the ANC adopted a strategy of sabotage and guerrilla war, but that proved ineffective. The nonviolent movement was taken up by the churches of South Africa, with leadership by Alan Boesak, Frank Chikane, a few white leaders like Beyers Naudé, and 1986 Nobel Peace Prize winner Archbishop Desmond Tutu. That church leadership, along with international sanctions and diplomatic isolation, led President deKlerk to break with his Afrikaaner history and party and begin secret negotiations with Nelson Mandela and others—lifting the ban on the ANC, releasing political prisoners, and working toward a new constitution, universal adult suffrage, and a peaceful transfer of power to the black majority with Mandela as the first president of a new South Africa.

In Eastern Europe, nonviolent revolutions toppled dictatorships in Poland, Czechoslovakia (the Velvet Revolution), East Germany (the Revolution of the Candles), Lithuania, Finland, Estonia, Hungary, and Bulgaria. In post-Communist Europe, Yugoslavia broke apart in huge civil wars and ethnic cleansing in Croatia, Serbia, Bosnia-Herzegovina, and then Kosovo and Albania. But in 1999, the Serbian dictator Slobodan Milosevic, the man responsible for much of that madness, was toppled with a nearly textbook nonviolent revolution—literally. In the PBS special, *Bringing Down a Dictator*, one can see copies of Gene Sharp's *The Politics of Nonviolent Action* being studied and passed around by students and workers during demonstrations! We argue that this nonviolent movement had been close to success earlier and was set back by the NATO bombing of Kosovo and Serbia: dissent disappeared for a while in the wake of the NATO attacks. The Kosovo Albanians also had a nonviolent movement, but NATO ignored it and chose to support the Kosovo Liberation Army. James Satterwhite's chapter in this volume explores that missed opportunity for nonviolent change.

In August 1991, hard-line Communists and the KGB staged a coup in Moscow to oust President Gorbachev, but Boris Yeltsin (no pacifist!) led a nonviolent movement that successfully repelled the coup—leading a few months later to the peaceful breakup of the USSR and the end of Communism in Eastern Europe and most of Asia.[40]

JUST PEACEMAKING THEORY

This narrative has featured the practice of nonviolent direct action, but other key practices of peacemaking that have developed, especially since World War II, have also played a crucial role—economic justice, conflict resolution, the United Nations, humanitarian intervention, the spread of democracy, and the action of churches and voluntary peacemaking groups like FOR and CORE. These practices need to be highlighted, lest we fail to notice the revolution of nonviolence that is changing our history. Twenty-three scholars have joined together to develop a new paradigm of ethics that names and describes these practices and unites them in a Just Peacemaking Theory, developed most fully in *Just Peacemaking: Ten Practices to Abolish War.*[41] It is important not to reduce the practices of nonviolence to a single practice, since they support and need each other. Together, working in synergy, the ten practices can achieve greater justice and prevent many wars. The more widely known they become and the more extensively supported, the more effective they can be in achieving justice and peace by nonviolent methods. Here are the ten initiatives of just peacemaking theory.

1. Nonviolent Direct Action

As narrated above.

2. Independent Initiatives

Developed by social psychologist Charles Osgood, independent initiatives: (1) are visible and verifiable actions designed to decrease threat perception and distrust but not leave the initiator weak; (2) are enacted independently of the slow process of negotiation but are intended to foster eventual negotiation; (3) have a timing announced in advance and carried out regardless of the other side's bluster; (4) have a clearly announced purpose—to shift toward de-escalation and to invite reciprocation; (5) come in a series; if the other side fails to reciprocate, small, continuing initiatives keep open the invitation to reciprocation.

3. Cooperative Conflict Resolution

Conflict resolution is becoming a well-known practice, seen dramatically in the work of President Carter in the Camp David Accords between Egypt and Israel, and in Haiti and North Korea. A key test of how seriously governments are seeking peace is whether they develop imaginative solutions that show they understand their adversary's perspectives and needs.

4. Acknowledgment of Responsibility for Violence and Injustice

Previously, nations thought acknowledging their own responsibility would be a sign of weakness. However, recent experiences show that acknowledging responsibility—Chancellor Willy Brandt and President Richard von Weizsäcker for the atrocities of the Third Reich, President George Bush Senior for the internment of Japanese Americans in World War II, President William Clinton for U.S. support of military dictatorship in Guatemala and neglecting justice in Africa, the Japanese Prime Minister for atrocities against South Korea, and the findings of Archbishop Tutu's Truth and Reconciliation process in South Africa—has lanced the boil of bitterness that could otherwise erupt into war.

5. Promotion of Human Rights, Democracy, and Religious Liberty

Extensive empirical evidence shows that pushing for human rights and religious liberty spreads democracy, and this in turn prevents wars. Democracies with human rights fought *no wars* against other democracies during the entire twentieth century. Some official democracies, such as the United States, are in danger of slipping into plutocracy (the rule of wealth) or military rule, or both, and do sometimes intervene imperialistically in other countries by proxy. But democracies generally devote lower shares of their income to military expenditures, and they produce significantly fewer terrorists, civil wars, and massacres.

6. Just and Sustainable Economic Development

Sustainable development occurs where the needs of today are met without threatening the needs of tomorrow—where those who lack adequate economic resources gain access and those who do have them learn to control resource use and prevent future exhaustion. Where this happens, war is less frequent and shorter in duration. Challenges to sustainable development are particularly evident in Latin America, which lacks real land reform and equality, and in the United States, where the wealth/poverty gap is growing dramatically.

7. Participation in Cooperative Forces in the International System

Four trends have been altering the conditions and practices of international relations so that the globe is becoming something of a society, though of course an anarchic society without anything like a world government—which very few want. These four trends are the decline in the utility of war; the priority of trade and the economy over war; the strength of international exchanges, communications, transactions, and networks; and the gradual ascendancy of representative democracy with human rights. Empirical studies in international relations show that where nations are more engaged in these growing international networks, they engage in war less frequently. Where they break treaties and disengage from cooperative trends, they experience war more frequently. The unilateralist policies of the second Bush administration, disengaging from peacemaking with North Korea and in the Middle East and withdrawing from several international treaties, are setbacks for these trends, but their war-threatening consequences also underscore the necessity of just peacemaking as the effective peaceful alternative.

8. The United Nations and International Efforts for Cooperation and Human Rights

International relations increasingly involve not only the traditional military-diplomatic arena but also the modern arena of economic interdependence, where governments are exposed to the forces of a global market they do not control. Additionally there is the increasingly important third arena of demands for "people power," or for "citizens' say." The information revolution makes it harder for governments to control people's minds, and popular pressures can now set much of the agenda of foreign policies. States float in a sea of forces from outside their borders and from their own people. Acting alone, states cannot solve problems of trade, debt, interest rates; of pollution, ozone depletion, acid rain, depletion of fish stocks, global warming; of migrations and refugees seeking asylum; of military security when weapons rapidly penetrate borders. Many multilateral practices are building effectiveness to resolve conflicts, to monitor, nurture, and even enforce truces and replace violent conflict with beginning cooperation. Multilateral agencies are organizing to meet human needs for food, hygiene, medicine, education, and economic interaction. Furthermore, most wars now happen within states, not between states (although the policies of the second Bush administration clearly contradict this trend). Therefore, *Just Peacemaking* argues, collective action needs to include UN-approved humanitarian intervention in cases like the former Yugoslavia, Haiti, Somalia, Rwanda, and East Timor, where otherwise massacres that shock the conscience of humankind are likely to occur.

9. Reduction of Offensive Weapons and Weapons Trade

Weapons have become so destructive that war is not worth the price. This is a key factor in the decrease of war between nations. The offense cannot destroy the defense before the defense does huge retaliatory damage. Reducing offensive weapons and shifting toward defensive force structures strengthens that equation. For example, President Gorbachev removed half the Soviet Union's tanks from Central Europe and all its river-crossing equipment. This action freed NATO to agree to get rid of all medium-range and shorter-range nuclear weapons in Eastern and Western Europe—the first dramatic step in ending the Cold War peacefully.

As nations turn toward democracy and human rights, their governments no longer need large militaries to keep them in power. As the ten practices of peacemaking reduce the threat in their environment, nations feel less need for weapons (although again the second Bush administration constitutes a setback to this worldwide trend). As they struggle with their deep indebtedness, they have less ability to buy weapons. The International Monetary Fund now requires big reductions in weapons expenditures before granting loans. For these reasons, arms imports by developing nations in 1995 dropped to one-quarter of their peak in 1988. But the power of money invested by arms manufacturers in politicians' campaigns is a major obstacle to reductions. So is the faith that the only reliable defense against violence is the power to do violence in return.

10. Grassroots Peacemaking Groups and Voluntary Associations

The existence of a growing worldwide people's movement constitutes one more historical force that makes just peacemaking effective. Citizen groups serve as voices for the voiceless, as they did in churches in East Germany and in women's groups in Guatemala.[42] They help to initiate, foster, or support transforming initiatives, where existing parties need support and courage to take risks to break out of the cycles that perpetuate violence and injustice. A citizens' network of NGOs and INGOs often is a source of information that governmental officials lack or resist acknowledging. They criticize injustice and initiate repentance and forgiveness. They nurture a spirituality that sustains courage when just peacemaking is unpopular, hope when despair or cynicism is tempting, and grace and forgiveness when just peacemaking fails.

Other summaries of effective nonviolent peacemaking initiatives exist besides *Just Peacemaking*.[43] They all show that nonviolence is an active practice of peacemaking initiatives that cannot be reduced to one or two of the well-known practices. Nor is nonviolence simply a set of ideals; it is actively preventing wars and achieving improved justice in many places in the real world, realistically perceived.

Now, with the chapters included in this volume, we can see the possibility of extending the practices of nonviolence beyond the spheres of social and political struggle into the very structures of knowledge and the methods for creating knowledge. Thus, the movements we have described—and the traditions of knowledge these movements drew from and developed—are bearing surprising fruit in that they have helped us to reevaluate our assumptions about the nature and character of truth itself—especially the Enlightenment version of truth which has perhaps more often than we have previously realized contributed to the legacy of modern violence, by imposing a regime of plausibility that can be described in many instances as authoritarian and certainly as a contributing cause for destruction, damage, and death to people. By seeking to change the worldviews that lead to wars and violence of all kinds, the chapters in this book provide compelling examples of an emerging practice of just peacemaking whose future has great promise. May peace break out.

NOTES

1. James Gilligan, *Violence: Reflections on a National Epidemic* (New York: Vintage Books, 1996), 5.

2. In personal conversation.

3. Ronald B. Miller, "Violence, Force, and Coercion," in *Violence: Award-Winning Essays in the Council for Philosophical Studies Competition,* ed. Jerome Shaffer (New York: David McKay, 1971), 25.

4. Miller, "Violence, Force, and Coercion," 20–21, 25, 31–32.

5. Miller, "Violence, Force, and Coercion," 27, 30–31.

6. Audi, "On the Meaning and Justification of Violence," in Shaffer, 45–100.

7. Audi, "On the Meaning," 52, 54.

8. Audi, "On the Meaning," 58–60.

9. Audi, "On the Meaning," 63, 65.

10. Audi, "On the Meaning," 66–67.

11. James C. Juhnke and Carol M. Hunter, *The Missing Peace: The Search for Nonviolent Alternatives in United States History* (Kitchener, Ont.: Pandora Press, 2001), 9–10.

12. Perry Yoder, "Introductory Essay to the Old Testament Chapters: *Shalom* Revisited," in *The Meaning of Peace: Biblical Studies,* ed. Perry Yoder and Willard Swartley (Louisville: Westminster/John Knox), 6–13.

13. E.g., Adin Ballou, *Christian Nonresistance* (Philadelphia: J. Miller M'Kim, 1845).

14. Among other places, Niebuhr makes this argument in "A Critique of Pacifism" (1927), "Pacifism and the Use of Force" (1928), "Why I Leave the F.O.R." (1934), and "To Prevent the Triumph of an Intolerable Tyranny" (1940), all reprinted in Reinhold Niebuhr, *Love and Justice: Selections from the Shorter Writings of Reinhold Niebuhr*, ed. D. B. Robertson (Gloucester, Mass.: Peter Smith, 1976).

15. G. H. C. Macgregor, *The Relevance of an Impossible Ideal* (1941), reprinted in his *The New Testament Basis of Pacifism and the Relevance of an Impossible Ideal* (Nyack, N.Y.: Fellowship Press, 1954).

16. John Howard Yoder, "Reinhold Niebuhr and Christian Pacifism," *Mennonite Quarterly Review* 29 (April 1955): 101–117. Also published as Church Peace Mission Pamphlet # 6 (Scottdale, Pa.: Herald Press, 1968). Cf. A. J. Musté, "Pacifism and Perfectionism," in *The Essays of A. J. Musté*, ed. Nat Hentoff (New York: Simon and Schuster, 1967).

17. Guy Hershberger, *War, Peace, and Nonresistance* (Scottdale, Pa.: Herald Press, 1953). In later years, however, Hershberger moved toward a more activist view.

18. Walter Wink, "Neither Passivity nor Violence: Jesus' Third Way (Matt. 5:38–42 par.)" in *The Love of Enemy and Nonretaliation in the New Testament*, ed. Willard M. Swartley (Louisville: Westminster/John Knox, 1992). See also, Walter Wink, *Engaging the Powers: Discernment and Resistance in a World of Domination* (Minneapolis: Fortress Press, 1992), 175–193. Decades ago Clarence Jordan and John Ferguson both argued for a similar conclusion using a different grammatical argument. See John Ferguson, *The Politics of Love: The New Testament and Nonviolent Revolution* (Nyack, N.Y.: Fellowship Publications, 1977); and Clarence Jordan, "The Lesson on the Mount II," in *The Substance of Faith and Other Cotton Patch Sermons*, ed. Dallas Lee (New York: Association Press, 1972).

19. Nancey Murphy and George F. R. Ellis, *On the Moral Nature of the Universe: Theology, Cosmology, and Ethics* (Minneapolis: Fortress Press, 1996), 136.

20. See the 2-volume study guide published by the (U.S.) Fellowship of Reconciliation, *Active Nonviolence: A Way of Life, a Strategy for Change* (Nyack, N.Y.: Fellowship of Reconciliation, 1991).

21. Some historians have questioned whether violent events are the dominant forces of change in history or if people, including historians, only believe them to be so. See American history from a nonviolent perspective in Juhnke and Hunter, *The Missing Peace.*

22. Josephus, *Antiquities* 18:3 (with a briefer parallel account in his *Wars of the Jews* 2:9); *Antiquities* 18:8 (*Wars of the Jews* 2:10); André Trocmé, *Jesus and the Nonviolent*

Revolution (Scottdale, Pa.: Herald Press, 1973; new edition with additional chapters and information forthcoming in 2003 from Plough Publishing; French original, 1961), 103–105; Milton Konvitz, "Conscience and Civil Disobedience in the Jewish Tradition," in his *Judaism and Human Rights* (New York: Viking, 1972), 164–166; John Howard Yoder, *The Politics of Jesus* rev. ed. (Grand Rapids, Mich.: Eerdmans, 1994; original edition, 1972), 89–92.

23. Ched Myers, *Binding the Strong Man: A Political Reading of Mark's Story of Jesus* (Maryknoll, N.Y.: Orbis Books, 1988).

24. Peter Brock, *Radical Pacifists in Antebellum America* (Princeton, N.J.: Princeton University Press, 1968); Carlton Mabee, *Black Freedom: The Nonviolent Abolitionists from 1830 through the Civil War* (London: Macmillan, 1970); Aileen S. Kraditor, *Means and Ends in American Abolitionism: Garrison and His Critics on Strategy and Tactics, 1834–1850* (New York: Pantheon, 1967); Peter Krass, *Sojourner Truth: Antislavery Activist* (New York: Chelsea House, 1988); Lewis Perry, *Radical Abolitionism: Anarchy and the Government of God in Antislavery Thought* (Ithaca, N.Y.: Cornell University Press, 1973); Valerie H. Ziegler, *The Advocates of Peace in Antebellum America* (Bloomington, Ind.: Indiana University Press, 1992).

25. Ellen Carol DuBois, ed., *Elizabeth Cady Stanton/Susan B. Anthony: Correspondence, Writings, Speeches* (New York: Schocken, 1981); Israel Kugler, *From Ladies to Women: The Organized Struggle for Woman's Rights in the Reconstruction Era* (New York: Greenwood, 1987); Pam McAllister, *You Can't Kill the Spirit: Women and Nonviolence* (Philadelphia: New Society Publishers, 1988); Henry David Thoreau, *Walden or Life in the Woods, and On the Duty of Civil Disobedience* (New York: New American Library/Signet Classic, 1980); Leo N. Tolstoy, *Writings on Civil Disobedience and Nonviolence* (Philadelphia: New Society Publishers, 1987).

26. Out of the many nonviolent resistance campaigns in World War II, *A Force More Powerful* focuses on the Danish campaign to save their Jews and resist the Nazification of their society; the Bulgarian campaign against deporting their Jews to death camps, which saved all of Bulgaria's Jews; and the campaign in Berlin of German (gentile) wives of Jewish men who successfully campaigned for their release from prison.

27. Peter Ackerman and Jack Duvall, *A Force More Powerful: A Century of Nonviolent Conflict* (New York: St. Martin's, 2000).

28. Clarence Marsh Case, *Non-Violent Coercion: A Study in Methods of Social Pressure* (New York: Garland Publishing, 1972; originally published, 1923). Murphy and Ellis, *On the Moral Nature of the Universe*, 151–156, use Marsh's spectrum of coercion to argue incisively that the greater the violence, the less the consent and long-term cooperation. This coheres with our attention to the overpowering, dominating, authoritarian means in violence—which cause resentment and resistance.

29. Graeme MacQueen, "Linking Gandhi to the Origins of Nonviolence: Edwin Arnold's *The Light of Asia*," in *Nonviolence for the Third Millennium: Its Legacy and Future*, ed. G. Simon Harak, S.J. (Macon, Ga.: Mercer University Press, 2000).

30. Ackerman and Duvall, *A Force More Powerful*, 6.

31. Mohandas K. Gandhi, *Satyagraha in South Africa* (Ahmedabad, India: Navajivan, 1961; originally published 1928); M. Swan, *Gandhi: The South African Experience* (Johannesburg: Ravan, 1985).

32. Judith M. Brown, *Gandhi: Prisoner of Hope* (New Haven, Conn.: Yale University Press, 1989). We owe insights about Gandhi's "positive program" of small-scale village

economics to Richard Axtell, Associate Professor of Religion at Centre College, Danville, Ky., and a scholar of Gandhi's religious, political, and economic thought.

33. Mohandas K. Gandhi, *An Autobiography: The Story of My Experiments with Truth* (Ahmedabad, India: Navajivan Publishing House, 1948; originally published 1927; later expanded.); Mohandas K. Gandhi, *Non-violent Resistance and Social Transformation,* vol. 3 of *The Moral and Political Writings of Mahatma Gandhi,* ed. R. Iyer (Oxford: Oxford University Press, 1987).

34. These African American leaders included at least the following: the Rev. Dr. Howard Thurman (1900–1980), a celebrated preacher-mystic-theologian, and his wife, Sue Bailey Thurman (1903–); the Rev. Edward Carroll (1910–), a church leader; William Stuart Nelson (1895–1977), the editor of Howard University's *Journal of Religious Thought;* Benjamin E. Mays (1895–1984), president of Morehouse College; Channing H. Tobias (1882–1961), a member of the NAACP Board of Trustees in the early 1940s.

35. Sudarshan Kapur, *Raising Up a Prophet: The African-American Encounter with Gandhi* (Boston: Beacon Press, 1992); Krishnalal Shridharani, *War without Violence: A Study of Gandhi's Method and Its Accomplishments* (New York: Harcourt Brace, 1939); James Farmer, *Lay Bare the Heart: An Autobiography of the Civil Rights Movement* (New York: Arbor House, 1985).

36. A. J. Musté, *Nonviolence in an Aggressive World* (New York: Harper and Bros., 1940).

37. Rosa Parks, *Rosa Parks: Mother to a Movement* (New York: Dial, 1992); Jo Ann Robinson Gibson, *The Montgomery Bus Boycott and the Women Who Started It* (Knoxville: University of Tennessee, 1987).

38. Martin Luther King Jr., "Pilgrimage to Nonviolence," in Martin Luther King Jr., *Strength to Love* (New York: Harper and Row, 1963), 146–154; Martin Luther King Jr., *Stride toward Freedom: The Montgomery Story* (New York: Harper and Row, 1964). Of the several biographies of King available, we find most helpful David J. Garrow, *Bearing the Cross: Martin Luther King and the Southern Christian Leadership Conference* (New York: Morrow, 1986); and Stephen B. Oates, *Let the Trumpet Sound: The Life of Martin Luther King Jr.* (New York: Harper and Row, 1982).

39. A good summary of this is found in Richard Deats, "The Global Spread of Active Nonviolence," in *Peace Is the Way: Writings on Nonviolence from the Fellowship of Reconciliation,* ed. Walter Wink (Maryknoll, N.Y.: Orbis Books, 2000), 283–295; and in Daniel Buttry, *Christian Peacemaking: From Heritage to Hope* (Valley Forge, Pa.: Judson, 1994).

40. Stephen Zunes, Lester R. Kurtz, and Sara Beth Asher, eds. *Nonviolent Social Movements: A Geographical Perspective* (Oxford: Blackwell Publishers, 1999).

41. Glen Stassen, ed., *Just Peacemaking: Ten Practices to Abolish War* (Cleveland: Pilgrim Press, 1998).

42. Paper by Duane Friesen. See Jörg Swoboda, *Revolution of the Candles,* trans. Richard Pierard (Atlanta: Mercer University Press, 1997); Michelle Tooley, *Voices of the Voiceless* (Scottdale, Pa.: Herald Press), 1997.

43. For example, see Robert Herr and Judy Zimmerman Herr, eds., *Transforming Violence: Linking Local and Global Peacemaking* (Scottdale, Pa.: Herald Press; copublished with Pandora Press U.S., 1998); and Gene Sharp, *The Politics of Nonviolent Action,* 3 vols. (Boston: Porter Sargent, 1973).

II

NONVIOLENCE IN THE BIBLE AND THEOLOGY

3

Violence in Christian Theology

J. Denny Weaver

Is Christianity characterized by the medieval crusades, warrior popes, the multiple blessings of wars by Christians over the centuries, wars religious and otherwise fought in the name of the Christian God, support for capital punishment, justifications of slavery, worldwide colonialism in the name of spreading Christianity, corporal punishment under the guise of "spare the rod and spoil the child," the systemic violence of women subjected to men, and more? Or does it reflect its eponymous founder, who is worshipped as "Wonderful Counselor, Mighty God, Everlasting Father, Prince of Peace" (Isaiah 9:6); whose Sermon on the Mount taught nonviolence and love of enemies; who faced his accusers nonviolently and then died a violent death; whose teaching of nonviolence inspired the first centuries of pacifist Christian history, was subsequently preserved in the justifiable war doctrine that declares all war as sin even when declaring it occasionally a necessary evil, and was also preserved in the prohibition of fighting by monastics and clergy as well as in a persistent tradition of Christian pacifism?

The fact that one could plausibly answer both of the previous questions in the affirmative points to the frequent disjuncture between Christian theology and ethics. Christian theology talks about Jesus, but Christian ethics takes its cues from elsewhere, so that Jesus is again and again proclaimed "not relevant" for social ethics.[1] To illustrate how accepting the relevance of Jesus' nonviolence impacts the study of Christian theology, this chapter outlines the way that a presumed standard Christian theology has accommodated violence, focusing especially on the central Christian doctrine of atonement, and concludes by sketching a specifically nonviolent understanding of atonement.[2]

I use broad definitions of the terms *violence* and *nonviolence,* akin to those developed in chapter 2 of this volume. *Violence* means harm or damage, which obviously includes the direct violence of killing—in war, capital punishment, and murder—but also covers such systemic violence as poverty, racism, and sexism.

Nonviolence is identified with a spectrum of attitudes and actions, from the classic Mennonite idea of passive nonresistance to the active nonviolence and nonviolent resistance pioneered by such leaders as Mahatma Gandhi and Martin Luther King Jr., which would include various kinds of social action, confrontations, and posing of alternatives that do not cause bodily harm or injury. That such commitments to nonviolence have generally become separated from theological abstractions can be seen from an examination of one particular sphere of Christian doctrine, the atonement.

STANDARD ATONEMENT MOTIFS

The standard account of the history of doctrine lists three families of atonement images. *Christus Victor*, the predominant image of the early church, existed in two forms, each of which involved the three elements of God, the devil or Satan, and sinful humankind. In the *ransom* version of Christus Victor, the devil held the souls of humankind captive. In a seemingly contractual agreement, God handed Jesus over to Satan as a ransom payment to secure the release of captive souls. The devil killed Jesus, in an apparent victory for the forces of evil. In raising Jesus from the dead, God triumphed over the devil, and the souls of humanity were freed from his clutches. This victory through resurrection provides the name Christus Victor or Christ the Victor.

A second version of Christus Victor pictured the conflict between Satan and God as a *cosmic battle*. In this struggle, God's son was killed, but the resurrection then constituted the victory of God over the forces of evil and definitively identified God as the ruler of the universe.

Satisfaction atonement has been the predominant atonement image for much of the past millennium. It suffices for present purposes to sketch two versions of satisfaction atonement. One reflects the view of Anselm of Canterbury, whose *Cur Deus Homo* (1098) constitutes the first full articulation of *satisfaction* atonement. Anselm wrote that human sin had offended God's honor and thus had upset divine order in the universe. The death of Jesus as the God-man was then necessary in order to satisfy God's honor and restore the order of the universe.

A change in this image of satisfaction occurred with Protestant Reformers. For them, Jesus' death satisfied the divine law's requirement that sin be punished. With his death Jesus submitted to and bore the punishment that was really due to us—humankind—as sinners. Since he was punished in our place, Jesus substituted himself for us and died a *penal, substitutionary* death.

Abelard (1079–1142) developed the *moral influence* atonement image. In this image the death of Jesus is a loving act of God aimed toward us. God the Father shows love to us sinners by giving us his most precious possession, his Son, to die for us.

DELETING THE DEVIL FROM ATONEMENT

These theories did not develop as isolated entities. Anselm and Abelard each responded to a previous motif. In the first book of *Cur Deus Homo*, Anselm specifically rejected the idea that Jesus' death was a ransom payment to the devil. Satan has no contractual rights that would obligate God to make such a payment. And even though humankind deserves punishment, Satan has no right to inflict that punishment. These considerations make it unworthy of God to deal with Satan via a ransom. Thus Anselm deleted the devil from the salvation equation.[3] Rather than seeing human beings as captive to the devil, Anselm made them directly responsible to God. Humans sinned against God, and the death of Jesus served to restore God's honor and thus restore order in the universe.

Abelard's school followed Anselm in rejecting the idea of Jesus' death as a ransom payment to the devil. But Abelard also rejected the idea of Jesus' death as a payment to God. It made God seem vengeful and judgmental. Instead, Abelard saw the death of Jesus aimed not at God but at sinful humankind. It was a loving act of God designed to get the attention of sinners and reveal the love of God for sinners while they were yet sinners.

Each of these images attempts to explain why "Jesus died for us." But recalling the object or "target" of the death of Jesus makes clear that these images suggest entirely different approaches to understanding the death of Jesus. For ransom and cosmic battle, the death of Jesus has the devil as its object. For satisfaction atonement, Jesus' death is aimed Godward—at God's honor or at God's law. Finally, for moral influence, the death of Jesus targets "us," sinful humankind, as its objects.

TWO MORE QUESTIONS

The description of the history of atonement thus far has followed the standard account. Two additional questions bring to the fore the intrinsically violent elements of these atonement images.

First, a nuance appears when we shift from asking about the object of the death of Jesus to inquire, *Who or what needs the death of Jesus?* For the ransom theory, one might say that the devil clearly needs the death—it fulfills God's part of the bargain when the devil releases the souls of humankind. For the cosmic battle image, the question makes little sense. For the satisfaction theories, it is God's honor or God's law that needs the death. Without it, the debt to God's honor remains unpaid or unsatisfied, or the penalty required by God's law remains unmet. Finally, for the moral theory, one might say that "we"—sinners—need the death since that is what enables us to perceive the Father's love.

A second question shifts the nuance again and produces an ultimately shocking answer. The question is: *Who arranges for or is responsible for the death of Jesus?* Or put most crassly, *Who ultimately killed Jesus?*

With the two forms of Christus Victor, it is obvious that the devil killed Jesus. But God the Father certainly appears to be something less than the source of all love and grace—handing the Son over for Satan to kill as a ransom payment to purchase freedom for God's other children. One can easily sense Anselm's distaste for this motif.

But the situation is not ameliorated when one poses the question for satisfaction and moral theories. Satisfaction atonement pictures a debt owed to God's honor. God's honor not only needs the death, but God also arranges for Jesus to die to pay the debt to God's honor. The image implies that God has Jesus killed in order to pay the debt to God's honor. Here is where we very pointedly see the result of Anselm's deletion of the devil from the three–cornered relationship involving the devil, sinners, and God. With Satan deleted, remaining in the equation are God and the sinners who have offended God. But these sinful human beings cannot save themselves by repaying God themselves. It is thus merely an extension of Anselm's own logic that leads to the conclusion that God is the only one left to orchestrate the death of Jesus in order to pay the debt owed to God's honor. In penal substitution, God's law receives the necessary death that it demands for justice. But again, since sinners cannot pay their own debt, God is the one who arranges to provide Jesus' death as the means to satisfy God's law.

One might ask, Wasn't the devil or the mob or the Romans responsible for killing Jesus? But answering "yes" to that question within the framework of satisfaction atonement points to a strange juxtaposition and non sequitur. Jesus, who is innocent and who does the will of God, becomes sin, subject to punishment. And the evil powers who oppose the reign of God by killing Jesus—whether the devil, the mob, or the Romans—are the ones who are actually doing the will of God, by killing Jesus to provide the payment that God's honor or God's law demands. The strange implication is that both Jesus and those who kill Jesus would be carrying out the will of God. In fact, asserting that both claims are true is nonsense. Attempting to avoid the implications of such mutually contradictory claims by cloaking them in a category such as mystery, or by claiming that the acts of God are too big for our categories to contain, renders meaningless any attempt to use theology to express Christian faith.

The moral theory fares no better. Remember that while Abelard rejected the idea that Jesus' death was a payment directed toward God's honor, Abelard agreed with Anselm in removing the devil from the equation. The result is an atonement motif in which the Father has one of his children—the Son—killed in order to show love to the rest of the Father's children, namely to us sinners.

These observations about the implied role for God the Father in satisfaction and moral atonement motifs help explain why a number of feminist and womanist writers have claimed that atonement theology presents an image of divine child abuse.[4] While none of the classic motifs escapes, the sharpest feminist and womanist critique falls on satisfaction atonement.

I cannot fault this feminist and womanist critique. The two questions (Who needs the death of Jesus? Who authors or arranges the death of Jesus?) reveal problematic dimensions of traditional atonement theology. The problems are particularly acute for satisfaction and moral theories, which have occupied most atonement discussions until quite recently. And these observations are not merely the result of feminist or pacifist radicalism. Most fundamentally, the observations about the role of God in satisfaction and moral atonement motifs simply draw out the implications of Anselm's own move to delete the devil from the atonement equation.

The conclusion from our first round of observations about classic atonement doctrine is that they portray an image of God as either divine avenger or punisher or as a child abuser, one who arranges the death of one child for the benefit of the others. Does it then surprise us that Christians envisioning a God who orchestrates violence as part of a divine plan might justify violence, under a variety of divinely anchored claims and images?

RETRIBUTION IN ATONEMENT

Another set of observations reveals additional violent elements of satisfaction atonement. The several versions all function with the assumption that doing justice or righting wrongs depends on retribution. Sin creates imbalance. Satisfaction atonement assumes that the imbalance is righted or balanced by the punishment of death.

One contemporary version and one historic version of this assumption make clear its presence in satisfaction atonement. The criminal justice system of the United States operates on the principle of retribution. Small crimes require small penalties, while a big crime requires a big penalty. The biggest punishment, namely death, is reserved for the most heinous crimes. The assumption that doing justice is equated with punishment appears in the public disapproval when what is perceived as a big misdeed receives only a "slap on the wrist" as punishment. With an apparent imbalance between deed and punishment, it seems that justice was not done. The assumption of retributive justice—that doing justice means meting out punishment—is virtually universal among North Americans and throughout much of the world.[5] The assumption that justice means punishment underlies satisfaction atonement, in particular the image of penal substitutionary atonement, with an innocent Jesus bearing the punishment we deserve.

The contemporary assumption of retributive justice has a medieval counterpart in the feudal system. I follow R. W. Southern's description of the feudal system and how Anselm's image reflects his feudal worldview.[6] The feudal world was hierarchical with a lord at the top who held the hierarchy together. The stability of the system depended on maintaining the honor of the lord at the top of the hierarchy. An offense against the lord's honor incurred a debt that threatened his authority and thus the stability of the system. In order to restore honor and stability, the debt had to be repaid. Inability to collect the debt challenged the honor and authority of the lord.

It's not difficult to see that Anselm's image of the atoning death of Jesus reflects the feudal worldview. Human sin has brought imbalance and disharmony into the universe. The restoration of harmony, order, and balance requires a payment to satisfy the offended honor of God. Anselm understood Jesus' death as the debt payment that satisfied the honor of God and thus restored balance and order in the universe.

Although Anselm's understanding of satisfaction atonement differs significantly from penal substitutionary atonement, each assumes some form of the idea of retribution. Whereas penal substitution pictures retribution in terms of punishment exacted by divine law, for Anselm it was the offended honor of God that required retribution in the form of the payment of death. The conclusion is inescapable that *any and all versions of satisfaction atonement, regardless of their packaging, assume the violence of retribution or justice based on punishment and depend on God-induced and God-directed violence.*

AHISTORICAL ATONEMENT

Satisfaction atonement accommodates violence in a third way. It structures the relationship between humankind and God in terms of an ahistorical, abstract legal formula. Thus it concerns a relationship that is outside of human history. Further, when visualizing the birth, life and teaching, death, and resurrection of Jesus, quite obviously satisfaction atonement actually needs or uses only the death of Jesus. These elements—positing a transaction outside of history and involving only the death of Jesus—make satisfaction atonement an image that (with one exception treated below) implies little or nothing about ethics and contains nothing that would challenge injustice in the social order. It is an a-ethical atonement image, with an understanding of salvation that is separated from ethics. In John Howard Yoder's language, it is theology that is "not relevant" for social ethics, or a theology that is quite compatible with the exercise of the sword, or a theology that accommodates slavery and racism.

The particular significance of these observations about the ahistorical and a-ethical dimensions of satisfaction atonement appears when they are considered against the backdrop of the changes in the church that are symbolized by emperor Constantine. These changes had already begun in the second century and extended through several centuries in evolutionary fashion. The end result of this evolution was that the church ceased being perceived as a dissident minority group and came to identify with the social order and thus to make use of and express itself through the institutions of the social order. Among other things, the exercise of the sword shows the change in the status of the church from a contrast with, to an accommodation of, the social order. Whereas before, Christians by and large did not wield the sword and pagans did, now Christians wielded the sword in the name of Christ. Rather than defining what Christians did on the basis of what Jesus said or did, the operative norm of behavior for Christians became what was good or necessary to preserve "Christian society." And in determining what was good for society, the emperor rather than Jesus became the instance of identification.[7]

I suggest that satisfaction atonement reflects the church after Constantine that accommodated the sword rather than the early church, which was primarily a pacifist church. The satisfaction motif's abstract, ahistorical, a-ethical formula permits one to claim Jesus' saving work while wielding the sword that Jesus forbade. James Cone, founder of the black theology movement, notes how such abstract formulas allowed slave owners to preach a salvation to slaves that preserved intact the master–slave relationship.[8] In other words, stated generally, satisfaction atonement separates salvation from ethics. In contrast, the atonement motif presented in what follows both reflects the nonviolence of Jesus and understands ethics as an integral dimension of salvation.

To this point, we have observed three levels of exhibiting or accommodating violence in satisfaction atonement. First, removing the devil from the atonement equation, as did Anselm and Abelard, leaves an image of God who saves by violence and of an innocent Son who passively submits to that violence. That is, its image assumes God-orchestrated and God-directed violence. Second, satisfaction atonement assumes the violence of retribution. Finally, its abstract, ahistorical character does not challenge and in fact accommodates violence and violent practices in the social order.

MORE VIOLENCE OF ATONEMENT

To this point, the argument has focused on the intrinsically violent elements of classic atonement formulas themselves. We now turn to observe additional problematic implications of the classic formulas and their application in the modern world.

Focusing on the violence of retribution that is intrinsic to satisfaction atonement brings to the fore the issue of the *image* or *role* of God. The logic of satisfaction atonement makes God the chief avenger or the chief punisher. In its worst case, as previously noted, it makes God a child abuser. This vengeful image of God led Abelard to reject the idea that Jesus' death was a payment to God's honor. However, the moral influence theory still leaves God the Father offering the Son's death to sinners as the example of Fatherly love. And classic Christus Victor has the Father hand over the Son as a ransom payment.

A further component of the violence in classic atonement images is the model of Jesus it presents. In satisfaction atonement, Jesus is a model of voluntary submission to innocent suffering. If the Father needs the death of Jesus to satisfy divine honor, Jesus as innocent victim voluntarily agrees to submit to that violence needed by the honor of God. Or as innocent victim, Jesus voluntarily agrees to undergo the punishment deserved by sinful humankind in order that the demand of divine justice be met. Because Jesus' death is needed, Jesus models being a voluntary, passive, and innocent victim, who suffers for the good of another.

It is important to underscore for whom these images of God as abusive Father and Jesus as an innocent and passive victim may pose a particular concern. It is an unhealthy model for a woman abused by her husband or a child violated by her father and constitutes double jeopardy when attached to hierarchical theology that asserts male headship.[9] A model of passive, innocent suffering poses an obstacle for people who encounter conditions of systemic injustice or an unjust status quo produced by the power structure. Examples might be the legally segregated South prior to the civil rights movement or de facto housing segregation that still exists in many places, or military-backed occupation, under which land is confiscated and indigenous residents crowded into enclosed territories, called "reservations" in North America and "bantustans" in South Africa and "autonomous areas" in Palestine. For people in such situations of an unjust status quo, the idea of "being like Jesus" as modeled by satisfaction atonement means to submit passively and to accept without protest that systemic injustice. James Cone links substitutionary atonement specifically to defenses of slavery and colonial oppression.[10] Delores Williams calls the Jesus of substitutionary atonement the "ultimate surrogate figure." After depicting numerous ways in which black women were forced into a variety of surrogacy roles for white men and women and black men, Williams says that to accept satisfaction or substitutionary atonement and the image of Jesus that it supplies is to validate all the unjust surrogacy to which black women have been and still are submitted.[11] Such examples show that atonement theology, which models innocent, passive suffering, supports rather than challenges violence in the contemporary context.

NARRATIVE CHRISTUS VICTOR

What I call narrative Christus Victor identifies the victory of Christ in terms of the narratives of the Gospels and Revelation and also distinguishes my formulation from classic Christus Victor. The final section of this chapter outlines narrative Christus Victor as an approach to atonement that expresses the nonviolence of Jesus, does not presume that justice depends on punishment, does not put God in the role of chief avenger, does not make Jesus a model of passive, innocent, voluntary submission to abuse, includes freedom from oppression in its understanding of salvation, and requires oppressors to cease oppression. Narrative Christus Victor features an understanding of salvation that includes ethics and begins in but is certainly not limited to the historical arena in which we live. In other words, narrative Christus Victor avoids all the problems of violence identified for classic atonement imagery.

Let us consider again the original survey of atonement images. In particular, let us recall the cosmic battle version of Christus Victor, which has received little attention in this chapter. This image featured the forces of God involved in a cosmic battle with the forces of Satan (or evil) for control of the universe. For present purposes, the important issue with classic Christus Victor is to recognize and understand what that cosmic battle consists of and where and when it took place.

The book of Revelation is replete with images of this cosmic battle. While many vignettes in Revelation portray this confrontation, chapter 12 contains the specific image of a heavenly battle between the forces of Satan represented by the dragon and the forces of God led by the angel Michael.

But one of the most important points is to see that this confrontation between Michael and the dragon was not an actual battle waged in the cosmos. The imagery and symbols of Revelation, both in chapter 12 and throughout the book, refer to people and events in the historical world of the first century. In other words, Revelation's symbols refer not to the distant future nor to cosmic events outside of history but to events of the first century in the historical world.

In the case of the seven-headed dragon in chapter 12, most scholars recognize that the dragon refers to the Roman empire, whose eponymous city by legend was founded on seven hills, with the horns and crowns referring to a sequence of emperors. The "battle" depicted between the forces of God and the forces of Satan was really the confrontation *in history* between the church, the earthly institution that represented the rule of God, and the Roman empire, the earthly structure used to symbolize the rule of Satan. Revelation uses cosmic imagery and symbols to depict the true nature of empire and to encourage the early church to confront it since the resurrection of Jesus has already defeated it.

The same kind of interpretation applies to the seven seals in chapters 6–7. I suggest that the seals correspond to the sequence of Roman emperors from Tiberius (14–37 C.E., seal 1), under whose rule Jesus was crucified, through Caligula (37–40 C.E., seal 2), Claudius (41–54 C.E., seal 3), Nero (54–68 C.E., seal 4), and Vespasian (69–79 C.E., seal 6), to the short reign of Titus (79–81 C.E.) or more likely Domitian (81–96 C.E., seal 7). Seal 5 coincides with the gap between Nero and Vespasian when three pretenders (Galbo, Otho, and Vitellius) carried the title but failed to consolidate imperial power.

Each seal contains a symbolic reference to elements from the reign of the corresponding emperor. The unsuccessful conquest by the rider on the white horse— he came out "conquering and to conquer"—makes an oblique reference to the death and resurrection of Jesus that occurred during the reign of Tiberius. Since Jesus did not stay dead, the imagery implies, the rider—Tiberius—had a victory in appearance only. Following symbols are more obvious. The blood red horse, the sword, and taking peace from the earth in seal two refer to the threats posed by Caligula. In addition to Caligula's provocations against the Jews, in 40 C.E. he sent an army to install a statue of himself arrayed as a Roman god on the altar of the temple of Jerusalem. This army posed a major threat to the city, but Caligula died before the threat was carried out. The symbols of famine in seal 3 refer to the famine during the reign of Claudius that is mentioned in Acts 11:28, while the double-ugly riders and multiple means of destruction in seal 4 portray Nero, whose infamy still lives. Changing the point of view from earth to heaven in seal 5 corresponds to the eighteen-month interlude between Nero and Vespasian, when the three pretenders each obtained the title but did not succeed in consolidating power as emperor. The multiple symbols in the first scene of seal 6 portray the breakdown of order and the overwhelming sense of despair and tragedy felt by the heirs of David when his city—Jerusalem—was sacked and destroyed in 70 C.E. by an army commanded by emperor Vespasian's son Titus.[12]

The entirety of chapter 7 also belongs to seal 6, which pointedly depicts the celebration of the two throngs as the counterpoint to the devastation of the first scene of seal 6. Twelve is the number of Israel's tribes, and 144,000 is the product of 12 times 12 times 1,000. It is a large number symbolizing that the people of God stand in continuity with God's people Israel. In the first century, this number would have seemed much larger than it does for us in the computer age on the cusp of the third millennium. Its size should be read as a parallel to the "countless multitude," which includes people of every ethnic and national group in the people of God. These two throngs, which show that the people of God includes both Israelites and gentiles around the world, celebrate the victory of the reign of God over the forces of evil. For those who perceive the resurrection of Jesus, the celebration loudly proclaims, the rule of God has already triumphed over the accumulation of evil experienced under the rule of Rome. In the midst of the worst imaginable tragedy from an earthly perspective—the destruction of the holy city—the two multitudes are depicted in celebration. For the reader of Revelation, the message of the cheering throngs is that for those who live in the reality of the resurrection of Jesus, the rule of God has already triumphed.

Finally, this celebration leads to the seventh seal, which does not advance the chronology but rather begins a new cycle of seven. Ceasing the count at seven and beginning a new series of seven places the time of the seventh seal in the author's present. According to my sequence, that would be perhaps during the short reign of Titus (79–81 C.E.) or more likely during the reign of Domitian (81–96 C.E.).

Putting the declarations of cosmic victory together with the historical antecedents of the symbols shows that Revelation delivers a cosmic and eschatological perspective on events in the history of the first century. The image in Revelation 12 depicts the same history in another way. Rome, the seven-headed dragon, whose ten horns and seven crowns encompass the emperors and pretenders just mentioned, confronts the beautiful woman with a crown of twelve stars. She is Israel, who produced Jesus the Messiah, and is also the church, who is pursued by Rome. In this set of symbols as well, the resurrection of Jesus gives the victory to the earthly representatives of the reign of God over the forces of evil symbolized by Rome.

The Gospels present the same story as that told in Revelation, but from a different standpoint. Revelation tells the story of Jesus from the perspective of the heavenly throne room and the future culmination of the reign of God. The Gospels narrate that same story from the earthly vantage point of the folks who got dust on their sandals as they walked the roads of Palestine with Jesus. Both accounts locate the victory of the reign of God on earth and in history—narrative Christus Victor—and make quite clear that the triumph occurred not through the sword and military might but nonviolently, through death and resurrection. The point is that the violence that causes Jesus' death comes from the side of evil, which means that the victory of the reign of God occurs nonviolently. The intrinsically nonviolent character of the victory eliminates what is usually called the triumphalism of the church. As intrinsically nonviolent, its stance to the other or toward those who differ and are different can only be nonviolent.[13] To be otherwise is to cease to be a witness to the reign of God and to join the forces of evil who oppose the reign of God.

At the same time, reading that story in the Gospels shows that Jesus was not a passive victim, whose purpose was to get himself killed in order to satisfy a big cosmic legal requirement. Rather, Jesus was an activist, whose mission was to make the rule of God visible. And his acts demonstrated what the reign of God looked like—defending poor people, raising the status of women, raising the status of Samaritans, performing healings and exorcisms, preaching the reign of God, and more. His mission was to make the reign of God present in the world in his person and in his teaching and to invite people to experience the liberation it presented.

And when Jesus made the reign of God visible and present in that way, it was so threatening that the assembled array of evil forces killed him. These forces include imperial Rome, which carried ultimate legal authority for his death, with some assistance from religious authorities in Jerusalem, as well as Judas, Peter, and other disciples, who could not even watch with him, and the mob that howled for his death. In the resurrection the reign of God is victorious over all these forces of evil that killed Jesus.

As sinners, in one way or another, we are all part of those sinful forces that killed Jesus. Jesus died making the reign of God present for us while we were still sinners. To acknowledge our human sinfulness is to become aware of our participation in the forces of evil that killed Jesus, including their present manifestations in such powers as militarism, nationalism, racism, sexism, heterosexism, and poverty that still bind and oppress.

And because God is a loving God, God invites us to join the rule of God in spite of the fact that we participated with and are captive to the powers that killed Jesus. God invites us to join the struggle of those seeking liberation from the forces that bind and oppress. This invitation envisions both those who are oppressed and their oppressors. When the oppressed accept God's invitation, they cease collaborating with the powers that oppress and join the forces who represent the reign of God in making a visible witness against oppression. And when the oppressors accept God's invitation, they reject their collaboration with the powers of oppression and join the forces who represent the reign of God in witnessing against oppression. Thus under the reign of God, former oppressed and former oppressors join together in witnessing to the reign of God.

Anselm removed the devil from the salvation equation. Narrative Christus Victor restores that deletion, but with a difference. In narrative Christus Victor, the image of the devil is not that of an individual, personal being. Rather "the devil" is the Roman empire, which symbolizes all the institutions and structures and powers of the world that do not recognize the rule of God. Following Walter

Wink's understanding of the powers, this devil is the symbol for the accumulation of all that does not recognize the authority of the reign of God.[14] In his contemporary construction of Christus Victor, James Cone wrote that the powers of evil confronted by the reign of God include "the American system," symbolized by government officials who "oppress the poor, humiliate the weak, and make heroes out of rich capitalists"; "the Pentagon, which bombed and killed helpless people in Vietnam and Cambodia and attributed such obscene atrocities to the accidents of war"; the system, symbolized in "the police departments and prison officials, which shoots and kills defenseless blacks for being *black* and for demanding their right to exist."[15] The victorious Christ has rescued us from the forces of evil and invites us to be transformed by the rule of God. While that transformation is never complete in the present eschaton, our participation in evil has now become involuntary and our lives take on the character of opposition to rather than cooperation with the forces of evil.

Earlier it was shown how Anselmian atonement correlates with feudal society and the ecclesiology that identified with the social order. It is now also possible to see that narrative Christus Victor belongs to, and in fact only makes sense when perceived within, the ecclesiological status of the early church that perceived itself to be different from the empire and the prevailing social order. This context is the setting for the confrontation *in history* depicted in narrative Christus Victor, which makes sense only if one assumes that the church, as a representative of the reign of God, confronts the social order or poses an alternative to the social order. According to my hypothesis, Christus Victor dropped out of the picture when the church came to support the world's social order, to accept the intervention of political authorities in churchly affairs, and to look to political authorities for support and protection. With the historical antecedents of Revelation soon forgotten, all that seemed to remain was cosmic imagery of confrontation that did not match the political reality. Thus eventually the motif I have called narrative Christus Victor could fade away without a sense of loss, to be replaced by Anselm's satisfaction motif, which reflected the medieval social and ecclesiological conditions.

The image of narrative Christus Victor avoids all the problematic elements in classic atonement images. It reflects the ecclesiological worldview of the early rather than the medieval church. It is grounded in assumptions of nonviolence—the nonviolence of Jesus—rather than violence. In particular, it does not assume retribution or that injustice is balanced by the violence of punishment. It does not put God in the role of chief avenger nor picture God as a child abuser. And it is abundantly obvious that God did not kill Jesus nor need the death of Jesus in any way. Jesus does suffer, but it is not as an act of passive submission to undeserved suffering. Jesus carries out a mission to make the rule of God present and visible, a mission to bring and to give life. When this mission threatens the forces of evil, they retaliate with violence, killing Jesus. This suffering is not something willed by nor needed by God, and it is not directed Godward. To the contrary, the killing of Jesus is the ultimate contrast between the nonviolent reign of God and the rule of evil.

Earlier, a question used to analyze the atonement motifs was Who needs the death of Jesus? Bringing that question to narrative Christus Victor focuses its profound difference from satisfaction atonement. The question has a nonanswer in narrative Christus Victor. God does not need the death because this motif does not make use of the idea of retribution. In narrative Christus Victor, the death pays God nothing and is not Godward directed. If anything or anyone "needs" the death, it is the forces of evil who kill Jesus. They "need" the death as part of the futile effort to annihilate the reign of God. The death of Jesus is thus very pointedly not something needed by God or God's honor. It is rather what the forces of evil—the devil—do to Jesus. Rather than being a divine requirement, the death of Jesus is the ultimate indication of the difference between the reign of God and the reign of evil. The reign of the devil attempts to rule by violence and death, whereas the reign of God rules and ultimately conquers through nonviolence.

If Christians are troubled by the violence associated with Christianity during its two-thousand-year history, the first step is to recognize the extent to which formulas of classic theology have contributed to violence both overt and systemic. This chapter has provided data for that acknowledgment. The second step away from Christianity as a violent religion would be to construct theology that specifically reflects the nonviolence of its namesake, Jesus Christ. As a suggestion in that direction, I offer narrative Christus Victor as both nonviolent atonement and narrative Christology. Finally, step three would be to live out the theology of its nonviolent namesake. That commitment is a call to every Christian. One dimension of enacting that call would be to make nonviolence an intrinsic and integrating principle across the curriculum of Christian colleges and within each discipline by anyone anywhere who seeks to follow the way of peace with mind as well as body.

NOTES

An earlier version of this article appeared in *CrossCurrents* 51, no. 2 (summer 2001): 150–176. Reprinted by permission.

1. John Howard Yoder, *The Politics of Jesus: Vicit Agnus Noster*, 2nd ed. (Grand Rapids, Mich.: Eerdmans, 1993), 5–8, 15–19.

2. Portions of this chapter draw on my article "Violence in Christian Theology," *CrossCurrents* 51, no. 2 (Summer 2001): 150–176. Both draw on my book *The Nonviolent Atonement* (Grand Rapids, Mich.: Eerdmans, 2001).

3. Anselm, "Why God Became Man," in *A Scholastic Miscellany: Anselm to Ockham*, ed. and trans. Eugene R. Fairweather, The Library of Christian Classics (Philadelphia: Westminster, 1956), 107–110.

4. Joanne Carlson Brown and Rebecca Parker, "For God So Loved the World?" in *Christianity, Patriarchy and Abuse: A Feminist Critique*, ed. Joanne Carlson Brown and Carole R. Bohn (New York: Pilgrim Press, 1989), 1–30; Julie M. Hopkins, *Towards a Feminist Christology: Jesus of Nazareth, European Women, and the Christological Crisis*

(Grand Rapids, Mich.: Eerdmans, 1995), 50–52; Rita Nakashima Brock, *Journeys by Heart: A Christology of Erotic Power* (New York: Crossroad, 1988), 55–57; Carter Heyward, *Saving Jesus from Those Who Are Right: Rethinking What It Means to Be Christian* (Minneapolis: Fortress Press, 1999), 151; and Delores S. Williams, *Sisters in the Wilderness: The Challenge of Womanist God-Talk* (Maryknoll, N.Y.: Orbis Books, 1993), 161–167.

5. For an analysis of retributive justice, with restorative justice as the suggested alternative, see Howard Zehr, *Changing Lenses: A New Focus for Crime and Justice*, A Christian Peace Shelf Selection (Scottdale, Pa.: Herald Press, 1990).

6. R. W. Southern, *Saint Anselm: A Portrait in a Landscape* (Cambridge: Cambridge University Press, 1990), 221–227.

7. The seminal treatment of the changes in the church symbolized by Constantine is John Howard Yoder, "The Constantinian Sources of Western Social Ethics," in *The Priestly Kingdom: Social Ethics As Gospel* (Notre Dame, Ind.: University of Notre Dame, 1984), 135–147; as well as John H. Yoder, "The Disavowal of Constantine: An Alternative Perspective on Interfaith Dialogue," in *The Royal Priesthood: Essays Ecclesiological and Ecumenical*, ed. Michael G. Cartwright (Grand Rapids, Mich.: Eerdmans, 1994), 242–261; and John H. Yoder, "The Otherness of the Church," in *The Royal Priesthood*, 53–64. H. A. Drake has shown that Constantine himself pursued a policy of tolerance and that the changes he symbolizes and the move toward enforcing one prescribed faith actually occurred in the decades following Constantine. H. A. Drake, *Constantine and the Bishops: The Politics of Intolerance* (Baltimore: Johns Hopkins University Press, 2000).

8. James H. Cone, *God of the Oppressed*, rev. ed. (Maryknoll, N.Y.: Orbis, 1997), 42–49, 211–212.

9. Brown and Parker, "For God So Loved the World?"; Hopkins, *Towards a Feminist Christology*, 50–52; Brock, *Journeys by Heart*, 55–57; and Heyward, *Saving Jesus*, 151.

10. Cone, *God of the Oppressed*, 211–212.

11. Williams, *Sisters in the Wilderness*, 60–83, 161–167, 178–199.

12. No scholarly consensus exists on the correlation of seals with emperors. While my particular suggestion here is quite plausible, the argument for narrative Christus Victor does not depend on accepting this particular interpretation. The vitally important point is to recognize that the antecedents of Revelation's symbols are located in the first century (however identified) and not in the distant future or our present age.

13. The chapter in this volume by Susan Biesecker-Mast uses rhetorical analysis to expose triumphalism and to display the necessity of a nonviolent stance toward the other.

14. For the full description of the powers, see the first volume of Walter Wink's trilogy on the powers, *Naming the Powers: The Language of Power in the New Testament*, The Powers, vol. 1 (Philadelphia: Fortress, 1984).

15. Cone, *God of the Oppressed*, 212–213.

4

The God of the Bible and the Nonviolence of Jesus

David Janzen

Biblical texts, located primarily but not exclusively in the Old Testament, where God is said to participate in and sanction violence, seem to legitimate violence for many Christians. I dissent from that supposed legitimation. This chapter suggests how to read such texts in a way that clearly retains them as an authentic part of the biblical canon but which nonetheless shows that the Bible's story as a whole teaches the nonviolence of God and the reign of God. The argument in part draws on the interpretive approaches that early Anabaptists, forerunners of the modern peace churches, brought to such texts.

For the past century, biblical scholarship has privileged interpretations that follow authorial intention, namely what biblical scholars believe the original authors meant when they composed these texts. While working with that position, my approach also appropriates the Anabaptist insight that understanding biblical texts happens within a context that assumes lived obedience to Jesus Christ. It is when one attempts actually to live in obedience to the God of Jesus Christ that one must account for those views of God and of divine commands that conflict with the life and teaching of Jesus. This chapter thus constitutes a biblical counterpart to J. Denny Weaver's chapter in this volume that expresses concern for lived theology in line with the life and teaching of Jesus.

THE PROBLEM: GOD AND VIOLENCE IN THE OLD AND NEW TESTAMENTS

The Old Testament provides the most obvious examples of passages where God is said to act violently and to insist that the people of God act likewise. The poem in Exodus 15:1–18, perhaps the oldest piece of literature in the Bible, calls God a "warrior" and recounts God's slaughter of the Egyptian army while freeing the

Israelites from slavery. The book of Deuteronomy, presented as Moses' final address to the people before they enter the land of Canaan, states that God demands genocide on the part of the Israelites. "When the LORD your God gives [the nations of Canaan] over to you and you defeat them, then you must utterly destroy them. Make no covenant with them and show them no mercy" (Deuteronomy 7:2). This God also demands capital punishment for certain crimes in Israel, such as working on the Sabbath or committing adultery. (Exodus 31:15; Leviticus 20:10). Such texts pose problems for peace churches, which reject the idea of divine sanction on warfare or capital punishment.

The Anabaptists, the earliest appearance of a peace church tradition in Protestantism, claimed that Jesus specifically annulled such laws in the Sermon on the Mount in Matthew 5–7. Because of their difficulty in reconciling the seemingly vast ethical gulf between the Old and New Testaments, Anabaptists believed that the New Testament witness superseded the Old, and they tended to insist that the Old Testament was authoritative only insofar as it was reconcilable with the New. In the Frankenthal debate of 1571, for example, Anabaptist leaders argued:

> We believe that the New Testament surpasses the Old. So much of the Old Testament as is not irreconcilable with the doctrine of Christ, we accept. . . . If anything that is necessary for salvation and a godly life was not taught by Christ and the Apostles but is contained in the Old Testament Scriptures, we desire to be shown.[1]

This position has a certain logic. If the church accepts Christ as the best revelation of the will of God, then all of Scripture must be read in light of this revelation. It also assumes that the life and teaching of Jesus Christ constitute the norm for living as a Christian, or what John Howard Yoder called "the politics of Jesus."[2] Anabaptists and their theological offspring have thus interpreted the Bible by what Ben Ollenburger calls the hermeneutic of obedience, the belief that a commitment to follow or obey Christ is a necessary prolegomenon to an understanding of what the Bible says about him.[3] In particular, this tradition has stressed the imitation of Jesus Christ's nonviolence, as exemplified in Matthew 5:38–39, 43–44. The ideas of imitating Jesus or of Jesus as an ethical norm are expressions of the commitment to obey him. The language of hermeneutics of obedience and of Jesus as ethical norm appears interchangeably in what follows. It is difficult to square such a presentation of discipleship to Jesus Christ and Jesus as a norm for ethics with the bloodshed demanded and divinely sanctioned in the Old Testament. Early Anabaptists thus rejected portions of the Old Testament as inapplicable to Christian life. Many who stand in the Anabaptist tradition today still adhere to that approach to the Old Testament.

But while the Sermon on the Mount clearly presents Jesus as demanding a life of nonretaliation, the New Testament also contains portrayals of God that are as disturbing to the peace church tradition as those found in the Old Testament. In a passage found in both Matthew and Luke, for example, John the Baptist tells those who come to him at the Jordan River that they must live righteously. "Even now the ax is lying at the root of the trees," he says; "every tree therefore that does not bear good fruit is cut down and thrown into the fire" (Matthew 3:10; Luke 3:9). This comment seems to place the life of nonretaliation that Jesus is about to outline in the Sermon on the Mount within a coercive framework of divine retaliation. In his writing to the church at Rome, Paul echoes this theme: "Beloved, never avenge yourselves, but leave room for the wrath of God; for it is written, 'Vengeance is mine, I will repay, says the Lord'" (Romans 12:19). And according to Matthew's presentation of the Sermon on the Mount, Jesus states that even those who address someone else as "fool" will "be liable to the hell of fire" (5:22).

While the New Testament texts just cited do not urge followers of Christ to engage in retaliation for wrongs done to them, and in fact they condemn human violence of any sort, they do seem to permit violence on the part of one party, namely God. That constitutes a problem when Christians confess Jesus Christ to be the incarnation of God on earth and the fullest revelation of the divine will. How closely does one wish to be associated with a God who, grimly or blithely, advocates divine capital punishment against those who have not lived up to divine standards, including the command to be nonviolent peacemakers? Or, is Jesus Christ, who modeled peacemaking and nonretaliation in his life and teaching, really the manifestation of this violent God of the New as well as the Old Testament? Moreover, a violent God and a system of ethics based on Jesus' nonviolence would appear to be inherently contradictory.[4] How can one say that God demands an end to violent coercion when some New Testament texts portray God as promoting violent coercion? Ultimately such an issue concerning the character of God cannot be resolved by simply saying that the New Testament has superseded the Old.

THE SOLUTION: A SELECTIVE TELLING OF TALES

Both testaments do present God as a violent character, but that is hardly the end of the story. God is also presented as a character who loves and promotes mercy and justice. In the hopeful future to which Isaiah and Micah point, God's rule of the world will make warfare anachronistic (Isaiah 2:1–4; Micah 4:1–5). God rejects the worship of Israel unless it is accompanied by social justice and concern for the poor (Amos 5:10–11, 21–24). God presents the people with laws that privilege the needy within the community and demands that debts be remitted every seven years (Leviticus 24:1–7), that wages to laborers be paid promptly (Deuteronomy 24:14–15), and that the poor not be prevented from gleaning what the harvesters have left (Deuteronomy 24:19–22). In depicting the coming reign of God, Jesus described a world where violence is not acceptable, where peacemaking is privileged, and where those marginalized in society are not neglected (for example, Matthew 9:10–13 and Luke 6:17–38).

Bible scholars today recognize that both testaments portray God and God's will for humanity and creation in a number of different ways. Walter Brueggemann writes in his theology of the Old Testament that the various portrayals of God and God's interaction with humanity actually function as different witnesses in the same court, each making its claim for its version of the way things are. Not all of these testimonies are compatible. The reader has to decide how to respond to the different witnesses about God.[5]

Can we reconcile these various pictures of God? Can the God who demands genocide in Deuteronomy be the same God who is revealed in the peacemaking of Jesus Christ? A part of the solution, I believe, is to pose the question differently. I do not believe that the answer is found in efforts to harmonize mutually exclusive images of God. The following poses the query about God and violence from a perspective informed by the Anabaptist hermeneutics of obedience to Christ, that is, by a hermeneutics shaped by the story of Jesus as ethical norm.[6] A somewhat similar approach appears in some circles of liberation theology, as when Gustavo Gutiérrez says that theological reflection is something that "limps after" the obedience that Christ demands.[7] And as Ollenburger said about Anabaptists:

> Jesus ceased to be, as he was for Luther, a forensic act of justification. The Anabaptists viewed Christ as one to be imitated as a judge of ethics. . . . Knowledge of Christ comes in walking *with* him, and only then can one understand what is written *about* him. A large part of "interpreting" the Bible is imitating it.[8]

One difficulty with the violent image of God is that it appears to construe God as a rather capricious being, changing the divine mind from one setting to the next, saying one thing about the ethical life to ancient Israel and another by means of the revelation of Christ. At this point, classic trinitarian theology comes to the aid of a hermeneutic shaped by the assumption of Jesus as ethical norm. However, classic trinitarian principles would seem to preclude such ethical duality in God. John Howard Yoder noted that according to this doctrine God, Christ, and the Holy Spirit cannot give differing revelations. It follows then that one should not say that the God of the New Testament and who is revealed in Jesus Christ differs from the God of the Old Testament. If we confess that through Jesus Christ God has revealed an ethic of peacemaking, then it cannot be that God would demand killing, or enforce capital punishment, or sanction genocide.[9] Reading the Bible through the hermeneutic of obedience to Christ and a trinitarian perspective means that the God of Jesus Christ is the same God who is revealed in the Old Testament. This is a Christocentric reading of the Bible that uses the narrative of Jesus as the lens through which to identify the stories of the Old Testament that most reflect the will of God as revealed in Jesus, and it is a reading through which God calls followers to acts of peacemaking and forgiveness, of social justice and mercy. And indeed, both testaments contain many passages describing this God.

However, such assertions have not yet dealt with the disturbing biblical portrayals of a God who commands and commends violence and other unsettling pictures of biblical ethics. While these disturbing elements are part of the biblical record, the Christocentric reading just described considers these problematic texts in light of the biblical stories and traditions that persuade us in the way of Christ and through argumentation about the priority of one over the other.[10] The stories that reflect the God revealed in Jesus Christ will then function as the lens through which we interpret the rest of the biblical material and will be our guide to a truer understanding of the character of God and God's relationship to humanity. This, essentially, was the approach of the early Anabaptists, who interpreted the whole Bible through the ethical picture of Jesus and gave that Jesus-focused ethical picture epistemological priority over the parts of the Bible that they could not reconcile with it.

However, reading through an ethical picture of Jesus differs significantly from saying that the New Testament supercedes the Old, which in effect constitutes abandoning much of the Old Testament. Unlike these Anabaptists, I do not want to ignore the parts of the Bible that do not fit a peace church morality. But instead of saying that the New Testament supersedes the Old, I read the problematic texts from the understanding that Christians are to live in the imitation of Christ. When interpretation happens through the lens of lived obedience to the peacemaking ethic of Jesus Christ and with the understanding that the character of God is revealed in Jesus Christ, then the violent texts and images are not being abandoned or superseded.[11] They remain as important parts of the record of Israel's varying attempts to understand God and their relationship to God—and are thus important to our understanding of the developing history of the people of God. Read in this way, then, these texts are not ethical injunctions that sanction violence by Christians today but are rather texts that underscore the difficult road toward the rejection of violence that is taken by believers when the reign of God is properly understood as revealed in the story of Jesus Christ.

I need to make two additional points about this approach to interpretation. First, I am talking not about what biblical texts mean, but about their *interpretation*. The distinction is an important one. Often, people write about what texts mean as if such an interpretation is the only correct one. However, it seems to be common knowledge that different people interpret the same biblical text in different ways. Thus I refrain from talking about meaning as something inherent in texts—except to criticize such a position—and instead will talk about interpretations of texts, that which people assign to texts. Second, while I have stated above and will argue below that we can read Old Testament texts concerning God's involvement in war, or New Testament texts about God's actions as an executioner, in ways that are consonant with a theology shaped by nonviolence, it is important to stress that one can also very easily read such texts in ways that support violence. In fact that is the prevailing mode of interpretation. Thus in the face of a long interpretative tradition of using a text to sanction warfare or capital punishment or the oppression of women or minorities or homosexuals, it requires courage to reinterpret the text and to say that the God of Jesus Christ could sanction no such violent actions or oppressions.

A TEST CASE: OBEDIENCE, HOLY WAR TEXTS,
AND JOHN HOWARD YODER'S HERMENEUTIC

This section illustrates the function of interpreting violent texts through a hermeneutic of obedience to Jesus Christ by putting that methodology in conversation with John Howard Yoder's method for dealing with those texts in his chapter on holy war in *The Politics of Jesus*.[12] Like my effort here, Yoder's *Politics* as a whole endeavors to show that the dominant ethic of the Bible is the peacemaking ethic of Jesus, and the chapter on holy war in the Old Testament in particular argues that even these apparently odious, violent passages can be used to make the same point.

Yoder states that the holy war texts that he examines in this chapter focus not on God's participation in or sanctioning of warfare, but on Israel's awareness that it should trust in God and not in its military might for survival. The authors of these texts, he argues, reject reliance on violence in a manner that in some fashion parallels Jesus' calls to nonretaliation.[13] I have chosen to deal with this particular chapter in this particular book for three reasons. First, it deals with Old Testament texts that Christians committed to nonviolence have traditionally felt ill equipped to read. Second, the book itself is well known across a broad range of Christian circles. Third, while I applaud Yoder's refusal to abandon such biblical texts, I believe that his hermeneutical approach to these texts is misguided and ultimately unhelpful and does not solve the problem of the character of God as presented in the holy war texts.

The Politics of Jesus makes an important contribution to Christian theology and ethics in general. It was Yoder who made the theological point that the Gospels articulate a radical ethic of peacemaking that their authors intended Christians to take up. I affirm Yoder's insistence on finding the political and social validity of the teachings of the Gospels, his ability to draw out the various traditions of the Bible that exhort an ethic of peacemaking within the people of God, and his attempts to deal with texts that appear hostile to a Christian ethic of nonviolence, even as I point out that the hermeneutic with which he approaches the biblical texts, the dominant hermeneutic of his time, is not entirely adequate for dealing with some of the texts of violence that one encounters in the Bible.

The basic hermeneutical difficulty is Yoder's insistence that interpretation must privilege authorial intention. "It is a general rule of proper textual interpretation that a text should be read for what its author meant to say and what its first readers or hearers would have heard it say," he writes.[14] And it is quite true that this was the basic rule of biblical interpretation among scholars when Yoder composed *The Politics of Jesus*. When we read the holy war texts, Yoder argued, we are concerned with the points the author intended to get across. The obvious difficulty with this approach, however, is that the authors and editors of the holy war texts in books such as Joshua, Judges, and Chronicles apparently found no difficulty themselves in believing that God could sanction and participate in warfare and genocide. Yoder's way out of the dilemma, however, was this:

Whether the taking of human life is morally permissible or forbidden under all circumstances was not a culturally conceivable question in the age of Abraham or that of Joshua. It is therefore illegitimate to read the story of . . . the Joshuanic wars as documents on the issue of the morality of killing. Although the narrative is full of bloodshed, what the pious reader will have been most struck by in later centuries was the general promise according to which, if Israel would believe and obey, the occupants of the land would be driven out little by little, . . . [and that Israel should not] think military strength or numbers had brought the victory.[15]

The holy war texts, Yoder thus concluded, are not about violence but about Israel's belief that God and not military force is ultimately responsible for victory in battle and for fairly successful conclusions to matters such as the attempted genocide of the Canaanites. This focus on God as source of victory, Yoder believed, is what these texts *mean*. Since the authors' cultural situation proscribed them from considering the belief that the taking of human life might be forbidden under all circumstances, it is "illegitimate" to read the holy war texts as comments on the morality of killing. Privileging authorial intention—what Yoder claimed as a general rule of interpretation—forbids it.

Yet once we privilege authorial intention—and should we come to the same conclusions regarding authorial intention as Yoder—we must ask why these texts should be important for us at all. Are advocates of peacemaking not interested in what the Bible has to say about God and the morality of taking human life under all circumstances? If these texts have nothing to say to us about such subjects, as Yoder claims, then they are worse than useless to us; they are actually extremely problematic, for there God commands warfare and genocide and participates in them. The character of God thus remains a problem. In fact, the authors of these texts do have something to say about God and the morality of taking human life: warfare and even genocide seem perfectly acceptable so long as they are sanctioned by God. Israel will succeed in battle, the stories say, so long as it remains faithful to God. We find nothing in these texts that condemns Israel's participation in warfare per se. It is true that ancient Israel understood its ultimate success in battle as dependent upon the beneficence of the divine, but this was also the case with the nations surrounding Israel, and Israel, no less than they, saw warfare as a valid function of the government. On the relation between God and warfare, the texts imply, we may safely say that warfare is perfectly acceptable whenever God commands it, as long as they recall that the victory depended on God rather than their own military prowess. The Christian tradition assumes that God is consistent, and a specific implication of traditional trinitarian doctrine is the consistency of God, or the belief that how God acts at one time is consistent with God's action elsewhere. Assuming that God is consistent, the hermeneutical approach that Yoder used makes it difficult for the peace church tradition to argue that God condemns violence, since the texts show God employing violence.

Perhaps because he was on some level aware of this shortcoming, Yoder left himself with a solution to this problem in the chapter on holy war. He writes that "[o]ur present concern is . . . with what it meant for Jesus and his contemporaries and his disciples to read this kind of [holy war] story in their Bible."[16] Given the content of *The Politics of Jesus* as a whole, this claim is not unexpected. However, it clashes with the first interpretive claim that Yoder makes earlier in the chapter. Jesus and his contemporaries were hardly the first readers or hearers of the texts that Yoder discusses in this chapter, and so by stating that he is interested in Jesus' understanding of these texts, Yoder has violated his own general rule of interpretation, which, he states, privileges authorial intention, or what the original readers of the texts would have understood the author to be saying.

I should stress that it is not Yoder's interpretation of the texts—his hermeneutics—but his method of interpreting the texts that I find unhelpful and self-contradictory. While I can only approve Yoder's refusal to abandon such holy war texts and his effort to retrieve them for the peace church tradition, I nonetheless believe that his approach is self-contradictory and leaves significant questions unanswered.

In more detail, I note four clusters of problems or unanswered questions from Yoder's hermeneutical approach:

(1) If our primary interpretive concern with these texts is how Jesus and his contemporaries read them, then that is, by the standard Yoder invoked early in the chapter, an illegitimate reading, for it does not privilege authorial intention.

(2) If our primary interpretive concern with these texts is how their original hearers would have read them, then just who were the original hearers? For example, Yoder mentioned a number of holy war texts from the books of Joshua and Judges, two works that fall within a larger original work that includes those books as well as 1 and 2 Samuel and 1 and 2 Kings. All together these writings constitute the Deuteronomistic History. The holy war stories to which Yoder refers once existed only in oral form, were then written down, and still later incorporated into the Deuteronomistic History, a work that was itself subject to a process of editing. At which point in this process should we begin speaking of original readers? To which of these stories' stages of development does Yoder refer?

(3) And even had Yoder specified one of these stages, why should he concern himself with their reactions if his interest was in the politics of Jesus? Why, moreover, assume that authorial intention or the reactions of original readers is the only legitimate way to read such stories? What, besides a vague mention of "a general rule of interpretation," might function as the warrant for such a claim? Although it is clear that this was the dominant rule of interpretation of biblical scholars when Yoder wrote, are we bound to follow it?

(4) For the moment, let us suppose that Yoder had specified that the holy war texts in Joshua and Judges to which he refers should privilege the interpretation of the first readers of the final edition of the Deuteronomistic History as it appeared sometime in the sixth century B.C.E. Is it true that these readers would have understood such texts of conquest and warfare to focus on Israel's reliance on God rather than its military might? The final edition of the Deuteronomistic History

emphasized that the destruction of Jerusalem by the Babylonians and the exile of the people from the land resulted from the failure of the Israelites to worship the God of Israel alone. The early readers of such texts, readers with firsthand knowledge of the slaughter in Jerusalem and the exile to Babylon, would have been struck by the fact that the God of Israel quickly moves to violent punishment should God's adherents not strictly follow the laws of worship. The picture of God's character that results from the interpretive principle of authorial intent still poses a problem for Christians committed to peacemaking. Moreover, none of the holy war texts that Yoder discussed in this chapter understand Israel's participation in warfare as anything less than legitimate. While Yoder is correct to claim that they see that ultimate success in warfare depends on God and not military force, the character of God still remains a problem. Why should Christians committed to nonviolence want to worship a God who promotes battle and genocide?

CHRISTOCENTRIC INTERPRETATION AND THE GOD OF HOLY WAR

In light of these four problem areas, how do those committed to nonviolence cope with texts where the character of God remains a problem? I invoke Yoder's principle of privileging the interpretation of holy war texts through the narrative of Jesus and his contemporaries,[17] which makes the rejection of violence revealed in Jesus Christ a primary interpretative criterion, along with the idea derived from trinitarian doctrine that the character of God as God cannot differ fundamentally from God as revealed in Jesus Christ. These two principles result in the conclusion that the God of Jesus Christ cannot condone violence of any sort. It then follows that despite what the original authors of these texts might have meant regarding the character of God and Israel's participation in warfare, we conclude that even if they may have correctly understood God's concern that Israel relies on God's power and not on chariots, they were mistaken in their assumption that God wanted them to slay their enemies in the first place.[18] These texts, as noted above, constitute one kind of testimony in Israel to who God is and what God commands, and all testimony to the divine mind—even if spirit-inspired—will be limited in some respect because humans are flawed creatures, conditioned by culture and history. While we can certainly acknowledge the scholarly reconstruction of what such biblical authors meant to convey about God's and Israel's participation in violence, we do not have to accept such scholarly reconstruction as an accurate reflection of the character of God and the kinds of actions God sanctions.

The two theological claims—of interpreting through obedience to Christ and accepting the trinitarian implication of the consistency of God—must take precedence over any reconstructed authorial intention. Of course, we may still conclude, with Yoder, that the holy war texts ultimately concern not the validity of military might or divine calls to warfare, but rather reliance upon God and not upon arms for survival. If we claim that the God of the Old Testament is the same as the God of the New Testament, then we may well arrive at the interpretation of the holy war texts that Yoder arrives at. But the path I suggest removes the character of God as a problem. This approach privileges obedience to Jesus Christ in the interpretation of holy war texts—a Christocentric reading—rather than scholarly interpretations of authorial intention.

Stated another way, the particular texts of the Old Testament but also the New contain a number of different statements and interpretations of stories about God and violence. These differing and even contradictory statements are part of the spirit-inspired efforts of God's people through history to understand what it meant to be God's people. Accepting them *all* as equally authoritative *for us* in effect makes the Bible into a flat book, ignores the tensions between the several statements, and results ultimately in a God who both practices and sanctions violence. Instead, I have suggested reading these texts through a lens focused by Jesus' rejection of violence and the belief encompassed in trinitarian teaching that God is consistent. Reading through this lens accomplishes two things: (1) it identifies the nonviolent strands as those that most reveal the will of God, but (2) it retains the entire canon as an authentic record of the effort of God's spirit-guided people to understand God and how to live as God's children.

NOTES

1. Cited in Cornelius J. Dyck, "Hermeneutics and Discipleship," in *Essays on Biblical Interpretation: Anabaptist-Mennonite Perspectives*, ed. Willard Swartley, no. 1 (Elkhart, Ind.: Institute of Mennonite Studies, 1984), 34.

2. John Howard Yoder, *The Politics of Jesus: Vicit Agnus Noster*, 2nd ed. (Grand Rapids, Mich.: Eerdmans, 1994).

3. Ben C. Ollenburger, "The Hermeneutics of Obedience: Reflections on Anabaptist Hermeneutics," in *Essays on Biblical Interpretation*, 45–61.

4. For example, accepting God's retribution while advocating Christian nonviolence would render hypocritical Jeff Gingerich's critique, in chapter 16 of this volume, of the retributive violence of the prevailing United States paradigm of criminal justice, or J. Denny Weaver's critique, in chapter 3 of this volume, of the divine violence of retribution that is intrinsic to all forms of satisfaction and substitutionary atonement.

5. Walter Brueggemann, *Theology of the Old Testament: Testimony, Dispute, Advocacy* (Minneapolis: Fortress, 1997), 117–130 and 317–324.

6. The argument is parallel to that of J. Denny Weaver in chapter 3 of this volume, in which he argues that the rejection of violence revealed in Jesus should shape the atonement paradigm.

7. Gustavo Gutiérrez, *A Theology of Liberation*, rev. ed., trans. Caridad Inda and John Eagleson (Maryknoll, N.Y.: Orbis, 1988), 3–12.

8. Ollenburger, "The Hermeneutics of Obedience," 58.

9. John Howard Yoder, "How H. Richard Niebuhr Reasoned: A Critique of *Christ and Culture*," in *Authentic Transformation: A New Vision of Christ and Culture*, ed. Glen H. Stassen et al. (Nashville: Abingdon, 1996), 61–65.

10. This strategy of identifying the persuasive stories also follows the American philosopher Richard Rorty, who uses this approach to speak about philosophical arguments. For a summary of the philosophical basis behind this tactic, see his "Introduction: Antirepresentationalism, Ethnocentrism, and Liberalism," in *Objectivity, Relativism, and Truth: Philosophical Papers,* vol. 1 (Cambridge: Cambridge University, 1991), 1–17.

11. Supersessionism poses a twofold problem here as a hermeneutical principle: it renders the Old Testament irrelevant or without authority for Christians, and it ignores the fact that the New Testament also contains apparently violent images of God. Supersessionism also presents problematic theological implications, particularly in relation to anti-Semitism, which are beyond the scope of the current discussion.

12. Yoder, *The Politics of Jesus,* 76–88.

13. Yoder, *The Politics of Jesus,* 78–79.

14. Yoder, *The Politics of Jesus*, 78.

15. Yoder, *The Politics of Jesus,* 78–79.

16. Yoder, *The Politics of Jesus,* 83.

17. This claim has its own interpretive minefield to pass through, since scholarly assertions about what Jesus might have actually done, said, or thought vary widely, and many scholars go so far as to suggest that any attempt to recreate a "historical Jesus" is doomed to failure. At this point, while learning from the scholarly discussion about "historical Jesus," I am following Yoder in working with the canonical picture of Jesus.

18. That the Bible contains and retains these contradictions is strong testimony to its authenticity. Their existence makes quite clear that no editor attempted to smooth over or systematize such material.

5

Nonviolence in the Biblical Struggle to Know

John Kampen

The struggle to know has always been part of the student experience. From my days as dean of Payne Theological Seminary, I recall the students' adaptation of the common athletic phrase, "No Payne, no gain." Hard work, long hours of reading, research, memorizing, and writing, have all been common to the student experience. Today at the beginning of the twenty-first century, we face a different struggle with respect to knowledge, one which bears only a remote resemblance to those factors we have traditionally associated with the struggle to learn. This chapter describes my understanding, in a global context, of that struggle and the place of nonviolence in it, especially as it is inflected through my reading of the biblical text which identifies truth with freedom.[1]

Scattered liberally throughout all the literature Bluffton College distributes and imprinted in its letterhead is the college motto "The Truth Makes Free." Immediately apparent is its biblical basis in John 8:32 "You will know the truth, and the truth will make you free." Freedom was a very important concept for the second half of the twentieth century as colonial entities were forced to accede to the loss of direct political control over the last vestiges of empire in the face of rekindled national and ethnic identities that demanded recognition and power. A similar and related movement was apparent within national borders as politically marginalized peoples called for recognition and attention to their concerns, in the name of freedom. The term has a longer history, of course, particularly as the concept was developed and achieved central significance within the postenlightenment tradition of Western thought.

At Bluffton College, as at many church-related institutions of higher learning, the identification of education with freedom took on a particular ethos throughout much of the twentieth century, one shaped by the assumption that there is a specifiable culture that characterizes the educated—the free—person. Like so many of their peers in the world of American and European higher education, Bluffton's leadership understood the purpose of education as creating the kind of person who will make a contribution to that culture and will lead society to achieve its highest ideals.[2] These educators also assumed that the basis for this culture of learning was the Enlightenment project which located truth within the epistemological triumphalism of science and philosophy as it developed in the West. When efforts to renew the peace church identity of Bluffton College took up concerns such as peace, service, and community outreach, these ideals were constructed on this enlightenment-focused philosophical base. This specific understanding of truth and the means by which it is accessed has certainly shaped the modern reception of John 8:32 among educators and those who treasure the "life of the mind."

However, advances in our perception of the ancient world and this particular biblical text along with the challenges of twentieth- and twenty-first-century life now open up new possibilities for its interpretation as well as for understanding the educational mission of historic peace church colleges like Bluffton College. These advances enable us to place the college motto in a new interpretive context that permits its use as a basis for facing the challenges of the twenty-first century.

TRUTH AND FREEDOM IN THE BIBLICAL STRUGGLE

When removed from its biblical context, the conventional understanding of the phrase "the truth makes free" stands in sharp contrast with the polemical paragraph within which it is found in John 8. A noted biblical scholar describes the problem: "The hackneyed use of this phrase in political oratory in appealing for national or personal liberty is a distortion of the purely religious value of both truth and freedom in this passage."[3] This verse appears not in the context of a refined philosophical discussion but rather in the heat of vitriolic name calling and struggle. The sentence which includes this phrase begins in the previous verse: "If you continue in my word you are truly my disciples . . ." Then the Jews, the designation for the opponents of Jesus in this Gospel, respond to the declaration about freedom: "We are descendants of Abraham and have never been slaves to anyone. What do you mean by saying, 'You will be made free'?" Jesus responds, "everyone who commits sin is a slave to sin. The slave does not have a permanent place in the household. . . . So if the Son makes you free you will be free indeed." The debate heats up in vv. 39–41: "If you were Abraham's children you would be doing what Abraham did, but now you are trying to kill me, a man who has told you the truth I heard from God." Then the tirade in vv. 43–44, the section that makes this passage a crucial text in the development of Christian anti-Semitism: "You are from your father the devil, and you choose to do your father's desire. He was a murderer from the beginning and does not stand in the truth, because there is no truth in him. When he lies, he speaks according to his own nature, for he is a liar and the father of lies." Recognition of the polemical nature of this material leads Leon Morris to comment: "There is, of course, a sense in which it is true that only by surrender to the facts is genuine freedom possible, be it in philosophy, science, or what you will. But that is not the point here." He then follows with a footnote of substantiation that begins, "For this reason parallels adduced from the Stoics and others to the effect that wisdom or the like liberates are misleading."[4] This passage reflects a passionate struggle, not a polite discussion, and we need to understand the significance of that realization.

Clues to the context of the struggle can be found earlier in this chapter in John 8:12. God as light was basic for many religions of the East, inherited by the gnostic systems present in the eastern Mediterranean during the period of the Roman Empire as well as in the mystery religions.[5] Erwin R. Goodenough, a historian of Hellenistic Jewish history, outlined the case for an intellectual approach to a Jewish version of a Greek mystery religion.[6] This semi-intellectual and mystic pursuit of individual truth in the mystery religions provided the background for biblical scholars to understand what Jesus meant when he said, "I am the light of the world." While the writer of John does seem to pick up the temple imagery of the four golden candlesticks lit in the Court of the Women on the first night of the feast of Tabernacles that give light to all the city of Jerusalem, we fail to understand the full significance of the conflict in this chapter if we do not also understand it in another perspective.[7]

Completely new ways of understanding the Gospel of John opened up in 1947 with the discovery of the Dead Sea Scrolls. While this discovery is now over fifty years old, we continue to probe the significance of these texts. The integration of this material into our conceptions of Judaism at the time of the Roman Empire as well as into biblical studies will continue to occupy us for some time. Some appreciation of their significance for the study of the Gospel of John came fairly early.[8] The War Scroll describes a war between the children of light and the children of darkness, which presumably lasts for forty years, even though the text we have of it describes only twenty-nine years—a Star Wars kind of scenario. In the Community Rule, also called the Manual of Discipline in some collections, the adherents of the Jewish sect that authored the scroll are known as the Children of Light and all of the rest of the Jews are the children of darkness. As in John 8, the Community Rule makes no attempt to find anything good to say about these opponents, no overtures to appeal to their good side much less to find common ground. These opponents are in the realm of evil, ruled by Belial, the prince of darkness. So we begin to see what John 8 means in the context of sectarian struggle: "You will know the truth, and the truth will set you free," free from the all-pervasive power of the realm of evil, free from the clutches of the prince of darkness. To know the truth is to take sides in a struggle, to declare boldly and forthrightly which side you are on. This is the nature of truth and the resulting freedom in the Gospel of John. So what does it mean to be engaged in the struggle to "know the truth" at the beginning of the twenty-first century?

THE PROBLEM OF EVIL

The legacy of the twentieth century has a profound impact on our understanding of truth at the beginning of the twenty-first century. The major realization and the most surprising discovery of the twentieth century is not the astounding advance in technology, even though the significant advances left the world considerably different at the end of the twentieth century than at its beginning. The most amazing discovery of the twentieth century is the recognition of the power of evil, and it will be our task in the twenty-first century to figure out what to do with this knowledge.

In the twentieth century the most well-known event that forced a recognition of the power of evil was the Holocaust, that occurrence in which the moral and political will to destroy an entire people was linked with massive technological experimentation and expertise such that this endeavor became an actual possibility. Six million Jews and an estimated total number of eleven to twelve million, including gypsies, homosexuals, and certain native populations, were destroyed in a disastrously misguided attempt to create the leadership for and chart the direction of a brave new world. While its precise nature and contribution is the subject of continuing analysis and debate, Christian anti-Semitism was an important factor in providing a foundation for a society in which this extermination effort became possible.

Substantial work has been done on the relationship between Christian sacred texts and anti-Semitism.[9] The most obvious questions center on texts such as the diatribes against the Pharisees in Matthew 23, the crucifixion account of Matthew 27:24–26 in which Pilate washes his hands in a declaration of innocence while the Jewish people "as a whole" cry out that "His blood be on us and on our children!" and John 8:31–47 in which the Jews are said to have their origin in the devil. The first response is to notice the very different meanings ascribed to these texts by Jews and Christians. Concerning Matthew 23 we might suggest that this text has more to say about hypocrisy within religious communities than about the Pharisees. But Jews see in that text a denigration of the particular group of persons who laid the foundation for Rabbinic Judaism, hence the formative social movement for modern Judaism.[10] There is ample historical evidence to suggest that these texts have been used to demonstrate the superiority of the Christian faith to Judaism, have provided the foundation for Christian triumphalism, and have functioned as the theological justification of the inquisition and the Crusades.[11] In the modern world they have provided a framework for evangelical efforts which targeted the Jewish people. Is it possible for us to develop a nonviolent biblical hermeneutic that challenges this kind of Christian triumphalism, thereby permitting us to approach Judaism in a different manner? In chapter 5 of this book, David Janzen suggests an affirmative answer to this question and demonstrates how such an approach might affect our understanding of biblical texts that seem to promote warfare. Might the hermeneutic of obedience Janzen proposes also assist us in challenging any kind of anti-Semitism, particularly that borne by Christian triumphalism?

In North America alongside anti-Semitism, a second social reality also points to the fundamental problem of the power of evil. At the beginning of the last century, after emancipation and the well-known failure of the promise of the Reconstruction era, W. E. B. Dubois writing in 1903 recognized that: "The problem of the twentieth century is the problem of the color line—the relation of the darker to the lighter races of men in Asia and Africa, in America and the islands of the sea."[12] Life behind the veil becomes the dominant motif of Dubois's book, probably the most important work on this subject ever written.[13] When he refers to the veil, he is not pointing simply to the difficulties immigrant groups know about from times when they moved into a culture or country where the customs were different from theirs or where they did not know the language. That kind of veil is penetrable because they gradually learn to understand something of the customs of the land as well as the language or at least the portions of it necessary to get by. What Dubois referred to was a separation not based on culture. This separation instead had its origin in legal mandates reinforced by the economic and political system that benefited from this enforced bondage, as well as by the social and religious forces that sanctioned it and continue to perpetuate it long after the legal mandates with which it began are no longer considered valid. In his book *Faces at the Bottom of the Well* Derrick Bell argues that racism is a permanent feature of American life, which can be resisted and defied but never defeated.[14] An analysis of racism's enduring hold is inadequate if it does not include the fundamental reality of the power of evil. How can we begin to comprehend the fact that an entire race of people could be enslaved because of the color of their skin without recognizing the problem of evil and asking the question: What is it about who we are as human beings that makes such an occurrence possible?[15]

This problem also cuts to the heart of the biblical roots of Christianity. With regard to the use of the Bible, it is possible to speak of the European coup, the manner in which Europeans co-opted the sacred book, made it speak their language and express their culture, and convinced the rest of the world to accept that Bible. Many are appalled by a heretical black Jesus while not recognizing the heresy of the European-looking figure that dots the walls of most homes and churches. A reexamination of the texts and the presuppositions with regard to those sacred traditions is in order for the purpose of uncovering some other viewpoints on that record.

A new reading of the biblical account suggests that Africa is much more important than customarily thought. Most people are only remotely aware of the Ethiopian kingdom which took over Egypt in 760 B.C.E. when Kashta, the Ethiopian ruler, began the twenty-fifth dynasty by assuming the title of pharaoh. This dynasty lasted until the ascension of Assyria in 664 B.C.E. Just as notable is the consolidation of a dynasty in the area of Ethiopia, later called Nubia, that halted the Persian, Greek, and Roman empires at its northern borders, remained an unhellenized kingdom, and established a continuous African kingdom that lasted a thousand years. Under the influence of the European coup, Western scholars tended to disconnect Egypt from the rest of Africa. Part of the "oriental" interest of nineteenth-century European scholars led to a great deal of research on Egypt, including archaeological work that still appears in major North American galleries. The analytical perspective within which this work was developed included the area known as the Fertile Crescent and its relationship to Mesopotamia. This work has lead African American scholars to note the manner in which European scholars appeared unable to imagine that black Africans were able to develop the civilization that was being uncovered in Egypt.[16] This scholarship has generated considerable debate concerning the African nature of Egypt and Egyptians.[17] How different from standard accounts this esoteric debate looks to an African American scholar reading Egyptian history!

Lest we be inclined to view the debate over these issues as insignificant, witness the furor caused by the work of Martin Bernal, the author of *Black Athena*.[18] This scholar of Chinese history, who dared to venture into a reevaluation of the African and Asian contributions to the formative stages of Greek civilization, has evoked an ongoing debate, frequently building on the work and perspectives of African and African American scholars of the last century. The major argument of Bernal's work is that many of the substantive elements that went into the formation of classical Greek civilization were adapted from Africa and Asia. While his reappraisal is frequently less radical than the work of some significant African American scholars, the controversy has been extensive simply because of the manner in which it undercuts the perceptions a Caucasian civilization has of itself and where it came from.[19] Also notable are two significant interpretive traditions in the African American community, the study of which are still in their infancy. Extensive research has begun on the particular usage of the biblical tradition that has sustained the African American community.[20] African American scholars also have been instrumental in the development of a second area, the ideological criticism of biblical texts. This particular method, related to the field of cultural criticism and rooted in the concerns of the black community, evaluates texts as to whether and how they contribute to the black liberation struggle.[21] Some implications of this method are described in more detail in chapter 3 of this volume by J. Denny Weaver. His analysis raises profound questions for how those scholars of European background appropriate and use biblical texts.

While there are those of European descent considered minorities within North American society, the circumstances are so vastly different for African Americans that respective fates within this system are difficult to compare. Members of the Caucasian race benefit from a system that was constructed precisely for their benefit. Their identities are formed and informed by this system. Not only are they the majority race, they are also the group in power and derive benefits including the maintenance of their lifestyle from that position.

The genocide of native peoples throughout the twentieth century speaks to the same reality of evil: Armenia earlier in the century, East Timor, Somalia, and other places. I know this from my own Mennonite experience: in my family a grandfather left to die in the Ukraine in his early twenties during the destruction of Mennonite society by the Red army during the Russian revolution, a grandmother who never spoke about those traumatic years of the revolution. To know the truth at the end of the twentieth century is to recognize the power of humanity to dehumanize, to enslave, to degrade, and to destroy. There is no naive knowledge left at the end of the twentieth century. With all my heart I wish it were not so. I wish we could make simple intellectual choices between abstract principles that did not have such grave consequences. But we cannot. It is in this context that we now need to address the question of learning in the light of a commitment to nonviolence.

NONVIOLENCE AND THE KNOWLEDGE CRISIS

The development and articulation of a strategy of nonviolence has never been easy or self-evident in most contexts. The recent popular and very significant collection of stories about successful nonviolent efforts in the twentieth century documents exceptions to that rule.[22] Persons who have developed philosophies and strategies of nonviolence have frequently had to challenge accepted wisdom and usually even the accepted presuppositions upon which a society operates.[23] In this effort, the development of strategies of nonviolence pose the same challenges for us as do the examples of anti-Semitism and racism cited above. These strategies call for a reassessment of the fundamentals of who we are as a society, the philosophical basis of how we live, and the theological underpinnings of the Christianity we espouse. The violence of our society and our world call for the same reassessment. An analysis of the violence in North America as well as throughout the world is a different piece of evidence concerning the power of evil. People are killing one another in new and different ways. Gun-toting teenagers in the schools of the United States are not carrying out state-sanctioned violence. They are, however, evidence of a deep-rooted evil that pervades more of our society than we want to recognize. Those political realities known as regional or ethnic conflicts continue to wreak havoc in communities and societies throughout the world because of the violence they promote and the peace they do not permit. A nonviolent approach to this reality should call for the same kind of reassessment as a serious attempt to address the implications of the Holocaust and slavery. We need to understand, to gain a new perspective on the realities of our world and its underpinnings, to engage in the struggle to "know the truth."

It is also true, however, that coming to terms with the problem of evil as posed in the examples above can challenge some of our strategies of nonviolence. A nonviolence that is based on a Christian theology that either intentionally or unintentionally promotes racism or anti-Semitism is not addressing the problem of evil or engaging in the struggle. This observation merely illustrates the major extent of the fundamental reassessment required. A veneer of nonviolence over a theology that continues to champion any brand of Christian triumphalism is inadequate and fails to address the basic problem. Any nonviolent strategy which justifies an exclusive Christian utopia that permits the justification of the debasement, dehumanization, and enslavement of any human beings outside of that perfect circle is to be suspect. Coming to terms with the power of evil is not simple. It requires the best minds and the most sophisticated analyses to engage in that struggle.

To know the truth is to join forces with peoples struggling for life and dignity, to join hands with others who look for ways in which we can create an environment that thrives in its support of a diversity of life-forms, to find effective ways to counteract those forces in a global economy that attempts to turn us into homogeneous consumers, to form alliances with the varieties of individuals and groups who are dispossessed by the growing massive disparity between the poor and the rich on an international scale, to be part of a coalition which creates a society that does not need more prisons.[24] This is the struggle in which we are engaged.

In taking up that struggle we begin to encounter the joy and freedom of the gospel. We are now not constrained by conventional perceptions or expectations, because we know their limitations. We have been made new, transformed into forces of liberation. We are free to enter into the lives of persons around the globe who are different from us, to hear their stories, to tell them our stories, to form bonds of allegiance that will unite us in a common struggle for dignity and humanity. Due to a commitment to nonviolence, we are free to accept the critique of cherished assumptions that have grounded our understanding of and engagement with the world. We are free, for example, to reject the racist underpinnings of both institutional and conceptional structures as we engage in the exhilarating task of transforming and building new and different frameworks for our lives. Because "the truth has set us free," we are free to enter into the lives and experiences of other peoples we were never even expected to encounter and who may now pose a serious challenge to comfortable habits of thought and practice. The challenge of the twenty-first century is an ominous one, but there is a way, there is a possibility that the twenty-first century can be a time of victory. The biblical statement that the truth makes free reminds us that our commitment to the struggle to really know is the condition for being really free. And truth, for people committed to nonviolence in the twenty-first century, is not something at which we arrive, it is something for which we struggle.

NOTES

1. This chapter is an elaboration of a sermon given at First Mennonite Church, Bluffton, Ohio, on April 30, 2000, and then published in *The Mennonite* 3, no. 33 (September 5, 2000): 6–7 and in *Scope*, vol. 88, no. 1 (September 2000), 8–9.

2. A short list of writing on this educational culture includes Stephen Toulmin, *Cosmopolis: The Hidden Agenda of Modernity* (New York: Free Press, 1992); Terrence W. Tilley, "In Favor of a 'Practical Theory of Religion': Montaigne and Pascal," in *Theology without Foundations: Religious Practice and the Future of Theological Truth,* ed. S. Hauerwas, N. Murphy, and M. Nation (Nashville: Abingdon, 1994), 49–74, 309–312; Charles

Scriven, "Schooling for the Tournament of Narratives: Postmodernism and the Idea of the Christian College," in *Theology without Foundations* (Nashville: Abingdon Press, 1994), 273–288, 342–344.

3. Raymond E. Brown, *The Gospel according to John I–XII: A New Translation with Introduction and Commentary,* AB 29 (Garden City, N.Y.: Doubleday, 1966), 355.

4. Leon Morris, "The Gospel according to John," in *New International Commentary of the New Testament* (Grand Rapids, Mich.: Eerdmans, 1971), 456, n. 64.

5. See the summary in C. K. Barrett, *The Gospel according to St. John,* 2d ed. (Philadelphia: Westminster, 1978), 335–337.

6. Erwin R. Goodenough, *By Light, Light: The Mystic Gospel of Hellenistic Judaism* (London: Oxford University Press, 1935).

7. Brown, *John I–XII,* 343–344; and Morris, *St. John,* 335. For the description of the light in the temple, see Mishnah, *Sukkah,* 5:2–4.

8. An early summary can be found in Raymond E. Brown, S.S., "The Qumran Scrolls and the Johannine Gospel and Epistles," in *The Sea Scrolls and the New Testament,* ed. Krister Stendahl (CBQ 17, 1955; reprint, New York: Harper and Brothers, 1957), 183–207, 282–291.

9. Important works include: Samuel Sandmel, *Anti-Semitism in the New Testament?* (Philadelphia: Fortress, 1978); John G. Gager, *The Origins of Anti-Semitism: Attitudes toward Judaism in Pagan and Christian Antiquity* (New York: Oxford University Press, 1985); Peter Schäfer, *Judeophobia: Attitudes toward the Jews in the Ancient World* (Cambridge: Harvard University Press, 1999).

10. Note that the question of the historical role of the Pharisees in the establishment of Rabbinic Judaism has no simple answer, and I will not investigate that topic in this paper.

11. The phrase "Christian triumphalism" was developed by Rosemary Ruether, *Faith and Fratricide: The Theological Roots of Anti-Semitism* (New York: Seabury, 1974).

12. W. E. Burghardt DuBois, *The Souls of Black Folk: Essays and Sketches* (Greenwich, Conn.: Fawcett, 1961), 23.

13. DuBois, *The Souls of Black Folk,* 16.

14. Recall that Derrick Bell is the attorney dismissed by Harvard Law School because of his protest of their refusal to hire black faculty members. He sets forth the following proposition:

"Black people will never gain full equality in this country. Even those herculean efforts we hail as successful will produce no more than temporary 'peaks of progress,' short-lived victories that slide into irrelevance as racial patterns adapt in ways that maintain white dominance. This is a hard-to-accept fact that all history verifies. We must acknowledge it, not as a sign of submission, but as an act of ultimate defiance." Derrick Bell, *Faces at the Bottom of the Well: The Permanence of Racism* (New York: Basic, 1992), 12.

On the origins of American racism in its Puritan past and the legacy of that tradition, see Paul R. Griffin, *Seeds of Racism in the Soul of America* (Cleveland: Pilgrim, 1999).

15. Portions of the following section are adapted by permission from my article "The Mennonite Challenge of Particularism and Universalism: A Liberation Perspective," *Conrad Grebel Review* 19, no. 2 (Spring 2001): 5–28.

16. Note the essays of Charles Copher, finally collected, in the volume *Black Biblical Studies: An Anthology of Charles Copher; Biblical and Theological Issues on the Black Presence in the Bible* (Chicago: Black Light Fellowship, 1993). Note also Cain Hope Felder, *Troubling Biblical Waters: Race, Class and Family* (Maryknoll, N.Y.: Orbis, 1989),

5–48; and the essays Felder has collected in *Stony the Road We Trod: African American Biblical Interpretation* (Minneapolis: Fortress, 1991), 127–184.

17. Along with the works cited in the previous note, see Frank Yurco, "Were the Ancient Egyptians Black or White?" *Biblical Archeology Review* 15, no. 5 (September/October 1989): 24–30.

18. Martin Bernal, *Black Athena: The Afroasiatic Roots of Classical Civilization,* 2 vols. (New Brunswick, N.J.: Rutgers University Press, 1987/1991).

19. A thorough analysis of the conflict with a citation of the relevant literature has been provided by Jacques Berlinerblau, *Heresy in the University: The* Black Athena *Controversy and the Responsibilities of American Intellectuals* (New Brunswick, N.J.: Rutgers University, 1999).

20. The results of the largest project of this nature ever undertaken can be found in *African Americans and the Bible: Sacred Texts and Social Textures,* ed. Vincent L. Wimbush (New York: Continuum, 2000).

21. Vincent L. Wimbush, "Biblical-Historical Study As Liberation: Toward an Afro-Christian Hermeneutic," *Journal of Religious Thought* 42, no. 2 (Fall/Winter, 1985–1986): 9–21; Renita J. Weems, "Reading *Her Way* through the Struggle," in *Stony the Road* (Minneapolis: Fortress Press, 1991), 57–77; Itumeleng J. Mosala, "The Use of the Bible in Black Theology," in *The Unquestionable Right to Be Free: Black Theology from South Africa,* ed. Itumeleng J. Mosala and Buti Tlhagale (Maryknoll, N.Y.: Orbis, 1986), 175–199.

22. Peter Ackerman and Jack Duvall, *A Force More Powerful: A Century of Nonviolent Conflict* (New York: St. Martin, 2000); also a PBS series and a feature film.

23. Note that I am here using the term "strategies" in a very comprehensive manner to include specific actions directed toward immediate goals, broader-based efforts which affect power and decision making in a society as well as philosophies, ideologies, and lifestyles that impact the entire lifespan of persons and the networks of relationship in a society.

24. One attempt to relate the Gospel of John to this struggle is found in David Rensberger, *Johannine Faith and Liberating Community* (Philadelphia: Westminster, 1988), esp. 138–144.

III

NONVIOLENCE IN HISTORY AND POLITICS

6

Violence, Nonviolence, and the Search for Answers in History

Perry Bush

"**A**nd you will pardon me if Bluffton College's recent class on becoming a conscientious objector leaves a nasty taste in my mouth. Freedom will never be free, and if we are willing to reap its rewards we should be willing to fight for them. Thank God our founding fathers were not conscientious objectors. If they had been, our country would never have existed in the first place."[1]

So wrote a local citizen "guest columnist" in the *Lima* (Ohio) *News* in the wake of the terrorist attacks on the World Trade Center in September 2001. Her comment reflects and expresses perhaps the preeminent American belief—that freedom depends on war. While such opinions particularly reverberated in the waves of national, patriotic chest thumping that accompanied the new War on Terrorism, they were but a newer expression of an older theme. That violence in general and war in particular has functioned to progressive and even redemptive effect throughout history is a truism that has largely proceeded without much questioning in American society and throughout the West. According to theologian Walter Wink, the "victory of order over chaos by means of violence" has been an integral part of the mythic structure of Western culture for millennia; "it is," argues Wink, "the spirituality of the modern world."[2] As the comments by the *Lima News* columnist illustrate, the linkage between violence and freedom has particularly deep roots in American society. Assumptions that violence and war have made American freedom possible are so central to our culture that nearly all Americans repeat them reflexively. The sociologist Robert Bellah found warfare so integral to American self-understanding that it was a key aspect of the national "civil religion."[3] The historian James Juhnke stated more simply that the linkage between warfare and freedom "is the creed of American history."[4]

Of all academic disciplines, perhaps this myth of redemptive violence engages history most inescapably. The personal experience of pacifists who live in a warrior culture may function as the best guide on this point. It is hardly possible for people of peace to debate nonpacifists for five minutes before the threat posed by a Hitler—or a bin Laden, a Saddam Hussein, a Slobodan Milosevic, or the monster of the moment—is raised as the ultimate, unanswerable sanction for warfare. In such an exchange it is not generally acceptable or persuasive to point out that "monsters" are products of particular historical contexts and that, except in fantasies like comic books or presidential speeches, evildoers do not attack us merely because they hate our freedom or because they have some kind of genetic predisposition to kill.[5] Rather, in such a conversation, history is presumed to begin when a conflict catches the attention of the American press or when the nation is attacked. Thus advocates of realpolitik present pacifists with a situation of violent conflict—with hatreds brought to a white heat because of years of realist intervention or imperialist manipulation—and demand that pacifists deliver an immediate, fail-safe method for peaceful reconciliation. When no such blueprint is forthcoming, nonviolence is usually dismissed as irrelevant or utopian. Of course people of peace do have answers to the problems of violence and injustice, but the answers are found to a significant extent in the past. Hence it would seem that an examination of history would be central in any effort to integrate nonviolence across the educational curriculum.[6]

IT MIGHT HAVE BEEN OTHERWISE

Before we can begin such an exploration, there are several methodological issues that demand attention, revolving most centrally around the question of human agency in history. At the outset I should state my own preference for historical perspectives that assume a significant role for human agents in historical outcomes, a preference that would challenge such modern historiographical approaches as Marxism or the Annales school, in which human actions are assumed to be primarily the effects of larger historical forces such as economics or geography. Such a preference, of course, is not unique to a pacifist historiography. Many contemporary historians maintain a firm belief that humans are capable of choices and that these choices have made a great difference in the making of historical events. This conviction has been especially harnessed in the traditional "Great Leader" vein of historical writing, in which the options chosen by the leader have proved centrally important in directing the flow of history into one channel or another. Such historians have even speculated quite freely about alternative futures that might have ensued had one or another leader chosen differently. To offer just one example, in his examination of Franklin Roosevelt's New Deal, William Leuchtenburg concludes with the observation that "it is difficult to gainsay the importance of Roosevelt. If, in Miami in February, 1933, an assassin's bullet had been true to its mark and John Garner rather than Roosevelt had entered the White House the next month . . . the history of America in the thirties would have been markedly different."[7]

The spirit of intellectual fair play must also grant to pacifist historians the freedom likewise to posit alternative futures or speculate on the outcomes of different historical decisions, especially when nonpacifist and even Great Leader historians themselves seem to fall victim to a sense of historical determinism regarding issues of war and violence. As he analyzed the origins of the American Civil War, for example, the biographer Arthur Schlesinger Jr. contended, "The unhappy fact is that man occasionally works himself into a log-jam; and that the log-jam must be burst by violence."[8] One service that a nonviolent reading of history might thus provide for the larger discipline of history is a recapturing and renewal of the power of human agency in history: the freedom that humans have had to choose different courses of action, to pursue different possibilities and different futures, so much so that nonviolent roads not taken may become a legitimate focus of historical attention.[9]

Given the importance of these alternative courses, the argument here must proceed upon two different tracks, one negative and one positive. First, on the negative side, if—as the unstated assumption proceeds—war and violence is sometimes necessary and delivers ultimately beneficial ends for people who harness such means, then one essential task in a nonviolent approach to history must be to critically examine this assumption. Second, on the positive side, it is necessary to discuss nonviolent alternatives: times and places where nonviolence might have or did avert war or worse violence or injustice, and episodes in which humans achieved beneficial ends through the use of nonviolence rather than violence.

WAR OUT OF CONTROL

Any comprehensive critique of modern war would run for volumes. For brevity's sake, I will confine my attention to two conflicts in American history—the Civil War and the Second World War—and focus on two key points. First, as these conflicts illustrate, modern wars often come to assume a momentum and trajectory that threaten seriously to reshape—and sometimes overwhelm—their original aims. Second, as a subpoint and consequence of the first point, modern war also assumes a ferocity of its own, so devastating that one may well question whether the ends which war makers set out to achieve actually justify the savagery of the means employed to obtain them.

"A singular fact about modern war," wrote the Civil War historian Bruce Catton, "is that it takes charge. Once begun it has to be carried to its conclusion, and carrying it there sets in motion events that may be beyond men's control. Doing what has to be done to win, men perform acts that alter the very soil in which society's roots are nourished."[10] Catton's observation holds true for all modern wars, especially for the Civil War and World War II. At the beginning of the Civil War, most Americans, North and South, expected a quick victory. Lincoln spoke and acted in ways that minimized the destructiveness of the war and created grounds for an easier reconciliation. "We are not enemies, but friends," he assured the South in his first inaugural address, ". . . though passion may have strained, it must not break the bonds of our affection."[11] The new president resisted early calls to emancipate slaves in order to render reunion more possible and told aides that this would not be "a remorseless revolutionary struggle."[12] Propelled into combat by a Victorian culture stressing key concepts such as duty, honor, and especially courage, officers and soldiers initially fought in ways consistent with Lincoln's early vision. Officers inspired their men through conspicuous displays of courage; soldiers often refused to shoot at enemies they deemed particularly valorous; prisoners of war were released and sent home upon only their solemn promises to leave the conflict.[13]

Yet this whole "constellation of values" among the troops and the early reconciling attitudes of war leaders like Lincoln were inexorably ground down by the new necessities inherent in modern war. Besides disease,[14] the reason the Civil War became such a slaughter pen is that officers and men remained wedded to the tactics of the Napoleonic War that were later refined in the American conflict during the war with Mexico and which stressed the head-on charge. Yet the new technology of the 1860s, principally the rifled musket and exploding artillery shells (grapeshot and canister) turned the traditional bayonet charge into a killing field. Attacking soldiers came under effective fire four hundred yards from the enemy, and rarely survived long enough to engage the enemy in the hand-to-hand combat of lore.[15] Three years into the war, armies had already engaged in a dozen of the most fearsome battles in human history to that point, and yet the war ground on in a bloody stalemate that had achieved little except frightfully long casualty lists.

The culture of combat began to shift as a result. Battles were no longer set affairs but, in anticipation of twentieth-century warfare, became continual engagements, as the armies of Grant and Lee grappled from the Wilderness to Spotsylvania to Cold Harbor to Petersburg. The soldiers learned elemental lessons: open displays of courage were a quick way to get killed; officers who ordered head-on charges were reckless fools; enemy soldiers were to be shot without qualm; and trees and mounds of earth could stop bullets.[16] Soon the dramatic but costly courage of a Pickett's charge gave way to the months of dreary trench warfare around Petersburg, in a nineteenth-century dress rehearsal for World War I.

Most important of all, as the armies stalemated and the new technology rendered a decisive battlefield victory both increasingly difficult and impossibly costly, the nature of the war itself changed. In the words of historian Russell Weigley, Union commanders pursued "a strategy of annihilation": new warfare directed not just at enemy soldiers, but also at the entire South, as a total society. The pioneers of this new way of total war were not dashing, Napoleonic figures like Lee and McClellan (with the latter's tender, solicitous concern for the lives of his men), but grim, hardened persona like Grant and Sherman. "(W)e are not only fighting hostile armies but a hostile people," Sherman reasoned, "and must make the old and young, rich and poor, feel the hard hand of war, as well as the organized armies."[17] In a perverse way, Lincoln's Emancipation Proclamation provided the ultimate moral sanction for this kind of warfare, infusing it with a new meaning—a war for freedom—that it had previously lacked. Lincoln himself caught the transformation. Contrast his earlier words of reconciliation with these: after the Proclamation took effect, he remarked, "The character of the war is to be changed. It will be one of subjugation . . . The (old) South is to be destroyed and replaced by new propositions and ideas."[18] The lesson to the troops in the field was crystal clear. After the commander-in-chief had already stripped away from Southerners their most valuable single piece of property—their slaves—invading soldiers felt it certainly within their rights to take such items as a chicken, a fence rail, or a family's food supply for the winter.

As Sherman burned a destructive path across Georgia and the Carolinas, in a strangely prophetic way he and Grant also began to sketch out the new ethical sanctions for total war that would echo through the twentieth century. First, it involved blaming the victims. Because the rebels "had forced us into war," Sherman argued, they "deserved all they got, and more." Secondly, in an eerie anticipation of justifications of Hiroshima, these architects of total war also reasoned that the terror they inflicted was ultimately the more ethical and merciful course, for it led more quickly to peace. In Sherman's words, "the crueler [war] is, the sooner it will be over"; Grant declared that "To conserve life, in war, is to fight unceasingly."[19]

Certainly, all the killing and destruction of the Civil War ultimately accomplished a number of positive ends. The nation provisionally settled several pressing political questions (like states rights vs. national authority); more important, four million enslaved individuals were freed. As historian Ron Wells has noted, pacifist historians who highlight the war's horrors without recognizing the issues of justice resolved by its outcome proceed on an ethical thin ice of their own.[20] However, a number of factors seriously erode the positive dimensions of these outcomes. While the war eliminated the institution of slavery, it did nothing about the underlying racism on which human enslavement was built. And given the continuing racism to which the reunited nation subjected its newly freed slaves in the century following the war—walling them off into a degrading system of poverty and segregation, stripping away nearly all their civil, legal, and human rights, lynching them by the tens of thousands—racial justice was clearly not central to the meaning or purpose of the conflict. Further, as noted below, there were other ways that the nation might have freed its slaves without resorting to the enormous costs imposed by war: 600,000 dead in a nation of 31 million people, another nearly 300,000 maimed, great Southern cities reduced to rubble. The effects of the war would mark the South for generations. Its financial institutions destroyed, it lay prostrate economically and came to function as a kind of internal colony for Northern capital. In such a desperate milieu millions of postwar Southerners would quietly enter the maws of the crop-lien system.[21] Culturally the South remained, argues one historian, "a notoriously violent place," as the massive waves of violence unleashed by the war became transfigured into a number of different horrible postwar manifestations.[22] Only the constraints of available technology limited the destructiveness caused by the war (imagine the horrors Sherman might have inflicted had he had access to a B-29 bomber).

The Second World War presents perhaps the supreme test case for the validity of a nonviolent approach to history. The evil posed by Hitler's genocide and Japanese fanatical militarism seems so apparent that the war appears the perfect example of "the good war,"[23] the Just War. Given the nature of the threat, traditional Just War theorists would certainly argue that the cause for which the Allies fought was just. Nevertheless, later historians and pacifist leaders [24] recognized that Hitler's fanaticism did not arise in a vacuum, that the seeds for it were laid in the humiliating, punitive peace and economic disintegration imposed upon Germany by the victors of World War I.

Moreover, even if the cause was just, the war proceeded in a manner that violated many other criteria of Just War theory, particularly the church's commands to limit destruction to the minimum required to win and to keep noncombatants immune from attack.[25] Like the Civil War, World War II began with high hopes about how its destructiveness might be limited and then spiraled downward into mass killing. When Hitler's air force bombed Warsaw, in the very beginning of the war, Franklin Roosevelt issued an "urgent appeal to every government that its armed forces shall in no event and under no circumstances undertake bombardment from the air of civilian populations or unfortified cities." For his part, British premier Winston Churchill denounced obliteration bombing as "a new and odious form of attack."[26] Yet the fine words and high thinking soon gave way to the logic of modern war, which meant that while maximizing one's own economic production and civilian morale, one concomitantly tried to destroy those of the enemy. By 1935, searching for a way of carrying the offensive to the enemy while avoiding the staggering casualties of World War I, the British government had focused its rearmament drive on the construction of long-range bombers. Even then they understood that such bombers would be used primarily against civilian targets.[27]

In the beginning of World War II, the Royal Air Force had aimed at specific military and economic targets; yet stung by German attacks on British residential areas, they began to retaliate in turn. Early in 1941 the British government officially abandoned "precision" bombing (which had never been especially precise anyway) and began regular nighttime bombing of German cities. The hope was to disrupt the German economy by displacing and killing workers and by terrorizing the general population far beyond its war workers. This destruction would damage enemy morale to the point they might give in. As a number of historians have related, initially American military leaders resisted such an approach, believing that attacks on strategic economic resources remained more effective. Yet as the costs of such daylight precision bombing mounted, Americans began to join the British in what was called "area" or "morale bombing." Often it took several raids to destroy a factory, they discovered, and Germans usually had them rebuilt within a few months. By destroying the entire town where a specific factory lay, one did not need to return.[28] As British bomber command head Sir Arthur Harris told an American general, "You destroy a factory, and they rebuild it . . . I kill all their workmen, and it takes twenty-one years to provide new ones."[29]

With fire insurance company officials working with the War Department to create new incendiary bombs that would catch the atmosphere on fire and consume everything underneath, the Allies embarked on a course that led quickly to the fire-bombing of Hamburg, Berlin, and Dresden, and then the saturation bombing of Japan in the spring and summer of 1945. On March 10, 1945, for instance, a fleet of American B-29 bombers selected a densely populated residential section of Tokyo and began dropping incendiaries in a regular grid pattern designed to ignite a firestorm. Twelve hours later, they had burned alive over 100,000 people; in a month of such bombings, they had destroyed over half the city, including the homes of half a million Japanese. Meanwhile the Army Air Corps high command leveled comparable assaults on a number of other populous Japanese cities such as Kobe, Nagoya, and Osaka, culminating in the atomic bombing of Hiroshima and Nagasaki. By the end of the war, such tactics had damaged sixty-six of Japan's largest cities, destroyed 2.3 million dwellings, and left 330,000 to 900,000 dead.[30] Meanwhile, given the ways of wartime hatred at home, large numbers of Americans greeted such developments with glee. In 1942, 67 percent of Americans polled thought the United States should wage "all-out" war on the Japanese people, not just on their military targets. Responding to the atomic bombings, another poll in late August 1945 found 22 percent wishing that "we should have quickly used many more of the bombs before Japan had a chance to surrender."[31] Once unleashed, the ways of violence cannot be easily channeled or controlled. Even if one accepts that the Allies began the fight with a just cause, by the war's end, they had come to embrace the genocidal tactics of their enemies, and simply ignored the Just War criteria of shielding civilians and winning with minimum destruction.

Nonpacifist defenders of allied conduct in World War II would certainly recognize the tremendous destruction of the war, but would argue that the ends—defeating fascist militarism, or saving the world's Jews—justified the means.[32] A nonviolent approach to history must address such arguments. A number of influential historians, for example, argue persuasively that, while the defeat of Hitler certainly brought an end to the death camps, in their purposes and actual conduct during the war, the Allies evinced very little interest in saving Jews. In none of the Allies' many conferences where they worked out war aims and strategy (i.e., Casablanca, Tehran, Yalta, among others) did any Allied leader mention a word about Jews.[33] Allied leaders certainly knew the details of Hitler's "final solution" early in the war.[34] At one point the Polish underground even smuggled one of their fighters, Jan Karski, in and out of a concentration camp and then to London and later Washington, D.C., to testify to officials (including British Foreign Secretary Anthony Eden and Franklin Roosevelt), presenting microfilmed documents which indicated that mass killing of Jews was occurring.[35] Yet outside of the efforts of a small number of American Jews, whose pressure on Roosevelt finally resulted in the important but limited efforts of the War Refugee Board, few officials in the Allied war effort exerted much effort to stop the Jewish holocaust.[36] Even with their total air supremacy over Germany and Poland by July, 1944, for instance, Allied air forces refused to bomb the gas chambers at Auschwitz-Birkenau—then liquidating thousands of people a day—though Allied planes were readily bombing German military installations less than five miles away. "The real obstacle" to the Allies' saving of hundred of thousands of European Jews during the war, concludes the historian David Wyman, "was the absence of a strong desire to save Jews."[37]

In sum, upon closer examination, it is difficult to argue that violence in general and modern wars in particular have had the positive results that nonpacifist historians ascribe to them. Indeed, since one side in any given dispute is bound to lose the war anyway, waging war brings victory to only half the participants. That is, violence and war is guaranteed to fail half the time. And as this brief chapter has illustrated, even the "winners" lose in a number of ways as well, making war less than 50 percent effective. Goethe once wrote a poem about a wizard's assistant who, by playing with his master's tricks, brought into being forces he could not control and ended up fleeing for his life. Viewed as a static snapshot, perhaps war seems to bring beneficial results. Viewed through the lens of history, however, those who wage war appear like the sorcerer's apprentice, conjuring up forces into the world, which they cannot control and which sometimes end up controlling them.[38]

NONVIOLENT ALTERNATIVES TO WAR

Yet it is not enough to merely critique the use of violence in history. A nonviolent approach to the study of history can also make a case for the power and effectiveness of nonviolence, both in terms of the nonviolent road not taken and also of places and times in history when the nonviolent alternative resulted in positive social change.

The ready use of violence has so permeated our national historical understandings that the nation has difficulty conceiving that our national wars were not inevitable and that nonviolent alternatives have existed. As the *Lima News* columnist quoted above indicated, Americans regard especially the War of 1776 as a kind of sacred, holy war for freedom, without which we would still be, two hundred years later, suffering from British tyranny and oppression.[39] Five minutes of reflection on Canada—apparently free and independent from England despite its meek and unwarlike heritage—should dispel such claims, but the religious nature of the myth of redemptive violence has seemingly placed it beyond the need to consider such matters as logic and historical truth. Later historians and, more important, political leaders on both sides of the Atlantic at the time of the Revolution produced a number of sensible political alternatives which, as Canadian history amply and aptly demonstrates, may well have resulted in freedom for the American colonies without the killing and heartache of revolutionary war.[40] As a cohort of historians have suggested, what may have transformed many colonists from contented and prosperous British subjects in 1763 to open revolutionaries in 1775 was their acceptance of a Whig ideology that led them irrationally to impute sinister and conspiratorial overtones to nearly every action of British imperial administration.[41]

Likewise historians have fully outlined the many different options through which North and South might have avoided war in 1861, had the two sides not allowed tensions to build to such a fever pitch that talking had largely ceased between them. Abolished in Russia in 1863 and in Brazil in the 1880s, slavery had already largely run its historical course, and the mechanization of agriculture in the Gilded Age might have hastened its death without the massive bloodletting of the Civil War.[42] Though shamefully delayed for a century, what the Civil War failed to accomplish—the legal inclusion of African Americans in a free and equal place in American life—was achieved through comparable bravery but with only a fraction of the cost in life by a nonviolent struggle in the 1960s.

Indeed, even if we ignore the more obvious examples of the campaigns by Mahatma Gandhi or Martin Luther King, history offers a multitude of instances in which nonviolent action served as a lever for important social change. The political scientist Gene Sharp has catalogued hundreds of examples of nonviolent action around the world. For example, in 1905–1906, spontaneous nonviolent revolution against the oppression of the Tsar shook Russia as major strikes resulted in substantial political reform. In Berlin in 1920 a rightist coup d'état against the Weimar Republic was defeated by a concerted nonviolent campaign that (temporarily) saved German democracy. In Guatemala in 1944, the longstanding dictatorship of General Jorge Ubico disintegrated in the face of a determined nonviolent campaign.[43] Nonviolence proved effective even against the Nazis during World War II. Much of the real saving of European Jewry did not occur at the hands of uninterested Allied military officials but instead transpired through the noncooperation and nonviolent intervention of a large number of ordinary citizens across Europe: in Norway, in Denmark, and in Belgium, where the police refused to cooperate with the Germans and railway men tampered with deportation trains. Not a single Belgian Jew was exterminated during the war, and similar campaigns of noncooperation saved large numbers of people elsewhere: 90 percent of the Jews in Fascist Italy, 80 percent in France, and virtually all Bulgaria's Jews.[44] Under the leadership of Protestant pastor André Trocmé, a concerted campaign of nonviolent resistance saved hundreds of Jews in Le Chambon, a region of France.[45]

Similarly, American history offers a number of examples of successful campaigns of nonviolence long before the civil rights movement. Abolitionists regularly employed a variety of nonviolent techniques to protest American racial discrimination: sit-ins and "stand-ins" in segregated schools and churches, "ride-ins" on segregated railroad trains; so did Native Americans in Minnesota in 1938 and North Carolina in the 1960s. Women's suffrage activists wrote a "People's Constitution" and created a parallel government in Rhode Island in 1841–1842.[46] Perhaps the most widespread movement of nonviolent noncooperation with governmental authorities in American history occurred during the colonial resistance to British regulations in the 1760s. In their angry and widespread boycotts and nonimportation campaigns from 1765 to 1773, the colonists may well have succeeded in winning some measure of independence in this manner without turning to a violent revolution.[47]

The mere suggestion that nonviolent alternatives may have been a better course than war and that justice may be better pursued through nonviolence rather than violence may strike many readers as something akin to heresy. Indeed, given the religious conviction with which the creed of redemptive violence is held, such arguments *are* heresy. It all depends on how one chooses to read the past. "(I)n the struggle for justice," the Mennonite theologian Duane Friesen writes, "what is enduring and powerful for history is persuasive love. If one begins with this premise, one will also interpret history differently" than realists such as Reinhold Niebuhr.[48] People of peace have all sorts of answers to the problems presented by injustice and evil but must resist being forced into a contemporary straightjacket which demands they consider only the crisis at hand and not how we got here. In responding to the "realistic" mandates of the apostles of redemptive violence, we would do well to keep in mind the wisdom of the old peace activist A. J. Muste, who used to say, "There is no way to peace; peace is the way."[49]

NOTES

1. Wendy Jones, "God Not Responsible for Attacks," *Lima News*, 30 September 2001, 8(A).

2. Walter Wink, *Engaging the Powers: Discernment and Resistance in a World of Domination* (Minneapolis: Fortress Press, 1992), 13, 16.

3. Robert N. Bellah, "Civil Religion in America," in *American Civil Religion,* ed. Russell E. Richey and Donald G. Jones (New York: Harper and Row, 1974), 29–33.

4. James C. Juhnke, "Manifesto for a Pacifist Reinterpretation of American History," in *Nonviolent America: History through the Eyes of Peace,* ed. Juhnke and Louise Hawkley (North Newton, Kans.: Bethel College, 1993), 2–3.

5. On the simplistic, comic book character of Bush's rhetoric following the September 11 attacks, see Michael H. Hunt, "In the Wake of September 11: The Clash of What?" *Journal of American History* 89 (September 2002): 418–423.

6. This task is much bigger than one chapter can accomplish. As the notes attest, I am deeply indebted to the work of James Juhnke and Carol Hunter, and also to much conversation with J. Denny Weaver for the analysis that follows.

7. William E. Leuchtenburg, *Franklin D. Roosevelt and the New Deal, 1932–1940* (New York: Harper and Row, 1963), 337.

8. Quoted in Juhnke, "Manifesto for a Pacifist Reinterpretation," 7.

9. Also on this point see John Howard Yoder, "The Burden and Discipline of Evangelical Revisionism," in *Nonviolent America*, 23–29.

10. Bruce Catton, *The Civil War*, quoted in Paul Fussell, *Wartime: Understanding and Behavior in the Second World War* (New York: Oxford University Press, 1989), 9–10.

11. Abraham Lincoln, "First Inaugural Address," in *A Documentary History of the United States,* 3d ed., ed. Richard Heffner (New York: The New American Library, 1976), 152.

12. James McPherson, *Battle Cry of Freedom: The Civil War Era* (New York: Oxford University Press, 1988), 558.

13. Gerald F. Linderman, *Embattled Courage: The Experience of Combat in the American Civil War* (New York: Free Press, 1987), 7–110.

14. This is admittedly a fearful omission. Occurring, as it did, at the end of the medical dark ages, deaths from disease in the Civil War outnumbered battle deaths two to one. On this point see Linderman, *Embattled Courage,* 115.

15. Grady McWhiney and Perry D. Jamieson, *Attack and Die: Civil War Military Tactics and the Southern Heritage* (Tuscaloosa: University of Alabama Press, 1982), 4–139; Linderman, *Embattled Courage*, 134–139.

16. Linderman, *Embattled Courage*, 139–186.

17. Russell Weigley, *The American Way of War* (New York: Macmillan, 1973), 128–152, quotation, 149. For a contrasting interpretation, see Mark Grimsley, *The Hard Hand of War: Union Military Policy toward Southern Civilians, 1861–1865* (New York: Cambridge University Press, 1995).

18. McPherson, *Battle Cry of Freedom*, 558.

19. Linderman, *Embattled Courage*, 180–215, Sherman and Grant quoted 213.

20. Ronald Wells, "Religion in American National Life: What Went Wrong," *Mennonite Quarterly Review* LXV (April, 1991): 125–127.

21. Lawrence Goodwyn, *Democratic Promise: The Populist Moment in America* (New York: Oxford University Press, 1976), 25–33; Steven Hahn, *The Roots of Southern Populism* (New York: Oxford University Press), 137–203.

22. Edward L. Ayers, *The Promise of the New South: Life after Reconstruction* (New York: Oxford University Press, 1992), 155 (quotation); George C. Rable, *But There Was No Peace: The Role of Violence in the Politics of Reconstruction* (Athens: University of Georgia Press, 1984).

23. The most noted user of this phrase is Studs Terkel in *The Good War: An Oral History of World War Two* (New York: Ballantine, 1984).

24. See, for example, John Haynes Holmes, "If America Is Drawn into the War, Can You, As a Christian, Participate in It and Support It?" *The Christian Century* 57 (December 11, 1940): 1546–1549.

25. For a convincing argument that World War II was an unjust war by Just War criteria, see Ken Brown, "Was the 'Good War' a Just War?" in *Nonviolent America*, 88–103.

26. Roosevelt and Churchill quoted in Roland H. Bainton, *Christian Attitudes toward War and Peace* (Nashville: Abingdon, 1960), 225. Also on this point, see Fussell, *Wartime,* 3–9.

27. Alan S. Milward, *War, Economy, and Society, 1939–1945* (Berkeley: University of California Press, 1977), 297–302.

28. Ronald Schaffer, *Wings of Judgment: American Bombing in World War II* (New York: Oxford University Press, 1985), 35–38, 66–70, 80–106; Conrad C. Crane, *Bombs, Cities and Civilians: American Airpower Strategy in World War II* (Lawrence: University Press of Kansas, 1993), 42–47; Michael Sherry, *The Rise of American Air Power: The Creation of Armageddon* (New Haven: Yale University Press), 116–117, 147–166.

29. Quoted in Wilbur Morrison, *Fortress without a Roof: Allied Bombing of the Third Reich* (New York: St. Martin, 1982), 37.

30. Schaffer, *Wings of Judgment*, 107–110, 127–148; Sherry, *The Rise of American Air Power*, 170–311; Crane, *Bombs, Cities and Civilians*, 120–142, 112–113, 159–160.

31. Polling data in Geoffrey Perrett, *Days of Sadness, Years of Triumph: The American People, 1939–1945* (New York: Coward, McCann and Geohegan, 1973), 223; and Paul Boyer, *By the Bomb's Early Light: American Thought and Culture at the Dawn of the Atomic Age* (New York: Pantheon, 1985), 183.

32. For an apt summary of the views of Just War theorists like Michael Walzer, see Brown, "Was the 'Good War,'" 93–100.

33. Henry L. Feingold, *The Politics of Rescue: The Roosevelt Administration and the Holocaust, 1938–1945* (New York: Holocaust Library, 1970), 311.

34. David Wyman, *The Abandonment of the Jews: America and the Holocaust, 1941–1945* (New York: Pantheon, 1984), 19–58.

35. Michael T. Kaufman, "Jan Karski Dies at 86," *New York Times* (July 15, 2000), at www.nytimes.com/library/world/europe/071500poland-karski.html (accessed October 18, 2001).

36. Wyman, *The Abandonment of the Jews*, 178–206, 311–340; Feingold, *The Politics of Rescue,* 230–274, 308–330. Also see Arthur Morse, *While Six Million Died* (London: Secker and Warburg, 1968).

37. Wyman, *The Abandonment of the Jews*, 288–307, quoted 339.

38. I have borrowed this metaphor from Mark Hertsgaard, *Earth Odyssey* (New York: Broadway Books, 1998), 14.

39. On this point see Juhnke and Hunter, *The Missing Peace: Nonviolent Alternatives in United States History* (Kitchner, Ont.: Pandora Press, 2001), 35–36.

40. Juhnke and Hunter outline such proposals concisely; see *The Missing Peace,* 36–41.

41. See, for example, Bernard Bailyn, *The Ideological Origins of the American Revolution* (Cambridge: Harvard University Press, 1967); and Drew McCoy, *The Elusive Republic: Political Economy in Jeffersonian America* (New York: Norton, 1980).

42. Juhnke and Hunter, *The Missing Peace*, 105–113.

43. Gene Sharp, *The Politics of Nonviolent Action* (Boston: Porter Sargent, 1973), 78–81, 87–93.

44. Gene Sharp, *Social Power and Political Freedom* (Boston: Porter Sargent, 1980), 79–81; Sharp, *Making Europe Unconquerable: The Potential of Civilian-Based Deterrence and Defense* (Cambridge: Ballinger Publishing, 1985), 106–107.

45. Philip Hallie, *Lest Innocent Blood Be Shed* (New York: Harper and Row, 1979).

46. Sharp, *The Politics of Nonviolent Action,* 371–376, 426–430.

47. Juhnke and Hunter, *The Missing Peace*, 42–43.

48. Duane Friesen, "Means and Ends: Reflections on Opposing Theologies of History," in *Nonviolent America*, 267.

49. Cited in Sanderson Beck, "The Way to Peace: Protests of A. J. Muste," at www.san.beck/org/WP25-Muste.html (accessed October 18, 2002).

7

Nonviolent Political Movements as Missed Opportunity in Kosovo

James H. Satterwhite

The conventional wisdom or usual presupposition in political science and in history is that in the so-called real world of international affairs, violence is both inevitable and necessary in order to stop truly evil people, groups, and nations. This presupposition is so common and pervasive that it is often not ever recognized as a presupposition. A corollary of the inevitability of violence is the assumption that the way things turned out was the necessary and inevitable way for them to turn out. Again, the presupposition of historical inevitability is so common as frequently to pass unnoticed. For all its invisibility, this presupposition is nonetheless real. This seeming inevitability appears in history when historians, who know how a specified story turns out, then examine the data of history to discover the causes of the final outcome. This search for causes both points to the apparent inevitability of the outcome and simultaneously covers over other, different but also realistically possible outcomes.

In this chapter I will challenge both the inevitability of violence in international affairs and the presupposition about the inevitability of outcomes in history.[1] I will pose these challenges via an examination of the recent war in Kosovo, for which the bombing of Serbia and Serbians by the United States and her NATO allies was presented to us in the United States as the only—that is, the inevitable—way to deal with the ethnic cleansing that Milošević and the Serbians were perpetrating against the Kosovar Albanian population.

For me this discussion represents the convergence of two strands in my own past: my scholarly involvement with Eastern Europe for the past thirty years and my pacifist convictions, which go back even further. Although the war in Bosnia caused me to think along similar lines, my reflections on the war in Kosovo brought these two strands together in a new way. An additional stimulus of these reflections came from my involvement for the past number of years with the Christian Peacemaker Teams (CPT), a nonviolent, peace activist organization.

Among my various assignments with CPT was eight weeks working with Serbian peace groups in Belgrade in the summer of 1997, with much of the work related to Kosovo.

In attempting to think through the question of "what might have been" in Kosovo if nonviolent efforts for change had been given more support and recognition in the years prior to the outbreak of war there in 1999, I am reminded of the historians' adage that "history does not like the conditional in the pluperfect." That is, historians understandably get nervous when asked to speculate on possible outcomes other than what actually did happen. Nonetheless, I think that it can be a valuable exercise to reflect on what course events could have taken had different choices been made. It is in this process of reflection that we can examine the assumptions that led to the actual outcome and thus observe that there were other, real choices.

KOSOVAR NONVIOLENCE

In the case of Kosovo we were presented by NATO with a stark choice early in 1999: either intervene militarily to do something about the ethnic cleansing being perpetrated on the Kosovar Albanian population by the Serb authorities, or stand by and do nothing—thereby allowing the mass displacement of the Kosovars to go unchecked. Leaving aside the question as to whether this stated rationale for intervention was indeed the true rationale,[2] it is possible to say that on the face of it, there seemed to be a compelling argument in favor of "humanitarian intervention." This argument had a powerful appeal among many people who otherwise would consider themselves sympathetic to a pacifist position. What is overlooked in this presentation of two alternatives is that at least until the time of the actual outbreak of fighting, other options were available. By the time fighting began, the Kosovars had been practicing a strategy of nonviolence in response to Serb repression for close to ten years. But the fact of this resistance was largely ignored by the outside world.[3] In order for us to better comprehend "what might have been," we need to reexamine that history and in the process try to see what role international participation in support of this nonviolent approach might have played.

Miranda Vickers commented on the Kosovar approach to nonviolence in her history of Kosovo, *Between Serb and Albanian*. "From the Spring of 1990," she wrote, "Albanians abandoned violence and embraced passive resistance, which became the hallmark of the next phase of the Albanian national movement in Kosovo."[4] What was particularly striking about this approach was that it was not understood as simply a set of tactics to be used against the repressive policies of Serbs, nor even merely as an overall strategy of nonviolent resistance to Serb rule. It was, first of all, a reflection of who or what the Albanians themselves wanted to be. As Vickers pointed out, "in response to . . . a sudden and forceful wave of Serbianization, Albanians began a long-overdue process of self-examination. In the midst of such a climate of violence, Albanians closed their ranks first by attempting to do away with violence among themselves."[5] In order to be sustained, this approach needed encouragement from outside sources as well. Sadly, for the most part, no such encouragement was forthcoming. Again, as Vickers put it:

> [the Albanian leader] Rugova's policies, while relying on the international community to appreciate the justice of the Albanian cause in Kosovo, had failed to change the situation. . . . As long as there appeared to be relative peace in Kosovo, the international community would avoid suggesting substantive changes. . . . Thus, by opting for non-violent resistance, the Kosovar leadership had reaped no benefits whatever. Instead they suffered humiliation and their people became even more desperate.[6]

Gradually, in the absence of any positive reinforcement from outside, growing dissatisfaction and frustration among the Kosovar Albanians led to increased pressure, especially among younger people, for a more active response to Serb repression. This sense of frustration was compounded by the Dayton peace agreements that ended the war in Bosnia. The Kosovar Albanians felt "snubbed and humiliated," "aware that their passive policy during the Yugoslav war had denied them an invitation to the peace talks."[7] As Howard Clark put it in a paper on "Nonviolent Solutions in Kosovo," written for the peace group War Resisters International, "the best chances to initiate a peace process in Kosovo happened when there was a Kosovar consensus to refrain from violence."[8] As he saw it, while both sides would have accepted partial solutions as late as 1997, pressure from the increasing radicalization of the Albanian population foreclosed this option. "The emergence of the Kosova Liberation Army, UÇK, changed all that. It rekindled the Serbian will to fight, and provoked horrific atrocities that united the Albanians more strongly than ever around the demand for independence."[9] Thus a cycle of violence was born that culminated in the NATO bombing and in the ethnic cleansing that paralleled the bombing (indeed, may even have been exacerbated by the onset of bombing), and served increasingly as its justification. And with the onset of bombing and ethnic cleansing, the prevailing response both inside Kosovo and among people looking on from the outside was that (a) violence in Kosovo was inevitable and (b) the NATO violence represented the only authentic moral response to the violence in Kosovo, specifically to the ethnic cleansing.

Thus far we have observed that, counter to the prevailing response, violence was not only not inevitable, but that it emerged after a long period characterized by a nonviolent approach. The violent response did appear to succeed. Refugees returned home, Serb repression in Kosovo was halted—seemingly a "Happy Ending."

THE COST OF "SUCCESS"

What is less often examined, however, is the other side of the issue: the cost at which it was achieved. The Albanian refugees returned to a homeland devastated by war and ethnic cleansing. The entire region was destabilized in the process, something the war was supposedly fought to prevent. These destabilizing effects are particularly evident in the conflict taking place in Macedonia in the years after the war in Kosovo. Of further consequence, that part of the opposition in Serbia that was genuinely democratic was discredited by the NATO actions, even though support of alternatives to Milošević was supposedly another aim of the war. As Clark noted:

> the NATO powers' response to the new mood among Albanians was not to look seriously at the option of independence, but to promise to defeat Serbia on their behalf. The result is that Serbs [were] now as united as ever behind Milošević and those most dismayed by the bombings and their consequences [were] the ones who [had] opposed his policy towards Kosovo. A statement by 17 Belgrade NGOs [said] "the NATO intervention has destroyed everything that has been achieved, and [threatens] the very survival of civil society in Serbia."[10]

The same sentiment was expressed by Staša Zajović, a representative of the Serbian opposition group "Women in Black," which had steadfastly opposed both the war in Bosnia and the Serb repression in Kosovo. As Zajović put it during the NATO campaign, "this conspiracy of militarism—global and local—dangerously reduces our space. Soon there won't be this space. With the horror the people of Kosovo are experiencing in this NATO intervention, they are paying a price even greater than before: NATO in the sky, Milošević on the ground."[11] Still further, the Albanian vision of an ethnically pure state—only this time without Serbs—was reinforced. The two nationalisms have been competing with each other since the mid- to late-nineteenth century, when modern Serbian and Albanian nationalisms began to take form. Already in 1913, the remarks of an Albanian representative to an international conference deciding the fate of the Balkans expressed some of this conflict: "When spring comes we will manure the plains of Kosovo with the bones of Serbs, for we Albanians have suffered too much to forget."[12] Since Serbs in Kosovo had the upper hand for most of the intervening years up to the present (except for the period from 1974 to 1989, when the Albanians enjoyed a greater degree of autonomy) and practiced quite repressive policies toward the Albanians for much of this time—especially and increasingly in the period under Milošević after 1989—those words could have been spoken at any point during the last year following the Serbian defeat in Kosovo. Certainly what we have seen after the end of the war in Kosovo is an attempt to induce all remaining Serbs to leave the area.

REAL ALTERNATIVES

This list constitutes only some of the negative consequences of the war, which should give us clear pause before we sing too loudly the praises of the violent international intervention. Yet to be examined, however, is whether there were specific ways that the international community might have supported the nonviolent Kosovar tactics and thus rendered a violent response less attractive. As James Douglass put it, "how could the struggling peace movements of Serbia and Kosovo have been effectively supported by the West, rather than ignored, driven to violence, and bombed into oblivion?"[13] As an example, Douglass cited a proposal for nonviolent intervention in Kosovo put forward by peace activists in Nashville. It is worth reproducing here in full as one example of alternative approaches to the whole conflict situation:

1. As the conflict began to develop, the United Nations Security Council would define the principles for UN intervention and a just settlement.

2. The Secretary General would begin to assemble a "nonviolent army" to be led by influential world figures such as (a) religious leaders, including bishops delegated by the pope, Orthodox patriarchs, and Islamic and Jewish leaders; (b) Nobel Peace Prize winners such as former Costa Rican president Oscar Arias, the Dalai Lama, Mairead Corrigan Maguire of Northern Ireland, President Nelson Mandela, and Archbishop Desmond Tutu of South Africa; (c) retired world leaders such as Jimmy Carter and Mikhail Gorbachev; (d) diplomats from Russia and all the other European neighbors of Yugoslavia; (e) experienced activists trained in nonviolent tactics, such as veterans of the civil rights movement and Christian Peacemaker Teams that have worked in the West Bank and Haiti.

3. In the case of Kosovo, this nonviolent brigade would have been divided into two units: one would have gone to Serbia to engage in dialogue with all sectors of civil society; the other would have gone to Kosovo to interpose itself between Serbian forces and the KLA and to begin dialogue and mediation between them.[14]

Another similar vision of what nonviolent alternatives might have looked like was developed by the Italian scholar Alberto L'Abate.[15] His paper dealt with what he terms "the negligence of official diplomacy concerning prevention" in Kosovo and constitutes an analysis of the "activity and proposals of seven Non-Governmental Organizations" that have been active in Kosovo. All these organizations had experience working to "prevent the explosion of conflict" there, as well as to "find just solutions which could lead to long-lasting peace and not only to a temporary agreement."[16] In this context he cites a proposal by an Italian organization, Campaign for a Nonviolent Solution to the Kosovo Problem (CSNK), which puts forward the idea of an intervention in Kosovo by a "European Civil Peace Corps." Such a group would be "unarmed and well trained in direct nonviolent action and in mediation and nonviolent resolution of conflicts," and "would be assigned to help the process of normalization of life in Kosovo and to stimulate the dialogue and the interaction between the two sides in the search for nonviolent solutions which would be correct for the problems of this region."[17] The same vision was articulated by veteran peace activist Kathy Kelly, who spoke of "large, well-trained but unarmed, 'nonviolent armies'—people who go into situations with the same understanding as a soldier: that they are putting their lives on the line."[18]

These proposals all start from the premise that two sides deadlocked over opposing views can benefit from an outside, third party to help break the logjam.[19] In the L'Abate proposal cited above, mention was made of "mediation" and "nonviolent resolution of conflicts" as contributions international third-party participants could make. However, more discussion is needed as to what such involvement would entail. L'Abate notes that it is necessary to define "what it means to 'mediate' in a situation like this where the power on the two sides is extremely unbalanced. . . . On the one side there is power based on arms, and on the other side the much more numerous Albanian population which has been defending itself for years with nonviolence, using that which is defined in terms of the theory of non-violence as the 'technique of a parallel government.'"[20] There is a danger, he writes, in just talking about "mediation," because to do so is to ignore the consequences of this power imbalance. If the power discrepancy is not addressed, any kind of mediation risks reinforcing the advantage held by the stronger party in the dispute. The prior issue of power thus has to be dealt with. "That is why, before going into the phase of 'negotiation,' or, in the case of the presence of a third party, of real 'mediation,' experts speak of the need to perform a task of awareness toward the weaker side and of helping them get organized in order to reduce the power gap ('empowerment'). Only later, when greater equality between the two sides has been achieved, is it possible to initiate the phase of 'negotiation,' or 'mediation.'"[21]

In the case of Kosovo in the 1990s, L'Abate envisioned this strategy played out as follows: "First, the Albanians themselves must try to overcome the strong differences in strategy and tactics in order to reach unity of action. . . . Second, third parties must be aware of the underlying aspects of the conflict and apply pressure on the stronger side (the Serbs) so as to bring the situation in Kosovo back to 'normality' and so as to reduce the military and police pressure on the Albanian population."[22]

It is precisely this strategy of empowerment that groups such as the Christian Peacemaker Teams have utilized in other conflict situations, such as in Haiti during the dictatorship, or in Hebron, West Bank, under Israeli occupation. One of CPT's annual reports states that "CPT offers a prayerful, nonviolent alternative to war and other forms of lethal violence. CPTers take the same risks as those waging war to demonstrate Jesus' way of self-giving love for neighbors and enemies. Following the Jesus way of peacemaking involves getting in the way of violence through active nonviolent confrontation and other forms of public witness."[23] Concretely, for CPTers this approach has meant interjecting themselves into confrontational situations, such as between soldiers and civilians in Haiti or between Palestinians and Israeli military or settlers in Hebron. The goal of these interjections is to forestall violence—as in attempting to block the demolition of Palestinian homes or in reporting on human rights violations and arbitrary arrests. In general the strategy is to put pressure on the stronger side (Haitian military, Israeli occupation) by standing as witnesses with those on the weaker side and by attempting to make people all over the world aware of the true situation.

Christian Peacemaker Teams were invited to put a team in Kosovo but were prevented by a shortage of personnel and resources. Had they and others been able to become more involved, might this have had an effect on the Albanian feeling of being ignored? If there had been a strong core of international monitors reporting from Kosovo on the Albanians' strategy of nonviolence, as well as on specific human rights abuses by the Serbian authorities, would the international community have responded differently? We will never know, but it is possible that such involvements would have made a difference. Certainly in Israel and Palestine the ability of CPT and others to bring the light of international awareness and response to bear on issues of injustice to Palestinians has had some impact on the policy of home demolitions practiced in the West Bank by the Israeli military government ("Civil Administration"). It is because of experience from this kind of involvement that the Nashville proposals envisioned a role in Kosovo for CPT and other "experienced activists trained in nonviolent tactics."

Another role that outside participants can play, and did do so on a very small scale in Kosovo, is to establish lines of communication "on the ground":

> Whoever has been in Serbia or Kosovo for a long enough time is very familiar with the difficulties of breaking down the "wall against wall" which exists between the Serbs and the Albanians. . . . The political isolation of the people and the groups that try to go against the current and sustain interethnic presence and dialogue between the two sides is well known. This is why it is difficult for both sides to "take

the first step." And for this reason, several projects consider the intervention of a third neutral party fundamental to starting this process.[24]

This role was played by Balkan Peace Teams, for example, in their efforts to establish a dialogue between Serb and Albanian young people in Prishtina.[25] Their efforts took place on a tiny scale. Could a larger presence, like the proposed European Civil Peace Corps, have made a difference? In addition, even the OSCE (Organization for Security and Cooperation in Europe) in effect served to some extent as a nonviolent presence in Kosovo prior to the bombing campaign and were able by their presence to deter some of the worst abuses by the Serbian authorities. It was not until the OSCE monitors were withdrawn and the bombing began that the worst of the mass ethnic cleansing gained in force.[26] Elsewhere Howard Clark wrote, "My vision would have been of OSCE teams in every municipality of Kosovo, strengthening the inhibition of human-rights violations by checking out incidents and monitoring trials but also encouraging some form of constructive programme among Kosovo Albanians (making better use of the resource created with parallel schools, putting up little bits of money for small-scale economic projects, etc.)."[27]

It is easy—too easy—to dismiss such nonviolent proposals and efforts out of hand, under the assumption that they are not "realistic." The problem with this easy dismissal is that its logic is circular. On the basis of the assumption noted in the beginning of this chapter that only violence can stop evil people and groups, nonviolent alternatives are dismissed as unrealistic by definition. And then with nonviolence dismissed as unrealistic, violence is touted as the only realistic course of action. But we would do well to give the matter a closer examination. Had the Kosovar nonviolent movement received the kind of international attention and support outlined above, it is quite possible that it could have gained momentum, rather than dissipating. It is arguable, I believe, that it was the widely held assumption that violence is the way to stop evil groups that prevented the United States and NATO from really seeing the Kosovar nonviolent movement as a real option. One who assumes that only violence works and that only violence constitutes a real option would not see anything real and workable when observing the Kosovar nonviolent movement. But for those with experience in nonviolence and eyes able to see nonviolence as realistic, the Kosovar nonviolent movement emerges as a very realistic but tragically lost opportunity. As Douglass further notes, "the realistic assumption behind the Nashville proposal is that the power of a government is dependent on the support and cooperation of its people. For that reason nonviolent resistance based on truth and supported by the world community can dislodge any unjust government's popular support."[28] And as we have seen, Milošević's hold on power was strengthened rather than reduced by the bombing campaign, because the bombing rallied people around his "patriotic" cause and discredited the opposition.

Some might still reply that nonviolent tactics are all very well and good in some circumstances but that when confronted by a massive breach of elementary human rights nonviolence must give way to more "effective" (i.e., violent) responses. Douglass also addressed this issue. He asked whether nonviolent intervention as outlined above can "begin to replace our reliance on vastly destructive weapons when we face an intolerable evil such as ethnic cleansing?"[29] His answer is that "thanks to the exemplary campaigns of Gandhi, King, and others, we can now make the life-sustaining choice of nonviolent action in visibly transforming ways. Serb and Kosovar peacemakers were developing such campaigns until Western policies and bombs blew them away. But when nonviolent initiatives are at last given the support, sacrifices, and resources we have previously devoted to war, they will be able to stop ethnic cleansing in its tracks."[30]

Noam Chomsky expressed a similar view. In answer to the argument that something had to be done, and that the only credible response was to use force, Chomsky put forth an alternative perspective. He reminds us that "one choice, always available, is to follow the Hippocratic principle: 'First, do no harm.'" He continues,

> If you can think of no other way to adhere to that elementary principle, then do nothing; at least that is preferable to causing harm—the consequence recognized in advance to be "predictable" in the case of Kosovo, a prediction amply fulfilled. It may sometimes be true that the search for peaceful means is at an end, and that there is "no alternative" to doing nothing or causing vast harm. If so, anyone with even a minimal claim to being a moral agent will abide by the Hippocratic principle. *That nothing constructive can be done must, however, be demonstrated.*[31]

Kathy Kelly articulated a challenge to those who favor nonviolent solutions to conflict situations. She stated that "we as a peace community need to improve vastly in our ability to move into situations of violence, to help persuade people that it is in their interest to lay down weapons and begin negotiation."[32] As Douglass noted, the issue is ultimately larger than Kosovo: "Martin Luther King put all such questions in the context of a post-Hiroshima prophecy: nonviolence or nonexistence." In a nuclear age, Jesus' principle, "Those who take the sword will perish by the sword" takes on new meaning.[33]

USING JUSTIFIABLE WAR CRITERIA

The logic of this appeal to Jesus' principle makes it incumbent on us to look again at the arguments advanced for the use of force in Kosovo. On the surface they seemed very compelling, and "humanitarian intervention" was touted as a new principle of international law. Whether or not, as Chomsky argued, this "new" intervention seems rather like older, more prosaic forms of intervention, the argument must still be grappled with. In a theological sense the principle seems to be simply a variation on the Just-War tradition, which as John Howard Yoder described it, consists of "an instrument for . . . discerning the morality of violence in the midst of a variety of interpretations." The criteria in this process of discernment, for what Yoder actually preferred to call "justifiable war," "are intended to allow some lethal acts, and exclude others."[34] "The mainstream of the [justifiable-war] tradition does not say that such military actions are morally imperative . . . but only that a case can be made for them and that those who find that they must do them are not to be treated as morally irresponsible."[35] The aspect of this tradition that is most often cited is that "a war may be fought only for a *just cause*" or for a "*right intention*."[36] Certainly this would be the way in which proponents of "humanitarian intervention" phrase their argument.

However, the justifiable-war position embodies other criteria, which are often overlooked by those adherents who are attracted to it for the reasons just mentioned. In the case of the intervention in Kosovo, one of the points in dispute had to do with whether NATO constituted "legitimate authority" for the conduct of the war. Another criterion that is particularly relevant to our discussion here is that "war must be a last resort, only after everything else has been tried. Refusal of other resources for redress invalidates an otherwise just complaint."[37] Another part of the same set of criteria holds that the war must cause less harm than the harm it seeks to prevent. As Pope Pius XII stated in 1953, "If the injury caused by warfare exceeds the injury suffered by tolerating the injustice done, one may be obliged to suffer that particular injustice."[38] Related to this point are several other criteria: that "the damage [inflicted] must not be greater than the damage prevented or the offense being avenged" or "disproportionate to the guilt of the offender," and that "the means used must respect the immunity of the innocent."[39] If these other justifiable-war criteria are taken seriously, then there is certainly room for doubt as to whether the conflict in Kosovo and the bombing of Serbia live up to the demands exerted by this tradition. For example, one has only to note the nonviolent Kosovar movement that went unrecognized and unsupported by the United States and NATO, and the nonviolent interventions suggested by the Nashville peace activists and by Alberto L'Abate, to show that the bombing was clearly not a last resort. And then one can note the actual worsening of the situation caused by NATO's bombing to show that the criteria were not fulfilled of doing less harm than the harm to be prevented. On the basis of such observations, one might want to argue that those who supported humanitarian intervention are not doing so out of the justifiable-war tradition. However, it would probably be more accurate to say that they are not *explicitly* following the criteria of justifiable war but rather are *implicitly* attempting to take only certain parts of the tradition (as outlined above) in order to provide a justification for intervention.

There might be more of a convergence between the justifiable-war tradition and the Hippocratic adage than at first meets the eye, but the discussion must go further. Douglass raises the fundamental issue when he asks: "Is the primary obstacle to nonviolent alternatives in Kosovo and elsewhere our own attitude that only violence can respond to violence?"[40] If we cannot even imagine the possibility of nonviolent solutions and the moral imperative of working toward such approaches, then this simply demonstrates the paucity of our imagination and its captivity to blind faith in violence as the ultimate problem solver. Using the "real world" case of NATO bombing in Kosovo, I intend for this chapter to stimulate our imaginative search for nonviolent solutions by showing the realistic opportunities that were missed when decisions were blinded by the assumption that only violent solutions could work.

NOTES

1. The first version of this chapter was a paper presented as a case study in the session "Unarmed Peacekeeping: New Models for Dealing with and Preventing Violent Crises," at the conference on "Re-imagining Politics and Society at the Millennium," Riverside Church, New York, N.Y., May 18–20, 2000. It subsequently appeared in the journal *Peace and Change*, October 2002.

2. Noam Chomsky explores this question well in his book, *The New Military Humanism: Lessons from Kosovo* (Monroe, Maine: Common Courage Press, 1999).

3. For understanding this phenomenon an essential resource is Howard Clark, *Civil Resistance in Kosovo* (London: Pluto Press, 2000).

4. Miranda Vickers, *Between Serb and Albanian: A History of Kosovo* (New York: Columbia University Press, 1998), 243.

5. Vickers, *Between Serb and Albanian,* 248; see also discussion in Clark, *Civil Resistance*, 66–68.

6. Vickers, *Between Serb and Albanian*, 281, 287.

7. Vickers, *Between Serb and Albanian*, 289–290.

8. Howard Clark, "Nonviolent Solutions in Kosovo," *War Resisters' International Balkans Archive,* War Resisters' International website, at www.wri-irg.org/news/1999/nvsolkos.htm (accessed April 11, 2003). Also published in their magazine, *Peace News*, June 1999. *Peace News* is available online at www.peacenews.info/, but this particular issue has not been archived as of this writing in spring 2002.

9. Clark, "Nonviolent Solutions."

10. Clark, "Nonviolent Solutions," 2.

11. Cited in James Douglass, "A Pacifist Response to Ethnic Cleansing," in *Kosovo: Contending Voices on Balkan Interventions,* ed. William J. Buckley (Grand Rapids, Mich.: Eerdmans, 2000), 366.

12. Vickers, *Between Serb and Albanian*, 85.

13. Douglass, "A Pacifist Response," 367.

14. Douglass, "A Pacifist Response," 367.

15. Alberto L'Abate, "Preventing War in Kosovo to Save the Balkans from Destabilization: Activities and Proposals Advanced by the Non-Official Diplomacy." The English version was received privately from the author. It is a translation of the Conclusion of the larger Italian version, *Prevenire la Guerra nel Kossovo per evitare la destabilizzazione dei Balcanni—attività e proposte della diplomazia non ufficiale.* Quaderno n. 33. della collana "Quaderni della Difesa Popolare Nonviolenta" (Molfetta [Bari]: Editrice La Meridiana, 1997). A new edition of the same book is *Kosovo: una guerra annunciata* [Kosovo: An Announced War] (Molfetta: Editrice La Meridiana, 1999). An abbreviated version of L'Abate's article appeared in *The San Francisco Chronicle*, May 27, 1999.

16. L'Abate, "Preventing War in Kosovo," 1.

17. L'Abate, "Preventing War in Kosovo," 8.

18. Pamela Schaeffer, "Human Rights, Peace Activists Split on Kosovo," *National Catholic Reporter* (May 21, 1999): 4.

19. L'Abate, "Preventing War in Kosovo," 3.

20. L'Abate, "Preventing War in Kosovo," 12, citing Gene Sharp, *The Politics of Nonviolent Action* (Boston: Porter Sargent, 1973); vol. 2: *The Methods of Nonviolent Action,* 423–425.

21. L'Abate, "Preventing War in Kosovo," 12, citing his work *Consenso, conflitto, mutamento sociale* (Milan: F. Angeli, 1990), 269; see also Clark, *Civil Resistance*, 131–133.

22. L'Abate, "Preventing War in Kosovo," 12.

23. 1997–1998 CPT Annual Report. Pamphlet published by Christian Peacemaker Teams, Chicago, Ill. Available online through the CPT website at www.prairienet.org/cpt/annrep97.php (accessed January 2, 2003).

24. L'Abate, "Preventing War in Kosovo," 18; see also Clark, *Civil Resistance*, 170.

25. Clark, *Civil Resistance*, 142.

26. See discussion on the role of the OSCE in Clark, *Civil Resistance*, 91, 178–180.

27. E-mail letter to author written on June 24, 2000.

28. Douglass, "A Pacifist Response," 367.

29. Douglass, "A Pacifist Response," 367.

30. Douglass, "A Pacifist Response," 368.

31. Chomsky, *The New Military Humanism,* 156; italics added.

32. Schaeffer, "Human rights," 4.

33. Douglass, "A Pacifist Response," 367–368.

34. John Howard Yoder, *When War Is Unjust: Being Honest in Just-War Thinking*, rev. ed. (Maryknoll, N.Y.: Orbis Books, 1996), 3.

35. Yoder, *When War Is Unjust*, 17.

36. See Yoder, *When War Is Unjust,* 147–161, for an elaboration of the traditional criteria in the justifiable-war position.

37. Yoder, *When War Is Unjust*, 154, citing John A. Ryan and Francis J. Boland, *Catholic Principles of Politics*, rev. ed. (New York: Macmillan, 1950), 150, 256–257.

38. Yoder, *When War Is Unjust*, 155.

39. Yoder, *When War Is Unjust*, 156–157.

40. Douglass, "A Pacifist Response," 368.

8

The Bush Doctrine and Pacifist Pedagogy

Daniel Wessner

The post–Cold War era has presented an engaging political dialogue, allowing space for a nonviolent, pacifist perspective in the areas of development and global affairs. This chapter critiques conventional perspective in these disciplines and responds with a pedagogy that both teaches and embodies a pacifist praxis. This pedagogy is "critically embodied studies."

For more than half of the twentieth century, the realpolitik of the Cold War dominated the disciplines related to development and global affairs. Realpolitik assumed that only state actors could address international peace and security. This paradigm, however, circumscribed humanitarian intervention, evolving human rights regimes, and goals of good governance and peaceful relations across borders. Following the demise of Soviet–U.S. tensions more than a decade ago, challenges and alternatives to realpolitik began to emerge. These unmasked the fiction that only sovereign states should deal with threats to peace and security for what it was—a power myth. From a number of sectors, a reassessment of contemporary political values by entities more peripheral to the realpolitik of the states began to close the gap of political participation between rich and poor parties, male and female discussants, majority and minority ethnic and racial groups, and powerful and subaltern state actors. Movements of poor people, of women, of non-European ethnic and racial groups in both first and third worlds engaged political and economic issues from nongovernmental contexts. Countries in the developing and non-Western world effectively challenged economic and political domination by European and North American governments.

THE BUSH DOCTRINE

Yet the world of post–September 11 is again muting these alternative perspectives. The United States government's forceful reassertion of domestic and global power underscores tense differences between realpolitik and populist empowerment. The people-centered gains of the last decade in contrast to Washington's present policies suggest a state-societal schizophrenia. Civil society is, on the one hand, still emboldened by the gains of nonstate, nonpowerful voices of the 1990s. The U.S. government, however, claims increasingly greater authority at home and abroad.

The events surrounding George W. Bush's articulation of reasons for war against Iraq illustrates this tension. Even as the president prepared to deliver the October 7, 2002, Cincinnati speech in which he sketched his case for war, peace rallies occurred in twenty U.S. cities that same weekend. On the night of his address, Bluffton College students joined several thousand other peace advocates outside the hall in which he spoke. Their presence exemplified a democratic republic grounded in a liberalist rule of law that protects alternative voices opposing war and dualism. They spoke, too, of Christian pacifist convictions of nonviolence (overcoming evil with good) and nonresistance (not resisting an evil doer). In Elise Boulding's words, they meant to help build a "culture of peace," standing up to "powered structure differentials." This process nurtures a mosaic of identities in our world. It examines transformative possibilities amidst conflict. It embraces the challenge of respecting and even loving one's alleged enemy.[1]

At the same time, much of today's political debate is reverting to the geopolitical myths posited by powerful states during the Cold War. In his Cincinnati address, Mr. Bush posited hyperrealist and unilateralist "might makes right" calculations of power and merit. Although Mr. Bush's rhetoric spoke of securing freedom, his stress of the word "terrorism"—thirty times in thirty minutes—was meant to produce fear and loathing.

> America must not ignore the threat gathering against us. Facing clear evidence of peril, we cannot wait for the final proof—the smoking gun—that could come in the form of a mushroom cloud . . .
>
> . . . [W]e have every reason to assume the worst, and we have an urgent duty to prevent the worst from occurring.
>
> . . . Failure to act would embolden other tyrants, allow terrorists access to new weapons and new resources, and make blackmail a permanent feature of world events. The United Nations would betray the purpose of its founding, and prove irrelevant to the problems of our time. And through its inaction, the United States would resign itself to a future of fear.
>
> . . . We refuse to live in fear. This nation, in world war and in Cold War, has never permitted the brutal and lawless to set history's course. Now, as before, we will secure our nation, protect our freedom, and help others to find freedom of their own.[2]

To put such assertions in historical context, the U.S. cause to "secure" itself and "find freedom" for others since World War II has meant its overt and covert warring in these countries: Afghanistan, Belgian Congo, Cambodia, Chile, China, Cuba, El Salvador, Guatemala, Grenada, Indonesia, Iraq, Korea, Laos, Libya, Nicaragua, Panama, Peru, Sudan, Vietnam, and Yugoslavia. The U.S. "contribution to freedom" in these states is remarkable, but mostly on account of its extensive reliance on disproportionate military intervention. Moreover, in the present Middle East and Central and South Asian context, the U.S. cause means a forward deployment of its troops, planes, munitions, bases, and military advisors in Afghanistan, Bahrain, Diego Garcia, Djibouti, Georgia, Israel, Jordan, Kazakhstan, Kyrgyzstan, Kuwait, Oman, Pakistan, Saudi Arabia, Tajikistan, Turkey, United Arab Emirates, Uzbekistan, and Yemen.[3] U.S. intervention for freedom actually means that "freedom" and grass roots movements that differ from the desires of U.S. government policy makers will be suppressed, often violently.

Mr. Bush's Cincinnati speech was also problematic in that he conflated events of September 11 with broader, independent foreign and economic policy objectives of his administration to preempt, prevent, and eliminate unsavory governments. In so doing, he ran roughshod over the charter of the United Nations. Its underlying principles are pacific, deliberative, collective, defensive, and self-determinative so as to preserve state, group, and individual fundamental freedoms and human rights. By contrast, Mr. Bush's words are the dark side of today's schizophrenia: threat, peril, smoking guns, mushroom clouds, worst-case tyranny, permanent blackmail, an irrelevant United Nations, and fear.

In contrast to these responses to the September 11, 2001, terrorist attacks—the present war in Iraq the October 2001 war against Afghanistan, the January 29, 2002, declaration of war against an "axis of evil," and the summer/fall 2002 construction of the Bush Doctrine of preemptive intervention or preemptive strike—"critically embodied studies" as explained below is a pacifist pedagogical alternative. It is not rooted in fear. Nor does it circumscribe "peace" within a narrow construct of "security." It is bold, relational, and as spiritual as it is political. Its multidisciplinary questions examine the U.S. "culture of politics," its global exertion of powerful forces, and the effect of its policies upon sustainable development.

The emerging Bush Doctrine is based on two pre-9/11 policy papers that argue for pre-emptive, preventive strikes against any entity that threatens the security of U.S. consumption and power. These two plans buttress limitless pursuit of oil, promise the growth of the American consumer culture, and project a global U.S. military and economic dominance.

As the first piece of the Bush Doctrine, the White House released the May 2001 *National Energy Policy Report*, also known as the Cheney Plan. Vice President Cheney's plan takes for granted the growing dependence of the U.S. and world economies on the Iraqi and Caspian Sea states' oil reserves over the next two decades. Combined, both proven and anticipated Iraqi reserves likely overshadow Saudi, Russian, and U.S. petroleum resources. The Cheney Plan posits that U.S. economic (hence national) interests must seek to control, if not possess, these Middle Eastern and Central and South Asian regions. This expanded sphere of U.S. influence stretches from Iraq and Iran, through Azerbaijan and Kazakhstan, and through Afghanistan and Pakistan, to the Arabian Sea. The deployment of U.S. forces after September 11 covers this terrain and begins to project unprecedented U.S. influence over European, Middle Eastern, and Asian economies dependent on these oil reserves. Simultaneously, the United States is positioned to secure its own growing demand for foreign oil.[4]

The second piece of the Bush Doctrine comes from a policy paper called "Defense Planning Guidance" and drafted in 1992 by Paul D. Wolfowitz for the first Bush Administration. More than a decade ago in the early post–Cold War years, as Under Secretary for Policy in Cheney's Defense Department, Wolfowitz sought to guarantee that no counterhegemonic superpower could threaten U.S. domination of geopolitics and global economics. Bill Keller reports that this *Pax Americana* imagined:

> [W]ith the demise of the Soviet Union the United States doctrine should be to assure that no new superpower arose to rival America's benign domination of the globe. The U.S. would defend its unique status both by being militarily powerful beyond challenge and by being such a constructive force that no one would want to challenge us. We would participate in coalitions, but they would be "ad hoc." The U.S. would be "postured to act independently when collective action cannot be orchestrated." The guidance envisioned pre-emptive attacks against states bent on acquiring nuclear, biological or chemical weapons. It was accompanied by illustrative scenarios of hypothetical wars for which the military should be prepared. One of them was another war against Iraq.[5]

Taken together, the Cheney and Wolfowitz plans are two of three pillars meant to secure the Bush Doctrine. It presumes the right to exercise military force globally, regardless of long-honored principles of international law (self-defense), state necessity (addressing genuine and immediate threats to survival and fundamental interests), or humanitarianism (consistent response to gross human rights violations).[6] This doctrine means either to manipulate or disregard U.N. principles favoring collective pursuit of security, fundamental freedoms and human rights, and tolerance. It mutes provisions in the U.N. charter for regional peace building, U.N. dialogue, and Security Council study, monitoring, decision making, and particular action in response to specific threats to international peace and security.[7]

A third and final pillar of the Bush Doctrine is a certain hubris that belies forward and backward looking consciousness. The Cheney-Wolfowitz projection for economic and military security presumes knowledge of "the other" into an indefinite future, along with ultimate faith in U.S. policy makers to control the "other's" responses. It is an audaciously presumed omniscience, but is it realistic? Consider the words of now Deputy Secretary of Defense Wolfowitz who laments, "There's an awful lot we don't know, an awful lot that we may never know, and we've got to think differently about standards of proof here."[8] Nonetheless, the presumption of control is accompanied by a clear-eyed willingness to kill—either directly or indirectly—to maintain U.S. hegemony and "security." Vice President Dick Cheney posits, "The risks of inaction are greater than the risks of action."[9] Near the end of the Clinton Administration, Secretary of State Madeleine Albright remarked that a U.S. foreign policy based on "coercion, the threat of coercion, sanctions, [and] the threat of sanctions" was simply practical, though clearly not aesthetic.[10] Asked whether U.S. policies could countenance estimates of one-half million Iraqi children dying from U.S. economic sanctions and military strikes, she concluded it was a "hard choice" over time, but one "worth it."[11]

These Bush Doctrine considerations raise a series of questions. Does the U.S. quest for security actually diminish its own, let alone others' justice, freedom, liberty, and equality? Does state-centered security increasingly take on an unabashed Machiavellian calculation of power? Does it presume the right to coerce and subordinate regional and international economic and political interests of others to the immediate desires of U.S. policy makers? Does this current policy exceed the hegemonic reach of Cold War realpolitik? The pedagogy of critically embodied studies seeks a teaching space for examining this and foreign policies that assume the necessity of violence in international affairs.

CRITICALLY EMBODIED STUDIES

My pedagogy begins with the truth of suffering in today's world. It accepts that the world is disfigured by the threats of rogue actors. Much more so, it is a world radically transfigured by the twining tendrils of fear, uncertainty, and consumer demands introduced by powerful states and societies. It is this world that critically embodied studies addresses.

Embodiment

Engaging such concepts as struggle, power, politics, and international relations places one among long standing religious concerns. Embodiment means that students are not asked merely to read stories and study their arguments, but to take them on. Consider the banishment of Hagar and Ishmael; or Siddhartha's sojourn; or the Hebrew enslavement in Egypt, the Babylonian exile, and the prophecies of Israel; or the birth and childhood refugee flight of Jesus, his peasant life under Roman rule, and his death and resurrection; or Gandhi's *antyodaya* (consciousness of suffering), his struggle against British imperialism, and his death by an assassin's bullet; or the five-hundred-year history of Anabaptist persecution, dislocation, and religio-political identity formation.

As much as these communities know struggle, they also reveal a hope to overcome struggle. Engaging the struggle becomes nonviolent through embodiment of the biblical stories of Jesus, who overcame death through resurrection, or stories of Anabaptist struggle and communal empowerment, or Gandhi's *antyodaya*. So, too, one's contemporary embodying of struggles can lead to the experience of transformative freedom, compassion, solidarity, responsible accounting of self, forgiveness, prophetic voice, giving and receiving. One hears this embodied response to suffering hope in Archbishop Oscar Romero's last sermon. He preached passionately, even as he named names of victims and devastated villages. He described torture and death. He admonished all Salvadorans, "Thou shalt not kill." Yet he understood the pastor's response to suffering to be a hopeful ministry for all people. Out of solidarity with suffering, one is prepared to insist upon and reach for liberation. Of this suffering hope solidarity, Romero concludes, "Christ desires to unite himself with humanity, so that the light he brings from God might become life for nations and individuals."[12]

If I take this embodiment seriously in any community—whether of faith, research, classroom, or family— then my presence contributes to another's change, just as others affect my life. Theologian Leonardo Boff explains that our most prescient insights occur as we encounter this first truth of suffering. We confront it not with distanced objectivity, but by human interconnectedness.[13] He goes on to posit a second truth, namely that there are paths of transformation beyond domination and needless suffering. Based on these two truths, the names and faces of real people intersect with and correct our methods, knowledge, service, and experiences.

Political Anthropology

The goal of embodiment changes the study of political anthropology. We best observe these suffering hope truths of diverse actors in states and societies by genuine immersion. Whereas the study of "political culture" looks for some general logic or snapshot of a state, a "culture of politics" approach via political anthropology allows for complex readings of state-societal relations, marginal actors, asymmetrical power relationships, and external forces contesting internal identities.

Even as one examines state-societal milieus, anthropologists Nancy Scheper-Hughes and Dorinne Kondo stress the importance of immersion in development service.[14] Beyond standard anthropological expectations of objectivity that inform any participant-observer status, an immersed researcher-teacher is intentional about social justice and peace. It means that the researcher-teacher must actually live out—embody—the justice and the nonviolence of the struggle that Christian faith envisions. During her years of research in a Brazilian barrio, for example, Scheper-Hughes and her family were fully engaged in dialogic community praxis, even as she pursued work as an anthropologist, feminist, and political theorist. Similarly, Kondo situated herself among confectionery assembly line workers in a Japanese factory. She joined the company's field trips, ethics training sessions, browbeating meetings before the management, and daily calisthenics. Through her immersion, she was exposed to gendered domination and compelled to participate in collective resistance.

According to Paulo Freire, the sort of dialogue essential to this embodying process has two constitutive elements: reflection and action. If cohered, they both form praxis, which feeds a quest for truth. If either element is underused, the other suffers too. One's supposed dialogue or knowledge becomes inauthentic.[15] Speaking to this authenticity, political anthropologists Nicole Polier and William Roseberry argue that if a scholar lives in the midst of crisis, then he or she must seriously think about it and be engaged in it.[16] But it is that engagement that is often lacking. John Paul Lederach charges that scholars and practitioners attached to development, international studies, and conflict resolution have too often *not* dared to address evident injustices.[17] He believes that participatory critical thinking and transforming moral agency among scholars and development personnel form a necessary corrective.

Critical Theory

As argued at the beginning of this chapter, the standard approach to political science and international relations deals primarily with state actors. Focusing on state actors frequently ignores or disguises the systemic violence imposed on subaltern states by the dominant economic and political powers. The critical dimension of critically embodied studies, therefore, has a scope far beyond state actors. It includes a country's culture, history, and political processes beside the dynamic effects of interstate and global forces. All of these inform the shape of state-societal relations, as well as the identities crafted by individuals, villages, cities, ethnicities, and political parties. Robert Cox diagrams this historical process of intersubjective learning in the tugs and pulls of state-societal global understanding.[18]

Social Forces

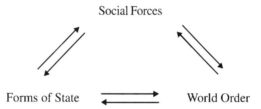

Forms of State   World Order

He posits that rather than political states, it is really state-societal complexes that are rightly viewed as the basic unit of analysis in international relations.[19] It is here, in the analysis of these state-societal complexes that the problems of systemic violence appear most acutely,[20] and it becomes most evident why working for justice requires attacking the roots of systemic violence. Intersubjective learning occurs between the successive forms of the state, social forces affecting these forms, and world orders. Critical theory also examines world orders that may be characterized as successive historical epochs. These eras overlap the above state-societal developments. Studying the evolution of state-societal cum global forces in other countries, one may address the effect of globalization on a particular state-societal development with components that are specifically structural violence.

Development Studies

There are at least four prevalent views of development. Three conventional interpretations regard development as synonymous with economic growth,[21] or economic growth alongside social change,[22] or elite-organized modernism that promises enlightened, market-oriented, technological paths of change. These three views may, in fact, serve certain forms of political and economic freedom, These conventional interpretations stress the benefits of change. For instance, they may produce material prosperity, efficient market processes, increased productive capacity, the fruits of higher consumption, improved housing and health services, greater educational options, choice of employment, or mobility.

Numerous scholars discern, however, that these views err uncritically in valuing efficiency, transparency, and the technical aspects of economics above all else. Stated differently, these three views of development may camouflage structural economic violence.[23] Denis Goulet summarizes that such "developmentalism" subordinates "value judgments about human goals to the achievement of economic growth, to the creation of new social divisions of labor, to the quest for modern institutions, or to the spread of attitudes deemed compatible with efficient production."[24] An example of an egregious spin on these benefits during the American-Vietnam War was Samuel Huntington's conclusion that extensive aerial bombing was developmentally beneficial to Vietnam since the consequent refugee resettlement and political change were thought to introduce modernization in place of old agrarian cultural orders.[25]

If conventional development presumptions value efficiency and social control, a contrasting fourth interpretation of "development as liberation" values social justice, human rights, and participatory people. Such liberating development does not discard empirical indicators. Rather, it examines quantitative facts in light of pathways for qualitative improvement in state-societal relations.

This development as liberation recognizes the distinctiveness of persons, communities, societal organizations, states, and regions, as well as their underlying values and goals for development. These assets will vary, as do each state's and society's development needs. One context, such as the European conquest and settlement of North America, may have provided ample space and time for establishing norms of politics and governance. Today, however, people in other contexts know better the constraints of prolonged war, civil strife, colonization, geographical challenges, and the too-swift sweep of international commerce, cybernetics, and mechanization. Critically embodied studies allows for these later contexts to become a part of the equation in ways that conventional development and global affairs schemes do not.

TEACHING APPLICATIONS

Critically embodied studies is both a tool of analysis and a teaching strategy. With it, I grounded a faith-based liberal arts study of global affairs in embodiment, political anthropology, critical theory, and development studies. For example, in my senior capstone course, called Christian Values in Global Community, students must not only study how the United States structures international trade but also ask how the U.S. government and society collectively influence the choices and hopes of people with less privilege. As argued in my critique of the Bush doctrine, the U.S. government's reach is now unprecedented. Similarly, American citizens, who account for only 4.5 percent of the world's population, reach a great deal themselves: they consume more than 30 percent of the world's product.[26] Or in my crosscultural class in Vietnam, students study that country's postwar economic and political system, as they come to appreciate the depth of another's suffering. They confront U.S. foreign policy in a new light. In the past, they likely learned that during the American-Vietnam war years, the United States lost 58,000 troops. Via critically embodied studies, they learn alongside Vietnamese youth who can explain how Vietnam endured 6.5 million casualties, 3.8 million deaths, 300,000 missing in action, 80,000 deaths in postwar landmine clearance, an unknown number of refugees, the bombardment by 7 million tons of ordnance, intergenerational deformities of Agent Orange, and lasting hazards from 350,000 tons of unexploded ordnance and landmines. Vietnam's many wars, hard-honed perspectives, and present-day speech are essential to these students' discernment of peaceful postwar development and future prevention of conflict.

CONCLUSION

Critically embodied studies is a pedagogy seeking peaceable paths for local and global security. Its response to struggle and hope is held together by a theological understanding of embodiment. This includes service, nonviolence, liberation, and solidarity among people who know too well the costs of war. The objective of my pedagogy, in Richard Falk's words, is a "politically engaged spirituality" that takes on modern warfare and domination. It "implies both the will and the capability to intervene nonviolently yet with behavioral consequences, in situations of conflict and oppression."[27] Let us work and pray for its success.

NOTES

1. Elise Boulding, *Abolishing War* (Boston: BRC for the 21st Century, 1998), 36.

2. "President Bush on Iraq," *Online NewsHour* at www.pbs.org/newshour/bb/middle _east/july-dec02/bushspeech_10-7.html (accessed October 8, 2002).

3. William D. Hartung, Frida Berrigan, and Michelle Ciarrocca, "Operation Endless Deployment," *The Nation* 275, no. 13 (October 21, 2002): 21–24.

4. Peter Grier, "Is It All about Oil?" *The Christian Science Monitor* (October 16, 2002): 1, 9–10; Michael T. Klare, *Resource Wars: The New Landscape of Global Conflict* (New York: Owl, 2002); and Michael T. Klare, "Oiling the Wheels of War," *The Nation* 275, no. 11 (October 7, 2002): 6–7.

5. Bill Keller, "The Sunshine Warrior," *New York Times Magazine,* September 22, 2002, 52.

6. Richard Falk concisely summarizes these aspects of international relations and law in "Rush to War," *The Nation* 275, no. 6 (August 19/26, 2002): 5.

7. Charter of the United Nations (as amended). Concluded at San Francisco, June 26, 1945. Entered into force, October 24, 1945. 1 U.N.T.S. XVI, 1976 Y.B.U.N. 1043; U.S.T.S. 993, 59 Stat. 1031; reprinted in Burns H. Weston, Richard A. Falk, and Hilary Charlesworth, *Supplement of Basic Documents to International Law and World Order,* 3d ed. (St. Paul: West Group, 1997), 11–31.

8. Quoted in Bill Keller, "The Sunshine Warrior," 50.

9. Quoted in Richard Falk, "A Dangerous Game," *The Nation* 275, no. 11 (October 7, 2002): 5.

10. Madeleine K. Albright, "The Testing of American Foreign Policy," *Foreign Affairs* 77, no. 6 (November/December 1998): 59.

11. Madeleine K. Albright, quoted in Noam Chomsky, *9–11* (New York: Seven Stories Press, 2001), 73.

12. Oscar Romero, "The Last Sermon," in *The Human Rights Reader*, ed. Walter Laqueur and Barry Rubin (New York: New American Library, 1989), 353.

13. Leonardo Boff, *Cry of the Earth, Cry of the Poor,* trans. Phillip Berryman (Maryknoll, N.Y.: Orbis Books, 1997), 26.

14. Nancy Scheper-Hughes, *Death without Weeping: The Violence of Everyday Life in Brazil* (Berkeley: University of California Press, 1992); and Dorinne Kondo, *Crafting Selves: Power, Gender, and Discourses of Identity in a Japanese Workplace* (Chicago: University of Chicago Press, 1990).

15. Paulo Freire, *Pedagogy of the Oppressed*, Revised 20th Anniversary Edition, trans. Myra Bergman Ramos (New York: Continuum, 1993), 68–69.

16. Nicole Polier and William Roseberry, "Tristes Tropes: Post-Modern Anthropologists Encounter the Other and Discover Themselves," *Economy and Society* 18, no. 2 (1989): 245, 250, 255, 260.

17. John Paul Lederach, "Keynote Address" for the founding of the doctoral program in Conflict Resolution, Graduate School of International Studies, University of Denver (May 4, 1999).

18. Robert W. Cox, "Social Forces, States and World Orders," in *Neorealism and Its Critics,* ed. Robert O. Keohane (New York: Columbia University Press, 1986), 221.

19. Cox, "Social Forces"; see also Cox, "Gramsci, Hegemony, and International Relations: An Essay in Method," in *Approaches to World Order,* ed. Robert W. Cox and Timothy J. Sinclair (Cambridge: Cambridge University Press, 1996), 124–146.

20. It is at this juncture, for example, that one can observe the violence of the marketplace that is described in chapter 15 of this volume.

21. Denis Goulet, "'Development' . . . or Liberation?" in *The Political Economy of Development and Underdevelopment,* ed. K. Wilbur and K. P. Jameson (New York: McGraw-Hill, 1992), 547.

22. This formula derives from United Nations General Secretary U Thant's phrase, "development = economic growth + social change" but suffers for lack of specificity. As Denis Goulet summarizes, "not any kind of growth will do, nor any kind of change." "'Development' . . . or Liberation?" 548.

23. For a nonviolence-shaped critique of the economic model that underlies the focus on growth and efficiency, see chapter 15 by James M. Harder in this volume.

24. "'Development' . . . or Liberation?" 547–548.

25. Samuel P. Huntington, "The Bases of Accommodation," *Foreign Affairs* 46 (1968): 652.

26. Mel Gurtov, *Global Politics in the Human Interest*, 4th ed. (Boulder, Colo.: Lynne Rienner Publishers, 1999), 5.

27. Richard A. Falk, *Religion and Humane Global Governance* (New York: Palgrave, 2001), 107.

IV

NONVIOLENCE AND THE HUMANITIES

9

Nonviolence, Anabaptism, and the Impossible in Communication

Susan Biesecker-Mast

In a sense, the discipline of communication is all about peace. This is so because the discipline seeks to explain the relationship between communication and understanding as well as to promote better understanding through instruction in effective communication practices. Thus, all the subdisciplines of communication—from organizational communication to public address to health communication—address both theoretical and practical questions about how communication assists or frustrates human understanding. To the extent that understanding serves as an antidote to human conflict, then, communication seeks to promote peace.

The discipline of communication is also one of the oldest academic disciplines. Already in the fifth century B.C.E., young Athenian men were receiving instruction in the strategies of persuasion.[1] Although in its earliest days the study of communication was called rhetoric, even then it was concerned with how human beings achieve understanding through communication. Thus we learn in Plato's *Phaedrus*, for instance, that it is possible to achieve understanding through dialogue between interlocutors who are essentially the same.[2]

If communication is all about peace and if practitioners, philosophers, and scholars of communication have been trying to figure out the relationships among communication and understanding for some 2,500 years, it might seem unlikely that a nonviolent perspective would have much to teach communication about peace. Nevertheless that is just what I want to argue in this chapter. As used here, a nonviolent perspective is a multifaceted worldview derived from Anabaptist Christianity with implications for any who seek to pursue peace through communication.

Informed by the sixteenth-century Anabaptist reformation, Anabaptist nonviolence understands that the future reign of God is breaking into the world in the person and life of Jesus and that discipleship to Jesus is constitutive of that

Christian life. Since Jesus' life and teachings instruct us in nonviolence and rejection of the sword, both commitments, realized in daily practice, are central to Anabaptist understandings of discipleship. Thus discipleship results in the church as a visible community that witnesses to the reign of God in the world through nonviolence. I believe that Anabaptism understood in this way has an important contribution to make to the study of communication by way of its distinctive understanding of peace through the teachings of Jesus. In what follows I will briefly introduce two primary perspectives on communication in the discipline today and then review critiques of these perspectives from a nonviolent viewpoint. Finally, I will argue that a nonviolent Anabaptist take on the question of the relationship between communication and peace would differ significantly from all these options and will suggest some implications of such a position.

CONTEMPORARY VIEWS OF COMMUNICATION

According to John Durham Peters, a prominent theorist of communication, two views of communication became dominant after the Second World War. One view takes a technical approach to communication and the other a therapeutic approach.[3] The technical view of communication holds that the problems humans experience in their efforts to understand one another are essentially technical problems. They are the effects of technical glitches such as a failing transmitter here or troublesome receiver there. For theorists and critics who take this view, the solution to misunderstanding is to repair existing communication technologies or to develop new technologies. The therapeutic view of communication takes a psychological approach that human understanding is contingent on the psychological health of the individuals communicating with one another. For theorists who work out of this perspective, misunderstanding is the effect of poor communication within the self. According to this view, I cannot hope to gain understanding from you until I first know myself. Only when I know myself well can I put my thoughts and feelings into words accurately thereby communicating effectively with you. The solution to misunderstanding for those who take the therapeutic view is, then, self-knowledge.[4]

There are a number of problems with these two views of communication.[5] One problem with the technical view is that it fails to notice that any technological solution merely introduces yet another mediating factor in communication. To introduce, say, the telephone to solve the problem of distance only complicates communication as it strips communication of face-to-face interaction. Another problem with both the technical view and the therapeutic view is that neither appreciates the difficulty in communication posed by the signs we are obliged to use in order to communicate. Insofar as communication is enabled by signs (the words, gestures, and images we use to communicate), it is also disabled by them since the meaning of any sign is always the effect of interpretation. But, most importantly for the concerns òf this chapter, neither view takes seriously enough the fact that communication always entails contact between the self (understood as a complicated entity that cannot fully know itself) and the other (who, to remain other, must also always remain somewhat of a mystery).

This is the most significant critique of these two views of communication for this chapter because we are called as Christians to love the other. Whether we look to the Sermon on the Mount, Jesus' parables of the good Samaritan and the prodigal son, or Jesus' teaching that all of God's commandments may be reduced to just these two—that we are to love God (who is perhaps more than anything else other) with all our heart, soul, and mind and that we are to love our neighbor (whether friend or alien) as ourselves—what we see is the centrality of love of other for the Christian life. Thus any adequate view of communication from a Christian perspective must consider paramount the way in which that view of communication theorizes the relationship between the self and the other.

TAKING THE OTHER MORE SERIOUSLY

Working out of Hans-Georg Gadamer's theorization of conversation, Michael King (a communication scholar and a Christian) seeks to take the other seriously. In his book, *Fractured Dance: Gadamer and a Mennonite Conflict over Homosexuality*, King analyzes and assesses the communication practices used throughout a conversation about homosexuality within the Franconia conference of the Mennonite Church. More specifically, King is interested to learn which communication practices enabled both conversational successes and failures among individuals who held significantly different biblical and theological positions. Thus, King's research focuses on the question of how we are to communicate with the other. He is interested to discover which communication practices make it possible for us to have meaningful conversations with an other whose difference takes the form of an alternative and presumably antagonistic set of religious commitments. Out of his study of Gadamer and his field research, King advocates what he calls "a third way" in which "we are called to ask what we might learn if our focus were less on defending a given stand and more on what it means to understand each other, even—or maybe especially— across polarization."[6]

Importantly, King uses Gadamer's theorization of conversation because Gadamer challenges us to take the other seriously in his or her difference from us even as he calls us to seek to understand the other. For Gadamer, understanding between human beings is difficult not for technical or therapeutic reasons, but because the other is different. Insofar as the other comes out of a necessarily different history than we do, we have difficulty understanding the other and vise versa.[7]

Still, Gadamer argues, even disagreement must presume understanding at some level. This is so since to have a thoughtful disagreement requires that the self and the other share at the very least some understanding of that about which they disagree. Thus, King argues, even in the context of fierce disagreement we ought "to ask what in the other's position, above and beneath the wrongness of it that seems so painfully obvious to so many, may nevertheless have its own valid contribution to make to our quest for truth."[8] For King (as for Gadamer), then, conversational success does not depend upon gaining agreement among interlocutors but, rather, is determined by the degree to which we seek to understand the other within their difference from us: *"Each speaker's ability to grasp why the* other *speaker finds her or his own position persuasive is what enables the true understanding that defines conversational success"*.[9]

King is no doubt correct that Gadamer's theory helps us to take the other seriously. Significantly for any Christian, which to my mind ought to mean a person who understands love of the other to be a question of discipleship, King's work via Gadamer calls us first to listen intently both to the similarities and differences with the other, also to seek agreement where we can with the other, and at the very least to pursue a basic commonality with the other even amidst disagreement. By engaging in this kind of open communication, King argues, conversation and even disagreement may become an occasion for two others to come together meaningfully: "As we allow our many different prejudices to intersect, interact, even combat, they lead us toward what Gadamer's thought might inspire us to view as the common music weaving our many different steps into one dance."[10]

But does Gadamer's theory enable us to take the other seriously enough? Indeed, what does it mean for the other to be other? For my part I have been persuaded that in order for the other to be and remain other, the other must remain always to some extent unavailable to the self. As philosopher John Caputo, whose book *More Radical Hermeneutics: On Not Knowing Who We Are* might be read as an extended essay on ethics within the problematic of the other, writes: "The alter ego [or other] . . . is precisely someone whose mental life I will never know or occupy, not because of some contingent limitation on my part that I might overcome later, but because it is in principle inaccessible. The alterity of the other would be destroyed if I had access to it; the other whom I would know would not be other."[11] For Caputo, the otherness of the other is not merely the effect of history (though it certainly is partly that) but has to do with the simple fact that the other is not the self. Moreover, for Caputo, remaining mindful of that intractable difference between the self and the other is crucial to any thinking about friendship, ethics, community, understanding, et cetera.

To put this concern for the alterity of the other into the context of communication raises some crucial questions. What does the quest for understanding—that is, for making the thoughts, intentions, and motives of the other accessible to the self—mean for the other? To what extent does the other remain other through that effort? Indeed, what does the search for commonality especially amidst disagreement do to the alterity of the other? If even in disagreement the other becomes accessible to the self, then to what extent does the other in any way remain other in the communication practices advocated by Gadamer and King? In order for the other to be truly other within any theorization of communication, doesn't that other have to be in at least the last instance inaccessible to the self?

John Peters, the communication theorist mentioned above, would argue that Gadamer and King have missed the point. Communication does not suffer from the problem of misunderstanding. Rather, for Peters, misunderstanding and its root cause, difference, are the conditions of possibility for communication.[12] Were it not for the difference between the self and the other—that is, were it not for the glitches, gaps, and gaffes that characterize our communication—he argues, there would be no need for communication. Indeed, were it not for the intractable difference among us, we would not seek to communicate with an other. So for Peters difference and misunderstanding are not an obstacle we ought to overcome: "The impossibility of connection, so lamented of late, may be a central and salutary feature of the human lot. The dream of communication has too little respect for personal inaccessibility. Impersonality can be a protective wall for the private heart. To 'fix' the gaps with 'better' communication might be to drain solidarity and love of all their juice."[13]

All this is not to say, however, that we do not or ought not seek understanding, argues Peters. On the contrary, all acts of communication are by necessity efforts at understanding: "All talk is an act of faith predicated on the future's ability to bring forth the words called for."[14] When we speak, we seek understanding. However, the fact that we seek understanding, even presume it whenever we speak, does not mean that we ever achieve understanding. For Peters, the difference that makes us others to each other and that thereby makes communication valuable also makes meaning and understanding elusive: "Meaning is an incomplete project, open-ended and subject to radical revision by later events."[15] Peters's point here is that understanding is never fully achieved because of difference and misunderstanding. All we ever achieve are contingent understandings. Again, for Peters, this is not a situation to be lamented since such "failure" is, among other things, precisely what keeps us talking.

Although communication, taken to be a kind of communion of minds, is not practically possible for those of us of this world due to history and difference, it is, according to Peters, theoretically possible. Or, put another way, though not possible in this world, it may be in another: "Communication is ultimately unthinkable apart from the task of establishing a peaceable kingdom in which each may dwell with the other. Given our conditions as mortals, communication will always remain a problem of power, ethics, and art."[16] As long as we humans are constrained by history, argues Peters, we cannot transcend difference. However, if we could ever escape our historicity and thus our difference, communication as understanding would be possible. But to escape historicity would be to leave this world for another.

Peters's theory of communication, focused as it is on protecting the other as truly other, makes two interventions into understandings about communication that are especially important from a nonviolent Christian perspective. The first is that this theory of communication considers the other to be central to communication.[17] First and foremost for Peters, putting the other at the center of communication means making sure that his theorization does not make the other the same. For Peters, the only way to truly honor the otherness of the other is to admit that our intractable difference cannot be bridged. This, of course, means giving up the "dream of communication" according to which we commune with the other. But more importantly for Peters, it means that the other does not become in the course of our communicative interaction some version of ourselves. Instead, the other remains other and, not incidentally, an interesting conversation partner. The second is that ethics, as action within history that is mindful of the otherness of the other, becomes the paramount question to be asked about any communicative event. Thus, the most important question is not whether I have been understood by an other or whether I have gained agreement from that other but whether through our communication I and the other have discovered ways to love one another: "The question should be not Can we communicate with each other? but Can we love one another or treat each other with justice and mercy. . . . At best, 'communication' is the name for those practices that compensate for the fact that we can never be each other."[18] Peters's theorization of communication, then, not only moves us away from questions about technology or self-knowledge and to questions of the other but also is intent upon protecting that other as an other and thus obliges us always to be paying attention to the ethics of our communication practices.

Because Peters's theory of communication calls us to pay close attention to the probability that our communication practices may violate the otherness of the other, it is helpful for thinking through communication from a nonviolent perspective. Still, as one who is committed to nonviolence through an Anabaptist theology, I cannot help but ask whether understanding must be put off to another world and time. A crucial theological point for Anabaptists is that the peaceable kingdom is not entirely an eschatological space. Although Anabaptists would, like Peters, say that total peace will only come at the end of history, they would also say that even now the kingdom is partly among us. As Menno Simons argued,

we teach that which Jesus the teacher from heaven, the mouth and word of the Most High God taught (John 3:2), that now is the time of grace, a time to awake from the sleep of our ugly sins, and to be of an upright, converted, renewed, contrite, and penitent heart. Now is the time sincerely to lament before God our past reckless and willful manner of life, and in the fear of God to crucify and mortify our wicked, sinful flesh and nature. Now is the time to arise with Christ in a new, righteous, and penitent existence, even as Christ says, The time is fulfilled, and the kingdom of God is at hand: repent and believe the gospel.[19]

The kingdom is among us, Anabaptists believe, insofar as God's people constitute the body of Christ in the here-and-now. If this is so, if the peaceable kingdom is not simply not-yet, but is also partially here through the body of Christ, then how should we be thinking about communication?

TOWARD AN ANABAPTIST NONVIOLENT VIEW OF COMMUNICATION

The Anabaptist nonviolent view of communication toward which I want to move would take the following two key presuppositions into account: (1) that the other is and should remain truly other; and (2) that the peaceable kingdom is already partly here. The former presupposition is important for protecting the other as other. It constitutes a radical nonviolent posture toward the other because it obliges us to communicate not in order to make the other understandable to us but rather to enable us to welcome the other as different from us.[20] Rather than seek to bring the other into our comprehensibility, this posture calls us to await their alterity. The latter presupposition is important because it obliges us to approach the other in anticipation of understanding. It demands patience from us within which we would strive to bridge the intractable gap between us and them. Rather than give up in despair at the difficulties posed by differences between myself and the other, this posture calls me to persist at the hard work that is communication.

In this short chapter, there is not space to offer a comprehensive theorization of a nonviolent approach to communication based in Anabaptist theology. However, in the space that I do have remaining, I would like to suggest what it might be like to communicate out of such a posture.

Anyone who would speak out of such a nonviolent Anabaptist posture would expect misunderstanding in any communicative event. If communication is taken to be the encounter of two others who, in order to remain other (as they ought), must remain something of a mystery to one another, then misunderstanding will be a dominant feature of any communication. Importantly, though, if misunderstanding were expected, then it would not be focused upon as the problem to be solved, the aberration to be eliminated, the obstacle to be overcome. Instead, it would be considered normal. This would be important, for if we were to take it seriously (as I am suggesting we should), it would mean that any time I approach a conversation, I should expect to be misunderstood. I should expect that the other will not take my meaning, will think I am saying something other than I think I am saying. Furthermore, such a posture would also demand that we expect to misunderstand the other.

Such a posture would radically transform our experience of communication. It would require of us a great deal of modesty. To make this more concrete, consider how any antagonists in a conflict would be obliged to change their communication practices if they assumed they were being misunderstood and were misunderstanding. How much more effort might they put into explaining themselves? How much harder might they listen to their interlocutor?

Yet, even as the first presupposition would demand of us that we expect misunderstanding (and speak accordingly), the second presupposition would require that we seek to understand the other nevertheless. Because the second presupposition assumes that the kingdom of God is already here, we would be obliged to talk out of an aspiration for understanding. That is to say, even as we expect misunderstanding, we must converse with an aim to understanding. Within a nonviolent Anabaptist perspective we could not simply assent to the first presupposition and give up on understanding altogether. We could not resign ourselves to misunderstanding and all that follows from it (such as cynicism, the will to power, etc.). Since in a nonviolent Anabaptist view the first presupposition would not operate without the second, we would strive for understanding even as we would expect misunderstanding. Thus it would be appropriate for us to speak modestly (since we would assume that we have not understood and are not being understood) yet earnestly, sensitively, and articulately in the hope of being understood (because the Kingdom is also among us). Out of such faith we would try to make sense of the discourse out of which the other speaks.

Finally, if we were to take the other seriously as other yet seek to understand that other, then we would become engaged in what I would call truly open communication. Communication of this sort would be truly open not because we would have solved the problems of understanding but because it would make us open to radical transformation. If we were to speak always in recognition of the normalcy of misunderstanding yet in anticipation of understanding, we might just succeed in welcoming the other to us. If that were to happen, if we were to invite the alterity of the other through our modesty toward understanding and our aspirations for understanding, I think we would make ourselves available to radical change.

Although what I am saying here may seem strange, it also strikes me as strangely familiar. That is because it reminds me of my experience reading the gospels. Whenever I read the Gospels I have a strong sense that I am encountering the other. Those texts do not make ready sense to me and indeed do not even seem to be addressing me. Yet still I am compelled to try to make sense of them. And somewhere in between my misunderstanding and my hope of the other we call Emmanuel, I believe I have been transformed. In a way, all that I am suggesting here is that a nonviolent Anabaptist view would embrace the frustration and the possibility of that experience of encountering the scriptures or any other who, by necessity, must confound us. Indeed, perhaps all I am trying to say in this short chapter is that a nonviolent Anabaptist view of communication would call us to engage any other as we must engage the Jesus of the gospels—in expectation of misunderstanding and in anticipation of a miracle.

NOTES

1. For a history of rhetorical teaching and practice, see John Poulakos, *Sophistical Rhetoric in Classical Greece* (Columbia, S.C.: University of South Carolina Press, 1995).

2. Plato, *Phaedrus*, trans. W. C. Helmbold and W. G. Rabinowitz (Indianapolis: Bobbs-Merrill Educational Publishing, 1956): 244–274.

3. John Durham Peters, *Speaking into the Air: A History of the Idea of Communication* (Chicago: University of Chicago Press, 1999). Peters writes, "The technicians of communication are a diverse breed, from Samuel F. B. Morse to Marshall McLuhan, from Charles Horton Cooley to Al Gore, from Buckminster Fuller to Alvin Toffler, but they all think the imperfections of human interchange can be redressed by improved technology or techniques. . . . The therapeutic vision of communication, in turn, developed within humanist and existentialist psychology, but both its roots and its branches spread much wider, to the nineteenth century attack on Calvinism and its replacement by a therapeutic ethos of self-realization, and to the self-culture pervading American bourgeois life" (29).

4. Interestingly, Peters attributes the emergence of both the technical and the therapeutic views of communication to the development of communication technologies such as the telegraph. With technology as the leading metaphor for communication process, questions focused on how to remove obstacles (whether technical or psychological) to improve communication. Previously communication had been understood as a process of interpretation across distance. See Peters, *Speaking into the Air,* especially 1–31.

5. For a summary of Peters's critique of these two views of communication, see *Speaking into the Air,* 263–271.

6. Michael King, *Fractured Dance: Gadamer and a Mennonite Conflict over Homosexuality* (Telford, Pa.: Pandora Press, 2001), 28.

7. Gadamer theorizes that differences emerge out of "prejudices" that are the necessary effects of our own historicity, or what he calls "finiteness." For King's review of these key terms in Gadamer's thought, see *Fractured Dance*, 38–40.

8. King, *Fractured Dance*, 29.

9. King, *Fractured Dance*, 30.

10. King, *Fractured Dance*, 40–41.

11. John Caputo, *More Radical Hermeneutics: On Not Knowing Who We Are* (Bloomington: Indiana University Press, 2000), 41.

12. For another study from within Communication (and the subdiscipline of Rhetoric) that comes to this conclusion through different means (namely, close readings of Kenneth Burke's works), see Barbara Biesecker, *Addressing Postmodernity: Kenneth Burke, Rhetoric, and a Theory of Social Change* (Tuscaloosa: University of Alabama Press, 1997).

13. Peters, *Speaking into the Air*, 59.

14. Peters, *Speaking into the Air*, 267.

15. Peters, *Speaking into the Air*, 267.

16. Peters, *Speaking into the Air*, 268.

17. "The other, not the self, should be the center of whatever 'communication' might mean." Peters, *Speaking into the Air*, 265.

18. Peters, *Speaking into the Air*, 268.

19. Menno Simons, "Foundation of Christian Doctrine," in *The Complete Writings of Menno Simons* (Scottdale, Pa.: Herald Press, 1984), 108.

20. This idea of welcoming the other as other, rather than seeking to make the other into something like the self, is borrowed from John Caputo's readings of Jacques Derrida's recent work on friendship. See, for instance, John Caputo, "Who Is Derrida's Zarathustra? Of Fraternity, Friendship, and a Democracy to Come," in *More Radical Hermeneutics*, 60–83.

10

Literature, Nonviolence, and Nonviolent Teaching

Jeff Gundy

Teaching nonviolence is important though difficult work. Practicing and modeling nonviolence in the classroom may be even more important and more difficult. This chapter explores the dance of teaching and learning as it might be undertaken by those committed to nonviolence as both means and end. I work with a keen sense of the long tradition of Anabaptist nonviolence in which I have lived my life, along with profound awareness that we make common cause with many other authors, traditions, and texts in the search to know how to live nonviolently. In the first section I will briefly describe my approach to teaching classic texts from a nonviolent perspective. In the second I will discuss an equally important and closely related issue—*how* we might go about teaching nonviolently—with special attention to some of theologian Stanley Hauerwas's ideas and practices.

TEACHING NONVIOLENCE

Peace underpins and influences every course I teach in one way or another, but I have also taught several classes that explicitly explored violence and nonviolence, under a number of titles and with various reading lists. As far back as *The Iliad* the glamour and intensity of war, as well as its terrible costs, have seized the human imagination. Writers at least since the Middle Ages have often been socially marginal and skeptical in one way or another. In their examinations of conventional wisdom, creative writers were often among the first to question militarism, nationalism, and other forms of violence and oppression in particular situations.

There is a long and rich literature, then, of work that explores and critiques the difficulties and disasters of violence as a way of solving problems. Relatively little of that work is driven by an explicit ideology of Christian nonviolence, but much of it lends itself quite readily to being read from such a perspective. One of my favorite

American literature courses is a Bluffton College offering entitled "Heroism and Humility," a course in which we look closely at visions and revisions of heroism in classic and contemporary texts. I typically begin by noting some classic American heroes, real and imagined, such as Daniel Boone, Davy Crockett, and the Natty Bumppo of James Fenimore Cooper's Leatherstocking novels—the last of which prompted D. H. Lawrence's famous observation that "The essential American soul is hard, isolate, stoic, and a killer."[1] Critics and historians such as Richard Slotkin, Sam Keen, and David Grossman have analyzed the need to apotheosize the hero and dehumanize the enemy in order to make war and the killing of enemies psychologically possible, and such texts combine well with more traditional pacifist authors to provide a theoretical background for the course.[2]

Much of the best American literature demonstrates a deep and persistent mistrust of heroic figures, a tendency to present them as problematic or doomed and to search for alternate models. One excellent example is Herman Melville's classic *Moby Dick*. Melville dramatizes the American struggle with the possibilities and perils of heroic action in his pairing of the fanatical Ahab and the contemplative Ishmael. Both seem clearly incomplete, yet both the grandeur of Ahab's megalomania and the melancholy of Ishmael floating on the coffin of his friend, escaped alone to tell us, are oddly attractive as well.

In a strange way, perhaps Ahab attracts because he incarnates so fully the worldview Sam Keen describes as paranoid: "an antireligious mysticism based on the feeling that the world in general, and others in particular, are against me or us."[3] Melville tells us that Ahab sees the white whale as the visible personification through which such "intangible malignity" might be attacked and defeated: "All that most maddens and torments; all that stirs up the lees of things; all truth with malice in it; all that cracks the Sinews and cakes the brain; all the subtle demonisms of life and thought; all evil, to crazy Ahab, were visibly personified, and made practically assailable in Moby Dick."[4]

We all recognize, to some extent, this sense that the world is against us and the desire to remove this opposition with one sudden, irrevocable blow.[5] Yet in our better moments, and surely as Christians, we must resist such selfishness and see the world more generously. Compare Ishmael's initial descriptions of the great white whale: "A gentle joyousness—a mighty mildness of repose in swiftness, invested the gliding whale. . . . not Jove, not that great majesty supreme! did surpass the glorified White Whale as he so divinely swam."[6]

Ishmael's sense of the whale's majesty is strikingly congruent to the view of life Keen poses at the other extreme from paranoia: "By contrast, the religious mystic experiences the ground of being as basically friendly to the deepest needs of the self. That which is unknown, strange, and beyond our comprehension is with and for rather than against us."[7]

Moby Dick offers no easy answer to pacifists seeking to understand the reality of evil and all the difficult conundrums of resisting evil without violence. Melville himself was deeply skeptical about the sort of mystic benevolence Keen proposes;

while he admits in a letter to Hawthorne that Goethe's "Live in the all" feeling contains some truth, he insists that "what plays the mischief with the truth is that men will insist upon the universal application of a temporary feeling or opinion."[8] To act as though there is no evil in the world, as though we have no enemies, may be naive; but to absolutize evil in the enemy and therefore justify anything we do in opposition as a necessary evil may be even more dangerous, as Ahab shows.

Texts such as *Moby Dick* may not provide clear road maps for nonviolent action, but they can be extremely useful as they help students to explore and critique the prevalent American notion that violence, however unfortunate, is also necessary and even, in Richard Slotkin's term, "regenerative." "An American hero is the lover of the spirit of the wilderness," writes Slotkin, "and his acts of love and sacred affirmations are acts of violence against that spirit and her avatars."[9] Through popular culture, family traditions, and even religious training, most young Americans absorb this ideology of necessary violence more or less unreflectively; they often find it startling that mainstream American texts call it into question.

American movies also both reflect and (less often) critique the myth of regenerative violence. Even a Western classic such as *Shane*, with its bare-bones plot and schematic characters, illustrates in stark clarity both the myth and its difficulties. Shane, a gunfighter who wants to retire, drifts into a small Western settlement only to find the honest small farmers there threatened by the local rancher and his band of thuggish cowboys (notably, the farmers all have families, while the ranchers all seem to be unattached males). Shane takes up the farmers' cause even though it means strapping on his gun again and taking out the hired gun and most of the rancher's men in the climactic shootout. There is no place for such a man once his work is done, however, as the barely concealed attraction between Shane and the head farmer's wife makes clear. Once his work is done he must ride off into the darkness, bleeding from a belly wound, presumably to die of peritonitis in some miserable back room a few days later.

Talking with students about such texts and films has several good effects. It enables and encourages them to reexamine myths and stereotypes, which often rule much of their thinking, and provides them with tools to do so. Whether or not they come to accept a pacifist, principled refusal of violence—and of course many do not—they may at least think more critically about the uses and effects of violence and thus become more critical viewers and readers in the future.

The critical, or at least thoughtful, analysis of violence can be found in unlikely places these days. The magazine *War, Literature and the Arts,* published at the United States Air Force Academy, recently carried an interview with poet John Balaban, a Vietnam-era conscientious objector. The interviewer, who teaches at the academy, says that his students appreciate Balaban's work, even his strongly antiwar poems: "They held you as the moral standard by which to judge our actions in the Vietnam War. Whether they agreed or disagreed with you, they felt your work raised essential questions that any military member must consider when thinking about the Vietnam War."[10]

Later in the interview Balaban admits that he "was never the kind of absolutist conscientious objector that one admires so much among the Quakers. Sometimes the sword, although 'a cursed thing,' saves us from greater evils."[11] It seems important to recognize that in defining himself as less than an absolute pacifist, Balaban places himself with the great majority of Americans, college students, and humans on the planet, who do not share the quirky, obstinate belief that Jesus calls for us not to kill anyone, ever, no matter what "greater evils" it seems we can escape only by doing so. Balaban's position, sometimes called selective conscientious objection, is in effect a Just-War position. Rather than dismissing it as merely compromised, however, pacifists might note that Balaban rules out more wars than is usually the case and even more important asserts the rights of individuals to apply Just-War criteria themselves rather than depending on government authorities.[12]

Absolute pacifists ought not understate the moral gravity of positions such as Balaban's. I believe that Christians are called to nonviolence and hope to persuade my students and the rest of the world to agree. I know the easy and shoddy variations of the argument for necessary violence, which are so deeply rooted in American history and mythology, and I will continue to press students to reexamine those myths and their own too-easy acceptance of them, and to point out alternatives and to emphasize the costs of even the most "effective" use of force. At the same time, as Balaban's action and writing make clear, it is necessary to recognize that absolute pacifism is not the only position on violence that one can hold with integrity. Furthermore, in both pragmatic and ethical terms it seems wrong not to make common cause wherever possible with people like Balaban, whose critique of the conduct of the Vietnam War is powerful, searching, and rigorous, even while we recognize that disagreements do exist.

Over twenty-some years of teaching I have found that I must be especially careful not to mock or deride those students who come to me with one or another version of Just-War theology. Even if that theology is not at all nuanced or sophisticated (and apart from theologians, whose theology is?), it often rests on a base of family history and personal loyalties that deserves to be acknowledged and respected. The family traditions students bring with them often include stories of considerable sacrifice and loss by their loved ones. When I ask students if they have a close relative or acquaintance who served in Vietnam, most raise their hands—and many students know that those wartime experiences still resonate strongly for their loved ones. To glibly dismiss their views on war and peace, then, is implicitly to devalue those stories and relationships. It is difficult to critique ideologies of necessary and redemptive violence while maintaining respect for individuals, many of them confessing Christians, who accept those ideologies. But the distinction is crucial. I have found that with time and patience I can woo many students seriously to consider nonviolence as a better way. But it does take time and patience, and learning on many levels, to overcome what many students have learned from school and family and church since childhood. It requires that they transform their views on patriotism and loyalty as well as their religious views. I rejoice when, as does happen, students become enthusiastic converts to pacifism. But I also rejoice when, as happens more often, they move a little closer to being pacifists without completely relinquishing their earlier thinking. One 2002 graduate wrote:

> I am proud to say that my four years at this institution have by no means undone the conservative political views that were founded in my previous eighteen years of life experience. . . . I will concede however, and comfortably so, that four years of exposure to such different ideas has softened me and allowed me to reevaluate some ideas and make compromises where I have felt convicted to do so. Though I by no means embrace pacifism, I have come to value pacifists for providing a balance with the war-mongering views of the NRA.

NONVIOLENT TEACHING

Having surveyed some of the ways that a nonviolent perspective reshapes the content of my teaching, I want to turn now to what I believe are the most crucial and difficult issues related to teaching and nonviolence, those which have to do with the manner in which this content is presented to students and discussed with them. There is no shortage of subject matter, and as this volume suggests, a comprehensive nonviolent worldview provides a workable perspective for examining and interpreting virtually all texts and events. Yet it is in pedagogy—in *how* we get our perspective on nonviolence across to students who are, by and large, at least somewhat resistant to it—that many of the most difficult issues lie. Ten years ago I explored some of these issues in a C. Henry Smith lecture,[13] in which I encountered a considerable body of literature on issues of nonviolence and pedagogy, including the well-known work of scholar-teachers such as Paolo Freire and Parker Palmer. Freire's links are to liberation theology and the effort to provide literacy education in South America that would be transformative rather than merely reinforcing oppressive social systems. His renown comes from his offering an "oppositional pedagogy" that would eliminate "banking education" in which teachers merely "deposit" information in passive students and would instead create a dynamic, democratic classroom in which the power relations between teacher and students are at least softened, if not equalized entirely.[14]

In one of his better-known formulations, Palmer suggests: "to teach is to create a space where the community of truth is practiced." Like Freire, he believes education should be the communal pursuit of holistic truth: "In truthful knowing the knower becomes co-participant in a community of faithful relationships with other persons and creatures and things, with whatever our knowledge makes known."[15]

Another writer, English professor and Quaker Mary Rose O'Reilley, published an influential book entitled *The Peaceable Classroom.* She describes her efforts to make the classroom a place where nonviolence is practiced, not just talked about, and writes with insight and candor about the difficulties and rewards of that effort. As O'Reilley points out, academics are not trained to be nonviolent; we learn to win arguments, defend positions, attack opponents, demonstrate that they are stupid or ignorant and we are not. Given the enormous advantages of experience and authority we have over our students, we can easily do so in the classroom—but O'Reilley suggests that it is both bad tactics and bad practice to use such techniques. "We have a lot to tell our students," she writes, "but I believe our primary job should be to bring them to asking, by whatever means we can devise, the question that will elicit what they need to know. Students do not really listen well to the answers to questions they have not learned to ask."[16]

To explore more thoroughly this problem—how we can teach nonviolently, as well as teaching about nonviolence—I engage Stanley Hauerwas's *After Christendom: How the Church Is to Behave if Freedom, Justice, and a Christian Nation Are Bad Ideas.* Hauerwas both responds to and, I think, exemplifies the difficulties of trying to teach nonviolence without slipping into coercive or even violent attitudes and practices.

The book continues Hauerwas's critique of American civil religion and especially of liberal pluralism. Among other sources, Hauerwas acknowledges his debt to the thought of Mennonite theologian John Howard Yoder. The problem with Christianity in America, says Hauerwas, is that it has been turned into "a set of beliefs to legitimate the false universalism of liberalism."[17] But since "outside the church there is no saving knowledge of God," Hauerwas argues, the church must distinguish itself from society and show why its identity in the narrative of Jesus is not expressed in terms of liberal concepts such as freedom, justice, and democracy. Hauerwas writes very confidently on what is wrong with all of these ideas, at least in their American versions, and much of his critique seems rather congenial and familiar to those with a believer's church perspective, such as me.

Hauerwas encounters a major problem, however, when he tries to envision a consistent and workable program for Christian and nonviolent education. The preface notes this difficulty without specifying the particular issues very clearly:

> The fact that the book ends with a challenge should be an indication that I write without knowing the answers. I realize this frustrates many, because "good authors" are usually thought to raise problems for which they think there is a solution. It frustrates me as often as it does my readers that I have few answers. I simply cannot, by the very terms of analysis, offer an alternative to those who conceive of Christianity as a strategy. I do not apologize for that, though I do know it is frustrating.[18]

This may pass as admirable honesty to Hauerwas's disciples, but his claim that it is the "terms of analysis" that create problems without answers does not hold up under scrutiny. The problems, I will demonstrate, are within Hauerwas's own theory and practice and can be addressed if not completely resolved by a different and more consistently nonviolent set of pedagogical assumptions and practices.

The preface of *After Christendom* concludes with a long quote from John Milbank, one of Hauerwas's favorite philosophers, on the joys of the radical Christian life. The passage ends this way: "Instead of a peace 'achieved' through the abandonment of the losers, a subordination of potential rivals and resistance to enemies, the church provides a genuine peace by its memory of all the victims, its equal concern for all of its citizens and its self-exposed offering of reconciliation to enemies."[19]

Hauerwas does not address here a problem implicit in his invocation of this rosy vision: its very generosity is seriously at odds with the divisive and exclusive elements of his own rhetoric and his famously abrasive way of operating in the academic world. Later in *After Christendom*, however, he does recognize the difficulty. For example, the chapter entitled "The Politics of Witness" issues a call for a Christian education that would be systematically and deliberately different from the standard American version.[20] Hauerwas duly notes the implicit imperialism of the usual narratives about Columbus "discovering" America. But less comfortably for his own argument, he quotes extensively from Tzvetan Todorov's *The Conquest of America* on the violence done to the Indians by their Christian conquerors: "Yet is there not already a violence in the conviction that one possesses the truth oneself, whereas this is not the case for others, and that one must furthermore impose that truth on those others?"[21]

Todorov's comment brings Hauerwas to an apparent crisis. To assert the truth of the narrative of Jesus does assert the superiority of the Christian story and thus presumes a need for conversion to it. The basis is there to justify coercion, even if the story is, as Hauerwas believes, nonviolent. Thus Hauerwas responds to Todorov, "We recoil at this suggestion. If it is true, it seems we are simply silenced. Moreover, we fear its implications. For it seems to imply the very histories that we teach our children as Christians . . . continue to legitimate the coercive imposition of the Christian story."[22]

I would suggest that Hauerwas recoils because what he proposes is still, in effect, an old-style master narrative that claims universal allegiance. He still wishes to claim that all salvation resides in a unitary entity he calls "the church," which for Hauerwas consists of all those who place their lives within the narrative of Jesus rather than within any of the prevailing narratives of the social order. According to this theology, the church can and must control the narrative through which salvation is found. Yet he has found from John Howard Yoder that nonviolence is indispensable to this narrative. Because Todorov's principle means that he cannot impose his narrative without enacting the coercion that the narrative itself forbids, Hauerwas is stuck in a contradiction. The coercive imposition of one's own version of the truth upon others, even for their own good, *is* still a form of violence.

Hauerwas's broad solution is the conventional postmodern one: to tell the narrative of Jesus as a "witness,"[23] proclaiming it as truth even in the absence of commonly agreed upon, universal axioms on which to establish its truth objectively. However, Hauerwas's ideas about teaching strain against such a nonviolent model of witness. He writes, for example, that students "do not yet have minds worth making up" and "my first object is to help them think just like me." Even when a footnote adds that as students read and discuss they will

"learn to think not only like me, but different from me," the implied right to coerce students and to disregard their status as independent human beings can
hardly be reconciled with rigorous nonviolence.[24] His "apprentice" model of
education assumes that students do not bring anything worth knowing and must
thus follow the steps of a "master," who defines what they need to know.[25] This
account understates, in both ethical and practical terms, the importance of the
stories and selves that students bring to the classroom. (I think the apprentice
model is salvageable with a more generous account of students, which I will
outline below.)

After Christendom concludes with an appended letter by graduate student
David Toole, which draws these problems into sharper focus. Toole notes "how
the universalism inherent in Christianity slips all too easily into the domination
or the extermination of the other"[26] and rightly notices that Hauerwas barely addresses the questions he himself raises about the violence implicit in claims to
possession of ultimate truth. "I don't think you do your own questions justice,"
he argues and suggests that silence might well play a larger role: "Perhaps Christians should learn to shut up."[27]

Toole seems to have gained the impression from Hauerwas that the "witness"
he describes is "in the manner . . . of the Mennonites."[28] But Hauerwas shows little familiarity with the kind of educational communities that Mennonites have
evolved, at least not the way educational practices at Mennonite schools like
Bluffton College offer of responding to this crisis.

The solution to Hauerwas's dilemma, I believe, begins with reconceiving the
church versus world dichotomy for educational purposes. In a church-related liberal arts college setting we are not "resident aliens," to use his phrase for the
church in a hostile or indifferent world.[29] While the church formed by the narrative of Jesus is of course different from "the world" (as Hauerwas uses the term,
all that is not ordered under Jesus), that dichotomy by itself does not adequately
conceptualize education in a church-related, liberal arts college. Within the college community, the faculty and administration are by and large at home, in a
space whose organizing principles we determine and can change if we wish. We
have limited but quite real control over many of the conditions of our lives together and a good deal of control over our students as well. If anything, it is the
students who join us for a few years who are the "resident aliens" in this community. We invite them to join us, and in simplistic terms perhaps they represent
"the world." But as we spend time with students, we learn that they hardly consist of a uniform mass of the hapless unsaved who come to us needing simply to
be converted and indoctrinated.

At Bluffton College, for example, the world comes to us as cohorts of mostly
young human beings with a wide range of religious backgrounds and experience,
even though the majority is from rural and suburban Ohio. (I will leave aside their
other sorts of diversity for the purposes of this chapter.) Some are thoroughly
evangelical and some quite secular, some Catholic and some charismatic, some

quite mature and some vastly naïve, some pacifists but most of them not. Some have grown up in "the church" and cannot imagine ever leaving, but even they have very different notions and experiences of what the church is and should be. Some have very little exposure to anything Christian; some are in various states of doubt or rebellion. Most are, like the rest of us, on a journey whose end point remains in considerable suspense. All of them change—from year to year, but sometimes from day to day as well—as they experience the joys, challenges, and confusions of college life.

Those students bring *something* with them, every one. They come to us voluntarily; we need them if we are to continue, at least as much as they need us. Both practical and Christian considerations require that we treat them, at the very least, with careful attention and the awareness that they are more than undifferentiated, formless blobs awaiting our shaping. In practical terms, many will leave if they feel abused or unheard. Furthermore, we do not—at least we should not—*want* to mold them uniformly into our notion of what the church should be. We are not the church and they are not the world, in any kind of neat way. We both have some knowledge of the truth and something to contribute to our joint pursuit of the truth, and we all have much to learn. As faculty we assume, usually correctly, that our training provides us with knowledge and experience that students will benefit from learning through us. But even if his tongue is partly in cheek, to claim as Hauerwas does that "students do not yet have minds worth making up" is to commit the same sort of nonphysical violence—that of reducing the other to an inferior object—that he notes uncomfortably in the Spanish conquerors' attitude to the natives they conquered and converted.

We should indeed talk with students about our particular versions of the story of the human and natural worlds, their history, meaning, and purpose under the reign of God. We should do this not because we know we are right and they are wrong, or ignorant, or both, but because we believe our version has value that will enrich their lives whether they come to embrace it totally or not. We must also listen to their stories, with all the care and patience we can muster, both because they will teach us things and because without the chance to tell one's story no one can be truly ready to expand, complicate, and deepen it.

This approach is not easy, nor is it very efficient. It requires constant attention, considerable self-scrutiny, and endless negotiations and adjustments. But it is coherent and practicable. It avoids making absolute claims while not giving in either to mushy relativism or civil religion. It allows us to believe and to assert that ultimate truth is best revealed in the life and teaching of Jesus, that nonviolence is inextricable from the gospel, and that our version of that truth seems to us the best available. But it also allows and requires that we not presume that our version is somehow definitive or beyond critique and revision.

If what I suggest here is still one more "master narrative," we can work at making it a modest and self-aware one, one whose truth claims are firm but not absolute. At a key moment of William Stafford's memoir *Down in My Heart*, a group of World War II conscientious objectors wonder how they might prove they are not merely weak or foolish for refusing to fight:

> One of the men asked, "When people say we are cowardly or dumb, and so on, for not joining in the war, how can we prove that it isn't so?"
>
> "Do not attempt to do so," said Gerald Heard. "We are each of us fallible, cowardly, and dumb. We can say, as great men have said before, 'Yes, it is true, I am a frail vessel in which to transport the truth; but I cannot unsee what I see.'"[30]

This response suggests that there is a way between helpless quietism and belligerent missionizing, a way that is at once humble and assertive both in its strategies and in its claims. Such an approach goes hand in hand with careful attentiveness to others. Mary Rose O'Reilley asks: "What if we were to take seriously the possibility that our students have a rich and authoritative inner life, and tried to nourish it rather than to negate it?"[31] When the signs of that rich inner life seem scant, I remember myself as a first-year college student, shy and unconfident and full of contradictory, barely articulable impulses. As I struggled toward some kind of clarity about who I was and what I believed, I heard a lot of authoritative, confident voices in classrooms, but really I remember very little of what they said.

What I do remember, and what did change me, is the way that some of those people carried themselves. The ones who changed me most, whose voices I came to respect and trust, were not always certain of themselves, though they were often passionate about what they believed and even more passionate about the questions they asked. They often confessed their uncertainties and the gaps in their knowledge. They pressed to know what I thought, sometimes, and did not deride me as stupid or ignorant even when they pointed out the weak spots in my reasoning or the limits of my knowledge. They made me want to join in the search for truth with them, rather than making me feel that they were possessors of a truth that I could obtain only from them.

The world is full of people who are ready to tell others exactly how to act and to believe. The world is full of people who are ready to make the world as it should be, by any means necessary. Although we may sometimes admire these people, even support them at times, we need to be and do otherwise. We need to learn that while convictions are necessary and passion is essential, patience and what Stafford once called "a certain courtesy of the heart" are equally vital. We need to have faith in our students, in the materials we ask them to explore, and in the ways that God works in people's hearts and minds, slow, subterranean, and mysterious as those workings may be.

NOTES

1. D. H. Lawrence, *Studies in Classic American Literature* (New York: Penguin, 1991), 62.

2. See Richard Slotkin's trilogy: *Regeneration through Violence: The Mythology of the American Frontier 1600–1860* (Middletown, Conn.: Wesleyan University Press, 1973); *The Fatal Environment: The Myth of the Frontier in the Age of Industrialization 1800–1890* (New York: Atheneum, 1985); and *Gunfighter Nation: The Myth of the Frontier in Twentieth-Century America* (Norman: University of Oklahoma Press, 1998). See also Sam Keen, *Faces of the Enemy: Reflections of the Hostile Imagination* (San Francisco: Harper and Row, 1986); and David Grossman, *On Killing: The Psychological Cost of Learning to Kill in War and Society* (New York: Little, Brown, 1995).

3. Keen, *Faces of the Enemy,* 100.

4. Herman Melville, *Moby-Dick* (New York: Bantam, 1967), 175.

5. On the proclivity within the American psyche to believe that the last evil is upon us and can be eliminated with one last war, see William G. McLoughlin, *Revivals, Awakenings and Reform: An Essay on Religion and Social Change in America, 1607–1977* (Chicago: University of Chicago Press, 1978).

6. Melville, *Moby-Dick,* 496.

7. Keen, *Faces of the Enemy,* 100.

8. Melville, *Moby-Dick,* 535.

9. Slotkin, *Regeneration through Violence,* 100.

10. Will Harris, "Remembering Heaven's Face: An Interview with John Balaban," *War, Literature, and the Arts* 11, 2 (1999): 10.

11. Harris, "Remembering Heaven's Face," 10.

12. On selective conscientious objection as a justifiable war position with individuals rather than authorities making the judgment, see John Howard Yoder, *When War Is Unjust: Being Honest in Just-War Thinking,* 2d ed. (Maryknoll, N.Y.: Orbis Books, 1996), 47–49, 83; John Howard Yoder, "'Selective Objection': The Moral Responsibility to Refuse to Serve in an Unjust War: The Movement of 1968–75 and Its Prehistory" (1993) at www.nd.edu/~theo/jhy/writings/home/ind-jw.htm (accessed December 14, 2002).

13. Jeff Gundy, "Beyond Conformity and Rebellion: Opposition, Community, and Mennonite Education," *Conrad Grebel Review* 8, 1 (1990): 35–52.

14. See Paolo Freire, *Pedagogy of Hope* (New York: Continuum, 1994); and Paola Freire, *Pedagogy of the Oppressed* (New York: Continuum, 1970).

15. Parker Palmer, *To Know As We Are Known: A Spirituality of Education* (New York: Harper, 1984), 26.

16. Mary Rose O'Reilley, *The Peaceable Classroom* (Portsmouth, N.H.: Boynton/Cook, 1993), 34.

17. Stanley Hauerwas, *After Christendom: How the Church Is to Behave if Freedom, Justice, and a Christian Nation Are Bad Ideas* (Nashville: Abingdon, 1991), 16.

18. Hauerwas, *After Christendom,* 21.

19. Hauerwas, *After Christendom,* 22.

20. This volume obviously attempts that task, as does James C. Juhnke and Carol M. Hunter, *The Missing Peace: Nonviolent Alternatives in United States History* (Kitchner, Ont.: Pandora Press, 2001), which is a revisionist history of the United States written from a nonviolent perspective.

21. Hauerwas, *After Christendom,* 139.

22. Hauerwas, *After Christendom,* 140.

23. Hauerwas, *After Christendom,* 148–152.

24. Hauerwas, *After Christendom,* 98, 180n8.

25. Hauerwas, *After Christendom,* 101–111.

26. Hauerwas, *After Christendom*, 154.

27. Hauerwas, *After Christendom,* 159.

28. Hauerwas, *After Christendom*, 158.

29. Stanley Hauerwas and William H. Willimon, *Resident Aliens: Life in the Christian Colony* (Nashville: Abingdon, 1989).

30. William Stafford, *Down in My Heart* (Swarthmore, Pa.: Bench Press, 1985), 45.

31. O'Reilley, *Peaceable Classroom,* 102.

11

Violence and Supernatural Justice in Gothic Literature

Cynthia L. Bandish

With plots distanced from everyday occurrences, Gothic novels often ask the reader to enter a world of unexpected happenings where fear and terror are the norm and violence and destruction repeatedly threaten the characters. Typically, the characters become victims of abusive authority: young women are imprisoned by tyrannical guardians seeking their property or personhood, men are separated from their beloveds or their possessions, with both facing persecution in a supernaturally charged world where ghostly figures appear to walk among the living. These precursors of the modern horror novel and ghost story allowed readers in late-eighteenth-century Britain to experience both mystery and terror. As such, they also provide an opportunity for contemporary critics to examine historical attitudes toward violence and sources of violence and to explore the theological implications of the violent supernatural worlds described in Gothic plots. Because the Gothic and numerous spin-off variations continue to be viable and popular genres in the twenty-first century of both novels and films, the messages of these early novels are important antecedents of our acceptance of violence as a condition of life and as a preferred response to injustice. But for those with the eyes to see, the violent paradigm of the Gothic novel also reveals the futility of the violence it portrays and thus points to the possibility of another answer.

As a subgenre of Romanticism (the European intellectual and artistic movement of 1750–1850), Gothic literature shares an interest in both the emotional and the psychological life of the individual, which privilege the world of imagination. However, Romanticism enables an individual to experience spirituality and extraordinary states of consciousness by turning inward, while the Gothic externalizes the intangible spiritual world. Because Gothic texts have a certain power to produce affective responses in captivated readers, literary critics have often used psychological models to explain the attraction of Gothic plots. However, by its invocation of the supernatural, Gothic literature situates the reader in

137

a theological as well as a psychological universe. While psychological interpretations of the Gothic are numerous, theological ones are scarce. Those critics who have favored theological interpretations have investigated the supernatural as the manifestation of a spiritual world but have not raised moral or theological questions per se about the violent world portrayed.

Both S. L. Varnado and Robert F. Geary examine the role of the numinous and its implications for the genre. Drawing on Rudolf Otto's *The Idea of the Holy*, Varnado suggests that the Gothic as a genre might be defined by its efforts to recreate the nonrational feeling of religious mystery.[1] For instance, feelings of dread, terror, and awe are inspired by the incomprehensible in the Gothic. In Geary's effort to explain the role of the supernatural in the Gothic, he theorizes that the numinous remains, but the "supernatural became disengaged from the earlier providential context."[2] Instead of Providence protecting the innocent, divine wrath scourges the guilty.

Among the historical-religious studies of the Gothic, Joel Porte's contribution "In the Hands of an Angry God: Religious Terror in Gothic Fiction" elucidates how Protestant theology, especially of a Calvinistic strain, shapes the Gothic universe. Calvinism provides a foundational paradigm in which people are doomed and God metes out deserved punishment.[3] In other early Gothic stories, this theological disposition and language are played out in Catholic settings. These writings often highlight the abuses of institutional power, the ineffectiveness of religious leaders, or the superstitious nature of the lower classes. Mark Canuel interprets the Gothic's negative portrayal of Catholicism as a reaction against a hierarchical rule that expects strict conformity and consensus.[4] As the protagonists of the Gothic move through these theological universes, they are, at times, persecuted by demonic forces from the spiritual realm or victimized by human antagonists among the ruins of a fallen world, or both. Anne McWhir suggests that the common basis between the supernatural and the rational, earthbound Gothic plots is fear, which accommodates the translation of demonic plots into human ones.[5] These analyses, however, address the violence of the villains but rarely question the victims' responses to violence as a theological problem concerning God and the spiritual realm. And from the nonviolent perspective assumed by this book, the presence of both earthly and supernatural violence in Gothic narratives is quite clearly a problem that ought to concern literary criticism.

From the standpoint of this commitment to nonviolence, then, I want to sketch the contours of the supernatural, theological world that is so central to the canon of Gothic literature. I use three texts from the early British Gothic to set up these parameters: *The Castle of Otranto* (1764), *The Mysteries of Udolpho* (1794), and *Frankenstein* (1818). An examination of *The Castle of Otranto* sets the stage by depicting a standard violent theological paradigm. Analysis of *The Mysteries of Udolpho* and of *Frankenstein* will then reveal some of the theological implications of the violent world of Gothic literature. Not only does the use of violence in the novels change but its theological foundation shifts to accommodate these changes. This theological foundation, which portrays God as condoning violence for a just cause, is so central to orthodox Christianity that writers can only escape it by removing God from the supernatural universe. The choice between condoning violence and removing God becomes evident when one examines this literature from a nonviolent perspective.

In *The Castle of Otranto*, Horace Walpole tells the story of how Manfred, the current owner of the castle, attempts to ensure the continuation of his family line and their illegally gained estate. Manfred possesses the estate through treachery committed by his grandfather Ricardo. Manfred's initial crime is the knowledge that his grandfather had poisoned Alfonso and used a fictitious will to gain Otranto, but Manfred soon adds to that guilty knowledge through his own efforts to keep the castle. Having received the estate through violence, he acts to retain Otranto through more violence. After the sudden death of his son, Manfred decides to divorce his wife and marry Isabella, his son's fiancée, in order to continue his line and thus produce an heir to Otranto. He casts off his wife, repeatedly threatens and bullies the clergy, and attempts to imprison Isabella until they can be wed. Thus in Wapole's version of Gothic, the story is about the roles that inheritance and property, including women, play in aristocratic life. Interpretations of the novel often focus on Manfred's obsession with begetting an heir, the criminal means he uses to maintain his authority, and his mistreatment of the women who are under his power. Manfred, not incidentally, becomes the paradigm for a long line of tyrants in Gothic fiction.

With this background in mind, it is instructive to see how Walpole constructs a solution to the abuses perpetrated by Manfred. Manfred cannot be forced by human means to relinquish his claim on the castle. He appears ready to defend his claim against all objections, but in the end, a number of supernatural occurrences convince him to relinquish his estate and repent his criminal actions. In both the first preface and the text of the story, Walpole establishes a theological context for understanding the actions of Manfred. Masquerading as the translator of the tale, Walpole assigns authorship to a Catholic priest around the time of the first crusade. He thus can identify the text as propaganda created to bolster the authority of the priests over their congregations, while simultaneously claiming that he offers the text to his British readers only on the basis of its value as entertainment and its examples of piety and virtue. He then suggests that the moral of the story is "that *the sins of fathers are visited on their children to the third and fourth generation.*"[6] With these two maneuvers, Walpole displays the common anti-Catholic sentiment of his time while offering the reader a theology in which God's primary function is to administer violent divine justice.

At the opening of the novel, Manfred's son Conrad is crushed by a gigantic helmet, and a similar, though smaller, helmet has disappeared from the statue of Alfonso in the church. With these events, the characters are situated in a violent and terrifying supernatural world that defies other explanations. Without this opening event, other occurrences in the novel might be ascribed to the wild imagination of the servants or the guilty conscience of Manfred—simple projections of emotional states. The appearance of the giant helmet, however, makes clear their supernatural origin. Both Manfred and his credulous servants initially interpret the ghostly, supernatural manifestations as the work of devils.[7] But as the story progresses, both the readers and characters come to see the supernatural not as the work of evil but as an agent of divine justice that killed the son Conrad in order to prevent Manfred's authority from continuing.[8] Father Jerome, the priest from the church of St. Nicholas, interprets the death of Conrad as an instance of heaven preventing the union of Manfred's line with that of Isabella; he even goes so far as to say that heaven "mocks" Manfred's desire for an heir.[9]

What is important about these interpretations and perceptions is that God's actions are indistinguishable from the devil's, a fact Manfred repeatedly acknowledges in his declarations that neither "Heaven nor hell" can stop him[10] and is also implicit in the initial thought of Manfred and the servants that it was the work of devils. Both God and Satan rely on intimidation, violence, and persecution. But in terms of the story line, the violence of vengeance, from whatever source, does not truly resolve an unjust situation; rather violence prolongs injustice and continues a cycle of violence and retribution.

As the prince of Otranto, Manfred plays the role of an almighty deity, a supreme authority. He is free to impose his will on his family and his subjects, he expects immediate and total obedience, and he punishes those who do not comply. Are Manfred and Otranto a microcosm for God's control of the universe or are they an example of a perversion of divine authority? Or more important, is violence intrinsically evil, or does the basis of authority determine the validity of violence? Is God's violence good?

If we examine how the role of divinely sanctioned violence leads to the reestablishment of the hereditary line in *The Castle of Otranto,* the plot would appear to function as an example of what Walter Wink has called "the myth of redemptive violence,"[11] namely the belief that violence is the ultimate arbiter of justice. The characterization of God as One who requires retribution replicates the image of God in standard atonement theology as described in chapter 3 of this volume. There is also the fact that justice was supposedly accomplished and order restored through the supernatural killing of the innocent son Conrad, which also parallels how justice is accomplished and the divine order restored in standard atonement imagery, as Weaver explained. The incongruity of these sequences seems clear when we observe that order and justice are reestablished by the killing of Manfred's son and heir, thus avenging the murder of Alfonso, which is also precisely the means by which grandfather Ricardo had illicitly acquired the estate from Alfonso, namely by killing him.

Along the path to establishing this order through supernatural violence, the reader encounters a variety of religious positions that accept or accommodate the vengeful god of the novel. Manfred's wife, Hippolita, believes that if she sacrifices her happiness and marriage, she might prevent Providence from ruining the principality of Otranto.[12] This stance seems to reflect the passive role of women vis-à-vis unjust suffering that chapter 3 in this volume says is modeled by satisfaction atonement and that modern feminist and womanist theologians have found so objectionable.[13] Hippolita further claims that women cannot "make election" for themselves, but heaven, husbands, and fathers must do so.[14] Father Jerome who claims that his "office is to promote peace" is guilty of lying to Manfred and inciting Manfred to turn his anger toward the innocent peasant Theodore. When Theodore's noble parentage and connection to Alfonso is finally revealed, Father Jerome explains that Theodore should be filled with "sensations of sacred vengeance."[15] The official orthodoxy of the novel insists on a violent god through whom justice is accomplished. But this supposed justice is really the continuation of a series of violent acts, each in response to and in vengeance of the prior one.

Although God does not directly appear, the spirit of Alfonso the Good, the rightful owner, finally forces Manfred to relinquish his illegal inheritance. Walpole gives us a story of revenge in which the wronged party, Alfonso, inhabits an afterlife where he has gained not peace and satisfaction but a superior capacity to exact revenge and inflict punishment, all with the blessing of St. Nicholas. As prophesied, the spirit of Alfonso grows too big for the castle and bursts through the walls, turning the castle into a pile of rubble. After a final proclamation about the legitimate heir of the property, he ascends into heaven. In setting up this resurrection scene, Walpole demonstrates that the path to heaven is also one of justice accomplished through violence. Alfonso's resurrection can only be completed after he has violently avenged his own death. But this resurrection to justice is merely the final act of supernatural violence. From a nonviolent perspective, the futility of violence—whether human or supernatural—to bring justice leaps from Walpole's story. Commentator Geary claims that by the end of the novel, "The supernatural . . . lose[s] its moral aspects as it manifests itself not as providential protection of innocence but as pure, numinous wrath."[16] Geary's observation does not challenge the idea itself of whether violent vengeance is the appropriate response to injustice, but his observation does suggest that we are left to choose either the conception of an immoral, avenging God or simply religious terror without a God to believe in.

The Castle of Otranto tests what the reader is willing to believe—not just through its incorporation of the supernatural but in its conception of how justice is accomplished. By identifying ultimate justice with supernatural violence and destruction, the story demands that the readers accept or reject a violent God who destroys in order to make things right.

One response to a problematic image of God is to reject the idea of God altogether. That is in fact one possible outcome of the standard discussion of theodicy, namely to deny the existence of God because the existence of evil proves that an omnipotent and good God cannot be in charge of the universe. A similar answer appears in some Gothic novels. While some Gothic novels repeat the paradigm initiated by Walpole, as the Gothic genre developed, other stories of violence emerge that transform God into an unseen partner or even a nonparticipant in the plane of human existence. In *The Mysteries of Udolpho*, Ann Radcliffe reconstructs the supernatural as imagined terrors created by the emotional and superstitious natures of the characters and as the sublime landscape of God's power. The heroine, Emily, often recognizes God's existence when she views nature: "From the consideration of His works, her mind arose to the adoration of the Deity, in His goodness and power; wherever she turned her view, whether on the sleeping earth, or to the vast regions of space, glowing with worlds beyond the reach of human thought, the sublimity of God, and the majesty of His presence appeared."[17] And while both Emily and her father, St. Albert, believe that God fills a providential role, God does not appear to intercede on behalf of justice. It is only through the happy reconciliation of Emily and her fiancé, Valancourt, and the reacquisition of her inheritance that the narrator suggests "that innocence, though oppressed by injustice, shall, supported by patience, finally triumph over misfortune!"[18] Violence is relegated to the human plane, where greed and lust motivate villains to commit fraud, kidnapping, and murder. It is important to note how Radcliffe chooses to deal with violence as a potentially corrupting force, so that violence is only part of the villains' demands, not part of the heroine's requests for justice nor part of God's control of the universe.[19] But it is also the case that Radcliffe's God is not an active, interventionist God. In this case, justice prevails without a real advocate other than the protagonists themselves.

By the time we get to *Frankenstein* in the early-nineteenth-century, the relationship between an offended God and the sinner Manfred has become the relationship between the doctor, Victor Frankenstein, and the creature that he created in his laboratory.[20] In moving the reader out of the supernatural realm and into science fiction, Mary Shelley nonetheless retains the psychological dimensions of Walpole's construction of the divine/human relationship rooted in the inherited theology of divine retribution as the basis for restoring order. Interpretations of this relationship in Frankenstein vary widely. Readings have focused on literary influences on Shelley, such as *Paradise Lost*, the myth of Prometheus, the writings of Shelley's parents, and the work of the Romantic writers. Psychoanalytical readings of the text have interrogated the work as Shelley's responses to her liaison with Percy Bysshe Shelley, her pregnancy and miscarriage, and her postpartum depression as well as analyzing the motives and developmental stages of the characters in *Frankenstein*. But beyond those discussions, of interest for this chapter is the question of how the violent relationship between Victor Frankenstein and his creature intersects with the violent theology captured in *The Castle of Otranto*. In the primary relationship, that of Frankenstein and his creature, as well as in the several characters' interaction with the legal system, violence in terms of retribution is the cornerstone of human justice. Shelley repeatedly critiques this justice system in the novel. She demonstrates how the system fails to protect an innocent Justine from execution for a murder committed by the creature and how it later falsely incarcerates Frankenstein for the murder of his friend Henry. But when Frankenstein seeks justice on his own, his actions also reflect the assumption of retribution, as he engages in a series of retaliatory exchanges with the creature, hunting him down in order to kill him. Is Frankenstein's desire to kill the monster justified by the fact that the monster is an unnatural creation and potentially without a soul? While Shelley's characterization of the monster has made this a difficult question to answer, the prevailing legacy of the text has been to overlook this question and simply to sanction violence against the alien. Violence is validated and justified if one accepts the paradigm represented in *The Castle of Otranto*. If we look at the story of Frankenstein as a parallel to God's creation of life, then we see a godlike figure who retains the right to reject and kill. If this is the image of God, what does it mean to aspire to be godlike? Here, being godlike is equated with power and particularly the power to kill.

Reading these texts from a nonviolent perspective makes the reader acutely aware of the propensity of Gothic novels to see violence as the way to solve problems and to enact justice. Though not the only solution offered, justice through violence is the one that predominates in the Gothic texts. And even though other types of stories, adventure tales, stories of political intrigue, and stories of crime and vigilante vengeance repeat the same solution—fighting violence with violence—they typically do not situate the reader at the intersection of the spiritual and material worlds. It is the Gothic realm that crystallizes how a theology wedded to violence sanctions violence as an answer and thus perpetuates a cycle of violence from which the popular imagination has yet to escape. As we have seen, however, Gothic violence is also deeply problematic even in the plots of writers who depict violence as a divine solution to injustice.

Becoming aware of the way that Gothic writers inscribe violence in the worlds of their stories can make us aware of the violence and the violent assumptions in the world around us—and more important, show us that violence and violent assumptions in literature and life are not inevitable but chosen. And that insight is the first step toward choosing an alternative to violence in the stories we tell and the lives we lead.

NOTES

1. S. L. Varnado, "The Idea of the Numinous in Gothic Literature," in *The Gothic Imagination: Essays in Dark Romanticism,* ed. G. R. Thompson (Pullman: Washington State University Press, 1974), 11–21.

2. Robert Geary, "From Providence to Terror," in *The Fantastic in World Literature and the Arts,* ed. Donald E. Morse (New York: Greenwood Press, 1987), 11.

3. Joel Porte, "In the Hands of an Angry God: Religious Terror in Gothic Fiction," in *The Gothic Imagination*, ed. G. R. Thompson (Pullman: Washington State University Press, 1974), 22–44.

4. See Mark Canuel, "Religion and Nationalism in the Gothic," *Studies in Romanticism* 34.4 (1995): 507–530.

5. Anne McWhir, "The Gothic Transgression of Disbelief: Walpole, Radcliffe and Lewis," in *Gothic Fictions: Prohibition/Transgression,* ed. Kenneth W. Graham (New York: AMS Press, 1989), 34.

6. Horace Walpole, *The Castle of Otranto: A Gothic Story*, ed. W. S. Lewis (Oxford: Oxford University Press, 1996), 7.

7. Walpole, *The Castle of Otranto*, 26, 34.

8. Geary and Ehlers also trace the pattern of Providential supernatural in the novel, which Geary argues is often contradictory. See Leigh A. Ehlers, "The Gothic World As Stage: Providence and Character in *The Castle of Otranto: A Gothic Story*," *Wascana Review* 14.2 (1979): 17–30.

9. Walpole, *The Castle of Otranto*, 49.

10. Walpole, *The Castle of Otranto*, 26.

11. See Walter Wink, *Engaging the Powers: Discernment and Resistance in a World of Domination* (Minneapolis: Fortress Press, 1992), 13–25.

12. Walpole, *The Castle of Otranto*, 90.

13. Among many examples, see Rita Nakashima Brock, *Journeys by Heart: A Christology of Erotic Power* (New York: Crossroad, 1988), esp. ch. 3; and Delores Williams, *Sisters in the Wilderness: The Challenge of Womanist God-Talk* (Maryknoll, N.Y.: Orbis Books, 1993).

14. Walpole, *The Castle of Otranto*, 91.

15. Walpole, *The Castle of Otranto*, 94.

16. Geary, "From Providence," 15.

17. Ann Radcliffe, *The Mysteries of Udolpho*, ed. Bonamy Dobrée (Oxford: Oxford University Press, 1980), 47–48.

18. Radcliffe, *The Mysteries of Udolpho*, 672.

19. This observation is part of a larger research project on the role of nonviolent resistance in the major Gothic novels of the 1790s.

20. Mary Shelley, *Frankenstein,* ed. Johann M. Smith (Boston: Bedford Books, 1992).

V

NONVIOLENCE AND THE ARTS

12

The Very Picture of Peace

Gregg J Luginbuhl

If one were to draw a picture of peace, what would it look like? Apart from the hackneyed dove, the quickly interpreted but overused peace sign, and the child-like butterfly or rainbow, what images convey the condition that peacemakers profess to seek? How might works of art depict or promote peace? Is there subject matter, shapes and colors, or abstract forms that represent the condition of peace? Historically, which artists are effective spokespersons for peace? Which key works form definitive statements for peace?

As an artist, I seek to infuse my own work with passion for issues that I care deeply about. I build around perspectives that are my own, vantages that have been attained through study, thought, and years of unique life experience. My perspective includes a paradigm of peace church theology nurtured and shaped through membership in a Mennonite congregation and through twenty years of teaching at a Mennonite college. So it seems that I should have quick answers to all of the questions posed above. But I confess that I do not have easy answers and certainly not definitive ones.

Reflecting on the history of Western art, it is easy to assume that antiwar statements, of which there are many, are statements of peace. Many works effectively depict the savagery of war: all manner of atrocity perpetrated on helpless citizenry and the senseless destruction of life, property, and culture. The prints and paintings of Francisco Goya (1746–1829), Picasso's *Guernica* (1937), and the drawings of George Grosz (1893–1959) and Otto Dix (1891–1969) leap to mind in this regard. But while antiwar statements are reactions against a condition, a barbaric one at that, they do not advocate for peace, except through inference. If there were no war, then there would be peace. But what would peace look like? What exactly is being advocated in even the most effectual antiwar statements?

None of these questions deny the eloquence, efficacy, or deterrent value of the artistic antiwar statement. A look at art produced by former faculty at our own

Mennonite college reveals the existence of many passionate and poignant works that speak against war.

John P. Klassen's career on the Bluffton College faculty spanned thirty-six years from 1924 to 1959. Much of the body of work he produced in those years comprises remembrances of his youth in the Ukraine. A large part of this work centered on the persecution of Mennonite people who had become successful farmers in that area, originally settling there at the invitation of Catherine the Great. A small sketch titled *Pleading Man and Soldier* (figure 12.1) displays the plight of these people of peace trapped in the politics of a conflict that was not of their own making. A bronze plaque (figure 12.2) documents the effects of war on society and culture as a mother pleads for food for her starving child. Klassen's powerful bronze sculpture *Modern Madonna* (figure 12.3), done soon after World War II, features a mother and child in a familiar maternal pose but incongruously

Figure 1. *Pleading Man and Soldier* by John P. Klassen. Colored pencil, c. 1930–1940, 7¼ inches × 4 inches. Photograph by Jon Stealey.

Figure 2. *Hardships* by John P. Klassen. Bronze, c. 1940–1950, 15½ inches × 16¾ inches. **Photograph by Jon Stealey.**

wearing gas masks. It is full of expressive irony and seems hauntingly relevant today in the climate of threatened biological terrorism and mass vaccination.

Darvin Luginbuhl, my father, a graduate of Bluffton College (1946) and an art faculty member there from 1959 to 1984, participated in Civilian Public Service and the United States Army medical corps as a Mennonite conscientious objector during World War II. Originally concentrating his efforts on the medium of photography, Luginbuhl eventually found ceramics, particularly ceramic sculpture, as the most responsive medium for the expressive work of his mature style. Many of these works decry war, and the majority of them rail against its destructive effects. His *Torso of a General* (figure 12.4) points to attitudes of pride and greed that make war possible, or perhaps inevitable. *In Memoriam* (figure 12.5), at once a rocketlike war machine and commemorative marker, documents the loss of life and creative potential in a stack of names and symbols incorporated as actual molded impressions from the gravestones of former soldiers. Later, his *Contemplating Catastrophe* (figure 12.6), which depicts an individual contemplating alone in a decimated landscape, points to the potential for total destruction of humankind through war in the atomic age.

Figure 3. *Modern Madonna* by John P. Klassen. Bronze, c. 1939, 17½ inches × 6 inches × 7 inches deep. Photograph by Jon Stealey.

Figure 4.   *Torso of a General* by Darvin Luginbuhl. Polychrome ceramic, c. 1964–1965, 22 inches × 14½ inches × 10 deep. Photograph by Jon Stealey.

Figure 5. *In Memoriam* by Darvin Luginbuhl. Ceramic, c. 1972–1974, 32½ inches × 14 inches × 11 inches deep. Photograph by Jon Stealey.

Figure 6.   *Contemplating Catastrophe* by Darvin Luginbuhl. Ceramic, c. 1976–1979, 20 inches × 17 inches × 12 inches deep. Photograph by Jon Stealey.

These works are sensitive, eloquent, poignant, and prophetic antiwar statements. But returning to our opening quandary, what does a picture of peace look like? Can the condition of peace be visually described only by denouncing war? Edward Hicks's *Peaceable Kingdom* (figure 12.7) c. 1834, shows an Edenic American landscape populated by docile and declawed beasts mingling amiably with cherubs and lambs, symbols of the meek and powerless. Far in the background, men in Continental dress negotiate with Native Americans over a trunk of beads and furs. Hicks's wide-eyed animals, an inventory of floating flat profiles on the right side of the composition, seem stunned or drugged. Their languid stupor is symbolic, but not convincing, as an image of self-denial or as a picture of peace suddenly visited upon savage temperaments. It is as though a twelve-step meeting for violent offenders of the animal kingdom is in progress, each participant seeking to repress instinct and elevate consciousness of a violent past as participants in the food chain. The encounter between the settlers and the natives is an equally uninspiring vision of the type of justice that forms the basis of a last-

Figure 7. *Peaceable Kingdom* by Edward Hicks. Oil on canvas, c. 1834, 29⅜ inches × 35½ inches. National Gallery of Art, Washington, D.C. Gift of Edgar William and Bernice Chrysler Garbisch. Photograph copyright © 2002 Board of Trustees, National Gallery of Art, Washington, D.C. Reproduced by permission.

ing peace. Even though I judge this work harshly in the contemporary context, Hicks must be lauded for his many works involving this theme. They are among the few major works of Western art that argue for the idea of peace, however disconnected the images might be from a reality to which one might ascribe today.

Is it possible that the most believable and convincing visions of peace are compositions which feature common acts of daily living, real human relationships, landscapes with and without human presence, domestic interiors, and still life arrangements? Living in a condition of peace, we are open to people around us, we have time to contemplate the gifts of creation that are readily available to us. We can celebrate beauty, take time to admire nature in all of its many forms, and have the freedom to be honest and just in our depictions of human interaction. We can incite pleasure, delight the eye, or inspire the aesthetic, intellectual, and moral sense. In short, we can engage in the visual dialogue that is the true province of the discipline of visual art.

Impressionism, dominant in France at the end of the nineteenth century, has never been advanced as a peace movement, but the subjects and compositions of these artists, taken as a whole, might be seen as a powerful vision of the condition of peace. Renoir's paintings of women and children, and of people joyfully interacting, represent positive human relationships and love itself on a number of levels. Monet depicts children romping in long grass, sensuous flowers, and landscapes which feature sensitive readings of the quality of light in different seasons and at various times of the day. Degas focuses on the beauty of the ballet in oil pastel drawings, paintings, and sculpture. Taken as a whole, the works of the Impressionists focus on the beauty of nature and the joy of human interaction. Where might we find a more convincing image of peace?

The still life composition emerged as conventional subject matter for painting in the seventeenth century. Artists in Holland and Spain developed this form contemporaneously, creating studies that fascinated viewers during the artists' lifetimes and for centuries to come. A collection of objects from the everyday environment, a still life might include dishes, flowers, fruit, vegetables, other foods, or a variety of diverse materials and objects gathered by the artist and set up for study. These objects are selected and arranged because of their fascinating colors, shapes, or textures; because of the harmonious relationships of these elements; or to exploit the interesting contrasts which are inherent in their relationships. A Francisco de Zurbarán still life, *Still Life with Lemons, Oranges and a Rose*, c. 1633 (figure 12.8), depicts objects selected for their textural contrast. A white-glazed ceramic cup contrasts with the reflective silver plate that it rests on. A basket adds another textural dimension. The viewer is even sensitized to distinguish between the textures of two similar citrus fruits: an orange and a lemon. This critical exercise of perception heightens the sensitivity of both the artist and viewer. It celebrates the beauty of often overlooked details in our everyday lives.

Taking the time to look this closely, to call attention to the subtle beauty that is apparent in common existence, is the privilege of people living under the condition

Figure 8. *Still Life with Lemons, Oranges and a Rose* by Francisco de Zurbarán. Oil on canvas, c. 1633, 24½ inches × 44⅛ inches. Norton Simon Museum, Pasadena, California. Copyright © the Norton Simon Foundation. Reproduced by permission.

of peace. Artists and their potential patrons living in war-torn countries may not have enough time or positive energy to engage in these simple acts of study and enjoyment. The landscape, the still life, the depictions of everyday human interaction are quickly consumed in the black cloud of war. There is rarely the will, the open frame of mind, or the sense of purpose that permits the cultivation of this heightened visual awareness, an act that might be seen as an affirmation of God's creation.

Healthy creative inquiry and free visual dialogue are the privilege of artists who live in peaceful settings. They are free to explore a variety of themes that reflect the positive interrelationships of people, the relationship of mankind and nature, and mankind's relationship with God. My own *Creation Series,* eight ceramic plates with modeled imagery based on the creation story of Genesis 1, reflects on the creation of the universe in which we dwell, but also on imitative creative acts of humankind and on the importance of these creative acts. Plate VII in the series (figure 12.9) was created in response to verse 20, "Let the earth bring forth living creatures of every kind." It began with an inventory of modeled animals but evolved into a visual fable titled *The Peaceable Kingdom.* The imagery shows the ape, most intelligent of the animals, making a strong and complex statement to the zebra, who can only see the issue in "black and white." The bird, a member of the parrot family, screeches a radical point of view while the lizard endures the tension, gripping the earth. These temperaments, like the conflicting temperaments of people, must coexist in delicate balance.

One might also argue that the quest to make a utilitarian object as useful and beautiful as possible is an individual craftsman's peace statement. A potter takes time to create a pleasing form by working a series of shapes until the dynamics and gesture of the object seem graceful and guileless to both the craftsman and

Figure 9. *The Peaceable Kingdom* (Plate VII from *The Creation Series*) by Gregg Luginbuhl. Ceramic, 1990, 24 inches × 20 inches × 7 inches deep. Yoder Recital Hall, Bluffton College, Bluffton, Ohio. Photograph by Jon Stealey.

patron and in so doing creates a vision of harmony and peace. This nonpolemic effort to insert an essential quality of humanness into the design of a utilitarian vessel is a humble statement but perhaps one of the most effective peace statements that might be made in this medium.

So the "picture of peace" is a very subtle image. It is untroubled, unobtrusive, noiseless, and nonpolemic. It reflects the freedom of friendly relations between people. It is marked by the absence of worry, open conflict, or fear. It is honest in its expression of content and devoid of artifice as subject matter is transformed, or as nonobjective form is realized, through a chosen medium. It shows invention and integrity in the handling of materials. It is emblematic of artists in pursuit of keen insight through critical perception, innovative creative thought, and the highest standards of craftsmanship. It is just as quiet, satisfying, elusive, and desirable as the condition of peace in human society.

13

Nonviolence in Actor Training

Melissa Friesen

Exposed to challenging play worlds in the acting classroom, some familiar and comfortable and some not, students discover that their own worlds are expanding. Since actors engage the world with their entire being—voice, body, mind, emotions, and spirit—an acting classroom inevitably involves risk taking and choice making. Thus the acting teacher must embrace both the responsibility and the opportunity for a safe but stimulating environment for students learning about the craft of acting and their own off-stage life performances.

These risks and choices also pose the potential for violation and abuse. As a theater practitioner and educator who embraces a nonviolent perspective, I am disturbed by the proliferation of both violent metaphors and violent practices in the contemporary acting classroom. This chapter analyzes the presence of violence in the training of actors, with particular focus on the American Method, arguably the most influential training system for actors in the United States. Based on this analysis, suggestions for a nonviolence-based acting pedagogy are given at the conclusion of the chapter.

The focus below on violent Method-based practices is not a blanket condemnation of the entire Method approach. Indeed, the self-interrogation called for by many Method practitioners can enrich our understanding of the world and inspire us to work for positive change. Nor does this chapter's focus on the Method imply that other acting systems are free of violence. They are not, and all pedagogical approaches should be interrogated for their potentially violent qualities.

THE ACTOR'S SELF IN STANISLAVSKY'S
SYSTEM AND THE AMERICAN METHOD

Much late-twentieth-century acting theory, influenced heavily by psychoanalysis, assumes the key to training actors lies in the interior life of the individual. According to this view, intense investigations of the self—one's emotions, fears, desires—mine the raw material out of which theatrical characters can be shaped. In the United States, the most influential training system for actors is the Method, an approach based on Constantin Stanislavsky's system for actor training and modified by American practitioners. Understanding how the actor's self is related to her role in these theories enables us to see how such pedagogical strategies may violate the delicate boundaries protecting the actor's self.

One of Stanislavsky's key principles is the strong correspondence between character and actor. Like "real" people, characters are psychologically complex. Actors are encouraged to embody their roles: "To play truly means to be right, logical, coherent, to think, strive, feel and act in unison with your role . . . we call that living the part. . . . You must live it by actually experiencing feelings that are analogous to it, each and every time you repeat the process of creating it."[1] This approach assumes that actors can indeed align themselves with their role and that there is something universal and recognizable within each character that an actor can access. Once actors have discovered these commonalities, they create their characters from the inside out. Actors create rich inner lives for their characters, while striving to remain open and receptive to the real and play worlds around them.

Stanislavsky utilized a wide array of exercises to help actors perfect their craft. Sharon Marie Carnicke breaks them into two general categories: exercises for the actor's "sense of self" and techniques for creating characters.[2] This chapter focuses on how the first category—the actor's sense of self—is treated in the Method. Since the actor uses herself to create the character, it seemed logical to Stanislavsky that the actor expand her own abilities in order to present a fully developed character. Actors expand their powers of observation by paying conscious attention to sensory experience in rehearsal and in daily life. Stanislavsky encourages actors to develop "emotional memory," working to recall with precision the sights, sounds, smells, tastes, and sensations of past experiences that generated an emotional response. Colin Counsell describes the desired effects of emotional memory as "calling up 'moods' and 'emotions' that can find a physical expression in the performance, while at the same time building a network of images and associations that actors can focus upon during performance, an internal 'reality' to hold them within the 'limits' of the drama."[3] Thus, the actor not only expands her capacity to recall emotions and express them physically but also uses these personal memories to inform her character.

The form of Stanislavsky's early ideas that took root in the United States during the 1920s and 1930s highlighted the actor's work on himself and the creation of a role through internal means. While American practitioners differed regarding specific exercises and the relative importance of various concepts for actors, they agreed on several general principles. Most relevant to our discussion are the conflation of actor and character, already suggested in Stanislavsky's early work. "Truthfulness" for Method actors involves matching the actor's internal emotional state to that of the character. Indeed, all aspects of the character's life and experiences, or as many as possible, are matched to the actor's personal and imagined experiences: "the actor personalizes the role, i.e. draws from the self, from his or her emotional, psychological or imaginative reality, bringing into view aspects of one's memories, life experiences and observations that correlate with the role."[4]

If, as Method teachers assert, the actors' own experiences, emotions, and imaginations form the "truth" of the characters they create, then one of the primary tasks of actor training is accessing and deepening these inner resources. Analysis of the rhetoric of Method teachers writing about their work and their classroom protocol reveals a belief in the imprisoning effects of culture. By simply existing in civilized society, human beings accumulate layers of restrictions regarding appropriate behavior that gag or label as immoral our "true" feelings and inhibit the actor's "true" expression of emotion. Method master Lee Strasberg asserts that the "strong conditioning" of social convention cripples human beings' abilities to express emotion, and Strasberg's task becomes "freeing the expression of the actor."[5]

METHOD POWER DYNAMICS

Although Method practitioners bemoan the stifling effects of polite society and attempt to unmask repressed emotion, existing societal power structures, such as male dominance, are left largely unchallenged. Descriptions of Method classrooms and workshops indicate a disturbingly violent quality—actors are "forced" to break through their emotional barriers, often at the hands of their acting teachers. Strasberg provides a representative example. In his "private moment" exercises, students develop concentration and attempt to eliminate inhibitions by performing an activity normally done in private. Strasberg describes his work with an actor with a monotonous vocal pattern. After she revealed her habit of dancing wildly to music at home, he instructed her to dance in front of the class, and the expressiveness of her performance was amazing. "We made her do it, and it worked and from that moment on her voice and action changed. We got through some kind of block by making use of the Private Moment."[6]

Strasberg, of course, highlights the effectiveness of his technique and the long-term results of this breakthrough. It is striking to note, however, his phrase "we made her do it." The Private Moment exercise was imposed on the actor, forcing her to work through her block. While we are not privileged with the actor's perspective in this example, the strategy of force suggested by Strasberg's language and process hints at the power imbalance circulating in the acting classroom. Strasberg, the famous male teacher, clearly dominated the classroom, requiring whichever exercises he deemed appropriate to free his students from their blocks. This approach measures "appropriateness" by its results—the ends justify the means. Since the actor is liberated from her internal blocks, the exercise is deemed successful. This approach ignores, however, the dangerous power imbalance that impacts the encounter, both from the standpoint of Strasberg's authority as a teacher and from his privileged position as a male in relation to female students. Apparently, the Method was not particularly interested in challenging or even acknowledging these layers of social convention. While Strasberg certainly utilized his exercises with both men and women, the societal imbalance in power based on gender alters the relative abilities of students freely to accept or resist coercive techniques in the acting classroom, as does the more general power differential between student and teacher.

Such exercises in power and coercion seem to contradict an assumption that lies at the heart of Strasberg's approach: the actor's free will. David Krasner argues that of all the major Method practitioners, Strasberg emphasizes to the greatest degree the importance of actor/character psychology as a motivating force—a concept directly related to that of free will. All Method theorists believe that the actor makes choices in creating a role. By exploring various objectives and motivations, the actor selects the ones that will evoke the strongest emotion and the clearest action in the play. It is the actor as a creative agent, freely choosing the building blocks of his character, who drives the acting process for Strasberg. He asserts that everything "the actor does demands some effort of will, thought, muscle, and emotion."[7] In this understanding, the actor's self exerts direct control over the performative events. Krasner explains, "The self is vulnerable, protean, and flexible in emotional content. Still, subject-actors are 'free' to interpret the role, a freedom that empowers them. They may conform to traditional views of the role or cut against the grain."[8]

While Strasberg's notion of free will illuminates the actor's process in creating a character, it does not apply as well to the process of training the actor. Actors are supposedly free to choose their own objectives and internal triggers, yet their efficacy is based on an audience's response. In actor training this audience consists of the other students and, most important, the acting teacher. Thus the actor's choices are limited by external factors, such as the power dynamics of the student-teacher relationship, as well as the circumstances and requirements of the text (ultimately determined by the teacher-director as chief interpreter of the text in realistic performance contexts). Strasberg's tenets ignore this very real dimension of actor training.

Sanford Meisner, another Method master, provides many examples of classroom modus operandi that efface the sociological, historical context in which he and his students are embedded. Like Strasberg Meisner begins with the actor's self rather than the character. Suggesting that talent comes from instinct, he utilizes the initial portion of his acting classes to access those instincts. While instincts are "spontaneous," the actors in Meisner's classes have plenty of trouble in expressing them to his satisfaction. The blocks, of course, stem from societal norms. Meisner encourages actors to be "open" and "honest," but "the tendency nowadays is to follow your instincts only when they are socially acceptable."[9] Thus he encourages actors to reject the control of social niceties that mask their true feelings for the sake of politeness. After telling Philip, a student, "you cannot be a gentleman and be an actor," Meisner asks Philip why he thinks he is a "logical gentleman." Philip replies, "People just kept saying, 'You're a gentleman, you're a gentleman,' and after a while I must have listened to them." Meisner responds, "Philip, do yourself a favor. Kick them in the ass!"[10] In other words, "good" actors are impolite, reactionary, violent, and abrasive, and do exactly the opposite of what polite society expects. Perhaps Meisner is implying that actors must be willing and able to do impolite, violent, and shocking things in drama, so this advice is readying their medium—their bodies, voices, consciousness—for that performative requirement. Yet Meisner does not address the character here; he seems solely focused on the actor.

Neither does Meisner fully interrogate the nature of "instinct." Judging from his examples, instinct is a spontaneous impulse triggered by an external force and leading directly to an action. His advice to Philip contrasts instinct with social restraint. Most important, intellect is antithetical to instinct. Meisner asserts, "all good acting comes from the heart, as it were, and . . . there's no mentality in it."[11] He consistently urges actors not to think, just to react instinctively, and he criticizes those actors who attempt to shape the exercises into scenes by intellectualizing the process. "I've been wary of your intelligence right from the beginning," he tellingly warns a student.[12] Meisner's rejection of intellect strips away some of the actor's power described by Strasberg. Meisner's actors react; they do not focus on creating purposeful action. Meisner tells an actor, "You've got control over what you're saying, and I say *he* [her partner in the exercise] has to have the control. What you're doing is self-manipulative."[13]

Theater practitioners must be wary of this approach, which objectifies actors and opens wide the door to manipulation and violation. Actors who do not think do not question the situations in which they are placed or the power structures in which they operate. While dangerous for everyone, this environment is perhaps most treacherous for members of oppressed groups, who are already positioned as the weak in society. While Meisner claims to be liberating actors from the restrictive bonds of social convention, he is paradoxically reinscribing them with passivity.

Actors who do not think will not challenge their acting teachers on sexist, discriminatory, or violent actions—all of which are done in the name of art. For example, note Meisner's use of two students to introduce his key concept of "the pinch and the ouch." John is instructed to use the text "Mr. Meisner," but only when something *makes* him say it or do something. With his back to the rest of the class, John shouts his text after Meisner pinches him on the back. Like a good student, John has demonstrated nicely a spontaneous reaction to an outside stimulus. Of course, no one questions whether the teacher should be physically violating his student—the audience laughs and applauds. Even more disturbing is Rose Marie's experience. Given the same instructions, she turns her back to the class. Instead of pinching her, Meisner "casually . . . reaches around her shoulder and slips his hand into her blouse. 'Mr. Meisner!' she giggles, drawing away from his touch. 'You see how true that acting is, how full emotionally,' Meisner says. 'I didn't know you were ticklish.'"[14] What in any other context would be considered sexual harassment is passed off as a clever, harmless example of acting pedagogy. Rose Marie is further objectified by Meisner's belittling quip about her ticklishness. But within Meisner's training system, nothing is wrong with his actions. He is simply accessing the "natural" instincts buried within the actors, while socially inappropriate methods become the preferred technique. Actors who might challenge his tactics would be guilty of intellectualizing or conforming to the stifling conventions of false politeness. Actors have no option for saying no.

Further, acting teachers like Meisner act as gurus who have the final say on what is "instinctive" and what is not. Meisner claims to seek spontaneous, natural reactions from his students, but it is he, not they, who can define spontaneity and authenticity. When a student overemphasizes a particular word while engaged in a repetition exercise, it is Meisner who stops her to explain how forced and unnatural her effort is. And his students, well trained by his repetition exercises, parrot back his advice—repeat, use my impulses, don't think, repeat. Actors are trained to react to their scene partners and to absorb the wisdom of their teacher but not to question the hierarchy in which they are subsumed or the violations to which they are subjected.

Eric Morris goes even further with the basic tenets of the Method's work on the actor's self. In *No Acting Please: "Beyond the Method," a Revolutionary Approach to Acting and Living*, Morris describes his classroom activities and his philosophy—"an integration of living and acting."[15] Dissatisfied with the Method's "lip-service" to the importance of actors' personal experiences in their roles, Morris advocates a radical program of self-discovery and "BEING." Like the previously mentioned Method practitioners, Morris seeks to peel away social conventions to find the "real" feelings within actors.

A typical Morris classroom exercise asks students to "express to individuals your perception of them in a way that you feel would be constructive or helpful to their growth. For example: 'You know, Sandra, I get the feeling that you don't really listen to what people say to you.'"[16] Morris reassures us that it does not matter if one has never spoken to the other person or does not know her well. In such an exercise, personal attacks are welcomed in the guise of honesty and constructive criticism. The instructor encourages the students to pose as therapists, diagnosing personal problems on the basis of first impressions. Of course, there are rules—do not "be cruel for the sake of being cruel" or "violate anybody's privacy without permission."[17] Yet who determines when cruelty or violation of privacy has occurred? Such techniques are inherently dangerous. Students are forced into an atmosphere of vulnerability and violation and required to make moral judgments of others and to submit themselves to the same treatment, while being reassured that this is the necessary pathway to self-discovery, truthful acting, and creativity. Educators committed to nonviolence must recognize the violent undercurrents at work.

NONVIOLENT ACTING PEDAGOGY

So far, we have examined several acting pedagogical strategies that contain tendencies toward either actual or metaphorical violence. Techniques that force students to expose personal experiences and emotions to the group, that promote aggressive or violent behavior under the guise of freeing the actor from social restrictions, or that actively belittle or harass students must be rejected by nonviolent educators. If peace church or pacifist educators accept J. Denny Weaver's statement that since "Jesus' teaching and his life reject violence and are intrinsically nonviolent, nonviolence should be a controlling influence in theology as well as in ethics," [18] then we must both challenge violent structures of knowledge and pose nonviolent alternatives.

We can now consider four characteristics of a nonviolent acting pedagogy. At its roots, such pedagogy acknowledges the fundamental social dimension of human existence. Instead of promoting a myopic, individualistic exploration of the actor's psyche, a nonviolent approach will enhance self-reflection within a broader examination of our interactions with each other and our world. In other words, a nonviolent pedagogy will recognize the intrinsic interconnectedness of human life rather than focus on presumably autonomous individuals.

A Questioning Spirit

A Christian nonviolent acting pedagogy sensitive to issues of systemic violence encourages a questioning and challenging spirit within an environment of love. As the introductory chapters to this book assert, a commitment to Christian nonviolence involves a commitment to struggle for justice and against oppression. In line with Jesus' challenge to prevailing societal assumptions, we must propose nonviolent challenges to a world dominated by oppressive gender, racial, ethnic, religious, and class hierarchies. Educators must acknowledge the complex power dynamics in which they, their students, their classrooms, and society are enmeshed. Nonviolent acting interrogates these structures. Why do they exist? Whom do they serve? In the acting classroom, students should be encouraged to question both the world of the play and the real world in which they participate as actors, students, men and women, believers, and so on. Rather than discouraging actors from using their intellect, as some Method (and non-Method) practitioners advocate, nonviolent educators should stimulate critical investigations. Why should students accept the status quo, when Christians are called to examine and challenge the world through the lens of God's love for every person? Similarly, students should be encouraged to investigate their roles in the world.

Rather than turning completely inward, attempting to discover "natural" instincts, emotions, and behaviors, actors in a nonviolent classroom might explore the ramifications their actions have on others.

Discovery and Growth

Nonviolent pedagogical practices encourage discovery and expansion rather than stripping away or breaking down. Certainly the process of self-discovery is a crucial one for any educational setting, including the acting classroom. Investigating our own experiences and perspectives enables us to personalize our education, testing new ideas against what we already know, challenging ourselves to strengthen our commitments, and opening ourselves to grow in new directions. However, many methods can be used to stimulate self-discovery. The pedagogical practices examined in this chapter are violent ones, stripping away socially developed behaviors and attitudes to expose the raw self underneath. The teacher occupies a position as the all-knowing superior who chips away at the students' defenses, forcing them to expose their inner feelings. Such a process is a violation of students, not self-discovery.

A nonviolent perspective enables educators to rethink the discovery process. While students are invited to interrogate their own beliefs and behaviors, more important they are given opportunities to explore and expand their views and skills. Students might do observation exercises, watching how other people behave in certain contexts. Classroom activities might incorporate nonmimetic, nonrealistic vocal and physical work to broaden their repertoire of skills. By discussing these experiences together in the classroom, actors discover new ways of behaving and thinking with which they may or may not agree. Educators can facilitate critical discussions that place these behaviors in social contexts and investigate them for political and ethical ramifications. Rather than breaking down a student's defenses in a quest for some true core, nonviolent educators might suggest that discovering an individual's experiences is not an ultimate goal but rather a starting point for additional growth.

Empowerment through Collaboration

Nonviolent acting pedagogy values actors as cocreators of meaning who work collectively to solve problems. Educators must be wary of construing students as passive recipients of knowledge. Violent acting techniques work from that assumption when they construe student actors as uptight, emotionally and physically inhibited objects ignorant of their own bindings and the way to escape them, which then requires an enlightened teacher-guru to solve the problem for the student by wrenching away the "blocks" that frustrate the actor.

By rethinking this approach, we recognize the goodness and capabilities within each person. While educators may guide and challenge the students, providing opportunities for exploration, the actors are active participants in this process. Furthermore, a nonviolent Christian approach might shift the notion of "obstacle" from the self or another person to an exterior problem. Rather than working against oneself or one's acting partner, students work together to solve the problem and achieve a goal.

Viola Spolin explores this idea of shared problem solving in her approach to acting based on game playing and improvisations, each of which focuses on a particular problem. As the students play the game, they use their own resources, imagination, powers of observation, and reliance on each other to solve the problem. For instance, after collectively creating a floor plan for a room, a small group of actors must improvise a scene in this room, finding ways to interact with each object and piece of furniture. Spolin suggests that this mode of learning destabilizes the student-teacher hierarchy, enabling students to focus directly on solving a problem instead of seeking approval or avoiding disapproval from the teacher.[19] Rather than bending other actors to one's will or privileging the instructor's viewpoint over all others, this nonviolent strategy recognizes that problems exist in the world and that many creative strategies can be employed to solve them.

Transformation

A nonviolent classroom can advocate the transformative power of theater. Rather than viewing the self and the world as static and irretrievably sinful, Christian educators can offer the hope and promise of God's transforming love. Radical nonviolence can make a difference in the lives of individuals and communities. Working cooperatively with others against violence and injustice in the world is daunting but necessary work for Christians. We can bring this commitment into our classrooms, embodying a theater of possibilities. A performance presents a picture of the world open to interpretation and criticism. Actors explore many possible ways to use their entire being to create the picture, making choices and selecting some options while rejecting others. In a nonviolent classroom, actors investigate the messages created by their stage pictures. Such investigations might lead to a radical rethinking of the structure of the theatrical experience itself. In a system he calls Theater of the Oppressed, Augusto Boal argues for a theater of change, a theater which addresses social injustice and prepares people to "act" in the real world. Instead of skilled actors performing plays before an unskilled, passive audience, Boal's theater breaks down the barriers between actors and spectators. "All must act, all must be protagonists in the necessary transformations of society," he argues.[20] Boal calls for "spect-actors" who participate in very real acts of liberation.

CONCLUSION

While popular acting pedagogy, materialistic modern culture, and current governmental policies advocate violent modes of thinking and acting, we do not have to participate in them. We can struggle against these violent entities, offering glimpses of the magnificent, transforming power of love that supports the weak, brings hope to the desperate, and empowers the oppressed. By challenging violent actor training assumptions and suggesting alternative approaches to theater, this chapter has described just some of the ways we might act nonviolently, both on the classroom stage and in the global theater.

NOTES

I am grateful to Michael Peterson for his comments on early drafts of this chapter.

1. Constantin Stanislavsky, *An Actor Prepares*, trans. Elizabeth Hapgood Reynolds (London: Methuen, 1980), 14.

2. Sharon Marie Carnicke, "Stanislavsky's System: Pathways for the Actor," in *Twentieth Century Actor Training*, ed. Alison Hodge (London: Routledge, 2000), 18.

3. Colin Counsell, *Signs of Performance: An Introduction to Twentieth-Century Theatre* (London: Routledge, 1996), 35.

4. David Krasner, "Strasberg, Adler and Meisner: Method Acting," in *Twentieth Century Actor Training*, 132.

5. Lee Strasberg, "Working with Live Material," *Drama Review* 9, no. 1 (1964): 123.

6. Strasberg, "Working with Live Material," 125.

7. Strasberg, "Working with Live Material," 119.

8. David Krasner, "I Hate Strasberg: Method Bashing in the Academy," in *Method Acting Reconsidered: Theory, Practice, Future*, ed. David Krasner (Bloomsburg, Pa.: Macmillan, 2000), 18.

9. Sanford Meisner and Dennis Longwell, *Sanford Meisner on Acting* (New York: Vintage, 1987), 30.

10. Meisner and Longwell, *Sanford Meisner on Acting*, 33–34.

11. Meisner and Longwell, *Sanford Meisner on Acting*, 37.

12. Meisner and Longwell, *Sanford Meisner on Acting*, 49.

13. Meisner and Longwell, *Sanford Meisner on Acting*, 30–31.

14. Meisner and Longwell, *Sanford Meisner on Acting*, 35.

15. Eric Morris and Joan Hotchkis, *No Acting Please: "Beyond the Method," A Revolutionary Approach to Acting and Living* (Los Angeles: Spelling, 1979), 1.

16. Morris and Hotchkis, *No Acting Please*, 66.

17. Morris and Hotchkis, *No Acting Please*, 67.

18. See chapter 3 in this volume.

19. Viola Spolin, *Improvisation for the Theater: A Handbook of Teaching and Directing Techniques* (Evanston, Ill.: Northwestern University Press, 1963), 20.

20. Augusto Boal, *Theatre of the Oppressed*, trans. Charles A. McBride and Maria-Odilia Leal McBride (New York: Theatre Communications Group, 1985), x.

14

Violence and Nonviolence in Choral Music

Mark J. Suderman

Music is common to all cultures and has been throughout history.¹ The art of choral music, in particular, has given voice to the emotions and thoughts of many people in varying situations. Music—created by the composer, combined with text, analyzed by the conductor, learned and internalized by the choral community (the choir), and presented to an audience—creates a powerful and often emotional influence that moves beyond the sounds heard or the text conveyed. This influence speaks not only to the listening audience but also to choir members and the conductor. While the choral piece may speak different messages to each person in the room, the most powerful impact occurs when musicians and the audience are all of one voice and one mind and one heart. My focus in this chapter is on that reconciling impact, which in my view points to the importance of discussing choral music from the perspective of nonviolence.

In what follows I examine violence and nonviolence in three areas of choral music: in the text of the choral work, in the music itself, and in the pedagogy of the choral rehearsal. Since the choral director usually involves herself in all three aspects—choosing the literature to be sung, comprehending the text, listening to the music, seeing how the music and the text combine, analyzing the work as a whole, and discussing both music and text with the choir and perhaps the audience—a nonviolent perspective from the conductor has the potential for great influence in the choral experience.

CHORAL TEXTS

Choral texts provide a vehicle for promoting a certain viewpoint or belief. For example, they can help the choir members see, discover, and hear about Christian faith. The choral text, its discussion and its internalization, can have this formative and transformative function in the classroom, and it can provide an opportunity for social interaction and change.

While discussing a text is one important way to understand its meaning, choir members also internalize the meanings of texts without discussing them. By rehearsing a piece over and over again, singers often grow into the text and its meaning. Consider, for example, how much theology has been communicated through the texts of hymns. Many people know hymn texts better than they remember biblical texts.

While many texts and pieces of music are appropriate in a Christian liberal arts college setting, for this chapter I will focus on music and texts that relate directly to violence and nonviolence. Many texts promote violence or the image of violence—certain pieces of popular music, patriotic pieces, even hymns.[2] Choosing a specific text can send a message to the choir members and to listeners about the priorities of the director's repertoire and alerts audiences and performers to the particular commitments found in whatever music is being rehearsed or performed. A director need not avoid a text simply because it deals with violence. Sometimes violence appears in the text as a way to shock the listener into thought. However, it can also promote a specific way of thinking and a particular lifestyle, which makes it imperative for the choir director to inspect carefully the texts used in a choral setting. Consider, for example, the different impacts of repeated singing of *The Marseillaise*, whose text is given here, and *Prayer of the Children,* which concludes this chapter.

Allons enfants de la Patrie	Let us go, children of the fatherland
Le jour de gloire est arrivé!	The day of glory has arrived!
Contre nous de la tyrannie,	Against us stands tyranny,
L'étandard sanglant est levé!	The bloody flag is raised!
L'étandard sanglant est levé!	The bloody flag is raised!
Entendez-vous dans les campagnes	Do you hear in the countryside
Mugir ces féroces soldats?	The roar of these fierce soldiers?
Ils viennent jusque dans nos bras	They come right into our midst
Egorger nos fils et nos compagnes!	To slaughter our sons and our comrades!
Aux armes, citoyens!	To arms, citizens!
Formez vos bataillons!	Form your battalions!
Marchons! marchons!	Let us march! Let us march!
Qu'un sang impur	That their impure blood
Abreuve nos sillons!	Should water our fields!

Some texts from choral pieces have responded to violence, literally and symbolically: slave songs and spirituals, songs of the Holocaust, and songs written during various struggles for freedom from oppression. In such literature one finds songs that advocate violence as well as songs advocating nonviolence.

FOUR PEACE PIECES

Here I examine four examples of choral music that promote nonviolence. The first and fourth come from "regional or ethnic conflicts" in chapter 5 of this book. The first choral piece, *Hope for Resolution: A Song for Mandela and de Klerk*, comes from South Africa. The choral octavo uses two songs, each representing one of the men from the title. On the score the arrangers wrote, "In its juxtaposition of a European chant melody and an anti-apartheid song from South Africa, this piece is a celebration of diversity. The arrangement reflects our respect for divergent musical styles and points us toward our innate (though sometimes neglected) potential for peaceful coexistence."[3] The texts (and music), one English and one South African, are first stated independently. By the end of the piece, both texts and both melodies have symbolically joined. Their music comes together in harmony both figuratively and musically, expressing desire for the nonviolent connection and community of one united South Africa, no longer separated by race, tradition, or class.

The second choral piece is Dale Grotenhuis's composition from the familiar St. Francis of Assisi text, *Make Me an Instrument of Your Peace*.[4] Numerous musical settings exist for these words. The message of the text encourages a personal commitment together with actions following for a life of peace and nonviolence. Grotenhuis's music enhances the text and provides an opportunity to hear it in a new way. The words from the title are set four times in this piece, twice at the beginning and twice at the end. The composer wanted to emphasize that this text consists of a request to God for help in making peace with others. No other phrases or words appear more than twice.

Kenneth Leighton has set to music the words of the poet Phineas Fletcher in *Drop, Drop, Slow Tears*.[5] The text speaks of the violence of the crucifixion and of the often-heeded call for vengeance following an injustice. But the poet responds with the words "Sin doth never cease." Almost the entire piece is soft in nature, with the prevalent dynamic markings consisting of pianissimo and piano. The only forte marking comes on the text just noted. The poet is asking for the tears to "drown all my faults and fears" with no further need for more violence. Whose tears are they? They are the tears of Christ, referred to in the text only as "Prince of Peace."

The fourth piece in this section is *Prayer of the Children*. Kurt Bestor composed both the words and the music.[6] When he lived in Yugoslavia during the 1970s, Bestor interacted with people who represented the various ethnic and religious factions in the war: Serbs, Muslims, Croats, and Christians. It occurred to him that those who suffered most in this war were the innocent children. He wrote *Prayer of the Children* as a tribute to them, expressing his hope that peace would be restored to their land.

These four pieces illustrate how choral texts can directly promote nonviolence by calling for peaceful responses to various forms of violence. Other vocal music genres, such as hymns and popular music, can also promote peace. For example,

Hymnal: A Worship Book lists sixteen hymns in the "Uses in Worship Index" under the heading "Peace Sunday."[7] And *Give Peace a Chance: Music and the Struggle for Peace* features American folk and rock music on peace since World War I.[8]

However, it is important to remember that choral music has both text *and* music. As the next section shows, the combination can move one beyond the text to a higher and deeper level of understanding and right living.

CHORAL MUSIC

While this chapter is not designed to examine musical structure in detail, one cannot address the use of violence and nonviolence in choral music without looking at the music itself. Music does contain moments of *violence*. A common understanding is that violence involves "great force or strength or intensity."[9] Much of music is designed in that way. Dissonance and suspensions (although not always associated with violence or violent texts) create tension. Dynamics can provide great power to the music. Unresolved chords or dissonant music can contribute to a sense of uneasiness and foreboding. Think of a film score played during scenes of violence. Such musical ideas can color and affect the text in choral music, as well as the emotions and feelings of the audience and the performers.

Much Western music does offer resolution to such tensions (dissonances are often followed by a consonance and suspensions are usually resolved), often implying a sense of closure to the concerns and issues raised by the text. However, music should transform the text, not just support it or provide closure. This explains, in part, why the combination of music and text can create something beyond the sum of each individual entity. As Ronald Pen says, "Song, the union of text and tune as expressed through the voice, marries two forms of communication—the concrete language of words and the abstract meaning of music."[10] Or as Joseph Machlis wrote, "Words are concrete; tone is fluid and intangible. A word taken by itself has a fixed meaning; a tone assumes meaning only from its association with other tones. Words convey specific ideas; music suggests elusive states of mind."[11] A study of people's musical experiences by Kropf and Nafziger resulted in such statements as, "Music makes the words speak a little louder" and "The music gives the text color, a human emotional dimension to the words."[12] These comments all point to a combination of the concrete and the abstract, or right brain and left brain, functions in choral music that provides a depth of meaning not available to either text or music alone.[13]

Through association even music without text can recreate the reality of violence. One recent example is in the controversy surrounding the playing of music by Richard Wagner in Israel by the renowned conductor Daniel Barenboim. Wagner's music was often used as a rally cry for a patriotic Germany during Hitler's regime. For a concert of Berlin's Staatskapelle orchestra in Jerusalem in July 2001, Barenboim had scheduled a composition by Wagner but agreed to drop it after Israelis protested. However, as a second encore, Barenboim did play a selection from Wagner, which was both applauded and denounced by people in the audience.[14]

CONDUCTING AND PEDAGOGY

A nonviolent perspective has the potential to impact the choral community in areas such as leadership style, decision making, pedagogy, and communication within the group. A dictionary defines *community* as "a group with common interests" or "fellowship" or "a body of people living in one place . . . and considered as a whole."[15] Those are appropriate definitions for a choral community, understood as choir members, accompanist, and conductor, who share common interests and goals in a Christian liberal arts college choir. The choir can experience fellowship together, confront challenges together, and live together while on tour. These elements make the academic course in choral singing more than a typical class. Memories and relationships are created. "The physical act of singing together creates a bond not only in the present but with memories of the past."[16]

The building of community in a choir can model the need for community building in the world today. Individuals who believe they can or should rely on themselves forget God while alienating themselves from others. This sense of individualism can easily add to the violence in the world, when people do not think beyond their own needs. The more individuals isolate themselves, the more they tend to see the world in terms of their needs only, often with expectations of forcing others, even violently, to supply those needs. In contrast, a caring community offers a model of peace among people, with nonviolent approaches to problems. Leonard Sweet, former chancellor of United Theological Seminary in Dayton, Ohio, speaks to how music can be helpful in the postmodern world: "Music is an absolute imperative if postmoderns are to move outside of themselves, connect with others, and build community. One can motivate and move individuals to an experience of God without music—perhaps. But to have a community experience of God's presence, to bring a community of faith to a 'catalytic moment,' . . . music is a must."[17]

The choral community of a liberal arts college encounters diversity. Music is not autonomous. It is diverse and always part of a culture and a history. Thus diversity may involve differing ideas on musical tone, literature selection, or rehearsal procedures. The diversity frequently includes religious, cultural, and ethnic backgrounds. Likely a college choir will encounter all these aspects and more. To create a good choral community, conductor, accompanist, and singers all need to function together to create community out of and in the midst of this diversity. This challenge presents an opportunity for the choral community—both conductor and student members—to model conflict resolution and decision-making procedures shaped by nonviolent perspectives that respect all voices.

There are a number of ways to structure the period during choral rehearsal. A conductor can teach only music, notes, and technique, without reference to what the music is about, with a goal of producing a program that sounds good to the audience while displaying the choir's expertise in musicianship. However, the conductor can also use the music to convey ideas, history, and beliefs and to provide a larger education for the students. Even more specifically, the conductor may use the music to witness to God's kingdom, including the nonviolence that is integral to the story of Jesus. The conductor should schedule some time for questions and discussion of the text and how it fits the music. Students need to understand fully what they are singing. Rather than coming from the conductor, who by means of his position has a soapbox from which to pronounce certain ideas and beliefs, the conductor can allow the discussion to develop naturally and informally during the rehearsal through promotion of a nonthreatening classroom atmosphere. But since this discussion does take time from rehearsal, conductors need to seek an appropriate balance between rehearsing and discussing.

Gerald Biesecker-Mast has noted the passive consumerist mentality of most American college students and proposed ideas for transforming them into actively engaged participants in the classroom.[18] Such participation requires open communication. In a choral rehearsal, the physical act of singing activates the mind. A nonthreatening classroom atmosphere will then encourage students toward further and deeper mental engagement. And if the conductor asks enough questions about the meaning, setting, and audience of the text, the students will begin eventually to ask questions on their own.

The conductor-teacher in this setting must be open to others' viewpoints. While the conductor works from a set of personal beliefs, openness to discussion and change models one dimension of a nonviolent worldview, namely that the outcome is not coerced or foreclosed. The community needs space for truth to happen. A dictatorial conductor, in contrast, does foreclose discussion and coerce consent—a form of psychological violence akin to that mentioned in chapter 13 of this volume.

Communication and understanding of the music does not end with the rehearsal. J. Denny Weaver speaks of the "activist alternative community" that proclaims the gospel, in part, "to transform the society."[19] The choir can be one model of that alternative community. The message of the music and the text is presented to the audience. If the choir has internalized the message and communicated it with sufficient musicality, both choir members and audience will see the world differently, through eyes focused by the nonviolent dimensions of the entire choral experience. The music thus offers a new view of the world from the composer, through the singers, and to the eyes and ears of the audience.

The axiom "actions speak louder than words" is very true for Christians and for the choir trying to communicate a message to its audience. "Faith without works is dead" (James 2:26). When a choir is on tour, the actions of the students outside the worship service are as important as what they hope to convey to their audience in the program. In chapter 3 J. Denny Weaver points out the difference between theology and ethics, calling them "different, but parallel expressions of the same commitment, namely to be Christian." The message of the choir (the theology) must be backed up by its actions (ethics), both on tour and in life beyond the choir experience. Music has a significant contribution to make in preparing both choir and audience for their ongoing life as Christians who espouse Jesus' nonviolence. Can anyone continue to espouse violence after singing *Prayer of the Children?*

Can you hear the voice of the children
softly pleading for silence in their shattered world?
Angry guns preach a gospel full of hate,
blood of the innocent on their hands.
Cryin', "Jesus help me to feel the sun again upon my face
For when darkness clears, I know you're near,
Bringing peace again."[20]

NOTES

1. "In every society, in every period of history, men and women have made music. . . . Music is not a fringe activity or a luxury one: it is a central and necessary part of human existence." Stanley Sadie, ed., *Stanley Sadie's Music Guide: An Introduction* (Englewood Cliffs, N.J.: Prentice Hall, 1986), 13.

2. Some examples include *The Marseillaise; The Star-Spangled Banner; Battle Hymn of the Republic; Onward, Christian Soldiers; Stand Up, Stand Up for Jesus;* and some rock and rap music (not typically sung by choirs).

3. Paul Caldwell and Sean Ivory, arrs., *Hope for Resolution: A Song for Mandela and de Klerk* (Corvallis, Ore.: earthsongs, 1998).

4. Dale Grotenhuis, *Make Me an Instrument of Your Peace* (St. Louis, Mo.: Concordia Publishing House, 1998).

5. Kenneth Leighton, *Drop, Drop, Slow Tears* (London: Novello, 1961).

6. Kurt Bestor, *Prayer of the Children,* arr. Andrea S. Klouse (Miami: Warner Brothers Publications, 1995). See www.kurtbestor.com/pages/prayer.html.

7. *Hymnal: A Worship Book*, managing editor Rebecca Slough (Newton, Kans.: Faith and Life Press, 1992), 879.

8. Marianne Philbin, ed., *Give Peace a Chance: Music and the Struggle for Peace* (Chicago: Chicago Review Press, 1983).

9. Eugene Ehrlich, Stuart Berg Flexner, Gorton Carruth, and Joyce M. Hawkins, *Oxford American Dictionary* (New York: Oxford University Press, 1980), 1038.

10. Ronald Pen, *Introduction to Music* (New York: McGraw-Hill, 1992), 129.

11. Joseph Machlis, *The Enjoyment of Music: An Introduction to Perceptive Listening,* 3d ed. (New York: Norton, 1970), 5.

12. Marlene Kropf and Kenneth Nafziger, *Singing: A Mennonite Voice* (Scottdale, Pa.: Herald Press, 2001), 76.

13. For a compelling example of the sustaining power of music, see the account of John Paul Lederach, who wrote that the air from the lips of a companion who serendipitously whistled Lederach's favorite hymn tune was like "the very breath of God blowing on my face" in a time of extreme danger. Kropf and Nafziger, *Singing,* 87–90.

14. "Israel Calls for Barenboim Boycott," BBC News, July 24, 2001, at news.bbc.co.uk/hi/english/entertainment/arts/newsid_1455000/1455466.stm (accessed

June 21, 2002); "Daniel Barenboim Conducts Wagner in Israel," World Socialist Website, August 1, 2001, at www.wsws.org/articles/2001/aug2001/wagn-a01.shtml (accessed June 21, 2002).

15. Ehrlich et al., *Oxford American Dictionary*, 171.

16. Kropf and Nafziger, *Singing,* 54.

17. Leonard Sweet, *Faithquakes* (Nashville: Abingdon, 1994), 63–64.

18. See Gerald Biesecker-Mast at www.bluffton.edu/~mastg/PEACE%20WORKS% 20.htm (accessed December 29, 2002).

19. J. Denny Weaver, "The Socially Active Community: An Alternative Ecclesiology," in *The Limits of Perfection,* ed. Rodney J. Sawatsky and Scott Holland (Waterloo, Ont.: Institute of Anabaptist-Mennonite Studies, 1993), 91.

20. Bestor, *Prayer of the Children.*

VI

NONVIOLENCE AND THE SOCIAL SCIENCES

15

The Violence of Global Marketization

James M. Harder

The rules governing human relationships that together comprise an economic system are among the most powerful determinants of the human condition. Economic systems push and pull on people over time, exerting tremendous impact on individual lives—sometimes positive, sometimes negative. In some cases, the negative outcome is strong enough that it leaves people in what development ethicist Denis Goulet has called a state of "inhuman" existence—one characterized by loss of the three most fundamental human needs: the security of basic sustenance, a sense of esteem, and the freedom of choice.[1]

Armed warfare is one way that a more powerful group can inflict inhuman conditions upon a weaker group. This chapter argues that a less visible form of violence, but with similar potential for causing "inhuman" outcomes, can occur within the realm of economic relationships. However, because economic assault is slow and its effect cumulative, it often goes unrecognized, as revealed by the examples of Mozambique and Mexico.

The decade-long civil war in Mozambique destroyed the fields, workplaces, and livelihood of that nation's civilian population. By the time a peace treaty was signed in 1992, Mozambique had become the most impoverished country in the world, with an annual income per capita of just $60.[2] The link between military violence and deepened poverty in Mozambique was both direct and evident.

By contrast, on January 1, 1994, when the North American Free Trade Agreement (NAFTA) opened the Mexican border to imported American agricultural products, few would have considered it to be a violent act. Yet that act destroyed the welfare of many Mexicans. Over the next several years, tens of thousands of Mexican campesino peasant farmers and their families faced the ravages of increased poverty that was a direct consequence of NAFTA.[3] The new free trade agreement doomed the small-scale production techniques of the campesinos. They soon lost out in a competitive marketplace to lower-priced products from American agribusiness that captured the markets in Mexico formerly served by local farmers. Many campesinos moved to squalid urban slums out of desperation, hoping against the odds to find jobs as day laborers. They had lost their previous security of basic sustenance, their sense of esteem, and their freedom of choice.

Were the signatories to NAFTA guilty of violence against the rural poor in Mexico in ways parallel to those who pulled the triggers of guns in Mozambique? Or was the decision to change economic policy under NAFTA—as most would argue—simply a value-neutral step toward greater global economic efficiency and enhanced total output of goods and services in the long run?

Few economists are willing to entertain such questions. This reluctance reflects the mainstream economic tradition, which by its very methods of analysis resists the thought that market-based economic relationships can be harmful. At its core, mainstream economics perpetuates the ideal but unrealistic assumption that the marketplace is a "level playing field," normally free of the one-sided advantages of power.

This chapter challenges the prevailing assumptions. It contends that real-world economic actions are to a significant extent about the exercise of power in the marketplace and that this power has the potential to perpetuate great violence on the already poor countries of the world and to the lower economic classes in wealthy nations. Economics studied and practiced from a nonviolent perspective will seek to counter this violence. Thus nonviolent economics will seek to create marketplace controls and "safety nets" against economic power abuse. In that way, a more responsible allocation of power in the marketplace can be achieved, reducing the potential for economic violence against vulnerable populations.

THE MANIFESTATION OF VIOLENCE IN ECONOMICS

Short of the occasional shooting war for the control of scarce natural resources (e.g., the Gulf War for oil in 1991[4] or the current regional conflict in central Africa for control of the Democratic Republic of Congo's valuable strategic mineral reserves[5]), economic violence is not often visible. It is normally necessary to look well beyond the barrels of guns to establish the existence of violence in economics.

As noted in chapter 2 of this volume, *violence* means harm or damage. It occurs in the process of the direct killing of others—as in war, capital punishment, or murder—as well as more subtly through relational systems that propagate dehumanizing outcomes such as poverty, racism, and sexism. It is primarily through the workings of such relational systems that contemporary economic practice is capable of inflicting violence on people.

Both *direct* and *systemic* violence in economics appear in the era of global colonization by European powers from the 1500s to the mid-1900s. The European powers achieved the initial colonization of Latin American, African, and south Asian populations by the deliberate and direct use of superior military force. Gunboats in harbors and thousands of armed troops established and maintained the colonial economic system. In India the British deliberately withheld malaria-suppressing quinine from the general population to ensure the physical superiority of their occupying forces.[6] There was considerable bloodshed of native peoples who dared resist this form of economic and political domination. European nations effectively enslaved entire populations for the explicit purposes of enriching the economic fortunes of the colonizing nations, and European nations used colonies primarily as sources of raw materials and cheap labor and as captive, guaranteed markets for the sale of European manufactured goods.

The era of militaristic economic colonization effectively ended during the 1960s as all but a handful of the remaining African colonies were granted their political independence. Yet today, some voices in the developing world argue that although these nations have achieved political independence, the economic domination by former imperial powers of former colonies continues. These voices argue that postcolonial systems of global trade and investment maintain the same destructive physical and psychological consequences for people as in the colonial era.[7] In their view, direct military colonization (which became politically incorrect) was simply replaced by the indirect control methods of its successor system of *neocolonialism*—defined as foreign exploitation of others through economic as opposed to military means. Thus, they argue, little has changed in the past five hundred years: a power advantage is still being exercised to maintain high living standards for some at the expense of others. The economic violence of colonialism continues, but in a more disguised form.

THE ORIGINS OF POWER BLINDNESS IN ECONOMICS

The mainstream economics tradition has difficulty in acknowledging the exploitative nature of the contemporary global market economy in the ways suggested by such critics. As a discipline, economics tends to be blind to issues of potential conflict and violence. At least three causes contribute to this blindness.

The first contributing element is the doctrine of "self-interested choice" in individual economic decision making, which is assumed to be absolutely foundational to the way in which market-based economic systems operate. For example, economic theory posits that individuals functioning in their role as consumers see a price tag and then react to it. They have the freedom to buy or not to buy the product at that price and will make the rational decision that most satisfies them based upon the interaction of their individual preferences, needs, income, and knowledge of their alternative choices as consumers. When functioning in their complementary role as workers, the same individuals are assumed to see a wage associated with a particular employment opportunity. Then in self-interested fashion, they react to it—freely accepting or rejecting the job depending upon their individual valuation of the importance of income, leisure time, and other employment options.

This process of self-interested free choice is presumed to operate in all other aspects of a market-based economic system. Owners of businesses have the freedom to choose whether to make a particular product, given their knowledge of production costs and product selling prices. And given knowledge of prevailing wage and benefit costs and a worker's expected contribution to production, owners can choose whether to hire another worker.

This model of self-interested decision making also applies to groups. For example, each nation of the world is depicted as being totally free to choose whether or not to participate in free trade agreements. No matter how small or how poor the nation, the model presumes complete sovereignty of choice.

The important point of this extended discussion of the presumption of free choice in every facet of economic life is that it rules out—by definition—the very possibility that market transactions can be harmful or exploitative. The model assumes that no one can force the purchase of overpriced or shoddy products. Underpaid jobs will simply go unfilled. International trade will be avoided unless *both* partners are convinced they will benefit (why else agree to it?). Thus by this reasoning, all transactions in the marketplace must be "win-win" scenarios—or they would not have occurred in the first place. In all circumstances, individuals or nations in a market economy are seen to be freely making self-interested and self-benefiting choices[8] and rejecting any arrangement that would leave them in a position inferior to where they started.[9] It is with this logic in mind that economists such as Milton Friedman champion the "free market" economic system as the ultimate guarantor of societal freedom and liberty from oppression.[10]

But construing reality in this way yields a very narrow and insufficiently analytical outcome. Missing from such an individualistic microlevel analysis is the element of a social perspective—the nature of *relationships* among and between *groups* and *categories* of people. Without this perspective, the idea of free choice in the market place masks much potential for violence.

An example taken to an absurd extreme can perhaps illustrate this shortcoming. Consider a public auction at which one very wealthy individual decides to bid whatever is necessary in order to purchase every item that comes up for sale. Even though everyone else in attendance would depart empty handed and frustrated, the individual choice model of economics would not allow recognition of that collective unhappiness, let alone acknowledge what model it actually was— the exercise of economically based privilege and power of one against many. Rather, under the individual choice model it becomes only a series of independent and rational decisions by everyone else at the auction that the items on sale were not worth their eventual selling prices. Socially based notions of power abuse, exploitation, or even violence can never enter that analysis because of its narrowly defined conception of individual choice.

Development economist Albert O. Hirschman offers another significant critique of the assumptions of the free choice model of economics. He points out that choice must occur in the context of realistic *alternatives*, or indeed it is no choice at all. Hirschman frames his discussion in terms of people having "exit" and "voice" options that allow them to withdraw from an unacceptable relationship with a person or organization. An individual or group has no exit or voice (and therefore no real choice) if a *different* relationship cannot be established because competitive markets are not functioning.[11] That no-choice scenario might well be the case, for example, when a multinational garment factory constitutes the only employment option in an impoverished region of the world. Without exit options for the factory's workers, various forms of economic violence can all too easily prevail.

A second explanation for the blindness of mainstream economics to issues of conflict and violence derives from the limited set of analytical tools used by the modern economist. Historically a social science rooted in the study of human behavior, economics has sought to distinguish itself from its historical cousins, political science and sociology. In that process—and especially during the latter-twentieth century—economics claimed for itself the scientific high ground of "objective" quantitative research. The individualistic "rational choice" paradigm described above meshes neatly with value-free mathematical modeling of quantitative research in ways that a more complex investigation into social issues of power and conflict cannot readily match because of the inevitability of subjective interpretation.

Hirschman has called attention to this divide in social scientific analysis between what he calls "synthetic views" and "whole views" of reality. The former are relatively "spare, parsimonious, elegant, [and] simple" enough to build into an economist's mathematical model. The latter are "sprawling, general, sometimes dripping with detail."[12] The informed richness of the whole view does not lend itself well to standard quantitative research methods but can much more readily open windows of insight into the potential for violence in economics. Unfortunately, economists interested in exploring such perspectives often find themselves at a professional disadvantage within a discipline that has tilted so far toward the limiting requirement of mathematical expression.[13] For that reason today, social power and conflict questions are almost always researched from outside of the formal discipline of economics.

Yet clearly the fundamental issues of such questions are most often economic in nature. As John Maynard Keynes, perhaps the greatest economist of the twentieth century noted, "The ideas of economists and political philosophers, both when they are right and when they are wrong, are more powerful than is commonly understood. Indeed the world is ruled by little else."[14]

Every generation of students in the introductory economics class recites the ideals of a market economy happily functioning under "perfect competition"—one that Adam Smith quite properly realized would contain effective checks on the abusive potential of market power.[15] Unfortunately, most modern texts seldom describe adequately the extent to which the reality of today's modern economy—and especially of the globally traded and financed economy—deviates from that much studied ideal of "perfect competition."[16] A much more accurate and honest depiction of reality would begin the study of economics with an analysis of the pitfalls of monopoly and monopolistic competition, with perhaps a footnote reference to the laudable but largely unachievable ideals of perfect competition. Only in the unattainable world of perfect competition is economic analysis justified in paying such short shrift to the dynamic of power.

There is a third and very different type of reason why the study of economics tends to avoid the dark sides of embedded, violent conflict. In many ways, economic doctrine has taken on near-religious qualities in the modern world. For many, economic ideology—specifically belief in the virtues of a free market system of private property rights—has replaced religion as the locus of ultimate meaning in life. Under such circumstances it is no easier to suggest a potential connection between that economic system and violent outcomes than it is to imply that a specific theology fosters social injustice.[17] The quasi-religious quality of economic thought compounds the difficulty of either discussion or objective research in such areas.[18]

For seventy years, the Cold War created an academic climate in which criticism of market economic processes from a social justice perspective risked a "leftist" or "Communist" or "unpatriotic" label for the author. Even today, it may be risky for an aspiring career economist to seek answers to questions that appear to challenge the dominant capitalist consensus of the day. By comparison, a chemist or musician faces no parallel risks for following questions of interest wherever they might lead.

For all of these reasons— the assumption of "free choice" in every facet of economic life, the limited set of analytical tools used by the modern economist, and the near-religious qualities of economic doctrine—issues of power and conflict seldom surface in mainstream economics discourse today. If the issue surfaces, the discipline as practiced today is ill-equipped to recognize it. In the remainder of this chapter, I build the case that more than ever before, the evolving global market economy carries with it the potential for significant economic violence. For that reason, it is high time for economists to pay attention to questions of power and conflict in economic systems.

THE SIGNIFICANCE OF ECONOMIC GLOBALIZATION

For the vast majority of humanity, economic life in the twenty-first century will unfold on a global economic playing field. Economic globalization is commonly understood to describe those advances in technology and communication that have made possible an unprecedented degree of economic interdependence and growth. With the integration of markets worldwide, investments can flow more easily, competition is enhanced, prices are lowered, and, at least in theory, material living standards everywhere can be improved by sharing the fruits of greater efficiency in investment and production.

David Held has identified the most distinctive features of globalization, including *stretched relationships* and *intensification of flows*.[19] Economic relationships have now become fully global in their reach, thanks to lower-cost long distance transportation (especially jumbo jets and containerized cargo ships) and ever cheaper telecommunications and data processing capabilities of computers networked via the Internet. These developments are critical because long distance relationships often require complex information exchange and management capabilities.

The same factors that have diminished the barriers of distance have converged to allow a tremendous expansion in scale of operation. Globalization creates ever larger markets that have given almost unimaginable value and market power to the best-known brand names—such as Coca Cola, McDonalds, Honda, and Nike—thanks to global media networks that can promote those names to the world's masses. As a result, four billion metric tons of merchandise are transported between nations each year—equivalent to the transportation of the complete Great Pyramid at Giza every twelve hours (one-sixth of a mile on each side and forty stories tall)—and just five hundred enormous corporations control seventy percent of world trade. Wal-Mart, the world's largest retail empire, sells more merchandise than its next several largest competitors combined. During the 1990s, McDonald's expanded so fast that a new restaurant opened somewhere in the world every four hours. Coca-Cola, now the most widely recognized word in the world, sells nearly half of all soft drinks consumed on the planet. If they were nation states, the annual output of several gigantic multinational corporations (such as General Motors, Exxon, and General Electric) would easily place them among the top twenty national economies of the world. The common feature in all of these examples: with size comes the ability to exercise tremendous power.

Held also notes that the stretched relationships and expanded markets of globalization require creation of a *global economic infrastructure.* As this happens, the traditional sovereignty of the nation-state is giving way to accommodate the needs of a global market economy, and more powerful roles are emerging for international economic agencies such as the World Trade Organization (WTO) and the International Monetary Fund (IMF). These organizations are successfully establishing new global market rules that supercede national authority.

MARKET POWER TRUMPS DEMOCRATIC POWER

Development of the new global economic infrastructure greatly expands the power of markets—and of those who can dominate markets. Simultaneously, the power of political processes, including democratic political processes, is being diminished. In fact, perhaps a more accurate label to describe the phenomenon of globalization is simply "marketization."

In their book, *The Commanding Heights: The Battle between Government and the Marketplace That Is Remaking the Modern World,* Pulitzer prize–winning author Daniel Yergin and Joseph Stanislaw weave a compelling historical account of how globalization represents victory by the marketplace over the once-formidable power that governments wielded to shape our economic life.[20] The ideological sea change championed by U.S. President Ronald Reagan, British Prime Minister Margaret

Thatcher, and German Chancellor Helmut Kohl in the 1980s, they suggest, effectively turned back the clock on the "government decades" of economic control that characterized the 1960s and 1970s. In its place began "an era in which the ideas of free markets, competition, privatization and deregulation are capturing the commanding heights of world economic thinking" in all corners of the world.[21]

Gone is the notion that governments can or should in any way seek to direct or redirect economic outcomes—a belief that had emerged out of the world's experience with global depression and postwar reconstruction during the mid-twentieth century. In its place, and coinciding with the rise to prominence of the global corporation, is a new "free market consensus" that prosperity is greatest when nearly all aspects of life are entrusted to the marketplace, with markets allowed to run according to their own logic.

Thus, modern economic life has meant the expansion of the *boundaries* of the marketplace. Profit-and-loss calculations have increasingly replaced political discernment of public needs as government services and tax collections are slashed and private companies move into the provision of education and health services, nursing home care, urban transportation and utility systems, parkland management, and neighborhood security services. The market solution as determined by mechanisms of supply and demand has become the response of choice to nearly every economic need—a growth-obsessed world order that has been labeled "economism" by some critics.[22]

Of concern to many critics of this expanded role for the market is the reality that access to goods and services in the marketplace corresponds directly to personal income and wealth—which quite often stands in marked contrast to access provided by former publicly provided goods and services. The market virtually guarantees that needs and desires backed up by superior purchasing power will be met first and foremost. Unlike decisions made democratically (one person, one vote), the market makes decisions based on economic power (one dollar, one vote)—and some people have far more say than others in that arena. In a world of scaled-back public services and public welfare programs, low-income people may no longer be able to afford to go swimming, enjoy police protection, see a doctor, or receive a basic education.

This economic liberalization has unleashed product and investment markets to function without impediment as never before, causing especially the economically vulnerable to experience market pressures in new, intense ways. There is reason to applaud the potential for enhanced opportunity and more choice that the market might bring. But, as Yergin and Stanislaw point out, the constant demands of the market "also brings new insecurities—about unemployment, about the durability of jobs and the stress of the workplace, about the loss of protection from the vicissitudes of life, about the environment, about the unraveling of the safety net, about health care and what happens in old age."[23] Employers can find it necessary to break the social contract with their workers as market competition heats up. And as taxes must be cut to maintain national competitiveness in the global business arena, governments of even the rich countries are less and less able to shield their vulnerable citizens from the market's potentially ugly downsides.

Kofi Annan, Secretary General of the United Nations, has written that "Globalization is seen by a growing number not as a friend of prosperity, but as its enemy; not as a vehicle for development, but as an ever-tightening [vise] increasing the demands on states to provide safety-nets while limiting their ability to do so."[24]

MANIFESTATIONS OF ECONOMIC
VIOLENCE IN THE GLOBAL MARKETPLACE

This expanding global market has great potential for economic violence. As global product markets have allowed business units to greatly expand in size, as production facilities are relocated amidst faraway reservoirs of cheap labor, as investment capital is given free reign to roam the world, and as more and more social decisions are left for market forces to resolve, at least four expanded possibilities for economic violence present themselves.

In the first instance, economic violence occurs in extreme cases of the income inequality that naturally characterizes market outcomes. Economist John Isbister observes that "The market allocates incomes to some people that are insufficient to provide a decent life, and it allocates incomes to others that are so lavish as to far exceed any reasonable need or dessert. These are injustices, not just regrettable occurrences."[25]

Fundamentally, a market economy operates in ways that tend to concentrate wealth and opportunity in the hands of a few, because success in the marketplace tends to breed more success and "bigness" usually (but not always) has its competitive advantages. Inheritances serve to further concentrate wealth and opportunity over time. Opening up materially poor areas of the world to international investment capital at this time is like starting a Monopoly game with half the properties already owned by one player. What are the odds of anyone else winning the game—let alone even being able to compete?

As the market system strengthens and extends its reach in the new global economy, economic inequality also increases. Countries with the strongest market economies tend to display the greatest inequalities. Of the top fifteen industrialized countries, the United States has the most skewed distribution of income. The top 20 percent of households now hold 85 percent of all wealth in the United States. The same phenomenon is occurring in the less developed nations, where together the three *billion* poorest members of the human race (including one billion who are living at the very margin of survival) can claim less combined wealth than is controlled by just 350 of the world's billionaires.

Inevitably, the discipline seldom addresses directly such glaring examples of economic injustice. Rather, the common mantra is that "more growth will solve the problem" for those at the low end of the economic ladder. Such an approach neatly avoids any discussion of the need for income redistribution. Yet it is far from proven that free markets can create new wealth fast enough to overcome the natural market forces that tend to increase inequality over time. Nonviolent economics cannot ignore what this portends for those on the bottom rungs of the socio-economic ladder, nor for the peace and stability of society in the long run.

A second opportunity for economic violence occurs as economic globalization works to reduce local control over economic decision making. It is not necessary to travel to the Third World to experience this phenomenon. A drive down the road in nearly any commercial district in the United States reveals the growing dominance of remote-controlled chain stores, franchises, branches, and subsidiaries. An increasing number of decisions that affect the quality of life in local communities around the world are being made somewhere else, by financial managers who are not members of those communities and who have no particular vested interests in the long-term welfare or quality of life of those communities.

Lost in this trend of long distance control are the social accountabilities of those who hold ultimate power in the marketplace.[26] Top corporate decision makers no longer need to look the majority of their workers in the eye or to know anything about them or the welfare of their communities. The children of decision makers attend schools disconnected from and unaffected by the local economies whose fates they control. In short, they do not need to live with the local consequences of their decisions—and amidst the intense pressures of business competition, the temptation to ignore those consequences is high.

For consumers as well, the global market economy acts to break down the social bonds that in the not-too-distant past were maintained through face-to-face exchanges with local producers. Now, a trip to any Wal-Mart yields a dazzling display of merchandise, the overwhelming majority of which was sourced from faraway places. The global market system allows one to know nothing about who made the product or how it was made—the living conditions of workers, methods employed to raise worker productivity, or how the environment was impacted by the product's manufacture. The only things that matter are price and quality. This arrangement means that consumers benefit, often without awareness, from violence perpetrated on workers and the environment in far-off places.

Nonviolent economics must insist that adequate levels of local control over the economy be retained and that foreign-sourced production is more closely monitored to ensure ethical treatment of low-wage work forces and the environment. Corporations must be held accountable through the political process for the welfare of workers and communities whose futures they increasingly control.

A third potential for economic violence exists in the growing trend toward use of nondemocratic decision-making processes in the domain of economic affairs. As already noted, markets are not democratic in the strict sense of the word. Democracy is based on the principle of the sanctity of every individual. Each person has an equal say. But in markets, some people have far more say in what transpires than others. In general, those with financial resources prefer control by markets; those without wealth find greater security in political processes. With market ascendancy, we are entering an era where markets overshadow government as the venue for deciding not only private but also traditionally public economic priorities.

The same lack of voice for meeting the interests of the poor can be observed in the workings of the world's dominant international institutions—the International Monetary Fund, World Bank, and the World Trade Organization. The rules of the global economy are determined at these institutions by nations with the most economic power, in spite of the superficial "democratic" appearance of having all nations at the table. Voting power within the IMF and World Bank derives from a nation's share of global economic output. (The United States currently has 18 percent of the votes—the only nation with enough votes to effectively block agenda items if it wishes.) As for the WTO, the bureaucratic system that determines world trade and investment rules is so complex that poor nations simply cannot afford to send the size of delegation that would be needed to play an influential role. In effect, the whole world must abide by new marketplace rules in trade and finance that are being determined by and in the interests of a small number of wealthy nations—and within them, by a minority of people who constitute the "investing class."

Nonviolent economics must insist that an imbalance of global financial power and responsibility today not be misused to perpetuate the lopsided status quo into the future. Voices from the currently disenfranchised need to be lifted up in the arena of open public debate. The future of the world must be determined more through democratic processes and less through processes controlled by money.

A final potential for economic violence exists in the market's treatment of the earth's natural resource endowment.[27] In this respect, many have concern for the additional pressures that globalization's growth and consumption bias places on scarce natural resources and fragile environments. Others have noted the environmental folly of shipping more and more products great distances in an era of global warming. The focus here falls on a different consequence of global marketization—the increasing power and ability of those with money disproportionately to control the fruits of nature, violating the principle that nature is a common heritage intended by the Creator for the equal benefit of all.

Data have long been cited that illustrate, for example, how each American's environmental impact (through consumption and waste disposal) is that of dozens of citizens in a typical materially poor country. But what enables this consumption? The answer is global markets. They ensure that Northern countries can continue to live beyond their own environmental means. By one study, it requires nine to thirteen acres of productive land to maintain the living standard of the average person living in a high consumption country, while only about one-third that much ecologically productive land area per person actually exists in the world today. With its dense population and small area, The Netherlands each year consumes an output equivalent to about fourteen times as much productive land as is contained within its own borders.[28]

The mechanisms of international trade allow countries to live beyond their environmental means through appropriation of resources from lower-income countries. In a world of inequality, markets are wonderful inventions for those with money. In this case, superior purchasing power guarantees that countries of the North will never experience natural resource shortages, as long as supply exists somewhere in the world. The first to notice impending shortages of fresh water, hardwoods, and fish stocks have been the poor. Long before the affluent must think about having to cut back on consumption, the poor will already have been price-rationed out of the market.

Those with the most purchasing power also have the ability to direct the global economy to produce what *they* want, to fulfill *their* desires first. I observed this principle in action during the three years I lived in Kenya during the 1980s. My travels there frequently took me past land growing the staple crop of corn for local consumption. But as American demand for specialized coffees grew during that same period of time, more and more land was taken out of food production for local markets in favor of the more profitable export crop of coffee. Through the workings of the market, the superior purchasing power of distant coffee drinkers effectively dictated land use priorities half a world away. The resulting diminished supply of local food only worsened the household nutrition situation of Kenya's most vulnerable people.

Similarly, the world's affluent population can use its money power to export their pollution and other environmental problems to low-income areas of the world. Many Americans wrongly believe that industrial pollution has largely been eliminated. In reality, much of it has simply been shifted by the global economy to new factory sites in China, Mexico, and elsewhere. Fortunately, recent restrictions on the international transportation of hazardous waste material have reduced the potential that poor nations, ill equipped to handle and monitor such wastes, out of desperation will mortgage their own environmental futures by selling themselves as dumping grounds.

In short, economic globalization means that we in the North do not have to cut back on our highly consumptive standard of living because of imminent environmental limits. We can force *others* to do the conserving for us, and we can rest assured that new WTO rules guarantee international access to natural resources under the same terms that they are available to a nation's own citizens. These impacts all exert economic violence by the North on the rest of the world. Nonviolent economics must advocate for the human rights of the world's poor when it comes to access to the fruits of nature's endowments.

The ways in which the global marketplace manifests economic violence will become increasingly apparent as the global economy expands and exerts its imprint on human economic relationships. Income inequality will worsen, local control over economic decision making will continue to diminish, financial power will increasingly replace democratic decision-making processes, and the earth's natural resource endowment will come under additional pressures from globalization's growth and consumption biases.

CONCLUSIONS

Although the potential for economic violence has always existed, it may be on the increase as the consequence of changed economic relationships in a global market economy. The ability to advocate and devise strategies that reduce economic violence must begin with a willingness to move beyond the traditional economic assumption that markets are generally fair and competitive to recognition that the global marketplace is all about the exercise of power in many forms. In and of itself, economic power is not a bad thing, but it certainly harbors the potential to inflict economic violence on vulnerable populations.

Economic globalization is an irreversible process—the inevitable result of technology shrinking time and distance. Contrary to a common assumption, however, the global marketplace need not run free of constraints. The often beneficial policies of market liberalization need not be an all or nothing proposition; they can be shaped and modified to achieve a better social and environmental outcome.

Calling for a reduction of the violence in economics will mean advocating that internationally negotiated "moral floors" be placed under the operation of global markets. Perhaps this moral floor will require some tradeoff in overall economic growth, but markets can still work their intended magic in the presence of meaningful minimum wages, more humane working conditions, stronger environmental standards, capital controls, consumption limits, and the like.

Nonviolent economics must concern itself with asking and researching some critical questions currently missing in traditional economic discourse—questions such as How much is enough for one individual or group to possess? and On moral and ethical grounds, how much inequality of income and wealth is the world willing to tolerate? Further, nonviolent economics must be more concerned with stewardship of natural resources.

The global market system has definite benefits for human welfare, but it carries a high price tag in the realm of social justice. Improving that record will require improved regulatory systems to control economic power abuse worldwide. Strong and sustainable safety nets must be crafted to shield the poorest and most vulnerable populations from the market's downsides. Transparent democratic control of our economic futures must balance the mechanisms of financial control.

"If globalization is to succeed," concludes Kofi Annan, "it must succeed for poor and rich alike. It must deliver rights no less than riches. It must provide social justice and equity no less than economic prosperity and enhanced communication. It must be harnessed to the cause not of just capital alone, but of development and prosperity for the poorest of the world."[29] This becomes the enduring agenda of those concerned with reducing economic violence in the world.

NOTES

1. Denis Goulet, *The Cruel Choice: A New Concept in the Theory of Development* (New York: Atheneum, 1978), 86–91.

2. World Bank, *World Development Report 1994* (New York: Oxford University Press, 1994), 162.

3. Diego Cevallos, "Trade-Mexico: NAFTA Equals Death, Say Peasant Farmers," Inter Press Service, December 3, 2002, at www.corpwatch.org/news/PND.jsp?articleid=5030 (accessed January 7, 2003).

4. See James M. Harder, "The Economics of War" in *Weathering the Storm: Christian Pacifist Responses to War* (Newton, Kans.: Faith and Life Press, 1991), 61–69.

5. See Dena Montague and Frida Berrigan, "The Business of War in the Democratic Republic of Congo," in *Real World Globalization* (Cambridge, Mass.: Dollars and Sense, 2002), 18–21.

6. This story is recounted in Lucile Brockway, "Plant Imperialism," *History Today*, 33 (July 1983): 31–36.

7. There are multiple vocabularies and analyses of the same essential argument. For example, see André Gunder Frank, *On Capitalist Underdevelopment* (London: Oxford University Press, 1975); or Samir Amin, *Imperialism and Unequal Development* (New York: Monthly Review Press, 1977).

8. As others have pointed out, this does not rule out the possibility that individuals can choose to include personal acts of altruism or charity in their own understanding of self-interest—perhaps for religious or humanitarian reasons.

9. The subdiscipline of welfare economics has developed a specialized vocabulary for these arguments. For example, a market transaction leads to a "Pareto-superior" outcome whenever it improves the welfare of at least one individual without decreasing the welfare of anyone else (see, for example, James Henderson and Richard Quandt, *Microeconomic Theory: A Mathematical Approach* [New York: McGraw-Hill, 1980], 286–291).

10. See Milton Friedman, *Capitalism and Freedom* (Chicago: University of Chicago Press, 1962).

11. Albert O. Hirschman, *Rival Views of Market Society* (Cambridge: Harvard University Press, 1992), 78.

12. Cited in Bruce Herrick and Charles P. Kindleberger, *Economic Development* (New York: McGraw-Hill, 1983), 5.

13. For a brief discussion of the problematic application of mathematical precision to questions of violence and war, see chapter 22 in this volume by Darryl Nester.

14. Quoted in Robert L. Heilbroner, *The Worldly Philosophers: The Life, Times, and Ideas of the Great Economic Thinkers*, 7th ed. (New York: Simon and Schuster, 1999), 14.

15. Adam Smith, *The Wealth of Nations*, Modern Library edition (New York: Random House, 1937), see especially 342–343, 118, 129.

16. For example, grain markets are often portrayed as approximating perfect competition. Seldom is it recognized, however, that today only a handful of corporate giants dominate the purchase of globally traded grain supplies. The world of Adam Smith's level playing field no longer exists.

17. For discussion of the link between specific theological claims and violence see chapter 3 by J. Denny Weaver in this volume.

18. Elsewhere, I have recounted how at a prestigious Christian college, the quasi-religious nature of economics is demonstrated in another way. The college's board of directors normally shows little interest in faculty-hiring decisions but made exceptions in two specific disciplines: religion and economics. In those instances, the board was known to request a face-to-face interview with the final candidate—presumably to ensure a fit with the institution's values. See James M. Harder, "The 'Anabaptist School' of Economics," in *Minding the Church: Scholarship in the Anabaptist Tradition* (Telford, Pa.: Pandora Press, 2002), 134.

19. David Held, ed., *A Globalizing World? Culture, Economics, Politics* (London: Routledge, 2000), 15–17.

20. Daniel Yergin and Joseph Stanislaw, *The Commanding Heights: The Battle between Government and the Marketplace That Is Remaking the Modern World* (New York: Simon and Schuster, 1998).

21. Yergin and Stanislaw, *The Commanding Heights,* 365.

22. The term "economism" was coined by process theologian John B. Cobb Jr. See his article "The Theological Stake in Globalization," at www.religion-online.org/cgi-bin/relsearchd.dll/showarticle?item_id=1095 (accessed January 7, 2002).

23. Yergin and Stanislaw, *The Commanding Heights,* 368.

24. Kofi Annan, "The Politics of Globalization," in *Globalization and the Challenges of a New Century,* ed. Patrick O'Meara, H. D. Mehlinger, and M. Krain (Bloomington: Indiana University Press, 2000), 126.

25. John Isbister, *Capitalism and Justice: Envisioning Social and Economic Fairness* (Bloomfield, Conn.: Kumarian Press, 2001), 89.

26. The points in this section are developed by David Korten, *When Corporations Rule the World,* 2d ed. (San Francisco: Berrett-Koehler Publishers, 2001). See also Herman E. Daly and John B. Cobb Jr., *For the Common Good: Redirecting the Economy toward Community, the Environment, and a Sustainable Future* (Boston: Beacon, 1989).

27. These concepts are developed more fully in James M. Harder and Karen Klassen Harder, "Economics, Development, and Creation," in *Creation and the Environment: An Anabaptist Perspective on a Sustainable World,* ed. Calvin Redekop (Baltimore: Johns Hopkins University Press, 2000), 3–26.

28. Study by William Rees, cited in Korten, *When Corporations Rule the World,* 40.

29. Annan, "The Politics of Globalization," 129.

16

Violence and Nonviolence in Criminal Justice

Jeff Gingerich

As it exists today the criminal justice system of the United States is steeped in violence, both overt and covert, both individual and structural. From arrest to incarceration, the system is filled with practical and moral directives that too often lead to the reinforcement of social inequalities, the degradation of human life, and the affirmation that violence is the ultimate solution to combating violence.

From the numerous media accounts of police brutality to the overwhelming evidence of racial profiling in the United States, the country is becoming increasingly aware of the fallibility of our contemporary system of justice. This fallibility is particularly apparent in the treatment of African American males, one out of three of whom is now under the control of the criminal justice system through incarceration, probation, or parole.[1] The past decade has witnessed a "get tough on crime" mentality that has bolstered public sentiment to build more prisons, creating a multibillion dollar prison industrial complex with gigantic "Supermax" prisons where inmates are placed in cells for twenty-three hours per day and treated as subhuman beings. Furthermore, the past three decades have witnessed a proliferation of offenders who have received the death penalty, one of the strongest pieces of evidence that the criminal justice structure relies on violence.

It would appear that working in the criminal justice system means learning to exercise violence. Given the intrinsically violent character of the criminal justice system, one can ask what role an individual committed to nonviolence can play in it and whether criminal justice is even an appropriate discipline to include in a college curriculum shaped by nonviolence. We would likely find it unthinkable to have an ROTC or any other type of military preparation at a peace church college—so why criminal justice?[2]

There are clear reasons why academics with a firm grounding in a nonviolent perspective *should* be engaged in the process of criminal justice education in undergraduate institutions. For one, there is a biblical mandate. It appears, for example, in the injunction "to do justice," Micah 6:8, and in Jesus' words, quoting from Isaiah 61:1, "to proclaim release to the captives and to set at liberty those who are oppressed" (Luke 4:18). Further, writings on theological understandings of justice and restoration are becoming increasingly prominent,[3] which presents a unique window of opportunity for a distinctive nonviolent Anabaptist perspective to be brought to the field. The field of criminal justice can and should be seen as a central arena for the practice of justice and peacemaking.[4]

RETRIBUTIVE JUSTICE AS CRIMINAL JUSTICE

The current system operates under a retributive model of justice.[5] Retributive justice defines a criminal offense as the breaking of the law and assumes punishment, or "just deserts," as the ultimate solution for dealing with criminal offenses. In other words, an offense—pain—inflicted by the lawbreaker is balanced by equivalent pain—punishment—inflicted on the lawbreaker. In line with public opinion, this system assumes that the harsher the crime, the tougher the penalty. This system thus operates under the assumption that violence responds to violence. Capital punishment is thus not an isolated case of violence within the system but rather the end point of a spectrum of increasingly violent responses. The justification of this system appeals both to the rhetoric of justice based on the application of pain and to the belief that harsh punishment deters future crime.

Another significant characteristic of the current legal system is the extent to which it removes both victim and offender from the process. First, the legal system is a complicated, technical process that requires the presence of highly educated attorneys to "represent" clients. The system thus puts both offenders and victims (when they are actually present) at the mercy of the attorney, while also conferring a significant advantage on the wealthy client—whether offender or victim—who has the means to purchase the most skilled lawyers. Victims rarely participate in the judicial process, for they are thought to be too emotional and too biased. In this retributive system, the two parties actually involved in the process are the state, whose law was broken, and the offender, who broke the state's law. The purpose of the trial is to determine whether the accused is guilty as charged. A verdict of guilty results in punishment. This system thus moves the victim, the one harmed by the offender, out of the process and onto the sidelines, a nonparticipant in the legal process and without redress for harm done by the offender.

This retributive paradigm has proved ineffective at reducing crime and in deterring repeat offenders. In many cases it is immoral. Studies show that crime rates fluctuate, not according to the severity of sentences given to offenders, but rather on the basis of broader social and economic trends. Recidivism rates remain high, and contrary to public opinion, punishment has not proved effective as a deterrent factor.[6] Historically, this system has not delivered what it has promised. It has not sufficiently prevented crime, rehabilitated offenders, or addressed the losses of victims. Public officials, system administrators, and the public at large should face some serious questions. Why has the system failed the public not only in terms of public safety but in failing to restore wounded people and fractured communities?

RESTORATIVE JUSTICE AS CRIMINAL JUSTICE

To approach the field of criminal justice from a nonviolent perspective, one must view both the causes and the consequences of crime from an entirely new perspective or, in Howard Zehr's apt metaphor, through a new lens.[7] Zehr borrowed from ancient practices to pose an entirely new paradigm for the present era. As noted above, the current system operates under a retributive model of justice. Ancient historical practices, on the other hand, operated under a restorative model of justice.[8] Restorative justice confronts crime but without continuing the cycle of violence. It empowers victims in their search for healing and holds offenders accountable for their actions by impressing upon them the real human impact of their behavior. Let's compare the assumptions behind retributive and restorative justice.

A restorative justice approach begins to deal with crime at a much different point than retributive justice. Restorative justice views crime fundamentally as a violation of people and relationships rather than a violation of the state or the state's law. Rather than treating a crime simply as a broken law, a restorative approach concentrates on the harm done to people, to relationships, and to communities. Instead of requiring the offender to serve a prison term to "pay a debt to society" for breaking the state's written rule, restorative justice focuses on the obligation of the offender to repair the harm to the victim. Thus the goal of restorative justice is actual restoration—as much as is humanly possible—to bring wholeness back to the situation and the people involved. From the perspective of nonviolence, it is evident that rather than responding to violence with violence, the focus on restoration changes the equation while also demanding that painful situations of wrongdoing be treated with humanness for all parties.

In a restorative process the key players are not limited to the state and the offender. Rather, a restorative process will include all victims who have been injured in the event, as well as the community and the offenders. Bringing victims back into the justice equation holds open the possibility for a deeper level of restoration. The traditional system of justice neglects and ignores the needs of victims. Victims need a chance to tell their story. For the sake of their recovery, they need to make statements and have their questions answered.[9] A nonviolent approach to crime requires consideration of these needs of victims in the process of working for restoration. Giving attention to the needs of victims may at times seem to conflict with the basic approach of many offender advocacy groups who feel the need to focus on the offender as a victim of societal injustice, such as the systemic violence of poverty or racism. Indeed, offenders frequently are victims of such injustice, but pursuing that kind advocacy without also focusing on the harm done to crime victims may "revictimize" the individuals who have been most directly hurt by the crime. A restorative approach addresses all these elements—the needs of individual victims, the needs of offenders and their obligation to make restitution, and the systemic and societal problems that contribute to criminal behavior.

One goal of the process of restorative justice is to bring offenders to understand their obligations so that they can be held accountable for their crimes. In this goal statement, notice the shift from a passive to an active involvement of the offender in the process. Instead of merely asserting forcefully that criminals must be punished ("do the crime, do the time"), the more sophisticated restorative approach requires the offender's participation in making amends for the wrong that was done. Braithwaite and Roche explain that the restorative justice paradigm requires the offender to take an *active* responsibility in the process of restoration in contrast to the *passive* responsibility implicit within the retributive paradigm.[10] In a restorative perspective, to be held accountable for one's crimes means that offenders are brought to understand the consequences of their decisions, then to move beyond the neutralizing strategies that downplay such actions, and finally to accept the responsibility and the obligation to take part in repairing as much as possible what was broken as a result of the crime.

Dialogue is a central premise of nonviolent peacemaking, and a central goal of restorative justice is dialogue between victim and offender. The current practices of victim–offender dialogue, family conferencing, and peacemaking circles[11] are a few of the methods that restorative justice practitioners have used to "encourage collaboration and reintegration, rather than coercion and isolation."[12] These practices not only provide a space of respect in which to address the wounds suffered by the offender they have also proved effective in preventing repeat behavior. Both victims and offenders report higher levels of satisfaction from participation in restorative justice processes in comparison with the current judicial system. At the same time, offenders are more likely to make restitution to victims after participation in the mediation process of restorative justice than if the offender is ordered by a court to make restitution.[13]

Finally, beyond new individual treatment models for dealing with the effects of crime on individuals, restorative justice also considers the underlying structural causes that lead to crime. In doing so, crime, violence, and conflict are viewed more broadly. The effects of a capitalist economy and of institutional racism are two examples of larger social problems that produce fertile ground for human conflict. Throughout history practitioners of nonviolence have actively confronted such larger systems of social injustice. Restorative justice must make this emphasis a priority as well.

RESTORATIVE JUSTICE IN UNDERGRADUATE EDUCATION

The field of restorative justice has been rapidly gaining attention and resources. Consequently, students of criminal justice need an earlier introduction to restorative justice principles. Currently, many people are learning about restorative justice theory and practice in a training format only after they enter their professional careers. Students would benefit greatly from learning to view crime and justice through a restorative lens *prior* to immersion in the traditional criminal justice system. Practioners will not have to make a paradigm shift if their initial paradigm is a restorative one.

This observation sets up two important observations about restorative justice in the undergraduate, liberal arts curriculum. The first concerns its applicability. Not only is it important to make students who want to work in the criminal justice system aware of restorative justice principles before they enter the system; it is equally important to impress on these students that restorative justice has immediate specific practical applications. Graduating students with an orientation in restorative justice need not wait for a complete systemic reform away from retributive justice to take place. The principles have immediate application. Persons working in the current criminal justice system can apply restorative justice principles on the authority of their office at whatever level they are working. Although it is sometimes difficult if this approach is not supported by the system as a whole, counselors, parole officers, prison administrators, lawyers, judges can all bring the insights of restorative justice to bear in their decision making.

Second, restorative justice fits within the purposes of a liberal arts education. It is a multidisciplinary subject in the social sciences. A goal for general education courses in those areas should be to expose restorative justice principles to *all* liberal arts students with a view to making them better informed citizens, who can recognize and support restorative justice initiatives in the criminal justice system of their communities. Exposing all students to principles of restorative justice in general education courses in the liberal arts curriculum will contribute to wider public acceptance of restorative principles in the future. For people concerned about the violence both overt and systemic in our society, exposing students to restorative justice is an important contribution of a liberal arts curriculum shaped by principles of nonviolence.[14] So what does it mean to have a criminal justice program within a curriculum shaped by principles of nonviolence? At Bluffton College, it means we offer "community justice" courses on conflict transformation, mediation, and restorative justice theory and practice. It means we discuss practices like peacemaking circles, community policing, and alternative types of probation and parole. And it means a central focus on encouraging students not only to understand how to deal with crime after it has occurred but also to develop a deeper understanding of why crime occurs in the first place.

Teaching restorative justice theory and practice, however, is not a simple matter of indoctrination. We also have courses that explain—as well as critique—the present retributive form of criminal justice in the United States. Before students can pose new and viable alternatives, they need to have a thorough understanding of the present system.

Difficult questions still remain regarding the teaching of restorative justice within an undergraduate criminal justice program and the liberal arts curriculum. Should we have courses in our program devoted to law enforcement? Stated differently, has the field of restorative justice actually developed enough alternatives to offer a complete curriculum focused on restorative practices in place of the current retributive practice of law enforcement? If the major is called *criminal justice,* does it convey too much the connotations of retributive justice? Or should a major in criminal justice shaped by restorative justice principles have another name, and should it be described as a major in peace or conflict studies? Further, given the wide scope that restorative justice brings to a victim and an offender, how does an academic institution actually maintain accountability to victims, offenders, and communities in its academic program?

Finally, a practical question about developing a program in restorative justice concerns the very viability of the program. If we build it, will they come? If we center an academic program on restorative justice, will we attract students? In an age of real-life cops shows and drama series that glamorize the lives of criminal lawyers and law enforcement officers, few incoming freshmen arrive on campus who want to learn more about peace and reconciliation *and* also major in criminal justice. And even when they do enter the program, we must also acknowledge that after studying in our curriculum, students may *still* decide to enter traditional criminal justice roles that perpetuate violence. Even though our program does not specialize in accommodating students to the retributive system, a part of our pedagogy is to teach about the current system and, in seeing that system, students can decide to reject restorative justice. This is a reality and a risk that we take in exploring a system that so often runs counter to nonviolent values.

The events of September 11, 2001, shifted the public dialogue about justice and crime toward vengeance and retaliation. Not surprisingly, this discussion has infiltrated our college classrooms as well. A nonviolent worldview pushes us to address the tremendous wounds of the individual victims and the wounds of a national community. How do we respond to this tragedy from a restorative justice perspective? The nonviolent criminal justice curriculum provides an opportunity for faculty and students together to search for alternative paradigms with which to address such attacks.[15] A restorative justice curriculum provides many opportunities for students to envision an "investigation" of the situation that does not merely focus on attempts to root out the terrorists. This investigation should also attempt to discover the underlying elements of a capitalist, globalized world that contribute to such terrorist actions;[16] to find a response to the victims of the attack that goes beyond financial needs to address psychological and social needs of victims; to develop an approach to the offenders that holds them accountable for their actions and the wounds that they have caused but without encouraging a martyrdom status; and to formulate a community and governmental response that fully addresses our fears about safety and wholeness by considering the underlying sources of broken international relationships.

And with this brief discussion of September 11, we see that restorative justice is really part of a nonviolent worldview that envisions the entire world.

NOTES

1. See David Cole, *No Equal Justice: Race and Class in the American Criminal Justice System* (New York: The New Press, 1999); Jerome Miller, *Search and Destroy: African American Males in the Criminal Justice System* (Cambridge: Cambridge University Press, 1996); and Robynne Neugebauer, ed., *Criminal Injustice: Racism in the Criminal Justice System* (Toronto: Canadian Scholars Press, 2000). For specific information on racial profiling among police, see David Harris, "Driving While Black: Racial Profiling on Our Nation's Highways," *An American Civil Liberties Special Report, June 1999,* at www.aclu.org/profiling/report/ index.html (accessed September 30, 2002).

2. Christian Peacemaker Teams have demonstrated a workable, nonviolent alternative model to ROTC programs on campus. See www.prairienet.org/cpt/index.html (accessed September 30, 2002).

3. Two examples are Timothy Gorringe, *God's Just Vengeance: Crime, Violence, and the Rhetoric of Salvation* (Cambridge: Cambridge University Press, 1996); and J. Denny Weaver, *The Nonviolent Atonement* (Grand Rapids, Mich.: Eerdmans, 2001), from which Weaver's chapter 3 in this volume is drawn.

4. An important step toward integrating the discussion of the justice system into the peace college curriculum was a 1998 meeting of Mennonite college representatives held at Bethel College in Newton, Kansas, to address the question Can a peace church college uphold its values while preparing students to enter into a system that uses violence as a basis for maintaining social control? The meeting reached a clear consensus—Mennonites can and should be educating on and about the criminal justice system, if operating within the historic values of the peace church. See Report and Minutes of Restorative Justice Palavar, September 1998. (In my possession.) I am indebted to this group for much of my own understanding of this issue.

5. The discussion of retributive justice, as well as of restorative justice to follow, comes from Howard Zehr, *Changing Lenses: A New Focus for Crime and Justice* (Scottdale, Pa.: Herald Press, 1990).

6. For example, the national incarceration rate doubled between 1985 and 1995 at the same time that every major category of violent crime, particularly violent youth crimes, was increasing. Elliot Curry, *Crime and Punishment in America* (New York: Henry Holt, 1998), 29.

7. See Zehr, *Changing Lenses.*

8. The roots of restorative justice can be traced back as far as the Code of Hammurabi, which prescribed restitution for property offenses, and to ancient Hebrew codes of justice, which were principally aimed at restoring wholeness to broken relationships. Such responses to crime require offenders and their families to make amends to victims and their families—not simply to ensure that injured persons received restitution but also to restore community peace. See Dan Van Ness, *Restoring Justice* (Cincinnati: Anderson, 2002), 8. For history of restorative justice in religion, see Michael L. Hadley, ed., *The Spiritual Roots of Restorative Justice* (Albany: State University of New York Press, 2001).

9. See Judith Herman, *Trauma and Recovery* (New York: Basic, 1997); Howard Zehr, *Transcending: Reflections of Crime Victims* (Intercourse, Pa.: Good Books, 2001); and Andrew Karmen, *Crime Victims* (Belmont, Calif.: Wadsworth, 1996). For more direct application of restorative justice to victim's needs, see Mary Achilles and Howard Zehr, "Restorative Justice for Crime Victims: The Promise, the Challenge," in *Restorative Community Justice: Repairing Harm and Transforming Communities*, ed. Bazemore and Schiff (Cincinnati: Anderson, 2001), 87–99.

10. John Braithwaite and Declan Roche, "Responsibility and Restorative Justice," in *Restorative Community Justice: Repairing Harm and Transforming Communities*, ed. Bazemore and Schiff (Cincinnati: Anderson, 2001), 63–84.

11. For more information on the practical application of restorative justice theory, see Susan Sharpe, *Restorative Justice: A Vision for Healing and Change* (Edmonton, Alb.: Edmonton Victim Offender Mediation Society, 1998).

12. Harry Mika and Howard Zehr, "Restorative Justice Signposts," *Conciliation Quarterly* 20, no. 3 (summer 2001).

13. Mark S. Umbreit, *Victim Meets Offender: The Impact of Restorative Justice and Mediation* (Monsey, N.Y.: Criminal Justice Press, 1994).

14. See chapter 5 by John Kampen in this volume.

15. J. Denny Weaver includes a restorative response to the September 11, 2001, terrorist attacks in his "Responding to September 11 — and October 7 and January 29: Which Religion Shall We Follow?" *Conrad Grebel Review* 20, no. 2 (spring 2002): 79–100.

16. For one element of that discussion, see chapter 15 by James M. Harder in this volume.

17

Psychology's Missed Opportunities for Teaching Peace

Pamela S. Nath

Both war and peace rest upon assumptions about the human condition. War is fueled by the assumption that violent conflict is inevitable—for protection and to ensure proper respect from others. A belief in justified violence can easily result from the assumption that the best way to deal with "bad," "wrong," and "unworthy" people is to defeat or even destroy them. Conversely, nonviolence and peacemaking can be fostered by other assumptions about the human condition—that the stranger has similar longings, hurts, and vulnerabilities as our own, that diversity is enriching, that aggression (from others) is fueled by fear or want, and that violence leads to more violence. Acceptance of these worldviews lays the foundation for nonviolent responses to the events of our world.

What does psychology, the science of human behavior, have to say about these sets of assumptions? Does it tend to favor one worldview over the other? Would accepting peace-fostering assumptions about human behavior change the discipline and the way a person committed to nonviolence would teach psychology? This chapter invites dialogue around such questions.

BASIC ASSUMPTIONS OF PSYCHOLOGY

Most introductory psychology textbooks describe psychology as the science of human behavior. This presumed empirical foundation for the discipline of psychology still leaves room for questions about the assumptions that shape the empirical "truths" that psychologists find and the theories developed to organize those truths.

The question of whether mainstream psychology works from assumptions that support nonviolence or violence is a complicated one. Diversity within the more than 155,000 members of the American Psychological Association (APA)[1] makes it difficult to say what constitutes the core of contemporary psychology or what the typical psychologist thinks. Differences abound both within specialty areas as well as within schools of thought. Different assumptions shape how a psychologist will approach the search for the causes of human behavior, including violence. For example the biological approach attempts to explain the potential for violent behavior through an exploration of biological factors, such as genetic inheritance, hormone levels, or activity or lack thereof in different regions of the brain. Freudians view aggression as a basic human motivation. The behavioral and social-cognitive approaches emphasize the role of environmental factors in shaping the likelihood of violence. Both within and across these approaches, researchers and theorists vary in terms of the extent to which they see violence as an inevitable reality of the human condition. In the midst of this diversity how does one approach the question of whether the discipline of psychology is rooted in violent assumptions?

In this chapter I begin to explore this question through an examination of the material to which students are typically exposed in an introductory psychology class. An examination of textbooks used in such classes can provide a glimpse into how the discipline introduces itself to newcomers. This first exposure can shape future understandings in subtle but powerful ways.

Cognitive psychology and the study of human perception has shown that in order to process information in the world around us, we develop schemas or cognitive structures that enable us to organize and make sense of the myriad of data that confronts us constantly. Too much novel information can overwhelm; we learn most easily when we have organizational categories and past experience to which we can connect new material. Once these schemas are developed, however, they can inhibit alternative ways of viewing the world. In my introductory psychology class, for example, I use a simple exercise to show students how schemas can limit our perceptions. On the board I write "time flies I cant theyre too fast" and then ask the students to add punctuation until these words make sense. They may not rearrange word order. The students quickly add the apostrophes to the contractions but then often get stumped. Sometimes one or two will happen upon the punctuation that makes sense: "Time flies? I can't! They're too fast!" And suddenly the meaning becomes obvious. These words refer to putting stopwatches on flying insects, not to the fact that days and hours pass too quickly.

This simple illustration demonstrates the extent to which we see what we expect to see and sometimes are unable to see anything different. Past experience and ways of thinking limit the ability to organize words (or facts) in new ways that might provide better solutions to a problem. In terms of our understanding of human behavior, the point is this: the initial theories that we develop to make sense of human behavior may have an enormous influence in shaping what we see in the world and how we make sense of it. And the initial theories may interfere with our ability to "make sense" in new, alternative ways. Thus psychological theories shape not only the discipline but also our culture.[2] In fact this introductory level of psychology may have the most widespread influence since many students will not be exposed to material from the discipline at a deeper level.

For all these reasons the question of what is taught to students in introductory psychology textbooks may assist in critical reflection on how psychology has shaped (and limited) our cultural understandings of human behavior. In particular, questions of violence, nonviolence, and peacemaking call for that critical reflection.

MISSED OPPORTUNITIES IN INTRODUCTORY PSYCHOLOGY TEXTBOOKS

So what does psychology say to new students about the human behaviors of violence and peacemaking? A review of a convenience sample of six textbooks suggests that they vary greatly in the amount of coverage they give to topics such as violence, aggression, conflict, conflict resolution, war, the military, and peacemaking.[3] Of these topics the most thoroughly covered is *aggression,* which is included in the index of all the textbooks reviewed and has the most pages devoted to it, a total of seventy. *Violence* is indexed much less frequently and appears on a total of only eleven pages in all the textbooks combined. Biological influences, interpersonal and media modeling of violence, and frustration and stress from such factors as noise, heat, pain, and aversive odors are the most frequently discussed causal factors in aggressive behavior. Several of the textbooks discuss research regarding how "cultures of honor" (cultures where small slights are viewed as insults to one's reputation that cannot be ignored) demonstrate higher rates of aggressive behaviors.[4] In a discussion of the way that narcissism can contribute to an individual's likelihood to respond aggressively, a textbook that otherwise ignores issues of war and peace mentions that some have suggested that nationalism is "narcissism on a grand scale."[5] Only one of the six textbooks discusses how social injustice (in this case a disparity between the rich and the poor) might contribute to rates of violence.[6] Overall, individualistic factors contributing to aggression are favored over explanations that focus on social or cultural influences.

The discussion of aggression focuses on individual acts of aggression rather than organized aggression between nations, or ethnic or religious groups. Half of the six textbooks fail to identify war as an important human behavior to be examined and explained. Only three of the six include the topic *war* in the index and none index the term *military.* In all of the textbooks combined, war is mentioned on a total of only ten pages, less than one-third of 1 percent of the total pages in the textbooks. Only one of the six textbooks contains a moderately thorough discussion of the psychology of war.[7] The failure of most of the textbooks to include a substantial discussion of the psychological factors that contribute to war is startling. Is war seen as so inevitable, necessary, and self-explanatory that a search for its psychological causes is an unnecessary avenue for a discipline that focuses on understanding human behavior? Perhaps, the beginning student might subconsciously assume, war is so natural that it is already understood—there is no need to raise questions about it.

Though several of the textbooks include a discussion of Posttraumatic Stress Disorder as one of the consequences of war, none of the authors of these textbooks discuss or analyze the role that military training and experiences of war may play in contributing to societal violence. That seems a significant omission since the military psychologist David Grossman has argued for the role of conditioning in overcoming a soldier's resistance to killing.[8] The issues raised by Grossman are particularly important in the light of the recent murder of four military wives by their spouses at Fort Bragg. Likewise, although all the textbooks discuss Bandura's research on the effects of social modeling, none raise the possibility that military action by a country may have a modeling effect on its citizens.[9]

At least as troubling is the exclusion of conflict resolution and peacemaking as topics of discussion in these introductory texts. Only one text includes a discussion of peace psychology,[10] while another refers explicitly to conflict reduction.[11] Taken together, peace and conflict reduction are included on only eleven pages in all of the textbooks combined, less than one-third of 1 percent of the total pages in the textbooks. One is reminded of the impact of the absence of the study of altruism in previous generations of textbooks. The underlying assumption of psychology seemed to be that all human behavior was self-serving[12] and the absence of a discussion of altruistic behavior allowed this assumption to go unchallenged. In much the same way, the absence of peacemaking and conflict resolution in today's textbooks may leave students with the impression that aggression, violence, and war are unavoidable human behaviors, particularly in situations of frustration or threat. Introducing the study of peace-promoting attitudes and actions to newcomers to the field might help to counteract this all-too-prevalent assumption.

The two textbooks that cover the topics of peace psychology and conflict reduction focus on several factors as important steps toward making peace between groups in conflict. Both of the texts include a discussion of the importance of contact,[13] whereas only one discusses the critical role that cooperation on mutual goals and equal power between groups—including economic and legal power—play in fostering the effectiveness of intergroup contact.[14] None of the textbooks includes any mention of nonviolent resistance as a possible response to violence. Especially in the U.S. context, students may be left with unchallenged assumptions that retaliatory responses demonstrating national force and resolve are the natural and perhaps the only way to respond to aggression toward one's self or nation. As recent historical writing demonstrates,[15] that assumption is invalid. Including research findings about recovery from violent trauma might encourage students to question this assumption in American culture. One of the most shattering consequences of violent trauma is an alarming recognition of one's vulnerability. Although one possible response to this vulnerability may be to strike back and thus to feel in control and reduce the uncomfortable sense of vulnerability, experts on trauma have found that over time, victims' increased recognition of their own vulnerability may in fact be the soil in which a deep appreciation for life's meaning and value develops.[16] A number of textbooks include other principles that might be helpful in fostering nonviolence and peacemaking, but they are not organized in any coherent discussion of the psychology of violence, conflict, war, and peace. For example, several of the textbooks include discussions of scapegoating and dehumanization of the enemy, deindividuation, and diffusion of responsibility as important contributors to human aggression. However, these topics are often scattered throughout the textbook rather than being presented in a unified discussion of our current understanding of the psychological factors that play a role in war and in peace.

In summary a review of textbooks reveals both the limited coverage of principles related to violence, war, conflict resolution, and especially peacemaking, and the failure to organize and integrate the findings of psychology that are relevant to these issues. As a result novice students may find it hard to identify these topics as important issues for the study of psychology or to recognize the possibility of utilizing psychological principles in promoting a less violent and more peaceful world.

TEACHING THE PSYCHOLOGY OF PEACE AND NONVIOLENCE IN A VIOLENT WORLD

Given that the topics of war, violence, and peacemaking are sometimes absent from introductory psychology textbooks, the first responsibility of academic psychologists committed to peace is to include supplementary material in their classes that introduces students to these topics and to the work of APA's Division of Peace Psychology. Current events, such as a campus conflict, highly publicized crimes, executions of capital offenders, terrorism, and war, all provide contexts for identifying important questions about human conflict and applicable psychological principles. A discussion of current events may also provide an opportunity to expose unnamed and unexamined assumptions about human behavior and to consider potentially more peaceful alternative assumptions. The events of September 11, 2001, provided such an opportunity in my own classroom.[17]

The attacks on the World Trade Center provided a particularly critical context for struggling with the question of teaching psychology in a manner that promotes peace. I identified several responsibilities about peacemaking as I entered the psychology classroom in the days following the attacks.

Given that there are alternative responses to trauma and alternative ways of explaining the causes that provoked the terrorists' actions, my first goal was to help students to recognize claims about the human condition as "theories," as human constructions that attempt to make meaning of the events that we encounter in the world. By emphasizing to my students the critical worldview of the discipline of psychology—the view that assumptions or theories about the human condition require empirical testing and support rather than being accepted as "givens" or absolutes—I hoped to encourage students to be critical consumers of the culture of nationalism and war that is prevalent in the United States and that has become much more prevalent in the days since September 11, 2001.

I also saw it as my responsibility to propose alternative theories about the human events that students are attempting to understand. For example, following the events of September 11, 2001, I emphasized to my students that the behavior of terrorists is *human* behavior that we ought to seek to understand in *human* terms if we hope to change it. Demonizing the enemy—seeing them as less than human—permits and promotes a warlike response.[18] In contrast recognizing the enemy's behavior as human challenges us to attempt to understand rather than simply to destroy.

Promoting peace in the classroom can go beyond intellectual endeavor, however. Some students will have psychological needs that if left unattended may make it difficult for them to choose peace. Developing peacemakers in the classroom means addressing these needs. War does not just happen. War occurs when arguments are made for war and then others accept these arguments. People are particularly vulnerable to arguments for war when they feel traumatized and vulnerable. Ronnie Janoff-Bulman and colleagues identified several ways in which trauma challenges our basic assumptions about the world that help us to feel safe and secure, such as that we live in a just and benevolent world.[19] As a result, trauma leaves us with a heightened sense of vulnerability. In the days following the terrorist attacks, I recognized such reactions in my students, particularly in students who had previously had little exposure to the reality that there is much violence and suffering in the world. Helping students to recognize and identify the trauma they have experienced and the ways it can influence and bias their thinking can help them to make active choices regarding their healing process. For example several students explicitly acknowledged a connection between their heightened sense of vulnerability and their desire for the United States to respond with a retaliatory military strike.

Those who have encountered trauma need to find ways to make meaning of their experiences and to reorganize their view of the world in order to cope with their newfound vulnerability. Here are two different approaches to this meaning-making activity. The first comes from the address of President George W. Bush to the U.S. Congress after the attacks of September 11, 2001. Bush said, "Freedom and fear. . . . Justice and cruelty . . . have always been at war. And we know that God is not neutral between them." The president's suggestion that the United States is allied with an ultimate good in a battle against ultimate evil provided the opportunity for those who feel vulnerable to respond aggressively or to support a violent response in order to demonstrate strength. Aggressive responses following trauma can be an attempt to reassert the just-world assumptions that have been shattered by the experience of one's own vulnerability. A different way of coping with similar feelings appeared in a posting in an Internet discussion forum following the attacks. The woman who posted the comment unapologetically recognized the pain and loss caused by recent events but simultaneously demonstrated an ability to recognize that further hatred would not resolve her feelings. She wrote:

> My best friend was in the South tower when this terrible tragedy took place. . . . She left behind a 5 year old daughter, a loving husband and family and many friends. . . .

Last night I spoke to her daughter, who is the same age as my little girl. . . . She asked me, whether, if she prayed really hard, her Mommy would come back to her. . . . Why does a five-year-old girl have to ask such a terrible question? Why did this senseless thing have to take place? I am crying and grieving for my friend that I grew up with, for all the victims and their families. I am praying for all their souls and the souls of those who did this. May God have mercy on them! There is so much hatred now, but this will not change what happened and it will not help how we feel. I cannot find forgiveness in my heart for the people responsible, but I am praying for the strength to do just that. Hate and revenge will only take this further and it will lead to a war that will leave the world in ruins. . . . How many more children have to pray for their parents to come home before this nightmare will end?

As this response to horrible loss and trauma demonstrates, seeing one's own vulnerability in light of the common frailty of the human condition can result in the development of a deeper and more rooted sense of the value and meaning of one's own life. Psychologists who work with trauma have described this potentially positive impact of trauma on individuals.[20] Exposure to the stories of others who have dealt with and overcome violence and suffering without the use of retaliatory violence can help traumatized people to find an alternative path out of their vulnerability. Helping students to understand these psychological dimensions of dealing with trauma will certainly counter the all-too-prevalent assumption that violence is an inevitable human behavior.

In introductory courses, teachers of psychology can help students to understand that the stories we tell and the theories we adopt to make sense of the world have a critical impact on how we live. Cognitive psychology emphasizes that our ways of making sense of the world shape both our emotions about and responses to the world. Telling stories that lead to peace will increase the possibility that those who hear our stories will behave in peaceful ways.

Psychologists and teachers of psychology have an important role to play in addressing violence in our society. If they can develop sense-making schemata that escape the blinders imposed by assumptions about the inevitability of violence, teachers of psychology can provide true, nonviolence-shaped schemas for students as well as assist them in responding to trauma and their sense of vulnerability with insight that counters the prevailing calls for violent retaliation.

NOTES

1. The size of the discipline is also revealed by the following numbers: in 1996 approximately 65,000 students graduated with bachelors degrees in psychology. In 1996–1997 2,116 individuals earned doctorates in psychology. See American Psychological Association, 2002, at www.apa.org/students/brochure/outlook.html (accessed October 6, 2002).

2. Philip Cushman, *Constructing the Self, Constructing America: A Cultural History of Psychotherapy* (Reading, Mass.: Addison-Wesley, 1995).

3. The following introductory textbooks were reviewed for this chapter: Robert A. Baron, *Psychology,* 5th ed. (Boston: Allyn and Bacon, 2001); Stephen F. Davis and Joseph

J. Palladino, *Psychology,* 3d ed. (Upper Saddle River, N.J.: Prentice Hall, 2000); Richard J. Gerrig and Philip G. Zimbardo, *Psychology and Life,* 16th ed. (Boston: Allyn and Bacon, 2002); Stephen M. Kosslyn and Robin S. Rosenberg, *Psychology: The Brain, the Person, the World* (Boston: Allyn and Bacon, 2001); David G. Myers, *Exploring Psychology,* 5th ed. (New York: Worth Publishers, 2002); and Carole Wade and Carol Tavris, *Psychology,* 7th ed. (Upper Saddle River, N.J.: Prentice Hall, 2003).

4. Gerrig and Zimbardo, *Psychology and Life,* 577; Myers, *Exploring Psychology,* 556; and Wade and Tavris, *Psychology,* 483–484.

5. Kosslyn and Rosenberg, *Psychology,* 456.

6. Myers, *Exploring Psychology,* 556.

7. Gerrig and Zimbardo, *Psychology and Life,* 589–591.

8. David Grossman, *On Killing: The Psychological Costs of Learning to Kill in War and Society* (Boston: Little, Brown, 1996).

9. Dane Archer and Rosemary Gartner, *Violence and Crime in Cross-National Perspective* (New Haven: Yale University Press, 1984); John Wilkes, "Murder in Mind," *Psychology Today,* June 1987, 27–32.

10. Gerrig and Zimbardo, *Psychology and Life,* 591–594.

11. Wade and Tavris, *Psychology,* 301–303.

12. Michael Wallach and Lise Wallach, "How Psychology Sanctions the Cult of the Self," *Washington Monthly* (February 1985): 46–56.

13. Gerrig and Zimbardo, *Psychology and Life,* 593–594; and Wade and Tavris, *Psychology,* 302.

14. Wade and Tavris, *Psychology,* 302.

15. See chapter 6 in this volume by Perry Bush as well as James C. Juhnke and Carol M. Hunter, *The Missing Peace: The Search for Nonviolent Alternatives in United States History* (Kitchener, Ont.: Pandora Press, 2001).

16. See for example Ronnie Janoff-Bulman and Michael Berg, "Disillusionment and the Creation of Value: From Traumatic Losses to Existential Gains," in *Perspectives on Loss: A Sourcebook,* ed. John H. Harvey (Philadelphia: Brunner/Mazel, 1998), 43; and Ronnie Janoff-Bulman and Andrea R. Berger, "The Other Side of Trauma: Toward a Psychology of Appreciation," in *Loss and Trauma: General and Close Relationship Perspectives,* ed. John H. Harvey and Eric D. Miller (New York: Brunner-Routledge, 2000), 29–44.

17. For additional information on psychological research relating to terrorism, see the recently published bibliography in the journal of APA's Division of Peace Psychology, Herbert H. Blumberg, "Understanding and Dealing with Terrorism: A Classification of Some Contributions from the Behavioral and Social Sciences," *Peace and Conflict: Journal of Peace Psychology* 8, no. 1 (2002): 3–16.

18. Grossman, *On Killing,* 156–170.

19. See for example Ronnie Janoff-Bulman and Michael Berg, "Disillusionment and the Creation of Value: From Traumatic Losses to Existential Gains," in *Perspectives on Loss: A Sourcebook,* ed. John H. Harvey (Philadelphia: Brunner/Mazel, 1998), 36–37; and Ronnie Janoff-Bulman and Cynthia McPherson Frantz, "The Impact of Trauma on Meaning: From Meaningless World to Meaningful Life," in *The Transformation of Meaning in Psychological Therapies: Integrating Theory and Practice,* ed. Mick Power and Chris R. Brewin (New York: John Wiley, 1997), 92–95.

20. Viktor E. Frankl, *Man's Search for Meaning* (New York: Pocket Books, 1963); and Ronnie Janoff-Bulman and Michael Berg, "Disillusionment and the Creation of Value."

18

War and Peace in Economic Terms

Ronald L. Friesen

The analytical methods of economics have many potentially fruitful applications to the issues of war and peace. However, these applications have yet to permeate mainstream economics. This chapter begins to fill this void by encouraging a more realistic, comprehensive definition of economics relevant to issues of war and peace, thus exposing some of the prevalent myths and half-truths related to these issues. The chapter uses standard economic theory and by using applications from typical course material and texts, shows that a peace analysis is not so much a highly specialized understanding as it is a simple willingness to bring a peace perspective to bear on standard data of economic analysis.

THE ECONOMICS PROFESSION AND WAR AND PEACE ISSUES

Writing in one of the most popular texts of economic principles, Campbell R. McConnell describes two kinds of economics:

> *Positive economics* focuses on facts and cause-and-effect relationships. It includes description, theory development, and theory testing . . . Positive economics avoids value judgments, tries to establish scientific statements about economic behavior, and deals with what the economy is actually like. . . . Policy economics, on the other hand, involves *normative economics*, which incorporates value judgments about what the economy should be like or what particular policy actions should be recommended to achieve a desirable goal.[1]

This chapter employs standard, often mathematics-based, economic analyses (positive economics), but it also interprets the results in terms of their implications for war and peace issues from a nonviolent perspective (normative economics). The war and peace applications have not been common within the economics professions, which generally work within conventional social parameters that assume the use of violence.

Three examples illustrate the need to display peace economics in a field dominated by violence-accommodating economics. First, despite the presence of several Nobel Prize winners in economics on its board, the Economists Allied for Arms Reduction (ECAAR), of which I am a charter member, has had great difficulty becoming a recognized group within the American Economics Association (AEA). Second, the precarious status of peace economics is made visible in the publication history of McConnell's best selling textbook just cited. In the 1978 edition only, the text included a chapter on the economics of war and peace. By the time the next edition appeared, more traditional and presumably more pressing economic issues had replaced that chapter. Third, publication of a compendium of economics reading lists, course outlines, exams, puzzles, and problems related to peace and war generated the creation of only seven peace economics courses throughout the world of American higher education, and two of those were Bluffton College courses.[2] The results were few in number despite a national effort to generate course materials. Many interested respondents indicated that since the economics of war and peace was not a major field in economics at their institutions, any courses generated in peace economics would not be helpful in promotion and tenure and hence such courses were not generated.

THE DEFINITION OF ECONOMICS

A brief survey of standard definitions of economics will lead to a definition that serves the analysis of war and peace issues. Standard definitions of economics typically focus on the "economic problem" of scarcity. But the nature of scarcity can be defined in different ways and hence be relevant to different issues. Both the scarce means and plentiful objectives can be defined simply and narrowly or defined broadly and in a more inclusive, complex manner. Although both narrow and broad definitions serve a purpose, the more comprehensive approach will be seen to have the best application to issues of war and peace.

A typical introductory definition of economics appears in McConnell's textbook.[3] As a beginning definition of economics he gives: "*the social science concerned with the efficient use of scarce resources to achieve maximum satisfaction of economic wants.*"[4] Later he expands the definition to include "two fundamental facts" that "together constitute the *economizing problem* and provide a foundation for economics." These facts are that the societal wants of all individuals and institutions "are virtually unlimited and insatiable," while the resources to meet these wants "are limited or scarce."[5]

This supposedly simple or limited definition of economics includes a number of assumptions. It concerns only *material* wants. At the same time note that "plentiful" wants and "scarce" means are relative terms. An economic problem exists any time means are scarce *relative* to the objectives to be achieved. Further, note that the definition presumably includes all citizens, including the disadvantaged, such as the poor, as well as the institutions responsible for their welfare. Thus the definition includes public and governmental institutions, as well as individuals and private property. Yet a further dimension of this definition is the assumption that economic analysis is irrelevant without relative imbalance of means and objectives. Most economists would argue, however, that in most circumstances for individuals and family households as well as for businesses, governments, and social institutions, there are always unmet needs that make economic analysis relevant.

The current task can make better use of an advanced definition from Robert H. Frank's intermediate microeconomics text: "Microeconomics is the study of how people choose under conditions of scarcity." Although it sounds simple, its complexity comes from the fact that scarcity applies to more than money and material resources. For example, "time is a scarce resource for everyone," which becomes apparent when we note that our free time, rather than the price of admission, determines the number of movies we see. "*Every* choice involves important elements of scarcity," sometimes of money but frequently not. "Coping with scarcity in one form or another is the essence of the human condition. . . . For someone with an infinite lifetime and limitless material resources, hardly a single decision would ever matter."[6]

The noteworthy contribution of Frank's definition is the broader interpretation of scarce means to meet individual and social needs. However, it still appears to be oriented toward meeting the needs of the self and does not take into account actions taken for the good of others or for society as a whole. Thus Frank says that his text "freely concedes the importance of the self-interest motive in many contexts" but adds that "it also devotes an entire chapter to the role of unselfish motives in social and economic transactions."[7]

Note that as definitions become more advanced, they emphasize a broad definition of scarcity, along with the benefits of cooperative behavior and the importance of other members of society. Synthesizing these definitions, I will define economics as the social science that deals with economic problems, which includes any situation of scarcity that necessitates making choices due to insufficient means of any kind to meet relatively plentiful objectives of all types. Those situations of scarcity could be for individuals, businesses, nonprofit organizations, or groups of any kind, including but not limited to local, state, or national governments, and international relationships and organizations. Economics as a discipline exists then to generate principles of decision making for individuals and groups of all kinds to meet as many of our world's needs and objectives as possible with the scarce means available in any given situation.

THE ECONOMIC CONCEPT OF
OPPORTUNITY COST IN WAR AND PEACE

The major economic consequence emerging from the discussion of scarce means and plentiful objectives is that some beneficial objectives cannot be attained and thus will be sacrificed. The objective sacrificed is the "cost" or, more precisely, the "opportunity cost" of the choices made. If students use the meager credit limit of their credit cards to purchase textbooks, they may sacrifice buying pizza. Or, if students use their evening hours to study or write a paper, they sacrifice playing tennis with friends. In these examples, the "opportunity cost" of buying textbooks is pizza, a monetary example, while the "opportunity cost" of studying is playing tennis, a nonmonetary example.

The familiar guns and butter economic analysis illustrates the relevance of the concepts of the economic problem and opportunity cost for war and peace issues. Several important points emerge. First, producing more guns requires sacrificing the production and consumption of the economically useful butter. The butter sacrificed is the opportunity cost of producing more guns. Second, if there is no scarcity and no economic problem, there is the theoretical possibility that producing more guns need not mean less butter. However, since all modern societies have full employment of their available resources as a social objective, there will be an economic problem and producing more guns will mean a sacrifice of butter. Even in the theoretical situation of underutilization of material resources, actually producing more guns would still mean that those resources were not available to produce more butter and, in this sense, butter is still a *potential* opportunity cost of producing guns.

Using the broader definition of economics identifies additional opportunity costs of producing guns instead of butter. The broader definition emphasized the scarcity of time. Increasing military production means less expenditure of the scarce resource of human time as well as the time of machine hours to produce butter. Both these time expenditures are thus opportunity costs of military production.

OPPORTUNITY COST OF MILITARY ACTION

The foregoing discussion of opportunity costs for production of military output did not consider whether the military products were ever used. Additional opportunity costs present themselves when a society engages in military action. Many of these additional costs are obvious materially—destruction of military hardware such as tanks, planes, and missiles as well as the "collateral damage" to civilian products such as factories and homes. And from the broader definition of economics, these costs also include the time expended in the war effort as well as the additional time required by civilians to meet their economic needs in the midst of fighting. National military actions also carry a diplomatic opportunity cost, as in the loss of international prestige when other nations condemn the aggressor. And tragically, there is the opportunity cost of lost human life, both civilian and military, in areas affected by military strife.

COMPARATIVE ADVANTAGE

In contrast to the very high opportunity costs of war and preparation for war, peaceful economic, social, and political relationships have much lower opportunity costs and can be mutually rewarding. The most common economic principle of potential mutually beneficial economic relationships between two parties is *comparative advantage*, whether applied to two individuals, two producers, two states within a country, or two countries. Rather than having each of the two parties attempt to perform all the needed services or produce all the needed goods, according to comparative advantage each of the parties would perform or produce what it does more efficiently and then trade what it does well and plentifully for what the other party does more efficiently. In one example, a carpenter and a plumber live next door to each other. Each could purchase all the tools necessary to do both plumbing and carpentry repair on his own house. However, it would be to the advantage of each of them if the plumber agreed to do the plumbing repairs for both houses while the carpenter agreed to do carpentry repairs for both. At the level of nations, think of a country in a cold climate suitable for indoor manufacturing and another country with a temperate climate suitable for agriculture. Rather than having each country produce both food and manufactured goods, it would be to the advantage of each to produce what it does more efficiently and then to exchange what each produces abundantly. This kind of analysis is called comparative advantage because each of the craftsmen or countries in these examples could produce what the other produces, but there is greater efficiency if each does what it does better when compared to the other.

What are some of the major implications of the comparative advantage analysis for peace issues? First, notice that the gain is available to be shared by both countries through trade, a win-win situation. In fact, the gain is available only if the trade is mutually beneficial and each side acts in good faith without efforts to gain an unfair advantage in the trade. Second, such trade produces dependency, and mutual interdependence holds incentives for neither party to act irresponsibly, which encourages the maintenance of peaceful relationships. Third, working from the principle of comparative advantage benefits both parties, even if one of them has the resources to act alone or without trade. Thus even if the United States were better at everything in an absolute sense (which it is not) when compared to any other country, whether Japan or North Korea or Mexico, there are still mutual benefits to be derived from international relationships, and it is in the interests of the United States to engage in them. Such relationships can make the world more peaceful and harmonious.[8]

COMPARATIVE ADVANTAGE AND COMPETITION

Although international trade is called *competition*, the economic definition is quite different from sports, where competition produces winners and losers and features one side striving for an advantage over the other.

Understanding the meaning of competition in an economic sense helps to clarify the peace benefits of analysis of opportunity costs. In an economic sense competition does not denote struggle or striving for an advantage against an opponent. "Pure competition" is defined as a situation in which no individual economic unit, whether producer or consumer, has a significant effect on price, and "imperfect competition" refers to a situation when either party can affect price. For example, a consumer at the supermarket checkout counter cannot negotiate down the price marked on her steak, and a farmer who takes a truckload of grain for sale to the elevator must accept the going price for her grain or not sell. In these examples, the consumer and the producer face a situation of pure competition, in that neither has a significant effect on price. Despite the common perception that economics is like sports, the relevant dimension of competition in an economic sense is the effect, or lack thereof, that an individual buyer or seller has on price in the market.

SOME POPULAR MYTHS AND MISCONCEPTIONS

Myths and half-truths abound concerning the positive economic effects of war and war preparedness. Most of these myths and half-truths focus on aspects of preparation for war that appear on the surface to be good for the economy. The strongest such argument would be the claim that capitalist economies must have war to survive. The following discussion uses the economic analysis of opportunity costs to expose the misleading or deceptive assumptions of four myths and half-truths about war and the economy.

Myth 1: War Is Necessary for Prosperity

One myth is that preparation for war brings with it the consumer goods of prosperity and the so-called good life of high consumption and great happiness. But we have already seen the refutation of this myth. The opportunity cost of war production is less, not more, consumer goods. When we think about it, that conclusion is intuitively obvious. Spending 100 billion dollars on a missile defense system or a "war on terrorism" means 100 billion dollars unavailable for domestic goods such as medical care for the elderly or hiring more teachers in order to reduce class size and thus provide better education for our children. In terms of actual military action, the comparative advantage argument demonstrates that producing military rather than consumer goods and the loss of human life destroyed by war make the opportunity costs very high for war as the basis of prosperity. Clearly there are more cost-effective ways to provide prosperity for American citizens.

Myth 2: War Increases the Employment of Labor

A second myth about war or war preparation is that it contributes to the economic good of society by utilizing human resources, that is, by creating jobs. First, note the very obvious point that more employment would result from greater expenditures by *anybody* on *anything*. The example presumes meaningful work. But even if the spending were only to pay people to dig holes one day and to fill them the next, the wages paid would get spent in the economy and thus stimulate it but provide no economically useful good or service. It thus becomes obvious that expenditures for the military are by no means the only way or even the best way to provide employment. Rather than spending for military procurement, the government could provide employment by improving roads, building low-income housing, providing job training for the unemployed, funding more teachers for overcrowded classrooms, and much more. At this point, readers should visualize their own favorite concerns. All of these possibilities, and more, would provide more meaningful employment and output than producing socially useless military products. The conclusion is quite clear that spending and employment for war and war preparedness make no special economic contribution. Any useful spending on anything would accomplish the same employment objective.

Further, the argument that an economy needs war expenditure is grossly inaccurate. It is a political rather than an economic argument. For some reason, arguing that new expenditures for military purposes will stimulate the economy tends to be much more popular than arguments that spending for other purposes will stimulate employment and improve civilian welfare. One example was the construction of the interstate highway system, which was originally proposed for the purpose of providing the military with roads to move military equipment efficiently around the country, whereas virtually all of its use was and continues to be for civilian purposes.

Myth 3: War Is Necessary to Provide Security

A third myth—argument—for war is that it is necessary in order to provide security. For this argument, one might say that the opportunity cost of security is war.

Economic analysis reveals serious flaws in this argument. The first flaw is evident from even a cursory reading of recent history, which reveals that war has frequently failed to provide peace and security. For example, note this list of countries that the United States has fought wars with or bombed within the living memory of writers of this volume: Yugoslavia (1999), Afghanistan (1998), Sudan (1998), Iraq (1991, 2002–2003), Nicaragua (1980s), El Salvador (1980s), Libya (1986), Cambodia (1969–1970), Vietnam (1961–1973), Laos (1964–1973). In none of these instances did military activity result in the formation of a government that the United States would call democratic. The much-vaunted "success" of toppling the Taliban and bringing peace to Afghanistan in the aftermath of September 11 is proving illusionary even as I write. This failure rate gives war an extremely high opportunity cost in the search for security, while alternatives to war tend to be less costly and to produce more stability. The opportunity cost in material goods and human lives to control another country is very high. In contrast mutually beneficial economic and political relationships could achieve the same ends at a much lower opportunity cost. For example building houses for the estimated three million Afghan refugees before the war on terrorism would have cost much less than the money spent to blow up mud brick dwellings in Afghanistan with expensive rockets that ended up killing more civilians than were killed in the World Trade Center towers in New York. Would building those houses or dropping those bombs be more likely to convince the Afghans that the United States could be trusted and that future terrorists should be controlled? Which option has the greater opportunity cost? The greater benefit?

Myth 4: The Military Is the Source of Beneficial New Technology

The fourth myth is that the general population benefits from military expenditures because military technology is ultimately modified and applied for civilian purposes. The key word here is *modified.* It would be more efficient for the government to directly support basic research for civilian uses than to support research to modify technology produced for military purposes. In other words, when viewed from the end point of a consumer good produced for civilian consumption, the opportunity cost is much greater when development passes through the military stages than if it were developed directly for civilian consumption. And note that the discussion here in terms of opportunity cost has taken place without even referring to the legendary cost overruns that accompany most military research and development.

As was also the case in myth 2, arguing for new weapons technology because it may have beneficial civilian spin-off is politically more popular than arguments that appeal only to the efficiency of civilian production. However, from an economic perspective directing research specifically to civilian needs clearly has the lowest opportunity cost.

IMPLICATIONS

The foregoing economic analysis points to an obvious conclusion. Using principles taught in any beginning economics course, it is easy to see that a military-based economy and fighting wars does not make sense and that those who advocate military spending and warfare would seem to be unintelligent. But in fact our national leaders are not stupid. It is rather that in spite of the foregoing economic arguments, there are certain parties and certain segments of the economy that benefit from war. The economic analysis does not get at the questions of who benefits from and who drives the military economy; however, by showing the high cost and limited gains of war, this analysis is still useful. It brings to the fore the question of what really does drive the military economy and the push for war.

One answer surely comes in the story told by Perry Bush in chapter 6 of this volume, namely the link forged in the public mind between freedom and war. When people truly believe that freedom depends on war, the economic analysis fades. At a more theological level, perhaps J. Denny Weaver's discussion of the "devil" and the "powers of evil" in chapter 3 of this volume offers an explanation. If the powers of evil include the structures of the social order that we live in, a part of their bondage to the devil may be continuing to believe in the goodness and the necessity of spending for war preparedness, even when those expenditures are the most expensive and the least efficient means to peace as demonstrated by standard economic analysis.

CONCLUSION

The discussions in this chapter constitute a brief but important beginning in applying the tools of economic analysis to peace issues. The analysis has demonstrated a very important point, namely that economic analysis reveals the futility of war. We have observed ways that presumptions in favor of war have actually covered over truths that economic analysis can make clear to anyone who has eyes to see. This analysis then assumes the rule of a stimulus to work at the real causes of war. And surely the answer is not more war to eliminate war but rather that Christians have the courage "to live out the theology of [their] nonviolent namesake."[9]

NOTES

This chapter is an extensive elaboration and extension of "The Pursuit of Peace, Prosperity, and Pebbles," a C. Henry Smith Peace Lecture originally presented at Bluffton College on December 8, 1981, and at Goshen College on January 15, 1982. Gratitude is expressed to the C. Henry Smith Trust for their early support of this interest in the economics of war and peace.

1. Campbell R. McConnell and Stanley R. Brue, *Economics: Principles, Problems and Policies* (Boston: Irwin/McGraw-Hill, 2002), 10.

2. Jurgen Brauer, Ronald Friesen, and Edward Tower, eds., *Public Economics III: Public Choice, Political Economy, Peace and War* (Chapel Hill, N.C.: Eno River Press, 1995), 158–240.

3. McConnell and Brue, *Economics*.

4. McConnell and Brue, *Economics*, 3.

5. McConnell and Brue, *Economics*, 22.

6. Robert H. Frank, *Microeconomics and Behavior,* 5th ed. (Boston: McGraw-Hill/Irwin, 2003), 3–4.

7. Frank, *Microeconomics*, x.

8. Comparative advantage does harbor another problem, however. In order for the smaller country to engage in mutually beneficial trade, it has to produce something or have a resource that is useful to the large country, which can by virtue of its size get along without the smaller country. Thus even if the larger country exerts no direct pressure, there is a very real indirect pressure for the small country to structure its economy around the needs of the larger country. This kind of indirect pressure can exist as systemic violence. For analysis of this kind of economic issue, see chapter 15 in this volume by James Harder.

9. J. Denny Weaver, chapter 3 in this volume.

VII

NONVIOLENCE AND THE SCIENCES

19

Violent Images in Cell Biology

Angela Horn Montel

Natural killer cells and T cells will seek out the foreign invaders and deliver a lethal blow through the use of perforin-mediated assault.

Macrophages have an arsenal of weapons available at their disposal, including reactive oxygen species and Tumor Necrosis Factor.

Cytotoxic molecules secreted in an attempt to bludgeon the enemy will sometimes destroy innocent bystander cells.

"**I** was intrigued by the metaphors you used in your presentation," a colleague said to me after a presentation to the faculty during my first year on the Bluffton College campus. Certainly most life scientists would not have made this observation, steeped as they are in the terminology like that above that characterizes disciplines such as mine (immunology). But this colleague was a trained rhetorician, and a pacifist. To him, the imagery of cells committing suicide (also known as apoptosis) or unleashing an arsenal of weapons (perforin, nitric oxide, Tumor Necrosis Factor, Fas Ligand—to name a few) was something new, intriguing, and troublesome.

At one point, early in my graduate career, I did acknowledge the violence of these metaphors, when I wrote a report summarizing the results of experiments I had conducted in a lab that investigated natural killer cells. Natural killer cells, a type of white blood cell, constitute a first line of defense against invading viruses or even "terrorists" from within (cancer cells). One experiment I conducted was called a "cytotoxicity assay" or a "killing assay." These experiments measure the ability of various types of white blood cells to kill target cells. In one exercise, I tested the cytotoxicity (ability to kill) of my own natural killer cells, and in my report to the principle investigator of the lab I distinctly remember writing: "I had to borrow some NK (natural killer) cells from Dr. Morse, as my NK cells turned out to be pacifists." My NK cells, it turns out, do not kill K562 (the classic target cell for testing NK cells in vitro) very well at all. Although I wrote the sentence about my pacifist NK cells somewhat tongue in cheek, I also wanted to counter the violent language confronting me during my first months of graduate school.

I later joined this lab and spent five years investigating how NK cells recognize and kill their target cells. By the time I gave my dissertation defense, I was a polished immunologist who could spew out violent metaphors with little thought about the implications behind the language. It took Gerald Biesecker-Mast's comment about the violent metaphors after my presentation that first year at Bluffton College to reawaken my disquiet.

These violent metaphors range far beyond my experience in my laboratory. Here are two additional examples from thousands easily available. In a highly regarded biochemistry textbook, the caption under the opening photo in the chapter entitled "The Immune System" begins: "Just as Medieval defenders used their weapons and the castle walls to defend their city, the immune system constantly battles against foreign invaders such as viruses, bacteria, and parasites to defend the organism."[1] Thus students of biochemistry are inculcated with the war metaphor. The second quotation not only sees the immune system as replete with killers but likens the microbes themselves to assassins: "The Anthrax spore lurks in the soil for months or decades, a patient assassin waiting for its sleep to be disturbed. One day, perhaps when a grazing cow yanks up a plant by its roots, the tiny spores shake loose and are eaten, or are sniffed into the cow's lungs, or dust its skin with a deadly bloom. Then begins a precise but terrible execution."[2] Since this comment came from *The New York Times*, it illustrates that the general public, as well as the life scientist, is inundated with violent images of the microbial world.

What does the presence of such terminology in my discipline mean? The terminology may be partially an effect of the violent metaphors that pervade society generally. Since such metaphors are deeply ingrained in our psyche, their use can draw a vivid picture of the relationship between host and pathogen. Most of us would probably stop short of saying that such violent metaphors in the discipline of immunology actually *cause* societal violence. But might such metaphors perpetuate the war mentality, the idea that a violent response to conflict is inevitable in human society?

Some would argue that the use of violent metaphors in immunology simply reflects the whole of the biological kingdom: "nature red in tooth-and-claw," "the survival of the fittest," the lioness's takedown of the graceful gazelle caught on camera by Marlin Perkins of Mutual of Omaha's Wild Kingdom. It might seem obvious that this violence extends to the microbial realm. And of course, microbes are dying daily, and our cells are doing the killing (or vice versa). But rather than visualizing a "war within" that reflects a broader tooth-and-claw struggle in which the biological world is perpetually engaged, might there be healthier ways for people in my discipline to consider the struggle of host against pathogen? And perhaps we need to ask even more generally: Is there really a "war" taking place inside the human body? The following does not provide a complete answer, but it begins a conversation, which shows that cell biology certainly belongs in the discussion of nonviolence across the curriculum.

WAR WITHIN OR A HEALTHY FORCE?

Let's start with the most basic question, Is there really a war taking place inside the human body? It is interesting that the same process that occurs inside of target cells (such as virally infected body cells) when "killer" cells give target cells the kiss of death also occurs inside of cells that are absorbed in the remodeling of the fetus. For example, human fetuses—as well as fetuses of nonhuman primates and chickens—begin with webbing between their digits, perhaps a remnant from our aquatic ancestors. Over the course of fetal development, the cells that make up this webbing slowly "commit suicide." White blood cells called macrophages comb the area and wrap their membranes around the moribund cell particles. Once engulfed, the cell particles are broken down inside the macrophages, and the useful building block molecules are recycled to construct new cell parts. This cell death gives rise to useful building blocks for new life. The same process occurs as millions of potentially dangerous, self-recognizing T cells are killed in the thymus during prenatal maturation of the human immune system. Thus not all cell death is the result of violent conflict; some is a necessary part of proper development.

Some immunologists and microbiologists describe higher-order life as a continual struggle against microbes that, alas, is lost at death. Ironically, the same scientists have found that artificially germ-free animals created in the laboratory are often unhealthy. These animals frequently succumb to normally harmless microbes when removed from their sterile chambers. Germs, it seems, are quite necessary for proper maturation and priming of the immune system, production of vitamins such as vitamin K and proper development of the intestinal tract. But sickliness is not limited to germ-free laboratory mice and guinea pigs. Human studies continue to show that allergic diseases such as asthma, which are dramatically more prevalent in industrialized than in nonindustrialized nations, are more likely to appear in children who grow up in an environment with few exposures to bacteria, viruses, or parasites.[3] Children who work with farm animals on a daily basis, for example, are less likely to develop hay fever and allergic sensitization than children from nonfarm families, even when the researcher controls for other factors such as air pollution, indoor air humidity, and use of heating fuels.[4] Several studies comparing Eastern Bloc countries to Western European countries have shown that asthma and positive skin tests to common allergens are *more* prevalent in the *less* polluted, *less* crowded Western countries.[5] A recent study has shown that young children with *higher* levels of a bacterial cell wall component called endotoxin in their mattresses have *lower* incidences of asthma, hay fever, and other allergic sensitization.[6] And a statistic to assuage the potential guilt of parents with children in daycare: because children in daycare are exposed to a wider variety of germs, they are less likely to acquire allergies and asthma than preschool children cared for at home (unless the family is large enough that siblings do the job of carrying home infections).[7]

One hypothesis for these striking observations is that a lack of repeated challenges to the immune system during early childhood changes the profile of cell-modulating substances (cytokines) produced and tips the balance toward the activation of antibody-producing cells and away from the activation of killer white blood cells.[8] Since allergy is mediated by one of the classes of antibodies, this tipping of the balance predisposes a person to the development of allergy. An alternative hypothesis suggests that a paucity of immune system challenges during childhood results in the underdevelopment of a network of regulatory cells that prevent the immune system from overreacting to harmless environmental substances such as dust mites and pollen.[9]

Although the specific details of the underlying immunological alterations have yet to be fully fleshed out, the data clearly show that living in a supersanitized, bug-battling world is not all it is cracked up to be. We cannot escape the obvious co-evolution of human hosts and microbial pathogens. Host and pathogen share an intimate dance whose steps are swayed by the lack of barnyard animals and privies in our backyards and even by childhood vaccination regimens, which also result in reduced immune system stimulation. This is no insignificant misstep in the host–pathogen dance given that the occurrence of asthma in industrialized societies has doubled in recent decades[10] and asthmatic attacks now precipitate one in every three pediatric emergency room visits in the United States.[11] Recent evidence even suggests that the dearth of childhood infections in industrialized nations has increased the prevalence of multiple sclerosis, insulin-dependent diabetes, and Crohn's disease—autoimmune diseases where the immune system mistakenly attacks the body itself.[12] We would do well to study and appreciate our dance with microbes rather than simply wage war against them. And if this *dance* actually contributes to our overall health, the terminology of *war* and *killer cells* is unwarranted.

ANOTHER HEALTHY DANCE

In addition to the necessity of germs for proper immune system development, nonpathogenic microbes are also required to keep us safe from pathogenic microbes. In other words, there also exists a dance between host, pathogen, and nonpathogen. In the absence of the competition from commensal microbes, pathogenic organisms can gain a foothold in the body. An adult human consists of approximately 10 trillion human cells and *100 trillion* bacterial cells.[13] Yes, a healthy human actually contains ten times more bacterial cells than human cells. (This may seem impossible until one considers that bacterial cells are typically a fraction of the size of human cells.) This amazing statistic points to the symbiotic relationship that has evolved between humans and nonpathogenic bacteria.

Many people are aware of the presence of "helpful" bacteria in products such as yogurt and wisely choose to consume these products when traveling to areas where bacteria-induced diarrhea may strike. In fact, a whole new industry is emerging to market food products and dietary supplements containing probiotics (helpful bacteria) or prebiotics (the compounds such as the sugar inulin that foster growth of helpful bacteria). Additionally, research is pursuing the therapeutic use of probiotic bacteria to displace pathogenic bacteria, as an alternative to antibiotics in the treatment of infection. Promising results have already occurred in studies examining middle ear infections, bladder infections, and the most widespread bacterial infection in the world—tooth decay caused by the *Streptococcus mutans* species of bacteria. Within a few years, baby formula may even be supplemented with compounds that encourage the growth of beneficial bacterial strains such as bifidobacteria. (Of course factors that foster bifidobacterial growth in newborns are naturally present in breast milk.)[14]

The irony is that while research shows the benefits of helpful bacteria, more than seven hundred *anti*bacterial products are currently marketed for home use. These include not only the familiar antibacterial hand soaps and dishwashing detergents but even such items as mattresses, sheets, towels, food storage containers, chopsticks, and toothbrushes impregnated with antibacterial agents.[15] Many microbiologists believe that these antibacterial products are useless or even harmful because they destroy the protective, competitive layer of nonpathogenic organisms that blanket our bodies. Further, these agents have been proven to select for bacteria that are resistant not only to the antibacterial agent itself but also to oral antibiotics. For example researchers selected for bacteria with increased resistance to triclosan, a common antibacterial agent found in most antibacterial soaps, and demonstrated that these bugs were cross-resistant to isoniazid, an important antibiotic used to treat tuberculosis, as well as to diazoborine, an experimental antibiotic.[16] Such studies indicate that the massive use of such products as antibacterial soaps and mattresses may actually exacerbate the already troublesome emergence of strains of harmful bacteria that are resistant to some, or even all, of the known antibiotics.

Thus, we see that only a small percentage of our interactions with microbes could actually be considered "battles." In fact, viewing ourselves as engaged in a constant war against bacteria has led to raising children in an oversanitized world where lack of exposure to microbes predisposes their immune systems to react to trivial antigens, resulting in allergies and asthma, and where antibacterial hand soaps destroy the good with the bad.

A NATURAL CYCLE

Turning our focus from the interaction of the human immune system with the microbial world to the broader lessons of ecology, we are reminded that bacteria and other decomposers are necessary for the functioning of the earth's ecosystem. Individuals only borrow the elements held in their bodies. At death, these nutrients are recycled back to the earth so that other living organisms can utilize them.

A carbon atom stored in Plato's liver glycogen, for example, could have been released in the form of CO_2 as his metabolic processes provided energy for him to pen Socrates' words, "The unexamined life is not worth living." This exact carbon atom could be incorporated into the structure of an olive tree through the process of photosynthesis. A pig could eat the tree's olives and incorporate the carbon atom into its body. At the death of the pig, decomposers could metabolize the pig, returning CO_2 to the atmosphere. (Or the carbon atom that was once a part of Plato could actually become part of the body of another person who eats the pig.) If bacteria, fungi, and other organisms that the war paradigm calls the enemy did not exist to carry out the decomposition process, the earth would literally fill up with dead bodies (sea weed, grass clippings, tree trunks, beetle and pig carcasses, and much more). And even if offspring organisms could find space to live amongst the debris, much of the supply of nutrients required for life would soon be locked up in the dead bodies and waste, making ongoing life impossible. Thus, the broad picture shows us that microbes are necessary for the cycling of life, and the image of a war against microbes greatly misconstrues the processes.

Although Native American cultures may not have known about microorganisms per se until recently, they have recognized the cycling of life for eons. As Cheyenne Peace Chief and Mennonite pastor Lawrence Hart writes, "The Native Americans' relationship to the earth is legendary; they have always maintained an intimate, spiritual, and personal relationship to the earth. Mountains, forests, streams, rivers, oceans, and the sky are a part of a circle. All life forms in the waters, on the land, and in the air are interconnected within the circle. Humankind is a part of that circle."[17] Perhaps it is the Western scientist's individualistic, temporal perspective that views microbes as the enemy.

THE STRUGGLE OF HOST AND PATHOGEN

Nonetheless, even with the realization that much cell death is not the result of microscopic conflict but is necessary for proper development, that most human interactions with microbes are friendly, and that microbes are necessary for the cycle of life, we cannot deny that our bodies do periodically work to destroy pathogenic organisms. I cannot argue, for example, that the Sabin and Salk polio vaccines are not great victories against the scourge of polio. And anthrax *does* "assassinate" cows, and—as we have recently been reminded—every once in a while anthrax also "assassinates" people. Further, a healthy immune system is constantly holding at bay normally nonpathogenic, symbiotic microorganisms, which becomes clearly evident when the scales are tipped in favor of the microbes, as when the human immune system is weakened by cancer chemotherapy, immunosuppressive drugs, or HIV infection. Given that our bodies are engaged in an antimicrobial struggle—however overexaggerated it may be by Western society—we are led to the second question posed above: Rather than visualizing a "war within" that reflects a broader tooth-and-claw struggle in which the biological world is perpetually engaged, might there be healthier ways for people in my discipline to consider the struggle of host against pathogen? This question touches upon the age-old question about God and suffering. Does the design of the natural world, all the way from the warring of humans against microbes to the bloody predation exhibited by the top mammalian carnivores, indicate that God is insensitive to suffering and that God created an inherently violent world?

Nancey Murphy has attempted to address this question from a nonviolent, Anabaptist perspective. Murphy compares the interaction of God with *humans* to the interaction of God with the *natural world*, asking her audience to conceptualize these two interactions as the uprights of a ladder. The points of similarity between the two relationships are then the rungs of this analogical ladder. Using the writings of Daniel Day Williams as her basis, Murphy contends that the essential characteristics of God's relationship with humans are (1) that "God creates genuine individuals, with their own created powers to participate in creation"; (2) that "God respects human freedom"; and (3) that "God accepts the cost of respecting the individuality and freedom of human creatures. This means that God's control of any particular event is limited; suffering and evil cannot always be prevented."[18] Murphy creates a parallel analysis of divine action in the natural world based on the suggestion that God acts in the natural world by influencing the behavior of subatomic particles such as quarks and electrons. The essential characteristics of God's relationship with the natural world, opines Murphy, are (1) that "God has created a universe which, at this point in its history, is made up of individuals, howsoever small and ephemeral. These subatomic entities have built-in capacities—types of behavior specific to their own kinds"; (2) that "while the what of such an entity's behavior is given by the kind of particle it is, the when is undetermined"; and (3) that "this is a *costly* withholding of God's power, since it means that God's scope for determining natural events is limited by respect for the integrity of these tiny creatures."[19] In other words, "God *is* acting in all created entities and events, and truly affecting the course of those processes, yet the scope of God's activity is constrained by God's free choice to respect the freedom and integrity of creatures, all the way from electrons to humans."[20] Under Murphy's paradigm, we might conclude that God undertook a costly withholding of power when God allowed pathogenic microorganisms to evolve along with the microbes that are helpful to humans, plants, and other animals. But God accepts the freewill of God's creation in order to meet the requirements of true love. True love must maintain the individuality of the one who is loved, allow the beloved individual the freedom to accept or reject the love, and acquiesce to the inevitability that the beloved will modify the lover. The costs that God incurs as a result of this nonviolent withholding of power include a "reduced effectiveness" and a "lack of control" because "the extent to which God can realize good plans is, by divine decree, dependent upon the cooperation of all-too-often-recalcitrant creatures, both human and non-human."[21] These costs also include "physical suffering." God is not the cause of struggle and suffering. Rather, suffering is the result of the proclivity of human and nonhuman creation to depart from the will of the Creator. God is not absent, however. God is with us through the struggles and transforms suffering into "something higher." A divine son who is often likened to a sacrificial lamb provides us with an image of God who is at work "not in the predator but in the prey."[22]

Murphy's work does not downplay the harsh reality of the natural world but instead emphasizes that God's very nature is to be with each creature through the suffering (even at the hands of nasty microbes). According to this model, God's nature is inherently nonviolent, which is evidenced by God's lack of violent coercion in turning humans toward God and in God's withholding of power exhibited in the crucifixion of God's Son. "Yet, if the death of Jesus is the ultimate act of God's withholding of power, then Jesus' resurrection is the promise and foretaste of final victory. The apparent ineffectiveness of God's suffering love must be judged in light of this unexpected and total transformation. It is an outcome that cannot be forced or seized by violence."[23]

Other Christians dispute the idea that nature is actually "red in tooth-and-claw." Instead, they claim that the natural order contains evidence of God's goodness. For example, "The actual suffering that occurs at death (measured in minutes) is *minute* compared to the years/decades of enjoyment and pleasure experienced by animals; . . . There is a definite tranquilizing system in prey animals, and one which mutes pain at time of death"; predators actually reduce the incidence of chronic pain and suffering in their prey by selecting the weakened members of a population and by keeping prey populations from outpacing their food supplies; and the vast majority of creatures on earth (for example, microbes!) lack nervous systems entirely or lack the type of nervous system that allows for pain recognition.[24]

Even Darwin's famous conceptualization of the "survival of the fittest" is not necessarily best viewed as a war among competing individuals. First, the biological definition of "fitness" is the ability to leave offspring behind. Thus, the fittest individual is not necessarily the most aggressive or the physically strongest. The fittest individual often emerges as the one who can, for example, better survive the stomach acid of a host organism or better survive a shift in climate or insolation. For instance, as the North American climate became warmer and drier twenty million years ago, forests gradually gave way—over thousands of years—to grasslands. It is not as if the grasslands killed the forests. The grasses were simply better able to survive and reproduce than the trees. During this climatic shift, those prehistoric horses whose genes happened to code for slightly longer than average teeth with slightly more ridges than average probably had an advantage as their diet shifted from soft forest leaves and shoots to tough grasses. These long-toothed animals were better able to acquire food and therefore better able to reproduce and pass on their long-tooth genes than their shorter-toothed relatives. Often, organisms are not killing each other in the struggle for survival of the fittest; instead, some organisms are just out-surviving and out-reproducing others.

Second, it has been suggested that although Darwin did declare that "all nature is war" and "the strongest ultimately prevail," his thinking was influenced by prevailing violent economic and social theories of his day such as capitalism, and all of these theories *presume* a violent human nature rather than actually *proving* a violent human nature.[25] If aggression always constituted a survival advantage, according to Darwinian logic one could assume that aggression would be genetically hard-wired into organisms such as humans since, by definition, the individuals who survived through the ages have been the most aggressive. However, altruism and love are just as real among humans, and even animals, as is aggression. Recent biologists have balanced Darwin's image of nature at war by proffering explanations for the evolution of altruism. When organisms sacrificially aid in the survival of others, they themselves may be killed and may fail to reproduce. Therefore their altruism genes fail to be passed on to their direct offspring. Traditionally, this fact has been construed to indicate that unselfishness could never evolve through the process of natural selection. Because closely related individuals share many genes in common, however, many of the altruism genes of the unselfish individual *can* live on in the relatives that he or she helps to survive.

Altruistic behavior is especially prominent in wolves, in various insect species such as termites and honeybees, and in the naked mole-rats of Eastern Africa. For example, most wolf packs consist of one breeding male-female couple and several nonbreeding relatives who aid the breeding pair in protecting and feeding the offspring. A similar arrangement is seen in naked mole-rats, with some nonreproducing members of the clan specializing as excavators who dig underground dwellings for the clan and other nonreproducing members specializing in protecting the clan from predators. Researchers have demonstrated that all members of the same mole-rat clan have extremely similar DNA fingerprints, whereas mole-rats from separate clans have dissimilar DNA fingerprints.[26] This finding supports the idea that self-sacrificing members of the clan are in fact aiding the survival of a high percentage of their own genes when they nurture their clan mates. "Survival of the fittest" *can* result in organisms being genetically programmed for unselfishness.[27]

These observations challenge the traditional conception of nature as the "survival of the most aggressive" or a "war" within the food chain. When coupled with the earlier point made in this chapter that most of our interactions with microbes are benign, these challenges suggest that alternatives to the violent metaphors are indeed appropriate.

DEPROGRAMMING VIOLENT ASSUMPTIONS

This leads us to my third question: Might violent immunological metaphors perpetuate the war mentality, the idea that a violent response to conflict is inevitable in human society?

In her essay "Roots of Violence, Seeds of Peace," Grace Jantzen argues that all major discourses—including political discourse, theological discourse, and biological discourse—*assume* that human nature is violent without really *proving* that human nature is violent. The founders of these disciplines have allowed the assumption of a violent human nature to underpin their theories because this assumption of violence is integral to the Western habitus, the sense of "how things are done" that we acquire through our upbringing. This habitus *feels* instinctual. "[I]ndeed *not* to behave in accordance with the habitus—to wear beach clothes to a funeral or to eat stew without cutlery—could only be done with deliberate forethought and to achieve some (perhaps shocking) objective."[28] However, the habitus is not instinctual in the same way that, say, the desires for food and sex are. Jantzen builds a convincing argument against the innateness of human violence based on the observations that 50 percent of the human population (the women) is generally far less violent than the other 50 percent and that many individual men, as well as whole cultures, eschew violence.[29]

Alan Gross writes in *The Rhetoric of Science*:

> Metaphors in science can disappear only when scientists can redescribe natural relationships in language free from metaphor. And they cannot; the cancer research papers typify this inability. Underlying their science is a way of talking that turns living cells and processes into their presumed mechanical and computer counterparts. . . . Initially, scientists imagine physical objects by thinking of them as machines or computers. Since they frame their causal hypotheses in these terms, it need come as no surprise that, in time, these objects seem more and more to *be* machines and computers.[30]

Extending Gross's analysis, we can say that as immunologists conceptualize the immune system in terms of war with the microbial realm, in time microbes seem more and more to *be* enemies and human cells seem more and more to *be* warriors. Immunology is only reflecting our violent habitus that "produces history on the basis of history."[31] But instead, immunology *appears* to join the other major Western discourses as yet another example of violence being "natural." And "if violence is naturalized, it is partly justified; if it can't be helped, it must be condoned," Jantzen aptly points out. "If, however, the assumption that violence is natural is destabilized, then so also is that justification. We have no choice but to take responsibility for it."[32] Humans must take responsibility for and confront violence.

However, as Gross indicates, natural relationships are difficult to describe in language free of metaphor. I might imagine a toning down of the violent metaphors that describe the immune system. For example, let's return to the opening statement at the beginning of this chapter: Natural killer cells and T cells will seek out the foreign invaders and deliver a lethal blow through the use of perforin-mediated assault. With minimal effort, I can transform this into the following: $CD16^+$ $CD56^+$ cells and T cells will seek out the unwanted bacteria, viruses, or parasites and will render them incapable of life and propagation through the use of perforin-mediated mechanisms. The second rendition conveys basically the same information as the first but without utilizing any violent metaphors. However, due partially to the lack of metaphor, it is less resonant to the ear. Perhaps, as I mentioned earlier, we could alleviate this problem by gradually replacing the military campaign metaphor with Nancey Murphy's metaphor of struggle, "a sacrificial suffering through to something higher."[33] But the nonresonance also reflects my habitus: as a North American and as an immunologist, my ears are trained in the rhetoric of violence. I have been programmed to be energized by the rallying cry of a fight against microbes.

I am not willing to give up the fight (oops, I mean *struggle*) toward reducing the suffering of humans at the hands of microbes. I believe in antibiotic and vaccine development. I believe in furthering our knowledge of how the human body protects itself from microbes and of how microbes foil the human immune system. But it is my desire to retrain my senses also to see the dance between microbe and host, to feel one with the great circle of life, and to appreciate the "sacrificial suffering through to something higher" that binds us to all creation and to the nonviolent, suffering Redeemer himself. This deprogramming is worth the effort.

NOTES

1. Jeremy M. Berg, John L. Tymoczko, and Lubert Stryer, *Biochemistry,* 5th ed. (New York: W. H. Freeman, 2002), 921.

2. Nicholas Wade, "How a Patient Assassin Does Its Deadly Work," *New York Times,* October 23, 2001, 1(F).

3. William O. C. M. Cookson and Miriam F. Moffatt, "Asthma: An Epidemic in the Absence of Infection?" *Science* 275, no. 5296 (January 3, 1997): 41–42; Maria Yazdanbakhsh, Peter G. Kremsner, and Ronald van Ree, "Allergy, Parasites, and the Hygiene Hypothesis," *Science* 296, no. 5567 (April 19, 2002): 490–494.

4. C. H. Braun-Fahrlander, M. Gassner, L. Grize, U. Neu, F. H. Sennhauser, H. S. Varonier, J. C. Vuille, and B. Wuthrich, "Prevalence of Hay Fever and Allergic Sensitization in Farmers' Children and Their Peers Living in the Same Rural Community," *Clinical and Experimental Allergy* 29, no. 1 (January 1999): 28–34.

5. Cookson and Moffatt, "Asthma," 41.

6. Charlotte Braun-Fahrlander, Josef Riedler, Udo Herz, Waltraud Eder, Marco Waser, Leticia Grize, Soyoun Maisch, David Carr, Florian Gerlach, Albrecht Bufe, Roger P. Lauener, Rudolf Schierl, Harald Renz, Dennis Nowak, and Erika von Mutius, "Environmental Exposure to Endotoxin and Its Relation to Asthma in School-Age Children," *New England Journal of Medicine* 347, no. 12 (September 19, 2002): 869–877.

7. U. Kramer, J. Heinrich, M. Wjst, and H. E. Wichmann, "Age of Entry to Day Nursery and Allergy in Later Childhood," *Lancet* 353, no. 9151 (February 6, 1999): 450–454.

8. Cookson and Moffatt, "Asthma," 41–42.

9. Yazdanbakhsh, Kremsner, and van Ree, "Allergy, Parasites," 490–494.

10. A. Seaton, D. J. Godden, and K. Brown, "Increase in Asthma: A More Toxic Environment or a More Susceptible Population?" *Thorax* 49, no. 2 (February 1994): 171–174.

11. Cookson and Moffatt, "Asthma," 41.

12. Jean-Francois Bach, "The Effect of Infections on Susceptibility to Autoimmune and Allergic Diseases," *New England Journal of Medicine* 347, no. 12 (September 19, 2002): 911–920.

13. G. W. Tannock, *Normal Microflora* (London: Chapman and Hall, 1995), 1.

14. Bob Beale, "Probiotics: Their Tiny Worlds Are under Scrutiny," *The Scientist* 16, no. 15 (July 22, 2002): 20–22.

15. Stuart B. Levy, "Antibacterial Household Products: Cause for Concern," *Emerging Infectious Diseases* 7, no. 3 Supplement (June 2001): 512.

16. Levy, "Antibacterial Household Products," 513.

17. Lawrence Hart, "The Earth Is a Song Made Visible," in *Creation and the Environment: An Anabaptist Perspective on a Sustainable World*, ed. Calvin Redekop (Baltimore: Johns Hopkins University Press, 2000), 170.

18. Nancey Murphy, "God's Nonviolent Direct Action" (Bluffton College Keeney Mennonite Peace Lectureship, Bluffton, Ohio, September 19, 2000), pages 7–8 of the typescript.

19. Murphy, "God's Nonviolent Direct Action," 8.

20. Murphy, "God's Nonviolent Direct Action," 9.

21. Murphy, "God's Nonviolent Direct Action," 15.

22. Nancey Murphy, *Reconciling Theology and Science: A Radical Reformation Perspective* (Kitchener, Ont.: Pandora Press, 1997), 70.

23. See Murphy, "God's Nonviolent Direct Action," 16. The nonviolent atonement motif of J. Denny Weaver makes more explicit than does Murphy that God is nonviolent and that the death of Jesus was a product of human evil, which makes the resurrection the triumph of the nonviolent reign of God over evil, however it is defined. See Weaver's chapter 3 in this volume, as well as his *The Nonviolent Atonement* (Grand Rapids, Mich.: Eerdmans, 2001).

24. Glen M. Miller, "Good Question . . . Does the Savagery of Predation in Nature Show That God Either Isn't, or at Least Isn't Good-Hearted?" at www.christian-thinktank.com/pred2.html (accessed August 8, 2002).

25. Grace M. Jantzen, "Roots of Violence, Seeds of Peace," *The Conrad Grebel Review* 20, no. 2 (Spring 2002): 4–19; and Murphy, *Reconciling Theology*, 64.

26. Hudson K. Reeve, David F. Westneat, William A. Noon, Paul W. Sherman, and Charles F. Aquadro, "DNA Fingerprinting Reveals High Levels of Inbreeding in Colonies of the Eusocial Naked Mole-Rat," *Proceedings of the National Academy of Sciences* 87 (April 1990): 2496–2500.

27. Chapter 20 in this volume, by Todd Rainey, provides additional challenges, in the realm of animal behavior, to the assumption that nature is intrinsically violent.

28. Jantzen, "Roots of Violence," 5.

29. Jantzen, "Roots of Violence," 4–19.

30. Alan G. Gross, *The Rhetoric of Science* (Cambridge: Harvard University Press, 1996), 81.

31. Jantzen, "Roots of Violence," 5.

32. Jantzen, "Roots of Violence," 18.

33. Murphy, *Reconciling Theology*, 71.

20

Nature's Tooth-and-Claw Conflict Resolution

W. Todd Rainey

Presumed aggressive conflict between baboons or chimpanzees is a common symbol of "nature red in tooth-and-claw" in some genres of popular science literature and television programming. Dominance hierarchies, competitive fights, and rare occasions of "murder" among primates frequently attract the focus of popular discourse. These interpretative emphases reflect American society's assumptions about the inevitability of violent conflict. In fact, as sensitivity to a nonviolent perspective enables us to see, the data on primate behavior actually point to a quite different picture. This chapter will consider the significance and importance of recent research on conflict, tolerance, and reconciliation behaviors among nonhuman primates.

Initially, the analysis uses definitions of conflict and aggression from the recent text *Natural Conflict Resolution*.[1] The authors define interindividual conflict as a "situation that arises when individuals act on incompatible goals, interests, or actions. Conflict need not be aggressive." They define aggression as "behavior directed at members of the same species in order to cause physical injury or to warn of impending actions of this nature by means of facial and vocal threat displays." My argument will eventually expand and adapt this definition of aggression.

A conflict, that is, a situation involving "incompatible goals, interests, or actions," can arise for primates in a variety of settings, such as competition for food and access to potential mates. Such conflicts also impact the social relationships of primates, the patterns of "friendship" between unrelated individuals, bonds between mothers and their offspring, and sources of protection for group members.[2] The consequences of "incompatible goals" can be exacerbated if competitors respond to the conflict with physical aggression. According to the prevailing paradigm, physical aggression can be considered a continuum with a range of intensity from single slaps to all-out biting attacks, in which the canines can cause serious gashes in skin and flesh and gnawing bites with incisors can cause substantial damage to muscles.[3] Conflicts between individual primates can result in anything from serious injury to mutual toleration.

RECENT INTERPRETATIONS

One of the most important transformations in the interpretation of animal behavior since the early seventies has been the recognition that some species of birds and mammals maintain long-term social relationships within discrete communities. These communities consist of individuals that recognize each other and apparently remember their history of interactions. These individuals participate in complex social relationships and display substantial diversity and flexibility in their behavior.[4]

S. C. Strum has documented an example of behavioral flexibility that is especially relevant for the analysis presented in this chapter.[5] Most adult male savannah baboons emigrate from their birth community at adolescence, and often from a second and a third community over their lifetime. Thus they are newcomers in a new community at least once in their life, relating to other adult males who already have long-term residency in this new home. Newcomers often use aggressive confrontations to establish a position in the new hierarchy and to try to replace males that have formed temporary consortships with females in estrus. In contrast, resident males tend to avoid these confrontations and are much less aggressive in their interactions with members of the troop. They have developed friendly relationships with one or more of the adult females and have developed nonaggressive, manipulative, or Machiavellian tactics for replacing males that are in consort. Pairs of the most experienced males even cooperate in the competition for access to females.[6] In summary, Strum states, "The current analysis of Pumphouse [troop] data suggest that nonaggressive social options are primary strategies when viewed across a male's lifetime. All adolescents and adult males shifted to nonaggressive tactics as soon as possible."[7] Aggressive tactics used by juveniles and adolescents challenging members of the dominance hierarchy or used by newcomers to new troops are replaced by more sophisticated tactics as soon as the individuals find a niche in social networks.

Such flexibility of behavior suggests that competition among these social animals does not have to be violent, that is, carried out for the purpose of physical injury or the threat thereof. Furthermore, for some of these species, additional evidence suggests that long-term relationships, between individuals that benefit mutually from life in their community, include substantial frequencies of friendly or tolerant behaviors. In many of these species, an animal's position within a dominance hierarchy controls much of its access to food items or mating opportunities. Dominant animals threaten subordinates that approach a nearby food item, and subordinates often avoid dominants even before threats are issued. Still, mothers tolerate their infant's and juvenile's foraging for morsels in her vicinity, and the male friends of these adult females can be equally tolerant of these young neighbors.[8] We have also mentioned coalition partnerships between pairs of long-term male residents of baboon troops. These partnerships can be the friendliest interactions observed between male baboons, since they tend to be tense around each other in most other pairings.[9] Finally, some species of primates maintain dominance hierarchies much less rigorously than others. Instances of a limited tolerance of successful begging by *unrelated* individuals around food sources or of some males attracted to estrus females are observed in at least some of these species.[10]

A preliminary analysis of findings given focus by a nonviolent perspective reveals evidence that the lives of primates exhibit many instances of tolerance that counterbalance images of aggressive competition, which seem to substantiate the old claim of "nature red in tooth-and-claw."

TYPES OF CONFLICTS

Nonetheless, despite these types of tolerance, conflicts—including aggressive conflicts—still occur within all species of primates, although the frequency or intensity varies substantially both within and between species. But at this juncture an important question surfaces: Are all conflicts the same? This question occurs in two versions. First, Is there a range of behaviors traditionally encompassed within the definition of conflict? Data exists for this question for a variety of species of primates, but especially thorough research exists for rhesus macaque monkeys. Since many investigators consider these monkeys to be among the most belligerent of primate species, the results are especially interesting for our purposes. Irwin Bernstein and Carolyn Ehardt quantitatively analyzed observations of two troops and have documented a wide range of behaviors during conflicts, from subordinates who "spontaneously" avoided approaching dominant individuals without a prior threat, to all-out fights that result in serious or fatal wounding.[11] Avoidance was the most common response, occurring in about 40 percent of conflicts. Specific submissive behaviors by subordinates were the type of interaction observed in another 17 percent of conflicts. The most common forms of aggressive expression were chasing and threatening, observed in about 15 percent and 12 percent of conflicts, respectively. Chasing rarely resulted in making contact with the victim, even when the victim was physically incapable of successful flight. Contact aggression consisted of hits and slaps in about 5 percent of conflicts. Nips or biting was observed in at most 5 percent of conflicts and sustained biting in only 1.6 percent of conflicts. Therefore, only about 2 percent of conflicts were likely to result in serious physical harm to a participant.

A second version of the question about the sameness of conflicts asks, Are all of these conflicts a part of a single continuum that measures increasing violence? Or are there different types of conflicts so that some are not violence as it is usually understood? Duane K. Friesen has developed definitions of coercion and violence among humans that are relevant for distinguishing kinds of conflicts. In

Friesen's understanding violence is "to violate the dignity or integrity of a person," including physical integrity.[12] However, coercion has a much different, potentially positive definition that emerges from the understanding that humans are inherently social.

> To be human, then, means to be acted upon by others, to be pressed to conform to patterns of behavior and speech. One takes on the patterns of others—their language, habits, attitudes, metaphors, rituals, and gestures. To become socialized means to have one's behavior ordered so that it is coordinated and patterned to fit into the group as a whole. . . . Some forms of coercion are violent if they are harmful to people . . . but there is also a coercive element in all social life which is not inherently evil. Coercion that "orders" [socializes] human . . . behavior into patterns of cooperation that is not exploitive is essential to human social life.[13]

In humans, this potentially positive coercion includes both psychological or social pressure, and physical force. Such pressure can include actions that impel a person to act in a certain way rather than another because of sanctions that range through various kinds of positive reinforcement, to expressions of disapproval from "social ostracism, and estrangement from others, political defeat, to strikes and economic boycotts. . . . Pressure permits persons to continue to act according to their desires as long as they are willing to take the consequences of their actions." Physical force, in Friesen's definition of positive coercion, includes "actions which physically restrict persons from continuing to do what they have been doing, or make them do something they would not otherwise do."[14] Friesen's analysis makes clear that acts of coercion, conflict, and confrontation can differ in both inner structure and ethical content and are not all of a piece that can be arranged on one continuum assuming only variations in intensity of violence. Borrowing from Friesen's distinction between violence and coercion brings new insight to analysis of primate behaviors and interactions.

PRIMATE CONFLICTS

Since nonhuman primates apparently do not have systems of communication that can exchange proposals with the nuances and clarity achieved in human negotiations, monkeys and apes depend much more on communication via physical actions. The putative socialization processes directed at juvenile and adolescent monkeys and apes may involve physical coercion. Bernstein and Ehardt have offered circumstantial evidence that aggressive behavior, especially by adult males, may shape how adolescent rhesus macaque males target their aggressive behavior and control the intensity and duration of any physical force they use. In another example, Chapais's extensive experiments have provided evidence that older Japanese macaques sometimes intervene on the side of both closely related and unrelated juveniles and adolescents that are aggressively targeting individuals of subordinate families of the troop. Young adults usually reach a level in the dominance hierarchy just below that already achieved by their older relatives.[15]

In these examples, physical coercion tends to contribute to the stability of the basic social structure and social relationships of a community over the years. These conflicts rarely result in serious wounding. Conflicts over material resources (which are often influenced by dominance relations) or access by males to females in estrus (which are less consistently influenced by dominance relations) are also embedded in the social network of the community and rarely result in wounding.[16]

Strum and Smuts, among others, have proposed that aggression can also be one option for animals "working out" or "negotiating" new relationships. Through these confrontations, juveniles and adolescents might learn about the personalities, fighting abilities, and networks of coalition partners of older individuals that are subordinates to their family. Similarly, animals that migrate into a new community face a whole set of individuals that do not yet have histories, personalities, or relationships, as far as they know. Strum suggests that baboons often use aggression solely to get another baboon's attention. "Aggression *said* something. [Scientists] had always assumed that when a large male employed it he meant 'I want what you have,' 'Get away from me' or some equally belligerent statement. But lacking human language, how else could a [baboon] even begin a negotiation with someone who wished to ignore him? [For example,] How else could a [newcomer to a troop] discover what he needed to know about other males? In responding to aggression—and it was difficult not to, in one way or another—Pumphouse [troop] residents gave away a great many secrets."[17] Thus what has been presumed to be aggression is actually a means for primates who lack spoken language to test and to provoke each other and to make each party's interests clear. To do so forcefully yet nonviolently (without harm), and to adjust one's objectives when the results become clear, is the key to mutually satisfactory coexistence.[18]

Apparently, much of the conflict in primate communities involves behaviors and social contexts consistent with Friesen's definitions of coercion, including the behaviors that Strum and Smuts called "aggression." These coercive acts are the way animals without language facilitate communication and respond to conflicts within their social structure. These interactions, while involving physical acts, do not need to be read as evidence of the violence of nature and by extension of the inevitability of violence in conflict.

Another category of aggression is harder to classify when we try to distinguish between appropriate physical coercion and violence that harms. Smuts identified a category of conflicts that included a disproportionate percentage of the severest attacks she observed. She was analyzing interactions between male and female baboons just before episodes of male aggression against females. Almost a quarter of these events were classified as "apparently unprovoked aggression" because "Neither the male nor the female were interacting with each other or with another baboon just before the aggression, and there was no apparent reason for the male's behavior." Smuts comments, "nearly all of the truly severe attacks that

I observed occurred in this context. These involved a prolonged, seemingly obsessive series of attacks on a female who, by the end of the incident, was often literally shaking with fear and choking on her own screams."[19]

Smuts described two events that suggest how long-term memories and retribution could explain at least some of these seemingly unprovoked attacks. In each case, a male wounded a female who had harassed a friend of the male several minutes to several hours earlier. Smuts concludes, "some—perhaps most—of these 'unprovoked' attacks are just the opposite: They are attacks in response to specific acts by the victim that the attacker observed and remembered; it is the [scientific] observer who does not know the reason for the male's behavior, not the baboons."[20]

Should we interpret a male's apparent retribution as physical coercion? Or should we interpret his action as violence because of the seemingly disproportionate intensity of these attacks?

One other situation poses similar difficulties of interpretation. As noted throughout this chapter, many species of primates have more or less rigorously defined dominance hierarchies that influence the access of individuals to material or social resources. We have also hinted at evidence that various coercive social interactions in these communities tend to keep the overall structure of their hierarchies consistent as new adolescents enter their ranks. These social structures often remain stable for several years. However, on occasion, substantial changes abruptly rearrange these orderly patterns of dominance and subordinance. "Rebellious" subordinates "depose" the highest ranking members of the hierarchy and at least some of the latter are severely wounded. Such rebellions have been described for a variety of primate species.[21] In most of these cases, scientists have not been able to define historical contingencies or social dynamics that would provide a convincing explanation for the initiation of these rare but dramatic events. These events tend to benefit most the members of the beta levels of the previous social hierarchies, while the former alpha members usually pay a high price. How should we interpret these rare events?

A final category of behavior poses the greatest difficulty in interpretation for the perspective developed here. Instances of infanticide by males, and much more rarely by females, have been observed infrequently in several species of primates but seem to be more common in a few species. Most of the latter have one-male-multifemale community structures or multimale-multifemale community structures with steep dominance hierarchies and short tenures for alpha males. Observations suggest that 30–40 percent of infants born in specific communities of these species have been killed over a few years. In most cases, the males that committed these actions had just gained the alpha position in a troop or would gain that position soon afterward. At the same time, a variety of behaviors of both females and males of these species apparently provide some protection to infants during these periods of transition. Intensive research is now focused on trying to understand the psychological and evolutionary origins of this violent behavior.[22]

CONFLICT RESOLUTION

Interpreting the role of aggression in conflicts requires analyses of both their social function and the consequences of these interactions. For decades, scientists recognized that dispersion of antagonists is the usual consequence of aggressive interactions, with the loser moving away from and avoiding the winner for a period of time. It was Frans de Waal's observations of the social dynamics among chimpanzees that led to the first recognition that substantial minorities of opponents establish nonaggressive interactions within five minutes of the end to a conflict.[23] Several subsequent studies demonstrated that these interactions substantially reduce the likelihood of immediate reinitiation of aggression and rapidly increase the level of toleration of the loser displayed by the aggressor. Further, individuals that have lost a conflict display behavioral signs of stress for at least a few minutes after a conflict but after a nonaggressive interaction with the winner, the loser's behavior relaxes back to resting levels.[24]

De Waal and several colleagues have hypothesized that many of these peaceful postconflict contacts constitute "reconciliations." That is, they may repair long-term relationships between kin or friends, as well as calm short-term relations between individuals.[25] However, only two sets of observations have been used to investigate the long-term consequences of reconciled versus nonreconciled aggressive conflicts. In one set of observations, a study of chacma baboons did not find the predicted difference in social relations over the ten days that respectively followed these two types of conflicts.[26] However, a recent study of Japanese macaques did find differences in the frequencies of aggressive and friendly behaviors, respectively, after these two types of conflicts, when they are compared to average frequencies of these behaviors over much longer periods of time.[27] The latter data are consistent with the hypothesis that reconciliations "repair a relationship," while nonreconciled conflicts are associated with increased rates of aggression and decreased rates of friendly interactions. Further research will need to be done to explain the difference in outcomes of these two analyses.

Interpreting the role of aggression in conflicts requires analyses of their social functions and consequences but also requires information on the process through which they end. To date we do not have evidence that helps us interpret the termination of conflicts between pairs of opponents. However, some conflict interactions end after a third member of the community becomes involved. Aggressive interventions (where the intervener threatens, hits, or bites one of the opponents of a conflict) are observed in a wide range of species but occur in only a small percent of conflicts for most primates. Active nonaggressive interventions (where the intervener directs friendly behaviors at one of the opponents) are observed only very rarely in most species but have been observed more frequently in Tonkean macaques and chimpanzees, two species that have relatively shallow dominance hierarchies and relatively high percentages of conflicts that are reconciled. A quantitative investigation of these two types of interventions was made for Tonkean macaques.[28] Of the total 934 conflicts observed, 74 were associated with aggressive intervention, 68 with nonaggressive intervention, and 18 conflicts received both kinds of intervention. Individuals initiating either type of intervention were more likely to respond to conflicts involving aggressive contact (slaps or grabs) than to intervene in milder conflicts involving only threat signals or charges. (Biting attacks are quite rare in this species.) Interveners preferentially targeted the initiator of the conflict, who was generally the more dominant of the two opponents. In many aggressive interventions victims received support from closely related interveners who provided protection or aided a challenge by an adolescent attempting to climb the dominance hierarchy. But in peaceful interventions the intervener was usually dominant over both parties and directed any of a variety of "friendly" signals toward the aggressor. Peaceful interventions were frequently followed by a friendly interaction, such as grooming, between intervener and the aggressor.

Aggressors reacted aggressively to the intervener in 59 percent of aggressive interventions. However, they reacted this way in only 5 percent of nonaggressive interventions. In addition, aggressive interventions were followed within five seconds by termination of all combat in only 20 percent of conflicts, while nonaggressive interventions ended combat within five seconds in 60 percent of conflicts. Therefore, the latter style of intervention was much more effective in terminating conflicts peacefully. In addition, nonaggresive interventions usually combined protection of a victim with the maintenance of friendly relations between intervener and aggressor.

One study raises the possibility that patterns of peacefulness can be shaped by the social dynamics experienced by maturing juveniles. De Waal and Johanowicz co-housed two groups of juvenile rhesus monkeys for several months with two groups of juvenile stumptail macaque monkeys, while other groups of rhesus were not co-housed. Observations of these groups continued after the co-housing was ended. Stumptail macaques reconcile a much higher percentage of their aggressive conflicts than rhesus macaques. De Waal and Johanowicz report a dramatically increased tendency for the rhesus to reconcile fights as an apparent result of their exposure to stumptail macaques. The rate of reconciliations among the rhesus progressively increased in frequency during the period of co-housing, until it reached a rate similar to that observed among stumptail macaques. This new rate was maintained during the six weeks of observations after the species were again separated. This increase in reconciliation behavior in the rhesus subjects was not paralleled by increases in their affiliative and grooming behavior. In addition, they did not acquire any species-specific behaviors of the stumptail macaques. Why reconciliation alone was effected was not obvious from this experiment. Nevertheless, de Waal and Johanowicz note, "All we can conclude—yet this seems both important and encouraging to us—is that the reconciliation behavior of juvenile nonhuman primates is susceptible to manipulation of the social environment."[29]

CONCLUSION

In summary, we have reviewed a variety of studies of primate behavior from a perspective informed by nonviolence. A particular feature of the analysis was to develop a distinction made by Duane Friesen between violence, which imparts harm, and social coercion, which can impel behavior but does not do harm to those involved. With this insight we have recognized that some primate activities presumed to be violent, if violence includes any physical action, are more properly characterized as positive social coercion as understood from Friesen. In addition the data from these studies reveal two types of actions that fall into the realm of conflict resolution.

The implications of these observations are twofold. First, when sensitized to see through nonviolent eyes, nature may not be nearly as red in tooth-and-claw as it is commonly assumed to be in popular culture. That insight can change how we look at a wide range of biological and zoological questions and raise the distinct possibility that many human observers have read their own violent assumptions into their observation of animal behavior. Second, this conclusion should then challenge humans to consider our own violence, as well as our assumptions about both the inevitability and the effectiveness of violence.

NOTES

1. Filippo Aureli and Frans B. M. de Waal, eds., *Natural Conflict Resolution* (Berkeley: University of California Press, 2000), 387.

2. For example: Jeanne Altmann, *Baboon Mothers and Infants* (Chicago: University of Chicago Press, 1980); and Barbara B. Smuts, *Sex and Friendship in Baboons* (Cambridge: Harvard University Press, 1985).

3. Irwin S. Bernstein and Carolyn L. Ehardt, "Age-Sex Differences in the Expression of Agonistic Behavior in Rhesus Monkey (*Macaca mulatta*) Groups," *Journal of Comparative Psychology* 99, no. 2 (1985): 115–132; and Thomas E. Ruehlmann, Irwin S. Bernstein, Thomas P. Gordon, and Peter Belcaen, "Wounding Patterns in Three Species of Captive Macaques," *American Journal of Primatology* 14 (1988): 125–134.

4. For birds, see: Stephen T. Emlen, Peter H. Wrege, and Natalie J. Demong, "Making Decisions in the Family: An Evolutionary Perspective," *American Scientist* 83 (1995): 148–157. For a primate example, see William J. Hamilton III and John Bulger, "Facultative Expression of Behavioral Differences between One-Male and Multimale Savanna Baboon Groups," *American Journal of Primatology* 28 (1992): 61–71.

5. S. C. Strum, "Reconciling Aggression and Social Manipulation As Means of Competition. 1. Life-History Perspective," *International Journal of Primatology* 15, no. 5 (1994): 739–765.

6. See also Smuts, *Sex and Friendship*, 134–150.

7. Strum, "Reconciling Aggression," 760–761.

8. For example, see Altmann, *Baboon Mothers*; and Smuts, *Sex and Friends*. For effects of a rigid dominance hierarchy on how individuals access resources, see Hanspeter

Schaub, "Dominance Fades with Distance: An Experiment on Food Competition in Long-Tailed Macaques (*Macaca fascicularis*)," *Journal of Comparative Psychology* 109, no. 2 (1995): 196–202.

9. See Smuts, *Sex and Friends*, 147–149. Also, see Barbara B. Smuts and John M. Watanabe, "Social Relationships and Ritualized Greetings in Adult Male Baboons (*Papio cynocephalus anubis*)," *International Journal of Primatology* 11, no. 2 (1990): 147–172.

10. (1) Tonkean macaque monkeys: Odile Petit, Christine Desportes, and Bernard Thierry, "Differential Probability of 'Coproduction' in Two Species of Macaque (*Macaca tonkeana, M. mulatta*)," *Ethology* 90 (1992): 107–120; (2) Brown Capuchin Monkeys: Frans B. M. de Waal, "Attitudinal Reciprocity in Food Sharing among Brown Capuchin Monkeys," *Animal Behaviour* 60 (2000): 253–261; (3) Chimpanzees: Frans B. M. de Waal, *Chimpanzee Politics: Power and Sex among Apes* (Baltimore: Johns Hopkins University Press, 1982); and Frans B. M. de Waal, "The Chimpanzees's Service Economy: Food for Grooming," *Evolution and Human Behavior* 18 (1997): 375–386; (4) Bonobos: Gottfried Hohmann and Barbara Fruth, "Food Sharing and Status in Unprovisioned Bonobos," in *Food and the Status Quest: An Interdisciplinary Perspective*, ed. Polly Wiessner and Wulf Schiefenhovel (Providence, R.I.: Berghahn Books, 1996), 47–67; and Amy Randall Parrish, "Female Relationships in Bonobos (*Pan panicus*): Evidence for Bonding, Cooperation, and Female Dominance in a Male-Philopatric Species," *Human Nature* 17 (1996): 61–96.

11. Each of the following statistics is taken from tables III and IV of Irwin S. Bernstein and Carolyn L. Ehardt, "Intragroup Agonistic Behavior in Rhesus Monkeys (*Macaca mulatta*)," *International Journal of Primatology* 6, no. 3 (1985): 209–226.

12. Duane K. Friesen, *Christian Peacemaking and International Conflict: A Realist Pacifist Perspective* (Scottdale, Pa.: Herald Press, 1986), 143. The following discussion based on Friesen's work is parallel to efforts to distinguish coercion, force, and violence described in chapter 2 by Stassen and Westmoreland-White in this volume.

13. Friesen, *Christian Peacemaking*, 60.

14. All quotations in this paragraph are from Friesen, *Christian Peacemaking,* 152.

15. (1) Articles about presumptive socialization among rhesus macaques: Irwin S. Bernstein and Carolyn L. Ehardt, "The Influence of Kinship and Socialization on Aggressive Behavior in Rhesus Monkeys (*Macaca mulatta*)," *Animal Behaviour* 34 (1986): 739–747; Irwin S. Bernstein and Carolyn L. Ehardt, "Modification of Aggression through Socialization and the Special Case of Adult and Adolescent Male Rhesus Monkeys (*Macaca mulatta*)," *American Journal of Primatology* 10 (1986): 213–227. (2) Article concerning intervention and social climbing in Japanese macaques: Bernard Chapais, "Alliances As a Means of Competition in Primates: Evolutionary, Developmental, and Cognitive Aspects," *Yearbook of Physical Anthropology* 38, (1995): 115–136.

16. For example, see Altmann, *Baboon Mothers*; and Smuts, *Sex and Friendship.*

17. Shirley C. Strum, *Almost Human: A Journey into the World of Baboons* (New York: W. W. Norton, 1987), 123.

18. See Frans B. M. de Waal, "Conflict As Negotiation," in *Great Ape Societies*, ed. William C. McGrew, Linda F. Marchant, and Toshisada Nishida (New York: Cambridge University Press, 1996), 159–172, especially 162.

19. Smuts, *Sex and Friendship*, 88, 93.

20. Smuts, *Sex and Friendship*, 94–95, quotation 96.

21. For example: Susan Perry, "A Case Report of a Male Rank Reversal in a Group of Wild White-Faced Capuchins (*Cebus capucinus*)," *Primates* 39, no. 1 (1998): 51–70; Amy

Samuels, Joan B. Silk, and Jeanne Altmann, "Continuity and Change in Dominance Relations among Female Baboons," *Animal Behaviour* 35 (1987): 785–793; Carolyn L. Ehardt and Irwin S. Bernstein, "Matrilineal Overthrows in Rhesus Monkey Groups," *International Journal of Primatology* 7, no. 2 (1986): 157–181; Lorenz Gygax, Nerida Harley, and Hans Kummer, "A Matrilineal Overthrow with Destructive Aggression in *Macaca fascicularis*," *Primates* 38, no. 2 (1997): 149–158; Frans de Waal, *Peacemaking among Primates* (Cambridge: Harvard University Press, 1989), 61–78.

22. See evidence reviewed in Carel P. van Shaik and Charles H. Janson, eds., *Infanticide by Males and Its Implications* (Cambridge: Cambridge University Press, 2000).

23. De Waal, *Peacemaking*.

24. See literature reviewed in the chapters by de Waal and by Aureli and Darlene Smucny in: Aureli and de Waal, *Natural Conflict Resolution*.

25. See literature reviewed in the chapter by Cords and Aureli in: Aureli and de Waal, *Natural Conflict Resolution*.

26. Joan B. Silk, Dorothy L. Cheney, and Robert M. Seyfarth, "The Form and Function of Post-conflict Interactions between Female Baboons," *Animal Behaviour* 52 (1996): 259–268.

27. Nicola F. Koyama, "The Long-Term Effects of Reconciliation in Japanese Macaques *Macaca fuscata*," *Ethology* 107 (2001): 975–987.

28. O. Petit and B. Thierry, "Aggressive and Peaceful Interventions in Conflicts in Tonkean Macaques," *Animal Behaviour* 48 (1994): 1427–1436.

29. See Frans B. M. de Waal and Denise L. Johanowicz, "Modification of Reconciliation Behavior through Social Experience: An Experiment with Two Macaque Species," *Child Development* 64 (1993): 906–907.

21

Nonviolence and the Foundations
of Mathematical Thought

Stephen H. Harnish

Mathematics is much more than the study of numbers and their operations. At its foundation mathematics is the study of axiomatic systems composed of undefined terms, axioms, definitions, and deduced theorems. Seen in this light, mathematics is very broad. All phenomena with observable patterns are natural candidates for mathematical modeling, axiomatization, and analysis. As Keith Devlin so aptly explains, mathematics can be considered the "science of patterns."[1] This chapter provides examples of how the systematic mathematical search for options and for logical consistency can contribute to a nonviolent worldview.

THE ROLE OF IMAGINATION

An ethics class I once took in seminary highlighted a place for creativity in ethical decision making. Although not a panacea, imagination can play an important role in suggesting previously unconsidered options in ethics. Perhaps the systematic thinking skills of a mathematician could play a significant role in developing alternative responses to violence or injustice. Let's consider an elementary example of one such skill. A basic organizational tool widely used by mathematicians (along with theorists in most other fields) is the use of tables. For example, many scholars use two-by-two tables (or larger n-by-n tables) to categorize choices. One elementary calculus example would be a two-by-two table with rows for continuous or discontinuous, and columns for differentiable or nondifferentiable functions of real numbers. This way, all combinations of the properties are considered. For example, the boxes of the table could include polynomials as both continuous and differentiable at all real numbers, the absolute value function as continuous but not differentiable at zero, and step functions as neither differentiable nor continuous at the x-values of the "steps." The fact that the box for differentiable but discontinuous functions is empty reflects a theorem of mathematics—that a function differentiable at a point must also be continuous there. As elementary as these examples appear to mathematicians today, there was a time in the history of mathematical concepts when such a chart could have sparked either inspiration or great controversy. Namely, prior to Fourier's work, few mathematicians had broadened their conception of "function" to include the discontinuous and nondifferentiable ones. An especially revolutionary example was Weierstrass's 1872 trigonometric series that was everywhere continuous, and nowhere differentiable. At that time, most mathematicians doubted that such functions were possible. Nevertheless, Fourier's and Weierstrass's ideas were eventually embraced and stimulated key developments in the study of real analysis—a foundation for understanding the modern theory of probability.[2] A mathematician's penchant for systematic consideration of all possible combinations just might prove helpful in uncovering ethical options that had been previously overlooked.

RELATIVE CONSISTENCY AND MEDIATION

My doctoral research was in mathematical logic—especially axiomatic and applied set theory. Key developments of twentieth-century logic were Kurt Gödel's proofs of the incompleteness theorems and the impossibility of completing Hilbert's goal of proving the consistency of key mathematical systems. In fact, Gödel showed that any logical system of sufficient complexity cannot be proven to be consistent *within that system*. The best that can be offered are relative consistency proofs—"If system A is consistent, we can prove that system B is consistent." Many of the key results in set theory during the twentieth century proved the independence of certain axioms (such as the axiom of choice and the continuum hypothesis) via relative consistency arguments.[3] In this section I argue that relative consistency and independence of axioms is a useful metaphor for the incompleteness of any given ideological framework. Each value system, culture, or worldview has its own "internal logic." In some conflicts, mediators may find it possible to bring competing parties together by embracing a new framework that preserves each side's legitimate concerns and ideals. Let's consider a mathematical analogue—an example of how two competing (even contradictory) axiomatic systems can be "reconciled."

For this analogy we consider two sets of numbers that mathematicians call the *integers* Z and the *positive rational numbers* Q^+. In mathematical notation these can be denoted by Z = {. . . , $-3, -2, -1, 0, 1, 2, 3, . . .$} and Q^+ = { p/q: p, q are positive integers}, which is read "Q^+ equals the set of all ratios p/q such that p and q are positive integers." Examples of positive rational numbers are $1/2$ (the ratio of 1 and 2) and $5/3$ (the ratio of 5 and 3). Mathematicians can easily provide two competing lists of axioms that capture the properties of the two sets Z and Q^+. Within each system some ideas are obviously true while others are obviously false. For example, within the "world" of the integers Z, the statement

A: there is a number x such that $5 + x = 4$

is true. A practical application of the equation $5 + x = 4$ comes from banking. To answer the question What transaction leaves \$4 in an account that started with \$5? we may solve for x to be the integer -1 that represents a one-dollar withdrawal. However, the statement

B: there is a number x such that $2x = 3$

is false. A practical use of the formula $2x = 3$ comes from making recipes. Consider the question If you know that two batches of a recipe make 3 dozen cookies, how many would one batch make? For the answer, we solve for x to be the rational number 3/2 or 1.5 dozen cookies. In other words, the world of the integers does contain the number -1—the necessary x value to make *A* true, but it does not contain the rational number 3/2—the x value that satisfies statement *B*. On the other hand, in the "realm" of Q^+, it is perfectly obvious that just the opposite is true. *A* is false while *B* is true since 3/2 resides in Q^+ and -1 and other negative numbers are not even conceived of within the "worldview" of Q^+.

How can we resolve the conflict of these two systems? There are several options. One scenario involves one side "caving in" under the persuasion (or coercion) of the other so that both worlds end up either accepting the existence of non-integer positive rationals or the negative counting numbers, but not both. A second approach is possible. With enough imagination one can devise a new set of principles that honor the strengths of both—negative numbers will be allowed and so will fractions. For example, the new set of principles might axiomatize the properties of a larger set such as Q (the set of all rationals—positive, negative, or zero) or even R (the elements of the real number line). In the expanded worlds of Q and R both statement *A* and statement *B* are true. This second approach in effect reconciles the two systems and actually mirrors the developments within the history of mathematics.

Most human conflicts and acts of violence do *not* revolve around competing systems of mathematics.[4] Nevertheless, this mathematical analysis of systems for Q^+ and Z displays two key principles: (1) both systems are equally valid, in that both are "just as consistent" as something as basic as Peano's axioms for the natural numbers; and (2) neither was the best answer to the question What objects should be called numbers? Today mathematicians accept the existence of numbers such as the square root of two and other irrational numbers left out by both systems. This mathematical analogy suggests the following principles for transforming human conflicts: (1) show respect for the internal logic and legitimate hopes and fears of opposing sides; and (2) look for options in the conflict, especially any alternative larger frameworks that might challenge the worst and embrace the best of all sides involved.

This mathematical model might have clear implications for the seemingly intractable search for a just peace between Palestinians and Israelis. Neither side appears willing to cave in, and Israeli expansion of settlements makes a two-state solution appear to be unreachable. But this mathematical logic would seem to support the solution sometimes proposed of a single territorial state encompassing two peoples. Similar situations would be the continuing presence of Native Americans and First Nations peoples in North America and efforts of blacks and whites to live together after the failure of apartheid in South Africa.

CONCLUSION

Without having specifically solved any international problems, the mathematical arguments of this chapter imply that it is logical to search for nonviolent solutions and for solutions that are third options between the usually assumed ones of giving in or fighting. Mathematics does belong in the discussion of nonviolence in the liberal arts curriculum.

NOTES

1. Keith J. Devlin, *Mathematics: The Science of Patterns* (New York: Scientific American Library, 1994), 1.

2. Techniques of real analysis are important tools in fields as diverse as economics, physics, engineering, and computer science. For more on the historical significance of Fourier's and Weierstrass's ideas see chapters 1 and 6 of David Bressoud's *A Radical Approach to Real Analysis* (Washington, D.C.: Mathematical Association of America, 1994).

3. More on issues of relative consistency and the implications of Gödel's work may be found on page 102 of the second edition of the classic text *Foundations of Set Theory* by Fraenkel, Bar-Hillel, and Levy (Amsterdam: Elsevier, 1984).

4. One notable exception was the violent internal struggle among the Pythagoreans of ancient Greece. Their philosophy related to Q^+ in that they revered natural numbers and their ratios. In fact, legend has it that they drowned Hippasus of Metapontum for devising a proof that some lengths are not rational. More specifically, this unfortunate Pythagorean had proven the irrationality of the square root of two—the length of the diagonal of the unit square. As the story goes, death threats prevented others in their school from revealing this damning mathematical fact. See Morris Kline's *Mathematical Thought from Ancient to Modern Times* (New York: Oxford University Press, 1972), 32.

22

Mathematics of Nonviolence

Darryl K. Nester

At least in fiction and popular discourse, the charge is often casually leveled that mathematics has little or nothing to do with "real life." If one accepts this idea, it may seem like irrelevance squared to ask what mathematics has to do with nonviolence. But skeptical readers should continue. Mathematics does belong in this book on nonviolence across the curriculum, and this chapter deals with mathematics and violence at several levels.

The mathematics community struggles against the perception of irrelevance by, among other things, attempting to incorporate real-life problems into the curriculum. By their choices of classroom examples and illustrations, teachers of mathematics convey messages about the ways that math is useful, and they shape the thinking of students about those subjects. Thus teachers who are advocates of nonviolence have a variety of ways to introduce students to issues of violence and nonviolence they might not otherwise consider.

MATHEMATICAL EXAMPLES

The goal in service and general education mathematics courses is often to teach particular skills and techniques, with enough theory to justify why they work. Examples used in such settings have the potential to teach more than the math involved. Illustrations can come from a variety of disciplines.

It seems reasonable to declare that many—perhaps most—mathematics examples are "violence-nonviolence neutral"—mathematical models for water sprayed from a drinking fountain, or plowing snow, or the traveling salesman problem. The boundaries of this category are somewhat fuzzy; those who object to the violence of sports might not wish to consider the flight of a kicked football, for example.

Other examples, however, do fall into categories that lend themselves to discussion of violence and nonviolence. Many textbooks that present models of projectile motion include one or more examples detailing the path of a bullet or a missile. Another violence issue appears when at least two rather common examples deal with a fictional application of the death penalty. A standard probability problem, the "prisoners paradox," has three prisoners in jail, with two slated for execution and one prisoner pumping the guard for information in an attempt to determine his chance of surviving. An illustration of mathematical induction involves a judge who sentences a prisoner to die within the next month, with the date to be kept a secret until the man is led off to his execution, while the prisoner tries to determine the death date inductively. Using these examples without comment appears to present violent activities—use of bullets and missiles, and the killing of prisoners—as normal activities.

The choice of a different kind of example can promote other kinds of activity or teach other lessons about normal life. For example, one could use mathematical examples that show racial inequities in the death penalty, the folly of playing the lottery, or the distribution of a country's wealth using the Gini Index or some other measure. When one realizes that such examples almost never appear in textbooks, it starts to become clear how mathematics texts do accommodate and teach the violence that is assumed in our society. Math books with different examples, or teachers with alternative illustrations, would show nonviolent values to students.

What kinds of examples are needed for an effective course? At the least, a course should balance violent examples with an equal number of specifically nonviolent ones. However, in some instances it is easy to go further. Teachers can revise the violent examples mentioned earlier—involving paths of missiles and bullets and the death penalty—to make them neutral or positive. Students can easily comprehend projectile motion problems in class using baseballs or pieces of chalk or dry-erase markers. The prisoners paradox can be told with three students sitting in the principal's office awaiting a decision on detention or suspension. The example of mathematical induction involving an execution date is sometimes told with a teacher warning her students of an impending pop quiz.

A promising example from probability is one I first encountered in the puzzle section of the magazine *Contingencies*, written for an audience of actuaries. At first glance it seems like a violent example, but it actually lends itself to teaching about nonviolence. In the problem Al, Ben, and Chad choose to settle a dispute by engaging in a somewhat peculiar duel. In a randomly chosen order, the combatants take turns shooting at each other. During his turn, that combatant can aim at one other person and attempt to shoot him. The rotation continues until only one man remains alive. Al is a 100 percent accurate shot, while Ben is 75 percent accurate, and Chad is 60 percent accurate. The question is, which shooter is most likely to survive the duel?

Intuition suggests that since Al is 100 percent accurate, he has the best chance to win this dual. Paradoxically, it turns out that by following a simple strategy,

Chad, the least accurate, is the most likely to survive (62.5 percent of the time). He should deliberately miss whenever his turn comes up, while Al and Ben each try to increase his chances by seeking to eliminate the most accurate remaining shooter. Even more paradoxically, if it should turn out that Ben shoots before Al, as occurs in half of the random orders, Chad's survival chances increase to 65 percent while Ben has a 25 percent chance of surviving and Al—the most accurate marksman—survives only 10 percent of the time. In any case, both Al and Ben should be eager to avoid the duel, because both are more likely to be targeted than the less accurate Chad.

Along with an interesting probability computation, this problem provides a possible moral: Being the strongest or most militarily prepared does not necessarily guarantee victory in a complex (or indirect) struggle. One can argue that this setting is highly artificial and vastly oversimplified compared to real conflict. It is nonetheless a mathematical model that challenges the conventional assumption that violence always works or security arises from strength.

The field of ethnomathematics—studying the mathematics developed and used by other cultures—might add a multicultural flavor to the classroom. In teaching probability, for example, use Native American stick games in place of dice. Such examples also serve to remind students and teachers that mathematics was not developed solely by rich, white, European males.

Mathematical problems can teach about national priorities. How many people could be educated or fed using the money spent on one $1.85 billion Seawolf nuclear submarine? How many new teachers could be hired? How many students could receive college educations? Solving such problems will start students thinking about the human costs that the nation is trading for military hardware. Or for a historical example with multiple ethical connotations, develop a problem set around freed slaves and free land after the Civil War. Have students calculate the number of freed slaves who could have received forty acres (and a mule), a suggestion rejected as impractical or impossible, if the 180,000,000 acres given to wealthy white men to build railroads from 1850 to 1871 had instead been distributed to the freed slaves. What percent of that land would have been used if each of the estimated four million former slaves received forty acres? If the four million former slaves were assumed to be grouped into families of four and each family received forty acres, what percent of the total would have gone to these families? Or devise similar problems with estimates of the hundreds of thousands of acres of plantation land leased to Northern whites and worked for wages by former slaves rather than distributing land to blacks that would have made them self-sustaining. A class studying exponential and other growth models can calculate the difference in the growth of the economy through several generations if the former slaves receive no land and thus contribute little and may actually hold the economy back versus scenarios in which freed individuals and families receive land and become self-sustaining contributors to the economy. (All the while the student mathematicians are contemplating that whether white or black men received the land, it was stolen from Native Americans.) Solving such problems will start students on the way to realizing that the Civil War did not solve the race problem in the United States and that in fact the nation is still reaping the consequences of its racist treatment of freed slaves. Such examples are easily available, if one asks a few historical questions or pays attention to reports of military spending in daily newspapers. And such examples developed and disseminated throughout math courses teach about issues of governmental choice, violence, and social justice as a product of learning mathematics.

THE PROBLEM OF MATHEMATICAL PRECISION

For those unconvinced about nonviolence or unconvinced of the value of such examples, or both, this might seem like the end of the story. Aside from the issue of which examples we choose, it may still be tempting to view mathematics as an innocent bystander in issues of nonviolence. There is more to say, however. In fact, the public image of mathematics may actually contribute to assumptions of violence in society. Mathematics is often viewed as a discipline that yields exact answers—an image first cultivated in elementary school classrooms, where we learn that two plus two is four and that six divided by three is two. In common perception, the precision of such answers is presumed to extend to every math problem.

The exactness of mathematics appears in Zeno's Paradox, often told as the well-known riddle about taking a letter to the post office. How long will it take to mail my letter if I go half the distance to the post office today, half the remaining distance tomorrow, and half the remaining distance on each successive day after that? The answer, of course, is that the letter will never get mailed—because half the remaining distance always remains. The answer reflects the precision of theoretical mathematics but clearly does not reflect the real-world application of mathematics. Even a child would say, "But can't you just reach over and drop the letter in the mailbox?"

This impression of math's exactness is further reinforced in the media, especially in the fictional glimpses of mathematics that arise in books, movies, and television. Many times, some clearly estimated value is stated as if it were exact. *Star Trek*'s Mr. Spock, for example, might quote the odds of some event to eight significant digits. In Isaac Asimov's Foundation novels, the science of "psychohistory" uses mathematics to predict the behavior of a galactic society, which allows experts to map out the future path of the Foundation in the coming centuries.

Calculators and computers exacerbate the problem, conveying as they do this false sense of precision. It is often difficult to convince students that an answer like "about 5.5 inches" is much more appropriate for many problems than the "5.461245927 inches" that might appear on their calculators. A calculator is not "smart" enough to automatically determine the real accuracy of a computed value; for example, a calculator will report 1.57^2 as 2.4649, even though the number 1.57

might have a margin of error of plus or minus 0.005 (which means the actual square could be as small as 2.45 or as large as 2.48). Students are often surprised when I spend a lecture or two showing them cases in which their calculators are not merely imprecise but incorrect. They may express dismay at the revelation that these tools will sometimes betray their trust, when it tells them, for example, that the square of the square root of 3 is different from 3. But for their own good, they need to learn this important lesson: No matter how sophisticated the technology, someone can come up with an example that will cause it to fail.

Even those with reasonably sophisticated mathematical understanding can fall prey to the trap of false precision. The computer scientist John von Neumann imagined that, with sufficient computational power available, the weather could be precisely predicted and controlled. He understood the calculus issues involved but could not imagine the impact of chaos theory (the so-called butterfly effect), which was yet to be developed. We now understand that complex systems often exhibit seemingly unpredictable behavior, simply because we cannot measure the variables involved with sufficient accuracy.

It seems reasonable to argue that the widespread belief in the assumption of mathematical precision contributes to the expectation in North American society that technology can solve moral and ethical problems. The assumption of mathematical certainty is one element of the belief that a missile defense system can protect the United States from nuclear attack by so-called rogue states. Almost certainly it cannot. Not only do complex systems often exhibit unpredictable behavior, but the number of calculations required would swamp the known computer systems.

The assumption of mathematical certainty also appears just below the surface in the search for demonstrable errors in the analysis of intelligence data, which would show that the tragedy of September 11 could have been prevented by more powerful computer analysis of the data; but again, almost certainly not. More importantly, the development of a "Star Wars" missile defense system and the search for what would have prevented September 11 are misguided efforts to solve moral problems with technological and mathematical solutions. Truly deflecting rockets and suicide bombers requires acknowledging and dealing with the causes of the anger that would launch missiles and send planes crashing into buildings. Addressing such causes requires moral searching and changes in behavior rather than more powerful computers and more precise mathematical analysis. Students would benefit from the observation that many problems require moral rather than (or in addition to) mathematical and technological solutions.

As a step toward debunking this fallacy of protection by perfect information and precise calculations, mathematicians must be more straightforward about the place of exactness in mathematics. There is a certain pleasure that comes from solving a problem and finding π in the answer, and students ought to glimpse these elegant examples. Nonetheless, students may actually be better served by seeing more cases in which the solution is noticeably approximate. I like to point out to my probability students, for example, that weather forecasters never predict a 73 percent chance of rain!

In fact we make many numerical calculations each day, and almost all of them are approximate. Will the money in my checking account cover the bills I need to pay this month? Will the change in my pocket cover a cup of coffee and a donut at this morning's coffee break? What percent of the minutes remaining until class time can I spend at coffee break and still have time to prepare today's lesson? How long an extension cord should I buy to plug in another computer in my office? Do I have enough minutes to walk to the library and back before my class? Such questions, and countless others like them, might have precise answers, but unless we are aiming a rocket at the moon, the approximate answers from rough calculations are quite sufficient. Perhaps greater awareness of the multitude of math approximations that we use daily would call into question the prevailing faith in the ultimate precision of mathematics and its ability to solve problems that do not have precise mathematical answers.

Mathematician George Pólya presents a seemingly simple, four-step process for solving problems:

1. Understand the problem;
2. Devise a plan to solve it;
3. Carry out the plan;
4. Look back.[1]

Step four is deceptively simple but important. In many cases, a crucial part of "looking back" is to examine the approach used to solve the problem and to determine whether some other plan might be simpler, faster, more efficient, or more effective. In other words, if done correctly, step 4 is where we determine if we learned anything from solving this problem. Here is precisely the point where the student of mathematics can observe and learn the limitations of mathematics in attempting to solve violence problems whose root is moral rather than technological.

NOTE

1. This process is now common knowledge for mathematicians. Its first appearance was in George Pólya, *How to Solve It: A New Aspect of Mathematical Method* (Princeton, N.J.: Princeton University Press, 1945), 33–36.

VIII

NONVIOLENCE AND THE PROFESSIONS

23

The Peaceable Educator

Gayle Trollinger

A couple of years ago the parent of a prospective student asked, "And what makes your teacher education program special? What makes it distinctive?" I launched into my usual answer about high standards yielding above average passage rates on the state's teacher assessments, excellent field-based experiences, individual attention to each student, sound pedagogical and content knowledge, and on and on. But her question stayed with me. What does make the teacher education program of a small, liberal arts, peace church college different from a teacher education program of a nominally affiliated religious college or a state university?

External requirements imposed by state departments of education and the influential national accrediting agent, the National Council for Accreditation of Teacher Education (NCATE), appear to allow little opportunity for teacher education programs to develop anything unique. In fact, there is a pervasive perception that teacher education programs are being held hostage to mandated courses, experiences, and additional added-on requirements. As a result of mandates, the perception continues, all teacher education programs look basically the same.

But this perception is badly misleading. NCATE actually provides, through its accreditation process, the framework by which a college should and must develop a unique teacher education program that holds the college mission in a central position. The conceptual framework is to reflect the college mission, its vision and direction for the program, and its work.[1] In fact, it is incumbent upon teacher education programs to embrace the conceptual framework as a living foundation that celebrates the college's distinctive qualities as they are infused throughout the teacher education program. In so doing, the teacher education program will join with the general education requirements and the cocurricular activities to give the teacher education candidates a cohesive educational experience based on the college's mission rather than external mandates.

This chapter will introduce NCATE and its state partnerships and propose ways a teacher education program can and must reflect the college's mission through the NCATE conceptual framework. Alongside examples of conceptual frameworks of several teacher education programs, the chapter will discuss the conceptual framework of the teacher education program of Bluffton College, a peace church college.

A recent report of the National Commission on Teaching and America's Future presented "a blueprint for recruiting, preparing, and supporting excellent teachers in all of America's schools." Based on two years of study, the commission identified seven "barriers" to achieving this goal, including "major flaws in teacher preparation."[2] In this regard, the report's first recommendation is that "Schools that are serious about preparing teachers should take the necessary steps to become accredited. Those that are not willing or able to develop a critical mass of intellectual resources for training teachers should turn their attention to doing other things well."[3]

The commission's argument that teacher education programs must be accredited (or, at the least, be held accountable to national standards) is at odds with the history of teacher education in the United States. In contrast to "professions such as medicine, nursing, architecture, accounting, and law," education has been slow to establish professional boards for standards and accreditation. This is true partly because teaching "has been governed through lay political channels and governmental bureaucracies rather than professional bodies." Legislators and school board members have "typically adopted a view of teaching as a relatively simple, straightforward work conducted by semiskilled workers."[4] On the other hand, "accreditation . . . assures the public across the board—parents, business leaders, policymakers— that candidates coming out of a particular institution have been prepared to teach using rigorous national standards that have been designed by the profession."[5]

Despite the importance of professional standards and accreditation, the reality is "Until the 1980s NCATE and the states did not collaborate in the review of teacher education programs." Each state planned and implemented the standards for the teacher education programs in its state, and "in 1990, NCATE had no discernable presence in national or state policy initiatives."[6] A variety of factors— costs, administrative time demands, and resistance to an external body dictating what the program should look like often deterred small liberal arts colleges from seeking national accreditation.

But over the past few years the once-chaotic world of teacher education standards and accreditation has become much more orderly. One indication of this burgeoning order is the tightening relationship between NCATE and the states. By 2000, NCATE had established some type of partnership program with at least forty-five states, with an "increasing alignment of state and professional standards." In fact, "as of 2001, 28 states have adopted or adapted NCATE unit standards as the state unit standards."[7] In 1998, Ohio became one of the states that requires all programs of teacher education to meet NCATE standards.

On the face of it, this requirement would seem to point toward the development of "cookie cutter" teacher education programs, with each program basically the same as all other teacher education programs. All programs would meet the state-mandated standards of excellence for field-based experiences and individual attention for each student, and all programs would be organized around sound pedagogical and content knowledge. And the program at peace church–oriented Bluffton College would look like the fifty other excellent teacher education programs in the state.

NCATE's 1995 publication, "Standards, Procedures and Policies for the Accreditation of Professional Education Units," seemed to bear out the suspicion of cookie cutter programs. These legislated standards were input based and fell into four Standards categories: Design of Professional Education, Candidates in Professional Education, Professional Education Faculty, and The Unit for Professional Education. Each of these Standards categories was broken into other Standards, which focused on such input-based facts as qualifications of faculty and assessing the progress of teacher education candidates.

In only one place was there opportunity for a teacher education program to express its unique identity. This place was the Conceptual Framework of the program, which was a subcategory under the Standards category of Design of Professional Education. However, the conceptual framework was but one of nine standards in this category and received no particular emphasis. In fact, based on the NCATE 1995 standards, a unit could receive accreditation even if the conceptual framework was weak.

Things have changed. NCATE 2000 Unit Standards acknowledge that all teacher education programs should not be the same. This change occurred by implementing a performance-based system and shifting the conceptual framework to the forefront of the standards. It is now impossible for a program to receive full accreditation or state approval without meeting the expectations for the conceptual framework.

Rather than being one of nine standards under another category of standards, the conceptual framework now shapes and guides the whole of the program of teacher education and must be visible in each of the six standards mandated by the unit standards for the year 2000. The six standards are based on: (1) the candidates' knowledge, skills, and dispositions; (2) the unit's assessment system and how the unit is evaluated; (3) field experiences and clinical practices; (4) diversity issues; (5) faculty members' qualifications, performance, and development; and (6) the unit governance and resources available to the unit.

The conceptual framework "provides direction for (all) programs, courses, teaching, candidate performance, scholarship, service, and unit accountability . . . [and] it provides the basis that describe the unit's intellectual philosophy, which distinguishes graduates of one institution from those of another."[8] In order to meet NCATE expectations, the conceptual framework must be knowledge-based, articulated, shared, coherent, and consistent with the unit. Finally, it must be continually evaluated.

The conceptual framework begins by describing how the unit prepares effective teachers and how it will demonstrate through valid and ongoing assessments that the teacher candidates are able to achieve high levels of learning in their future classrooms. It also requires that the teacher education program be rooted in sound research; that the program's students complete course work and experiences that include professional commitments and dispositions; and that programs address diversity and technology.

But there is more. The conceptual framework must be linked to the mission of the college. This provides colleges and universities the unique opportunity to infuse their particular mission into the teacher education program in an up-front, no-apologies way. The conceptual framework is the way in which the link between the college mission and the teacher education program is articulated. This linkage must be found throughout the six standards.

The conceptual framework must be articulated, shared, and coherent. This coherency means, for example, that when a Board of Examiners Team visits a campus, all students and faculty should be able to talk about the conceptual framework and what it means in the teacher education program. A teacher education program often coins a phrase that encapsulates the conceptual framework. This phrase should appear on syllabi, in class discussions, in publicity materials, and the Title II Report. This phrase may be found printed on pens and pencils, and perhaps on tee shirts, mugs, and hats. How to make the conceptual framework public and "shared" is up for some debate; whatever methods are used, however, they should enhance the conceptual framework and not reduce it to a catchy phrase with no substance. Used appropriately, the phrase is a helpful way of getting a handle on the conceptual framework.

It is instructive to examine the phrases that summarize the conceptual frameworks of several schools. For example, Cedarville University is a conservative university affiliated with the General Association of Regular Baptists, a fundamentalist denomination. The conceptual framework for their teacher education program clearly delineates who they are within the context of the mission of Cedarville: Christian Educators Who Demonstrate a Biblical World and Life View, Excellent Academic Preparation, and the Ability to Teach Effectively and Serve Compassionately in a Diversity of Setting.[9] On the other hand, Wilmington College is a Quaker school. Its conceptual framework, Reflective Practitioners for Peaceful Schools,[10] clearly reflects the Quaker traditions of the school.

The conceptual framework of the Bluffton College Teacher Education Program is embodied in the phrase Educators Nurturing Communities of Learning and Respect. Each word of this conceptual framework was carefully chosen. Our teacher education candidates are educators. These educators do not simply teach, control, or run classrooms; they nurture communities. Nurturing builds from Nell Noddings's models of caring.[11] A community is "safe and supportive. It consists of a close-knit group of people who share some common goals and values and who have a built-in capacity to respect each other, even in the midst of profound disagreement."[12] These communities focus on high levels of student learning (based on national and state outcomes) and mutual respect, which at Bluffton College is rooted in its peace and justice heritage.

In practice the Bluffton College Teacher Education Program is rooted in a strong liberal arts preparation, which focuses on critical thinking skills and the development of a cross-cultural understanding, all within a broader context of peace, justice, and service. From these roots our program "branches out" to a program focusing on inclusive classrooms where all children are valued for the unique gifts they add to a community. Our program values strong content knowledge, effective teaching strategies, effective use of technology, on-going assessment, and professionalism.

Of course, claiming these values is one thing, implementing them is another. What does it mean to argue that we must integrate our commitment to respect, nonviolence, and justice into the teacher education program?

Using a model in which nonviolence is one particular class session or requirement in the program, we could require students to take a course on nonviolence or to visit Bluffton's Lion and the Lamb Peace Arts Center. We could also ensure that all students attend forums and special events that deal with peace and justice issues.

More than this, we could focus a particular course around these issues. An ideal course for including a peace component is classroom organization. The traditional way to teach classroom management and organization is to make it a "how to" course. The goal in such a course is for the prospective teachers to figure out how to "make" students do what the teacher wants, that is, to control them. To do this the teacher focuses on power techniques, and any problem rests with the child who does not do what is requested. Alfie Kohn in *Beyond Discipline* challenges us to consider who benefits from these models: it is usually the teacher and not the student.[13] Alex Molnar emphatically states, "If we are to construct a more peaceful world, we have work to do. As educators, it is logical for us to begin with questions of classroom method. We should ask ourselves the extent to which our classroom practices promote and strengthen peaceful relations among our students."[14]

If we do require some sort of nonviolence component, if we completely redesign our classroom management course, we are doing something significant and something that will set our program apart from most teacher education programs in the state. This is good. But this approach is still clinging to the 1995 NCATE standards that made the conceptual framework one part of the program. Instead 2000 NCATE standards invite us to infuse the conceptual framework throughout the entire Bluffton College Teacher Education Program.

To accomplish this infusion, we must go beyond the model that locates nonviolence in one particular class or requirement in the program and develop a model with nonviolence as a worldview. If we believe in nonviolence, peace, and justice, we must examine again how we view children and how we view education in society and the world around us. With this model, peace and justice issues would be so much a part of every course in our department that students would have difficulty isolating them out. Students would address issues like inclusive classrooms, where all children are welcome and valued from a peace and justice perspective, not just from a utilitarian perspective—"does it or doesn't it work?"

Students would talk about access to education from a peace and justice perspective, not just from a perspective based on cost. Students would truly embrace diversity and not see it merely as one more roadblock to high test scores. Students would refuse to exclude children from their classrooms and from access to the education that children from families in the wealthy suburbs expect. And of course teacher education students would be in ongoing discussion about the future application in their classrooms of the peace and nonviolence issues that this book raises for other academic disciplines.

We—the department members and the teacher education candidates—would also begin to understand that a peace and justice stance, exotic until September 11, 2001, and subversive thereafter, is not accepted in most public school classrooms across the nation. Although we believe that schools should be "places where students learn the knowledge and skills necessary to live in an authentic democracy,"[15] students (and teachers) are often rewarded for conforming to the norm and are punished for speaking out. However, teacher education graduates from a peace church college should emerge with skills in meeting the challenges they will face in teaching nonviolently and teaching about nonviolence, and these new graduates should be prepared to "empower students . . . [to] educate them for transformative action. That means educating them to take risks, to struggle for institutional change, and to fight both against oppression and for democracy."[16] This also means that our classes should address issues of diversity and how essential it is to the maintenance of a healthy democracy.

Have we fully arrived at this program for teacher education fully infused by nonviolence, peace, and justice? No, of course not. But using the conceptual framework as defined by the NCATE 2000 standards, we are expected and thus empowered by the state of Ohio to keep moving toward a teacher education program that is firmly rooted in the peace and justice mission of Bluffton College. We are committed to preparing educators who are nurturers of communities of learning and respect. While this process is ongoing and never truly finished, we can confidently tell the parent of the prospective student what uniquely distinguishes teacher education at Bluffton College.

NOTES

1. National Council for Accreditation of Teacher Education, *Professional Standards for the Accreditation of Schools, Colleges, and Departments of Education (Revised 2002)* (Washington, D.C.: NCATE, 2002), 5.

2. Report on the National Commission on Teaching and America's Future, *What Matters Most: Teaching for America's Future* (New York: The National Commission on Teaching and America's Future, 1996), vi.

3. *What Matters Most*, 70.

4. Linda Darling-Hammond, *A License to Teach: Building a Profession for 21st-Century Schools* (Boulder, Colo.: Westview Press, 1995), 7–9.

5. NCATE, *The Importance of Being Accredited* (Washington, D.C.: NCATE, 2001). Available at www.ncate.org/resources/boyceqa.htm.

6. NCATE, *A Decade of Growth 1991–2000* (Washington, D.C.: NCATE, 2001), 8. Available at www.nate.org/newsbrfs/dec_report.htm.

7. NCATE, *A Decade of Growth*, 9.

8. NCATE, *Professional Standards*, 2.

9. Ohio Department of Education, *Report on the Quality of Teacher Education in Ohio, 1999–2000* (Columbus: ODE), 45.

10. ODE, *Report on the Quality*, 173.

11. Nel Noddings, "Teaching Themes of Care," *Phi Delta Kappan* 76 (1995): 675–679.

12. Renate Nummela Caine and Geoffrey Caine, *Education on the Edge of Possibility* (Alexandria, Va.: Association for Supervision and Curriculum Development, 1997), 160.

13. Alfie Kohn, *Beyond Discipline: From Compliance to Community* (Alexander, Va.: Association for Supervision and Curriculum Development, 1996).

14. Alex Molnar, "Too Many Kids Are Getting Killed," *Educational Leadership* 50 (1992): 4–5.

15. Henry Giroux, *Teachers As Intellectuals: Toward a Critical Pedagogy of Learning* (Granby, Mass.: Bergin and Garvey, 1988), xxxii.

16. Giroux, *Teachers as Intellectuals*, xxxiii.

24

The Peaceable Manager

George A. Lehman

George Marsden argues that any scholar inevitably will and should evaluate truth claims from a particular perspective or perspectives. He suggests that this perspective shapes the scholar's response to the following questions:

1. "What do I think is important enough to study?
2. What questions do I ask about it?
3. What currently fashionable interpretive strategies are compatible with my religious outlook?
4. How do I, implicitly or explicitly, evaluate various developments as positive, negative or something in between?
5. How do these evaluations shape my narrative?" [1]

In light of this structure of inquiry, my question is: How does a commitment to nonviolence impact my understanding of how we should both understand and teach management principles at a peace church college?

Let us consider two different options for approaching this question. One option is to treat knowledge about business as a set of facts or truths and thus to teach students to behave ethically within this factual environment. Indeed Marsden says, "Religious perspective will change some things but not everything."[2] Certainly my students wish to know about the world "the way it really is." If we assume that the content of management should be essentially the same no matter where it is taught, a kind of standard or universal business-as-such, then we would need to teach norms for business practice that are both ethical and consistent with those universal management principles. In this case the idea of nonviolence would be something added to the core of standard or universal business principles.

A second option is to question the universal management principles from the perspective of nonviolence. This approach assumes that all knowledge is perspectival and thus that even the most commonsensical features of business and management philosophy are not simply describing the "factual" world but are also making those descriptions from a particular perspective, one that either accepts or disregards nonviolence as a crucial commitment. In this view, the idea of nonviolence would be intrinsic to assumptions about what business is. In my view, although both options can make a useful contribution to the conversation about nonviolence in management practices, in a time of epistemological crisis and perceived need for ethics in business, the second option has more potential to challenge supposed common sense about the business and management environment.

NONVIOLENT ETHICS UNDER
UNIVERSAL MANAGEMENT PRINCIPLES

A commitment to nonviolence that seeks to operate within conventional wisdom about universal management principles at the very least would explicitly reject the use of overt violence as a business strategy. While it might be tempting to say that business use of violence is an issue only for drug dealers and the Mafia, we can find many relatively recent historical examples of business organizations that were directly involved in violence for their own ends. For example, numerous sources have documented the role of ITT in the overthrow of the democratically elected Allende government of Chile. Certainly the business community provided substantial opinion support for the Gulf War in the early 1990s as a way of protecting access to oil. The Heritage Foundation and individual business leaders gave substantive support to rebel groups during the decade long civil war in Mozambique. Various forms of private business support for the Contras in Nicaragua during the 1980s have been well documented.

Furthermore business and commerce in the United States have been closely connected to the violence of slavery, the exploitation and ill-treatment of Chinese railroad workers, forcible suppression of labor unions, and the violent displacement of native peoples. In all these business ventures, nonviolence clearly did not belong to the supposed core of standard business principles. Surely if managers and business leaders placed off limits the use of violent means either directly or indirectly to achieve business ends, something significant would be accomplished.

But of course business ethics can and should go beyond not using violence. Aristotle argued for positive virtues that are utilized in creating a better community. If this is desirable then it is important to teach students that the corporation is rooted in a public benefit arising from the creation of a corporate entity. In view of the various financial scandals among major companies during 2002, it is again important to address the broad social impact and social responsibility of a public corporation.

While most of us are aware of the large sums that are sometimes awarded aggrieved persons in civil lawsuits, we forget that corporate officers are by and large protected from criminal prosecution for their corporate acts. If I were to sneak over to my neighbor's house every night and secretly spray poisonous chemicals into my neighbor's house and if my neighbor died from breathing those chemicals, I would certainly be charged with murder. But asbestos manufacturers knew that asbestosis was killing workers for many years before they cleaned up the air in their plants. Lawsuits related to this behavior have certainly been very expensive, but no one has gone to jail for murder. Members of a corporation receive certain legal protection because the corporation is expected in some way to serve the larger public good. Note that one legislative response to the corporate malfeasance discovered during 2002 was the initiation of procedures to make CEOs and CFOs criminally liable for misrepresentations of corporate finances. The point of all this is that it is reasonable that the creation of the legal entity of the corporation can legitimately be tied to the expectation of some larger public good emanating from such an entity.

Milton Friedman, in particular, has argued that the sole social responsibility of the corporation is to stay within the law and to make a profit. The church-related college with a commitment to pacifism and social justice will likely wish to describe and define a broader understanding of the social responsibility of business than Friedman does. For example, the story is told that in the early days of Quakerism, George Fox taught his adherents that even though the local business culture was based on the principle of caveat emptor they should consistently deal in an honest, above the board manner and give fair value in the exchange of goods and services. This set of practices actually helped Quaker businesspeople to become the traders of choice in some parts of England and hence to become quite profitable.

While Fox likely did not think in strategic terms and say "there is a market niche for honest traders," this illustration does suggest that high ethical standards and success in the business arena are not incompatible. Thus acceptance of the social vulnerability demanded by an ethics of nonviolence can contribute to the understanding and decision making of all managers, even those whose first commitment is not to Christian nonviolence. It is not illogical to think about adding a concern for ethics, even a concern for nonviolence, to the core of supposed standard business principles. Teaching nonviolence and vulnerable honesty as a good business practice is thus a way of describing ethical behavior within an orderly system and, as such, should be valued as one approach to the ethical training of managers.

MANAGEMENT PRINCIPLES UNDER NONVIOLENT ETHICS

But what if the principles of management rather than having an existence independent of human creation are in fact a uniquely human, ongoing creation. In such a context Marsden's questions above do not shape our discovery of *existing* truth but rather shape our discovery about what can *become* true in a particular context. Perhaps a personal illustration can clarify this point.

As a management theorist I have made modest attempts to understand the workplace and the social impact of the *maquiladoras* in Latin America. Although some people are uniformly critical of the growth of the maquiladoras, my own reading and personal contacts lead me to a position of cautious optimism about the potential benefits to the local communities and the foreign countries involved in these manufacturing operations. There are of course some concerns that need to be raised about maquiladoras. In particular, the nature of the manager–worker relationship is an area of frequent concern. Unhealthful working environments, exceptionally long working hours, excess charges to workers for services that must be purchased as a condition of employment, and physical abuse seem to occur frequently in many *maquilas*.

As part of my own research I visited with a staff person for an international relief agency who reported visiting with a Mennonite-college-trained manager of a maquila about various working conditions. The agency staff person suggested that improving working conditions could lead to the possibility of substantial gains in worker productivity. The manager simply responded "that's not the way we do it here." Note that the response was not that the organization could not afford to create a better working environment or that such an environment might not be more profitable but simply "that's not the way we do it here."

What is going on when a manager trained in a presumably highly ethical environment manages in a way that appears to be legal but not ethical? I suggest that the implicit assumption in many management curricula and in ethics discussions is that it is important, and perhaps even essential, that the manager be "realistic." For example, the ancient Chinese strategist Sun Tzu and his book *The Art of War* are particularly popular as a focal point for management development programs. Sun Tzu opens his book by describing a setting in which a commander kills two of the king's concubines as part of a process of creating discipline within a group of servants. The king was distressed by this action, to which Sun Tzu replies, "The King likes only empty words. He is not capable of putting them into practice."[3] The common phrase "whatever it takes" is the contemporary equivalent of this perspective. When we accept the responsibility of teaching students to be realistic, we are implicitly granting the existing social order an inevitability that it does not need to have. The story of the maquila manager illustrates the downside of limiting our ethical teaching to questions about how one struggles to make good decisions within a given framework of presumed universal management principles.

But the story of the maquila manager also implies that what is called "good management" or even simply "effective management" is not based on some immutable laws of science but rather on "the way we do it here." "The way we do it here" is actually a series of specific choices about how things should function made at a particular time and place by particular people. From this perspective the nonviolent manager faces the challenge of creating "the way we do it here" in a manner consistent with a commitment to nonviolence. And with this insight in mind, it becomes apparent that the so-called realistic approach to management is no more real than an approach shaped by nonviolence. The so-called realistic approach is actually the attribution of inevitability and functionality—a quasi-ultimate validity—to structures and social norms about management that are simply conventions that have been broadly accepted within a specific cultural context but that have no inherent inevitability or functionality. Put differently, my approach suggests the need to remind managers that in understanding business and management the only real world is the one we humans create through our own study and practice. And we can work to create a real world shaped by nonviolence.

Such an approach to knowledge is obviously influenced by the assumptions of postmodernity that knowledge is limited and perspectival and that truth is shaped more by "paradigm shifts" than by a progressive accumulation of facts. While the purpose of this chapter is not to elaborate extensively on the problems and possibilities of postmodernity in general, it does seem that some postmodern theory helps us understand the process of knowledge creation in organizational settings.

For example, Heckscher contrasts bureaucratic and "post-bureaucratic" models of management by asserting that "in bureaucracies, consensus of a kind is created through acquiescence to authority, rules or traditions. In the post-bureaucratic form it is created through institutionalized dialogue," and furthermore this dialogue is based on influence arising from trust rather than power.[4]

The nonviolent business manager who accepts postmodern insights such as these is a person who is clearly aware that core values can and should be used to design new approaches and structures that work within and ultimately modify currently practiced approaches and structures toward a less violent organizational marketplace. For the person and institution committed to nonviolence and social justice, this means actively searching for ways to extend thinking already done by authors like Robert Greenleaf (servant leadership), Peter Block (stewardship), and Peter Senge (learning organizations), who write as scholars of organizational life and who seek to transform the common sense assumptions about "the way we do it here."

Additionally, such a rethinking of management theory from the standpoint of nonviolence will benefit from the work of theologian Walter Wink. Wink uses the phrase "the Powers That Be" to describe "the systems . . . the institutions and structures that weave society into an intricate pattern of power and relationships."[5] According to Wink, "The Powers That Be are not merely the people in power or the institutions they staff. Managers are, in fact, more or less interchangeable. Most people in management would tend to make the same sort of moves."[6] This ordering of our lives and daily praxis by the "powers" can be the basis of both good and evil.

Most of Wink's work is based on the negative aspects of The Powers That Be, as characterized by a "domination system" that is deeply embedded in the overall culture and has been for most of modern history. Indeed Wink argues that the personification of good and evil as angels and demons in the Bible is simply an alternate way of describing the broad impact of The Powers That Be on our daily lives. In like manner Wink argues that the New Testament phrase "powers and principalities" refers to this embedded web of relationships that sets the stage for and frequently delimits much of perceived range of potential action. The maquila manager who says "that's not the way we do it here" is describing the grip of The Powers That Be on him, the factory in which he works, and on the larger society.

In my mind the postmodernist understanding of the paradigmatic nature of management theory is consistent with Wink's understanding of "the Powers." The Powers are simply those practices that have become embedded in organizational life through those paradigms and structures that guide the daily life of an organization beyond individual intent or desire. Wink's concept of The Powers is in essence an alternative theological analysis of the conventional wisdom that shapes the "way we do it here."

Given these assumptions about the paradigmatic nature of knowledge and the importance of prior worldviews and assumptions in generating knowledge about organizational management, it seems apparent that there is room for nonviolence as a philosophy of management, not merely an ethics or practice. The task then of an educator who is committed to nonviolence is to create a picture of how management works (or at least *can work*) that is consistent with the values and beliefs that are part of that peace perspective. At the most ambitious level this task can be seen as attempting to reshape The Powers That Be from a negative violence-generating force to a positive peace-building one. How is the scholar to approach this daunting task? Marsden's five questions are helpful in approaching this endeavor

1. What Do I Think Is Important Enough to Study?

I pay attention to scholarship that attempts to describe a broad picture of management and of organizational life since I think that how we see the world at these broad levels influences the praxis of daily organizational life. How we understand the world in which we live influences the range of options we have for "the way we do it here." Or in Wink's language we need to learn to "name the powers." Thus when I study something like Total Quality Improvement (TQI) I look for the patterns of relationship that such a system creates more than at the proposed steps to implement TQI.

2. What Questions Do I Ask about It?

What kind of people does a given organizational pattern tend to create? Does the leadership style being promoted create relatively egalitarian relationships or needless hierarchy? Is a particular pattern of leadership and organizational life sustainable for the employees, for the community, for the planet? Does the leadership and organizational theory in question create good relationships within and without the organization? Does the leadership pattern support both profitability and community responsibility? Does the theory encourage destructive or transformative practices of conflict and competition?

3. What Currently Fashionable Interpretive Strategies Are Compatible with My Religious Outlook?

A trip to the business section of the local supersize bookstore can be a discouraging event. The most visible titles alternate between cheery positive thinking books about the importance of good attitudes, and strategy books on how to demolish one's opposition. I do not recall seeing anything about having a good attitude while demolishing the competition. Perhaps that book is just waiting for an author. And of course there are plenty of self-congratulatory books by the likes of Jack Welch and Rudy Giuliani.

Fortunately there are also other voices. Robert Greenleaf's book *Servant Leadership* is still selling well even though it was first published in 1977. Greenleaf argues, "the great leader is seen as servant first and that simple fact is the key to his greatness."[7] Furthermore Greenleaf's original examination of the nature of leadership has been highly influential for numerous current writers including Peter Senge, Peter Block, Peter Koestenbaum, and Margaret Wheatley. In their own way these writers are attempting to influence the practice of leadership in the direction of creating workplaces that build the internal community, support and nourish the individual worker, make a profit, and provide a significant service to the larger community.

Although none of these management writers works within an apparent pacifist perspective, they certainly do appear to be creating new knowledge about "what can be." We do not have to live and work in organizations based on Wink's "domination system." All of this suggests that we are at a point in our understanding of management in which a more overtly peace-oriented approach to management could be appropriated by others as "having truth." The task will be to extend the analyses of these thinkers into a better understanding of the way that various forms of violence within organizational life can be critiqued and subverted.

4. How Do I, Implicitly or Explicitly, Evaluate Various Developments As Positive, Negative, or Something in Between?

I tend to evaluate developments in the field of management positively if they open up the possibility for enactment of new more-life-giving ways of relating among people at work and across cultures, between people and the natural environment, and between people and God. Put differently, I am interested in management theory that promotes peacemaking and reconciliation as a basic strategy and experience of corporate life.

5. How Do These Evaluations Shape My Narrative?

This question really homes in on the knowledge creation concept with the suggestion that the final product is a narrative. Language like this reinforces the idea that the "best practice" of management is not a fixed proposition but rather that of a provisional narrative. A recent speaker on the Bluffton College campus told the faculty "those who tell the best stories create the future." What stories do we tell? Do we talk about the rough and ruthless CEO who achieves great success as he destroys the opposition or do we tell the stories of the people who create a profitable company by creating an atmosphere in which workers are able to develop themselves and increase their contribution to the larger purposes of the organization? Do we tell stories about successful international ventures that sustain appropriate development or do we tell stories about the worldwide conquests of Microsoft?

One of my own hopes is that peace church colleges like Bluffton College can become settings in which stories of how managers have served well can be collected, interpreted, and retold. Our graduate students in management tell us that after studying at Bluffton they are clearer about the contribution they can make to their organizations and they are clearer about maintaining a life style that balances work, study, leisure, and service to others on and off the job. We are trying to create a network of people and stories about what organizational life can be at its best. Such a project, if successful, will certainly create peace alternatives at multiple levels in our workplaces, our communities, and our world.

For example, if the manager of the maquiladora had been working within a story that stressed the contribution of that organization to human flourishing—both the workers and the company itself—then it might have been possible for him to reconceive the status quo not in terms of "the way we do it here" but rather according to the "the way it might be." There are solid precedents for such a reconception. Robert Owen in seventeenth-century Wales developed workplace alternatives to the dreadful spinning mills of that era, based on his conviction that exploitive workplaces were neither ethical nor necessary. Peter Block moves in this direction when he first of all challenges the status quo with "The governance system we have inherited and continue to create is based on sovereignty and a form of intimate colonialism. . . . We govern by valuing, above all else, consistency, control, and predictability."[8] His approach challenges the whole notion of the traditional hierarchy as an essential for the successful organization. Instead he argues that "real accountability and service seek equity in relationships."[9]

Such a reconstrual of the organizational story, not just by a maquiladora manager but by the people who provide us with universal management principles, could open the doors for peaceable organizations around the world to rethink their missions, their structures, their habits of relationship along the lines of the biblical vision of shalom. Human energy, creativity, and collective enterprise would be mobilized, first of all, for the sake of human well-being, power would circulate in a way that empowered rather than enslaved, and violence of any kind would be definitively rejected as a valid strategy, even for dealing with a global marketplace that is still full of violence.

NOTES

1. George M. Marsden and Bradley J. Longfield, eds., *The Secularization of the Academy* (New York: Oxford University Press, 1992), 45–46.

2. Marsden, *The Secularization*, 46.

3. Sun Tzu, *The Art of War* (London: Oxford University Press, 1963), 59.

4. Charles Heckscher and Anne Donnellon, eds., *The Post-Bureaucratic Organization* (Thousand Oaks, Calif.: Sage Publications, 1994), 25.

5. Walter Wink, *The Powers That Be* (New York: Galilee Doubleday, 1998), 1.

6. Wink, *The Powers That Be,* 2.

7. Robert K. Greenleaf, *Servant Leadership* (New York: Paulist Press, 1977), 7.

8. Peter Block, *Stewardship* (San Francisco: Berrett-Koehler Publishers, 1993) 7.

9. Block, *Stewardship,* 28.

Index

275

About the Contributors

Cynthia L. Bandish is associate professor of English at Bluffton College. She has a Ph.D. in nineteenth-century studies from Drew University, with a dissertation on "Mary Elizabeth Braddon and the Bohemian Circle of *Belgravia*." Her published research includes the application of Bahktin's dialogical theory to literary periodicals, and her current research focuses on the role of violence and nonviolence in British Gothic novels written during the French Revolution.

Gerald Biesecker-Mast is associate professor of communication at Bluffton College. He is coeditor, with Susan Biesecker-Mast, of *Anabaptists and Postmodernity* (2000) and has published numerous essays about Anabaptist-Mennonite persuasion. He is presently completing a book on arguments against the sword in sixteenth-century Anabaptist rhetoric. His Ph.D. in communication and rhetoric is from the University of Pittsburgh.

Susan Biesecker-Mast is associate professor of communication, chair of the Communication and Theatre Department, and director of the Honors Program at Bluffton College. She coedited *Anabaptists and Postmodernity* (2000) with Gerald Biesecker-Mast and is currently working on a book that explores why middle-American tourists are drawn to Amish Country and discusses what possibilities tourism may enable for radical witness by Amish to tourists. Her Ph.D. is from the University of Pittsburgh.

Perry Bush is professor of history at Bluffton College. He is the author of two books, *Two Kingdoms, Two Loyalties: Mennonite Pacifism in Modern America* (1998) and *Dancing with the Kobzar: Bluffton College and Mennonite Higher Education 1899–1999* (2000), as well as numerous articles on Mennonite history and modern American evangelicalism. He received his Ph.D. in history from

Carnegie Mellon University. He is currently working on a book of urban history dealing with the impact of economic globalization on an Ohio city.

Melissa Friesen is assistant professor of theatre and communication at Bluffton College. A Ph.D. candidate in theatre research at the University of Wisconsin–Madison, she is researching the intersections of nonviolent perspectives and theatrical texts.

Ronald L. Friesen is professor of economics at Bluffton College. After he completed his doctorate at Columbia University, he developed his interest in the economics of war and peace as a way to integrate his professional interests in economics with the peace church tradition of Bluffton College. He is a coeditor of *Public Economics III: Public Choice, Political Economy, Peace and War* (1995).

Jeff Gingerich is assistant professor of sociology at Bluffton College where he serves as coordinator and instructor for the criminal justice major. He received his Ph.D. in sociology from the University of Pennsylvania. His research interests include the emerging field of restorative justice, and racial segregation within religious organizations.

Jeff Gundy is professor of English at Bluffton College, where he has taught writing, literature, and general education since 1984. He has published three books of poems, *Inquiries* (1992), *Flatlands* (1995), and *Rhapsody with Dark Matter* (2000), and two books of creative nonfiction, *A Community of Memory: My Days with George and Clara* (1996) and *Scattering Point: The World in a Mennonite Eye* (2003).

James M. Harder is special assistant to the president and professor of economics at Bluffton College. His Ph.D. in economics, with a specialty in the economics of developing countries, is from the University of Notre Dame. He has authored several book chapters and numerous articles on topics related to global economic justice and environmental issues. Dr. Harder chaired the Department of Economics and Business at Bethel College in Kansas from 1990 to 2001 before coming to Bluffton College.

Stephen H. Harnish is associate professor of mathematics at Bluffton College. He wrote his Ph.D. thesis at the University of Illinois under proof theorist Gaisi Takeuti—a protégé of Kurt Gödel. He has also studied theology, ethics, and peace studies at the Associated Mennonite Biblical Seminary. He has published in journals of mathematical logic. His research interests include the relative consistency and applications of set theories without a foundation axiom, and applications of geometry and logic in theoretical physics.

David Janzen was assistant professor of religion at Bluffton College from 2000 to 2002. In the fall of 2003, he began teaching in the Bible Department of SEMILLA, an Anabaptist seminary in Guatemala City. He has published *Witch-Hunts, Purity, and Social Boundaries: The Expulsion of the Foreign Women in Ezra 9–10* (2002) and is currently working on a book on Old Testament sacrifice and ethics.

John Kampen is vice president and dean of academic affairs and professor of religion at Bluffton College. He has done extensive research and writing on Second Temple Judaism, especially on the Dead Sea Scrolls. He has coedited or written three books, including *Hasideans and the Origin of Pharisaism: A Study in 1 and 2 Maccabees* (1988). Present research projects include a commentary on the wisdom texts from the Dead Sea Scrolls and a volume on social history related to the Gospel of Matthew. Before coming to Bluffton he was professor of New Testament and academic dean at Payne Theological Seminary.

George A. Lehman is professor of business; chair of the Department of Economics, Business, and Accounting; and director of the Master of Arts in Organizational Management Program at Bluffton College. He earned an executive doctor of management from Case Western Reserve University in 2000 and an MBA from the University of Pittsburgh in 1978. Dr. Lehman had twenty-five years of administrative experience in nonprofit organizations prior to joining Bluffton College.

Gregg J Luginbuhl is professor of art and chairman of the Art Department at Bluffton College. He has exhibited art in regional and national exhibitions. He has received numerous awards, and his work is included in many public and private collections. An installation of eight large ceramic plates with modeled imagery, *The Creation Series,* and two bronze sculptures, *Jonah and the Whale* and *The Last First Draft,* are permanently displayed on the campus of Bluffton College. Mr. Luginbuhl received the M.F.A. degree in ceramics from the University of Montana in 1975 following a B.A. in art from Bluffton in 1971. Mr. Luginbuhl taught at the University of Findlay, 1976–1984, before returning to Bluffton College.

Angela Horn Montel is associate professor of biology, Bluffton College. She has a B.A. from Manchester College and a Ph.D. from Indiana University School of Medicine. Her dissertation was titled "Fas/Fas Ligand and B7/CD28 Interactions in Human NK-Mediated Lysis of Virus-Infected Cells." She has coauthored nine peer-reviewed articles and numerous abstracts on the subjects of natural killer cells and gene therapy.

Pamela S. Nath is associate professor of psychology at Bluffton College. After earning her doctoral degree from the University of Notre Dame, Dr. Nath worked as a clinical psychologist in community mental health and private practice settings before returning to academia in 1996. She is currently involved in a large, collaborative research project studying faith development in college students.

Darryl K. Nester is professor of mathematics at Bluffton College. He has written many supplements for math and statistics textbooks, including solutions manuals for instructors and for students and manuals illustrating the use of graphing calculators. His research deals with probability, differential equations, and creative problem solving.

W. Todd Rainey is professor of biology at Bluffton College. He earned a Ph.D. in comparative neuroanatomy at the University of Chicago, followed by two postdoctoral research projects in neurobiology. He began teaching at Bluffton College in 1989. A generalist by choice, his course topics include anatomy and physiology, genetics, and developmental biology. Another course concerns animal behavior, with a focus on the plasticity and complexity of primate social behavior, including primate use of conflict resolution behaviors.

James H. Satterwhite is professor of history and chair of the Religion and History Department at Bluffton College. He has written *Varieties of Marxist Humanism: Philosophical Revision in Postwar Eastern Europe* (1992) and edited a collection of essays by the Czech philosopher Karel Kosík. He is currently interested in the phenomenon of nationalism in Eastern Europe. Since 1996 he has served summers with Christian Peacemaker Teams in Chechnya, Serbia, and five summers in Hebron, West Bank (Palestine).

Glen H. Stassen is Lewis B. Smedes Professor of Christian Ethics at Fuller Theological Seminary and a member of the Board of Peace Action. He is the editor of *Just Peacemaking: Ten Practices for Abolishing War* (1998) and of *Capital Punishment* (1998), and author of *Kingdom Ethics: Following Jesus in Contemporary Context* (2003) and *Just Peacemaking: Transforming Initiatives for Justice and Peace* (1992).

Mark J. Suderman is professor of music and director of choral activities at Bluffton College. His undergraduate degree from Bethel College is in voice performance and music education. At the University of Iowa, Dr. Suderman received master's and doctoral degrees in choral conducting. Besides working as a musician in academic settings, he is very active as a choral clinician, adjudicator, and church musician.

Gayle Trollinger is chair of the Education Department, director of the Master of Arts in Education program, associate professor of education, and director of teacher education at Bluffton College. She taught for fourteen years in public schools in special education and general education classrooms. Her Ph.D. is from

Pennsylvania State University, and her dissertation focused on inclusive middle school education. She is president of the Ohio Association of Colleges of Teacher Education, and her most recent work focuses on teacher education issues especially as they relate to independent colleges.

J. Denny Weaver is professor of religion and is the Harry and Jean Yoder Scholar in Bible and Religion at Bluffton College. He is editor of the C. Henry Smith Series. He has written four books, including *The Nonviolent Atonement* (2001) and *Anabaptist Theology in Face of Postmodernity: A Proposal for the Third Millennium* (2000), as well as many articles and chapters in edited books. Following a doctoral dissertation on Anabaptist history at Duke University, his research interests in recent years have focused on understanding how a nonviolent perspective can shape interpretations of a wide range of theological and historical issues. He served with three Christian Peacemaker Teams in Haiti.

Daniel Wessner is associate professor of history and international studies at Bluffton College and adjunct professor of international law at Pettit College of Law, Ohio Northern University. His research concerns political systems in subaltern states. His dissertation, "Monkey King and Sage: Hanoi's Political Syncretism," examined Vietnam's postwar reconstruction. He reports often at international conferences on topics of Vietnamese–American relations and development studies and is working with Vietnamese and American universities in establishing virtual information technology classrooms that address sustainable development needs. He holds graduate degrees in theology (Princeton Theological Seminary), law (University of Virginia), and international relations (University of Denver).

Michael L. Westmoreland-White is research associate for the School of Theology, Fuller Theological Seminary. Westmoreland-White has a Ph.D. in Christian ethics with a dissertation in theological ethics called "Incarnational Discipleship: The Ethics of Clarence Jordan, Martin Luther King, Jr., and Dorothy Day." From 1994 to 1999, he was the pacifist cochair of the "War, Peace, Violence, and Revolution" Interest Group of the Society of Christian Ethics. He is both an activist for issues of peacemaking, nonviolence, and human rights and a writer whose publications include scholarly and popular articles on human rights, nonviolence, peacemaking, capital punishment, ethical theory, and ecological ethics.